"In this remarkable book, Franca König delivers probably the most comprehensive account of the dynamics of European integration in the field of police cooperation to date. A must read for anyone interested in how policing and internal security cooperation has evolved in Europe."

Florian Trauner, *Vrije Universiteit Brussel, Belgium*

"Ms König has provided an excellent and comprehensive analysis on international police cooperation in the EU. I highly recommend reading this book to better understand how this process has influenced recent decisions on the European internal security."

Catherine De Bolle, *Executive Director of Europol, The Hague, The Netherlands*

"This book comes on the heels of an important reform of the Europol Regulation and of the proposed EU Police Cooperation Code. It is a key contribution to understanding the underlying integration dynamics in this field."

Cathrin Bauer-Bulst, *Head of Unit "Security in the Digital Age", European Commission, Belgium*

THE RISE OF EU POLICE COOPERATION

This book provides an in-depth empirical analysis and theoretical history of the institutional development of EU police cooperation, with a focus on the creation and integration of Europol.

Presenting a thoroughly comprehensive analysis, the book systematically traces integration dynamics and the evolution of EU police cooperation over a 40-year period, assessing the influence of cross-country interdependencies, politicisation and policy entrepreneurship on Member States' behaviour and institutional choice. By combining a wealth of sources including previously unpublished sources and personal insights from key decision-makers, it explores which driving factors shape processes of differentiation and integration in this sovereignty-sensitive policy domain, and how, and attempts to explain state preferences on international police cooperation in the light of major theories of European integration.

The book will be of key interest to students, scholars and practitioners working in or on the fields of police cooperation, Justice and Home Affairs policy, EU governance and security studies, both at national and European level.

Franca König is EU Policy Officer at the Berlin Senate Department of the Interior, where she currently heads the Task Force on the Berlin Presidency of the Standing Conference of Germany's Interior Ministers. She is also a Consultant at The Counterterrorism Group.

Routledge Studies on Government and the European Union

Edited by Andy Smith, University of Bordeaux, France

European Values
Challenges and Opportunities for EU Governance
Edited by François Foret and Oriane Calligaro

Governing Sustainability in the EU
From Political Discourse to Policy Practices
Ekaterina Domorenok

Decentring European Governance
Edited by Mark Bevir and Ryan Phillips

Subsidiarity and EU Multilevel Governance
Actors, Networks and Agendas
Serafín Pazos-Vidal

Governance and the European Social Dimension
Politics, Power and the Social Deficit in a Post-2010 EU
Paul Copeland

EU Socio-Economic Governance in Central and Eastern Europe
The European Semester and National Employment Policies
Mario Munta

Value Politics in the European Union
From Market to Culture and Back
Edited by François Foret and Jana Vargovčíková

The EU's Government of Worker Mobility
An Interdisciplinary Discussion
Edited by Hélène Michel and Mélanie Schmitt

The Rise of EU Police Cooperation
Governing Differentiated Integration
Franca König

THE RISE OF EU POLICE COOPERATION

Governing Differentiated Integration

Franca König

Routledge
Taylor & Francis Group
LONDON AND NEW YORK

First published 2023
by Routledge
4 Park Square, Milton Park, Abingdon, Oxon OX14 4RN

and by Routledge
605 Third Avenue, New York, NY 10158

Routledge is an imprint of the Taylor & Francis Group, an informa business

British Library Cataloguing-in-Publication Data
A catalogue record for this book is available from the British Library

ISBN: 978-1-032-20092-7 (hbk)
ISBN: 978-1-032-20094-1 (pbk)
ISBN: 978-1-003-26217-6 (ebk)

DOI: 10.4324/9781003262176

Typeset in Bembo
by KnowledgeWorks Global Ltd.

To all Europeans at heart.

CONTENTS

LIST OF FIGURES

LIST OF TABLES

ACKNOWLEDGEMENTS

A book is never a one-person show, something I learned very early on in my doctoral research. Although it was ultimately just me who spent countless hours in front of my laptop, I could not have done it without the support of everyone who has helped me complete this book and the dissertation on which it is based. I look back on the years between 2016 and 2022 with a feeling of tremendous gratitude and humbleness – I have learned so much. My thanks go to the Hertie School of Governance and the Konrad Adenauer Foundation for having supported me financially and ideationally throughout the creative process. From 2016 to 2017, the Hertie School of Governance provided financial support to my doctoral research. This book is based on the dissertation I submitted to the Hertie School in autumn 2019. In this context, I also received a doctoral stipend from the Konrad Adenauer Foundation between 2017 and 2019. I would like to extend a heartfelt thank you to both institutions for making full-time research possible for me.

I would also like to thank Markus Jachtenfuchs for his invaluable guidance through my doctoral journey. His supervision and support, especially in my first year, have contributed significantly to the successful completion of my doctoral research within three years. It goes without saying that this likewise applies to the help and encouragement of Florian Trauner and Christine Reh as well as many others at the Hertie School of Governance and beyond who listened, advised me and ultimately encouraged me to publish this book. I am also tremendously grateful to a number of people outside academia who have provided assistance and ideas along the way. My special thanks go to the helpful archivists of the German Federal Archives in Koblenz, particularly Michael Weins, and to the EUCARIS Secretariat, especially Idske Dijkstra. Additionally, I am deeply indebted to everyone who kindly agreed to being interviewed by me and made my research better by giving suggestions, establishing contacts and helping me think outside the box. It was such a pleasure to bounce ideas off people who share my enthusiasm for the topic!

On a personal note – although it is perhaps expected and may sound trite – I want to thank my parents for having nurtured a profound curiosity about the world in me and sparked my passion for the international sphere and my love for Europe. On a more trivial note, large parts of the dissertation preceding this book have been written at Café Roberta whose friendly team eventually started to prepare my coffee whenever I walked through their door. You always made my day! Many friends have likewise contributed to the successful completion of my research and this book. I greatly appreciate all the pep talks and emotional support I have received over countless cups of coffee. Marie, I am so happy to have had you by my side (at least in spirit if not in person). Thank you, Adina, Enora, Alexandra, Luis and Daniel, for reviewing substantial parts of my dissertation and this book, and providing helpful feedback when I could no longer see the wood for the trees. I am indebted to everyone who has kept me grounded throughout this academic journey – you know who you are. Finally, my thanks go to all those working and believing in European cooperation who have inspired me along the way and who understand my passion for Europe. You are the core of what the EU is and you will shape what it becomes. Let's do this!

Franca König
Berlin, June 2022

LIST OF ACRONYMS AND ABBREVIATIONS

AA	German Federal Foreign Office (*Auswärtiges Amt*)
AFSJ	Area of Freedom, Security and Justice
AHWGE	Ad-Hoc Working Group on Europol (as part of Trevi)
AML	Anti-Money Laundering
AMLA	Authority for Anti-Money Laundering and Countering the Financing of Terrorism
APIS	Advance Passenger Information System
ARO	Asset Recovery Office
ASU	Active Service Unit (a type of IRA cell)
AWF	Analysis Work File
BDK	Federation of German Detectives (*Bund Deutscher Kriminalbeamter*)
BfV	German Federal Office for the Protection of the Constitution (*Bundesamt für Verfassungsschutz*)
BKA	German Federal Criminal Police Office (*Bundeskriminalamt*)
BMI	German Federal Ministry of the Interior (*Bundesministerium des Innern*)
BND	German Federal Intelligence Service (*Bundesnachrichtendienst*)
BNDD	US Bureau of Narcotics and Dangerous Drugs
BR	Red Brigades (*Brigate Rosse*)
CARIN	Camden Assets Recovery Inter-Agency Network
CEPOL	European Union Agency for Law Enforcement Training (*Collège Européen de Police*)
CERT	Computer Emergency Response Team
CFT	Countering the Financing of Terrorism
CoE	Council of Europe

COSI	Standing Committee on Operational Cooperation on Internal Security
CTC	EU Counter-Terrorism Coordinator
CTG	Counter Terrorism Group
CTIRU	Counter-Terrorism Internet Referral Unit
DDoS	Distributed-Denial-of-Service
EAW	European Arrest Warrant
EC	European Community (also: European Communities)
EC3	European Cybercrime Centre
ECAB	Europol Criminal Assets Bureau
ECCP	European Cyber Crime Platform
ECD	Europol Council Decision
ECIM	European Criminal Intelligence Model
ECJ	European Court of Justice
ECRIS	European Criminal Records Information System
ECST	European Convention on the Suppression of Terrorism
ECTC	European Counter Terrorism Centre
EDIU	European Drug Intelligence Unit
EDPS	European Data Protection Supervisor
EDU	Europol Drugs Unit
EEAS	European External Action Service
EEC	European Economic Community
EFIPPP	Europol Financial Intelligence Public Private Partnership
EIS	Europol Information System
EMSC	European Migrant Smuggling Centre
ENU	Europol National Unit
EPC	European Political Cooperation
EPE	Europol Platform for Experts
EPPO	European Public Prosecutor's Office
ETA	*Euskadi Ta Askatasuna*
EU	European Union
EUCARIS	European Car and Driving License Information System
EUROPOL	European Police Office (European Union Agency for Law Enforcement Cooperation)
FATF	Financial Action Task Force
FBN	US Federal Bureau of Narcotics
FCO	British Foreign and Commonwealth Office
FIU	Financial Intelligence Unit
FMI	French Ministry of the Interior (*Ministère de l'Intérieur France*)
FP	Focal Point
GA	General Assembly
GDPR	General Data Protection Regulation
GTAZ	German Joint Counter-Terrorism Centre (*Gemeinsames Terrorismusabwehrzentrum*)

HENU	Head of Europol National Unit
HO	British Home Office
HTCC	High Tech Crime Centre
IMK	German Standing Conference of State Interior Ministers (*Ständige Konferenz der Innenminister und -senatoren der Länder*)
INTERPOL	International Criminal Police Organisation
IRA	Irish Republican Army
IRU	Internet Referral Unit
IS	Islamic State (also see ISIL and ISIS)
ISIL	Islamic State of Iraq and the Levant
ISIS	Islamic State of Iraq and Syria
ISS	Internal Security Strategy
JHA	Justice and Home Affairs
JIT	Joint Investigation Team
JMLIT	Joint Money Laundering Intelligence Taskforce
JOT	Joint Operational Team
JPSG	Joint Parliamentary Scrutiny Group
LEWP	Law Enforcement Working Party
LKA	German State Criminal Police Office (*Landeskriminalamt*)
MPS	Metropolitan Police Services (London)
NATO	North Atlantic Treaty Organisation
NCSS	National Cyber Security Strategy
NDIU	National Drug Intelligence Unit
NGO	Non-Governmental Organisation
NRA	National Risk Assessment
OCTA	EU Organised Crime & Threat Assessment (Europol)
OPEC	Organisation of the Petroleum Exporting Countries
PFLP	Popular Front for the Liberation of Palestine
PJCCM	Police and Judicial Cooperation in Criminal Matters
PNR	Passenger Name Records
PWGT	Police Working Group on Terrorism
RAF	Red Army Faction (*Rote Armee Fraktion*)
RCI	Rational Choice Institutionalism
RDW	Dutch National Vehicles and Driving Licences Registration Authority (*Dienst Wegverkeer*, formerly *Rijksdienst voor het Wegverkeer*)
SEA	Single European Act
SIENA	Secure Information Exchange Network Application
SIS	Schengen Information System
TCA	EU-UK Trade and Cooperation Agreement
TEU	Treaty on European Union

TFTP	Terrorist Finance Tracking Programme
TG	Target Group
TGN	Transgovernmental Network
TREVI	Trevi Group
TWP	Terrorism Working Party
UK	United Kingdom of Northern Ireland and Great Britain
UN	United Nations
US	United States (of America)

INTRODUCTION

On 13 November 2015, more than 100 people were killed and over 350 injured in six coordinated terror attacks instigated in Paris by the so-called 'Islamic State' (IS). In the following days, French President François Hollande called the attacks an 'act of war' and declared a national state of emergency, which would be extended six times by Parliament and remain in place for almost two years (Hollande 2015). The attacks were not only deeply unsettling from a human point of view, but they also unearthed fundamental albeit long-standing questions about European cooperation in the fight against terrorism. The Belgian authorities had possessed evidence of a concrete threat since mid-2014: plans for an "irreversible act" by the Abdeslam brothers who were significantly involved in the Paris attacks (Paravicini & Cerulus 2016). However, comprehensive surveillance of the suspects did not occur due to a lack of capacity, and information exchange with the French authorities failed. When this became known in the aftermath of the attacks, it gave rise to a heated debate about internal security cooperation in the European Union (EU) and how to improve it.

There can be no doubt about the significance of EU internal security and particularly police cooperation. Events like the recent terrorist attacks in Paris, Brussels, Berlin, Vienna and other places all over Europe demonstrate time and again the need to strengthen common efforts and collective action on a transgovernmental if not European level. Additionally, public polls show consistently high citizen support across EU Member States for a stronger role of the EU in internal security (Special Eurobarometer 432 & 290). Finally, EU heads of state or government have likewise reiterated the importance of this undertaking. They largely agree that coordination and cooperation at the EU level are vital in related issue areas, especially with regard to information exchange (Bigo et al. 2015; Council 2015a). Streamlining communication channels and integrating approaches have been especially emphasised by policymakers with a

DOI: 10.4324/9781003262176-1

view to improving the efficiency and effectiveness of European internal security governance and police cooperation. What is more, the latter has increasingly become associated with EU policy venues. This can be seen in the expanding role for supranational actors in police cooperation, most notably the European Commission and of course the European Police Office (Europol). In December 2020, European heads of state and government welcomed the Commission's detailed proposal for a new EU Counter-Terrorism Agenda and backed the amendment of Europol's legal framework to strengthen the agency's mandate and improve law enforcement cooperation across the Union. At the time of writing, EU Member States are additionally discussing an ambitious proposal for an EU police cooperation code, which seeks to boost cross-border operational cooperation, information exchange and automated data-sharing.

Nevertheless, many different formats and types of police cooperation still coexist and continue to mushroom, causing inefficiencies at best, duplication and waste at worst. Informal networks grow side by side with, but are often not linked to, official institutions and formalised platforms for cooperation. Similarly, intergovernmental modes of working together coexist with transgovernmental and supranational ones but are for the most part neither integrated nor coordinated sufficiently or at all. It appears puzzling that EU Member States should on the one hand agree on the merits of enhanced cooperation and an integrated EU approach, and at the same time advance an incredibly complex governance environment with overlapping and diffused structures that often make cooperation let alone governance rather inefficient and difficult. This is arguably even more striking when considering that police cooperation is a predominantly operational policy domain, and related issue areas should be primarily driven by effectiveness concerns.

This book sets out to investigate which causal factors drive the national preferences of EU Member States on integration in the area of EU police cooperation. While the analytical focus lies on the explanatory power of the factors that shape state integration preferences, the qualitative nature of this assessment and its relatively long temporal outlook might additionally shed light on trends and patterns behind institutional choice and differentiated integration[1] in this policy domain. Drawing on existing theories of European integration, the role of interdependence, politicisation as well as supra- and subnational policy entrepreneurship are traced throughout the institutional evolution of EU police cooperation, beginning in the 1970s. While there is high confidence that these factors play a substantial part in shaping state preferences and thus integration outcomes, few studies have actually unpacked to what extent they do so and how precisely they function as causal conditions. This book attempts to unpack how and to what extent these conditions affect state preferences within EU police cooperation at the example of concrete institutional 'milestone' agreements.

In the following, it first provides an overview of the state of affairs in EU internal security and concretely EU police cooperation. This includes a brief account of the historical development of this policy domain and the current empirical state of play. Chapter 1 sketches the evolution of EU police cooperation along three 'waves' of institutional development. It then turns to possible explanations and what we possibly know about why this field evolved in the way it has. Departing from key theories of European integration, it identifies three potential driving factors of governmental integration preferences that serve as this book's theoretical framework: issue-specific interdependencies, politicisation and policy entrepreneurship from above and below. The subsequent chapters (2 through 5) investigate whether and to what extent these factors can help explain how EU police cooperation came into existence and has increasingly developed a dynamic of its own. They analyse EU police cooperation through four comparative case studies. Each one was conducted through a qualitative, process-tracing approach and supplemented by problem-oriented expert interviews. Each chapter focuses on one instance of significant change in the nature of European police cooperation and the degree of EU integration. Accordingly, Chapter 2 scrutinises the initiation of the Trevi Group in the 1970s, the first semi-formal cooperation venue comprising all Member States. Chapter 3 resumes a few decades later, tracing the process that led to the creation of Europol in the 1990s. The third case study – investigated by Chapter 4 – comprises Europol's institutional development in the early 2000s, particularly its integration into the EU framework and subsequent establishment as the EU's official law enforcement agency. The last empirical chapter, Chapter 5, studies the development of EU police cooperation between 2010 and today. Amongst other things, it investigates the adoption of the Europol Regulation in 2016 – an institutional milestone that changed the organisation's legal framework yet again, barely seven years after the previous change. It also looks at the development of specialised centres at Europol and at the agency's development post-Brexit. This includes the 2020 proposal for a revision of Europol's mandate. All four case study chapters trace the role of interdependence, politicisation and policy entrepreneurship, and assess their importance as shapers of state preferences on EU police cooperation. Finally, the conclusion summarises the overall findings from the analysis of EU police cooperation between 1976 and 2022. It lists a number of broader conclusions that can be drawn from the case studies with respect to drivers of state preferences as well as differentiation and integration processes in this policy domain.

This book argues that EU police cooperation has long been on the rise and is increasingly developing a dynamic of its own. Despite persisting differentiation, this policy domain has become progressively integrated and established within the EU framework. Not only has law enforcement cooperation become institutionalised at European level, it has become tightly embedded in national settings and networks. As a consequence, relevant EU structures and actors have more and more assumed a role as principals rather than mere agents. And they continue to do so. Nevertheless, interdependencies primarily shape governmental preferences in favour of integration. While external interconnectedness in common threats acted as largest driver to this end in the early stages of European police cooperation, internal institutional linkages have become increasingly important since at least the mid-1990s. Both challenge Member States with collective action and coordination problems and thus produce functional pressure on governments to cooperate if not integrate.

Whereas interdependencies seem to prominently drive pro-integration preferences, politicisation often acts as enabler of other driving factors rather than having an independent effect. At the same time and contrary to common conception, its impact can be relatively strong in the area of EU police cooperation. Whether high politicisation affects state preferences negatively or positively hinges on contextual factors, most notably the framing by EU and subnational actors. The single or aggregate effect of 'politicising events'[2] frequently presents a window of opportunity for policy entrepreneurship. Especially shocks and crises generate high salience and visibility of related topics or issue areas in EU police cooperation. In doing so, they often illustrate existing interdependencies and produce significant public pressure and political momentum that tends to push states to act on their preferences. This book demonstrates that high politicisation more often than not yields pro-integration preferences, especially in conjunction with supranational policy entrepreneurship.

By comparison, policy entrepreneurs harness the functional and public pressure from interdependencies and politicisation in their efforts to drive state preferences towards integration. Whereas subnational officials from domestic law enforcement and security authorities initially rather pushed Member States towards differentiation, their advocacy is progressively moving from bureaucratic resistance towards the promotion of integration within EU police cooperation today. However, this book finds no strong evidence for the universal influence of subnational policy entrepreneurship on state preferences. Its impact was highly asymmetrical in line with the different security cultures and political systems of Member States. By contrast, the analysis in this book clearly demonstrates the significant and growing role of EU actors as shapers of pro-integration preferences. They have benefitted from rising internal interdependencies within the EU. Spill-over effects and a gradually emerging path-dependency increasingly enabled supranational policy entrepreneurs to successfully promote integration within European police cooperation. Especially since 2010, EU actors have harnessed functional and public pressure to cultivate spill-overs and shift state preferences towards centralisation in this field. Whether they will be able to maintain and expand their influence into the future and thus advance further integration within EU police cooperation remains to be seen.

Finally, this book asserts that differentiated integration matters. Or differently put: EU police cooperation is a matter of governing differentiated integration. Rather than straightforward integration this field has evolved through parallel processes of differentiation and integration. And it continues to do so. This book's empirical chapters illustrate how instances of differentiated integration are often driven by asymmetry, that is, the asymmetrical effects of driving factors across governments and integration dimensions. When interdependence, politicisation and/or policy entrepreneurship do not generate similar levels of functional or public pressure across Member States, their asymmetric effects prevent preference convergence. This asymmetry frequently produces different integration pressure on different levels or dimensions of cooperation: the extent of centralisation, territorial extension and functional scope. Member States may for example see a need to cooperate across the full territorial extension of the EU or across all issues related to terrorism or organised crime, yet may not see a need to centralise powers at the EU level. Where asymmetrical levels of 'affectedness' lead to diverging state preferences, yet generate enough pressure on some Member States, the latter favour instances of differentiated integration. The case studies of this book demonstrate how governments and practitioners deliberately advocate temporary differentiation when lack of preference convergence prevents full integration. Rather than presenting an explicit preference, flexible integration and avant-garde group approaches seem to constitute temporary, operations-driven strategies in EU police cooperation. While Member States often employ avant-garde groups as short-run tactics to cope with the relatively stronger effects of driving factors at home, this book finds that they rarely prefer differentiation but usually advocate it with the aim of achieving some degree of long-term integration through flexible, 'multi-speed' models.

Since its beginnings in the 1970s, EU police cooperation has evolved significantly. While it has become increasingly integrated over the years, especially in the past decade, it continuous to be marked by differentiation and variable geometry. However, the study of this policy domain suggests that these trends do not necessarily conflict with integration, even present a tool for advancing police cooperation among European Member States in the long run. How exactly this will play out in the future ultimately hinges on the impact of interdependence, politicisation and policy entrepreneurship on state preferences and on the dimensions of vertical and horizontal integration as well as the functional scope of EU police cooperation.

Notes

1 The simultaneity of differentiation and integration processes that result in integration in the long run.
2 Events that significantly raise the salience of an issue, sparking public and political debate.

1

EU INTERNAL SECURITY AND POLICE COOPERATION

Putting Theory into Perspective

Since its creation the EU has grown steadily and developed into an unprecedented showcase of supranationalism.[1] Yet, today differentiation rather than straightforward integration has become a key concept in many areas of EU governance. Beside the increasingly complex institutional reality, the political situation in Europe requires not only recognising but also politically incorporating this phenomenon and seeking ways to reconcile differentiation with further integration instead of making them mutually exclusive. This is more important than ever before, as recent developments demonstrate such as the 2016 'Brexit' referendum in the United Kingdom (UK) or the widespread surge of right-wing populist parties that generally oppose European ideas and have been able to expand public support in the course of the COVID-19 pandemic. Some argue that this does not concern the area of internal security as much because it remains a competence of national Member States rather than EU institutions or supranational regulation (Block 2011; Friedrichs 2008; Herschinger et al. 2013; Kirchner & Sperling 2007). Yet, European cooperation on issues of internal security has intensified tremendously over time and has developed more and more of an integration dynamic, especially in recent decades.

Internal security may be understood and conceptualised in many different ways. Definitions vary not only within the theoretical literature but also across national systems, depending on the domestic judicial or political tradition. Over the years, the area of EU Justice and Home Affairs (JHA) has undergone significant changes and along with it the different approaches to and understandings of components and issue areas falling within the domain of internal security. While broader concepts of internal security exist and may undeniably be well-justified in some regards, for the purpose of a focused, comparative study of the drivers behind the integration preferences of Member States, this book employs a more narrow, traditional definition. With a view

DOI: 10.4324/9781003262176-2

to EU internal security cooperation, it limits itself to the aspects of police and policing activities. EU police cooperation especially demonstrates the integration trend in the area of JHA and thus lends itself to an analysis of integration drivers. A continuously growing number of common channels and fora, often at the EU level, enables Member States to work together on a wide range of topics, including international terrorism or serious and organised crime. The empirical literature clearly illustrates that increasingly dynamic developments have been at work in the field of EU police cooperation since at least the 1990s and have led to modes of cooperation that go beyond mere intergovernmentalism through formally established channels. However, even in this smaller area of JHA, different understandings and interpretations persist, deriving from diverging national security and police cultures.

An Empirical Overview of the State of Affairs

Many accounts have been written on the evolution of European policing and EU internal security cooperation (Anderson et al. 1995; Andreas & Nadelmann 2006; Bigo 1996; Busch 1995; Fijnaut & Hermans 1987; Knelangen 2001). Therefore, this chapter limits itself to a brief historic overview. It highlights broader trends, milestones and major developments of cooperation, which it structures along three 'waves.' From no EU-level policy coordination before the 1970s, internal security cooperation gradually developed across multiple stages, including a period of enhanced intergovernmental coordination, first outside the framework of the European (Economic) Community (EC or EEC), then within the EU pillar of JHA in the 1990s, to finally become increasingly integrated into EU modes of joint decision-making and the community method in recent decades.

When evaluating the historic evolution of internal security cooperation in the EU, two observations stand out. Although European intergovernmental and police cooperation may retrospectively seem like a linear process, these developments were neither clear-cut nor straightforward. Instead, the history of internal security cooperation consists of multiple, often reciprocal processes of differentiation and integration that occurred simultaneously and interacted on various levels of governance (police, governments, institutions). As former Europol Deputy Director Willy Bruggeman (2016: 30) reflects: "Looking back, police cooperation emerged as a series of ad-hoc developments, best characterised as 'a crowded police space'." The historic development of EU police cooperation can be divided into three broader 'waves' (see Figure 1.1). The first occurred in the 1970s and 1980s with the establishment of the first substantial intergovernmental cooperation arrangements, albeit outside the EEC framework. This period was marked by a beginning regularisation of cooperation. The second wave of cooperation developments took place around the 1990s, including the formal creation of a JHA pillar as one cornerstone of the EU legislative framework and the foundation of Europol and its predecessor, the Europol Drugs Unit (EDU). Finally, a

1970s **Trevi Group (1976)** - WG 1 on terrorism - WG 2 on police technical matters & training (1980s) - WG 3 on transnat. organised crime - Trevi '92 (in relation to Schengen)	***1st wave*** *rather informal, network-based cooperation:* *intergovernmental*
1990s - Trevi ad-hoc WG on Europol (1991) ***Maastricht Treaty (1992)*** *creation of JHA as Third Pillar of EU* **Europol Drugs Unit (1994)** - Ministerial Agreement (1993) - Joint Action (1995) **Europol Convention (1995)** ***Amsterdam Treaty (1997)*** *targeting an EU AFSJ (Art. 1(5)) & PJCC as own EU pillar*	***2nd wave*** *beginning shift into EU framework:* *beginning formalisation and institutionalisation, intergovernmental*
2000s **Prüm Treaty (2005)** - gradual integration into the EU framework within three years ***Lisbon Treaty (2007)*** *dissolution of pillar structure and subsumption under single consolidated EU framework* **Europol Council Decision (2009)** - establishing Europol as EU agency **Europol Regulation (2016)** - further institutionalisation and more operational flexibility **Revised Europol Regulation (2021)** - further strengthening of the mandate	***3rd wave*** *increasing centralisation:* *intergovernmental, but increasingly 'supranational' modes of decision-making* ***Beginning of a 4th wave?***

FIGURE 1.1 Three Waves of EU Internal Security Cooperation

third wave emerged around the turn of the century with the Amsterdam Treaty and an increasing shift of cooperation into the EU framework as well as towards supranational fora and modes of decision-making.

The First Wave: Beginnings of European Police Cooperation

EU police cooperation can be said to date back to the 1970s. A wave of national terrorist acts across a number of EU Member States in the late 1960s and early 1970s – mainly Germany, Italy, France and the UK – sparked various intergovernmental meetings (Anderson et al. 1995: 170–171; Bunyan 1993; Knelangen 2001: 97). The rather nationally oriented terrorism of that time differs significantly from the more recent international 'fourth wave' terrorism that it is often religiously motivated and confronts EU Member States with new threats such as radicalisation and 'homegrown terrorism' (Rapoport 2013; cf. Bossong 2013). Yet, radical separatist groups as well as left- and right-wing extremists like the French *La Gauche Prolétarienne*, the Irish Republican Army (IRA) in the UK or the Red Army Faction (RAF) in Germany provided an unprecedented momentum for European intergovernmental cooperation on terrorism (Bell 2013; Crelinsten & Schmid 1993; Von Hippel 2005).

Accordingly, a multitude of different initiatives were established throughout the 1970s (see Figure 1.2 for an exemplary albeit not exhaustive overview), ranging from the Club de Berne and the Pompidou Group to the Vienna Club and the Trevi Group. Although TREVI was kept outside the EEC framework, it can be argued that it laid the foundation for enhanced European police cooperation and thereby EU integration in the policy domain of internal security, since it presented a path-setting European functional response to terrorism where the International Criminal Police Organisation (Interpol) had been unwilling or unable to react (Fijnaut & Hermans 1987; Giering 1997: 117). While TREVI was initially merely one of many cooperation arrangements, its semi-institutional

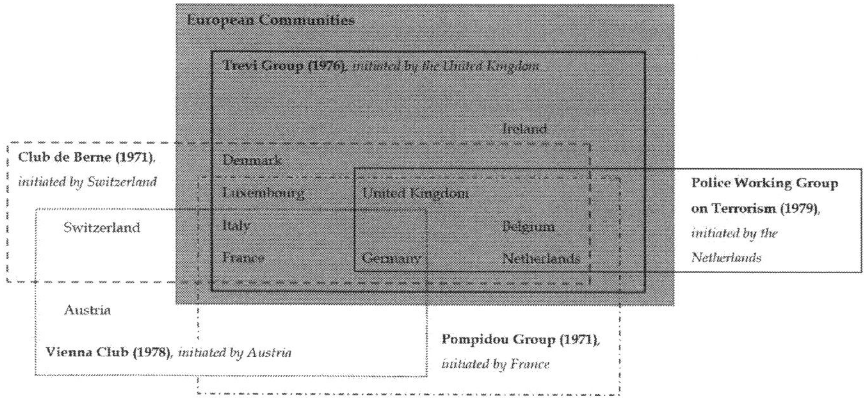

FIGURE 1.2 Mapping European Cooperation Arrangements in the 1970s

character and degree of formalisation make it a historic milestone of European police cooperation – the first attempt at regularised cooperation between macro-levels of security governance in addition to informal cooperation between micro-levels (Fijnaut 1992b: 103; Knelangen 2001: 98).

For almost two decades EEC Member States frequently met and cooperated on different levels (ministers, senior officials, police officers) in the framework of the Trevi Group and its working groups (WGs) (Benyon et al. 1993: 154; Bunyan 1993: 2–3). Already during this period the group's functional scope gradually expanded from terrorism to drug trafficking and transnational crime (Aden 1998: 77–80; Fijnaut 2016: 51).

The Second Wave: Associating Police Cooperation with the EU

The second 'wave' of security and police cooperation in Europe emerged in the 1990s, ushered in by the Maastricht Treaty, also known as Treaty on European Union (TEU). Signed in 1992, Title VI TEU established JHA, including police cooperation, as one of the central pillars of the EU (Monar & Morgan 1994). Although this Third Pillar remained on an intergovernmental basis, the decision of European policymakers to move JHA cooperation into the EU's legal and single institutional framework presents a remarkable change compared to the cooperation of the 1970s and 1980s. This development marks the beginning shift of EU police cooperation away from TREVI as a single intergovernmental cooperation platform and towards a first formalisation of working and coordination arrangements at European level (Peek 1994). Initially, EU bodies and supranational actors had little or no say in related matters and JHA policies, especially in the early 1990s. They remained overall excluded from decision- and policy-making in this field, which stayed a Member States' competence (Kaunert et al. 2015). Yet, the Maastricht Treaty laid the foundation for the further institutional developments and cooperation structures that exist today in European internal security governance (Siegele 1992). Article K.1, for example, stipulates the creation of Europol by listing an area of 'common interest' for all EU Member States:

> police cooperation for the purposes of preventing and combating terrorism, unlawful drug trafficking and other serious forms of international crime, including if necessary certain aspects of customs cooperation, in connection with the organization of a Union-wide system for exchanging information within a European Police Office.
>
> *(para. 9)*

Accordingly, an additional Ad-Hoc working group on Europol (AHWGE) was founded and mandated with its realisation as part of TREVI. As a first step, the EDU was launched as a Europol forerunner. It was operational by January 1994 and marked the institutional beginnings of the second wave of centralising police cooperation in the EU. The AHWGE was however also responsible for preparing and drafting the Europol Convention that formally established Europol. It was signed by all 12 Member States on 26 July 1995 and debatably presented a provisional culmination of the second-wave formalisation and institutionalisation process that had been initiated at the end of the 1980s. As stipulated by Art. 43(5) of the Europol Convention, the EDU seized its activities, and its resources were integrated into the new institution. Europol under the Convention was still an inherently intergovernmental body with a limited mandate that needed to be implemented and further developed by the Member States, most notably through their representatives in Europol's Management Board (Europol 2016a: 32–35).

In the context of the historic evolution of EU police cooperation, two other significant events must be mentioned in addition to the entry into force of the Europol Convention: the Treaties of Amsterdam and Lisbon. When the Amsterdam Treaty was signed by the European Council on 2 October 1997, it effectively amended the TEU, most notably through envisaging the establishment of an EU Area of Freedom, Security and Justice (AFSJ), under which JHA policies would fall (Art. 1(5) & (11)). The Amsterdam Treaty thus further strengthened the role of the EU in the transnational governance of internal security (Kirchner & Sperling 2007). A significant number of policy areas were transferred from the intergovernmental third to the supranational first 'Community pillar' (cf. Art. 61–64). The focus of Title VI – previously cooperation in the area of JHA – was dramatically narrowed and renamed to Police and Judicial Cooperation in Criminal Matters (PJCCM) (Art. 1(11); cf. Lavenex 2010; Schütze 2015: 28–29). This change matters because it presents a substantial move away from purely intergovernmental to more joint modes of decision-making in the wider area of EU internal security (Leuffen et al. 2013: 222 ff.). Yet, it should take another ten years and another treaty before Member States would make a major institutional choice that further advanced EU police cooperation.

The Third Wave: Moving Police Cooperation into the EU Framework

The Lisbon Treaty (2007) presented a 'game changer' for EU police cooperation. It dissolved the former pillar structure and merged the supranational first with the intergovernmental second and third pillars under the consolidated single framework of the EU. This opened the floodgates to a rising trend towards supranationalisation, for example, through the application of community decision-making methods to internal security governance such as the ordinary legislative procedure rather than unanimity (Herschinger et al. 2013: 210 ff.; Leuffen et al. 2013: 222 ff.). Lavenex (2010) additionally highlights the emergence and persistence of a multitude of 'semi-autonomous' agencies and bodies in the AFSJ, including in the area of police cooperation (cf. Aden 2015). Finally, the EU itself obtained legal personality under the Lisbon Treaty, a significant gain in power for a 'construct in between state and international organisation' (Leuffen et al. 2013: 8–9).

Of course, this process was not a linear one and accompanied by instances of differentiation and flexible integration. For example, on 27 May 2005 merely seven of the 25 Member States at the time signed an intergovernmental convention on intensifying cooperation on terrorism, cross-border crime and illegal migration. When the so-called Prüm Treaty was signed that year by Austria, Belgium, France, Germany, Luxembourg, the Netherlands and Spain, it already contained as a concrete target the expansion of the provisions to all EU Member States through the transfer of the agreement into the EU framework within three years (Art. 1(4)).[2] While various Member States had already joined the Treaty in the following years, in 2008 – roughly 12 months after the adoption of the Lisbon Treaty – a number of provisions were indeed formally integrated into the structure of PJCCM through the 'Prüm Decision' (Council Decision 2008/615/JHA, 2008; cf. Balzacq et al. 2006; Niemeier & Zerbst 2007; Schober 2017). This development is relevant for the overall course of EU internal security cooperation because it marks a role model case of differentiated integration a concept that has become ever more important since the Lisbon Treaty and arguably constitutes a core element of the third wave of EU internal security and police cooperation (Tekin 2015).

Two more 'milestone' decisions must be mentioned here as part of this third wave: the Europol Council Decision (ECD) and the Europol Regulation (2016/794). The ECD was adopted by the Council in 2009 and replaced the intergovernmental convention that had governed Europol until then. It established the body as the EU's official law enforcement agency, making it subject to the Union's legal framework and budget (Council Decision 2009/371/JHA; cf. Europol 2016a: 36–39). Not only did this decision formally integrate Europol into the supranational institutional structure of the EU, but it also expanded the role of EU actors in police cooperation. The Commission, for example, gained a regular seat on the otherwise intergovernmental Management Board of Europol (Art. 31(1)). The ECD (Art. 48) also granted the European Parliament the power to request hearings with the Presidency of the Council, the Chairperson of the Management Board and the Europol Director on matters concerning Europol.

Whereas other developments have unfolded as well since the entry into force of the Lisbon Treaty and the ECD, this book limits itself to finally mentioning the Europol Regulation adopted on 11 May 2016. Compared to the changes from the Europol Convention to the ECD, this regulation does not represent as much of a substantial transformation. Nonetheless, the choice of a regulation – a legal instrument that is binding throughout all Member States – presents a remarkable step-up. It can be argued to continue the institutionalisation process of European police cooperation, illustrated for example by the shift in voting rules of the Europol Management Board from two-thirds majority voting to the regularisation of majority voting (Art. 15(1)). Other than that, the Europol Regulation embodies a macro-level reaction to new and operational security requirements, perceived as 'European,' which is reflected in many of its provisions. For example, under the Regulation Europol gains flexibility to act in response to changing circumstances. Concretely, this means that the European Commission may authorise measures by taking 'adequacy decisions' in response to arising needs as pointed out by the Council and the Europol Management Board (ibid.). While these provisions imply a greater role for the Commission, they of course also leave considerable room for further institutional development of the organisation by Member States and in relation to operational requirements. This has especially mattered in recent years and continues to matter today, as ambitions for a European FBI resurface amidst negotiations on a revised Europol mandate and new regulation as well as in the context of designing the future of EU police cooperation after the UK finally exited the EU on 1 January 2021. We may well find ourselves at a crossroads, the brink of a fourth wave in the integration and institutional development of EU police cooperation.

Five Observations on the Empirical State of Affairs

While integration is clearly taking place in this domain of 'core state powers,'[3] integration preferences are asymmetrical and variable, and differ across states, issues and time. The empirical literature additionally demonstrates that politicisation, interdependence as well as sub- and supranational actors matter as driving forces of EU internal security and police cooperation. With the narrow understanding of internal security as police activities in mind, five observations may be highlighted with regard to the empirical state of affairs in EU JHA.

First, the EU's governance of internal security and police cooperation faces an inherent tension between integrating structures and policies at the EU level on the one hand and state sovereignty and the monopoly on the use of force on the other (Herschinger et al. 2013; Jachtenfuchs et al. 2008; Rittberger et al. 2014). For a long time, security has been a core power and responsibility of the state but is recently becoming an area of pluralistic governance, thereby challenging traditional conceptions of the state. Policing practice has been transformed by the option to privatise security governance and the technological capacity for large-scale and cross-border monitoring, both of which go against entrenched ideas of state sovereignty and territorial integrity (Sheptycki 2002). Integration in this domain of core state powers thus seems to create a growing tension between EU cooperation and national sovereignty.

Second, no agreement exists with regard to what recent changes in internal security governance mean for the nature of EU governance more generally and the relationship between EU actors and Member States. Do national interests and governments, as many studies argue, still primarily drive (and correct) European and transnational cooperation developments as well as the process of internationalisation of EU internal security (Friedrichs 2008; Herschinger et al. 2013; Kaunert & Léonard 2012; Van Buuren 2012)? Or is EU police cooperation moving towards supranationalism with a progressively "expanded operational role and greater autonomy" for EU actors like Europol (Occhipinti 2015: 239; cf. Busuioc et al. 2011)? It remains unclear whether EU governance in this policy domain is moving towards intergovernmentalism or supranationalism, differentiation or integration.

Third, the importance of the public sphere in the governance and scrutiny of JHA policies has evolved in line with the EU's role in internal security. This can be seen in the growing importance of politicisation, understood here as social contestation and deliberation processes, in European integration dynamics more generally (Leuffen et al. 2015; Zürn & Ecker-Ehrhardt 2013) or in the societal construction of security and the relationship between discourse, securitisation and identity in particular policy areas like drugs and terrorism (Friedrichs 2008; Herschinger et al. 2013; cf. Balzacq & Léonard 2013; de Graaf 2010a, 2015; Lange 1999; Selchow 2016). Nonetheless, few accounts prioritise or target more general, theoretical conclusions about the implications of this trend for European integration. Leuffen et al. (2013, 2015) argue that the interplay of politicisation, interdependence between countries and state preference compatibility determines the degree of differentiation or integration in a policy field. The empirical literature confirms this statement and simultaneously questions the assumption that politicisation acts either as an integration driver or obstacle. Counterterrorism is for instance regarded as an area of limited supranationalism and few formal institutions. It is frequently highly politicised and relies on the distinct national cultures of security and intelligence specialists (Bures 2012; Fägersten 2010; Occhipinti 2015). All of these factors appear to pose obstacles to integration. Yet, police cooperation on this issue has been pushed strongly towards a more integrated approach, including the creation of a specialised common counterterrorism database and institutions such as the ECTC. Carrapiço and Trauner (2013: 357) show how the "different legal systems and policing traditions" of Member States have impeded EU police cooperation on organised crime but simultaneously enabled Europol to establish itself as 'point of reference' and successfully 'Europeanize' national policies. The policy domain of EU JHA is increasingly and visibly open to the influence of politicisation and to the scrutiny of private actors and the public sphere.

Fourth, empirical studies on the evolution of EU JHA extensively document the parallel evolution and existence of hard and soft modes of governance. The relevance and practical involvement of sub- and supranational actors are growing in areas and levels of cooperation previously reserved for states (cf. Frevel & Rogers 2016; Jones & van Steden 2013). Understood through the lens of policy entrepreneurship, international policing, police cooperation and security governance are primarily shaped by organisational self-interest and considerations of bureaucratic autonomy and survival *vis-à-vis* the state (Deflem 2002; Lavenex & Wagner 2007). While the majority view persists that national governments are the primary drivers of European integration, executive stakeholders such as security professionals and police officials also influence this process. Subnational levels may mould collective action at the EU level through horizontal transgovernmental cooperation with equivalent levels, for example, within the police and practitioners networks that often generate political impacts in addition to operational benefits (Anderson 1989; Bigo 1996; Busch 1995; Nadelmann 1993). A look into the practice of EU policymaking confirms that 'grassroot transgovernmentalism' often plays a role in the formation of state preferences in JHA. Domestic security experts and practitioners' networks often possess significant agenda-setting powers in this intelligence-driven policy domain and are able to complement or steer high-level agenda-setting from 'above' (cf. Princen & Rhinard 2006). Although formal *de jure* decision-making remains in the hands of the Member States, this relies largely on the *de facto* involvement of actors below and above the national level. The blurring of different governance and decision-making levels as well as the network character of transgovernmental cooperation in the area of JHA makes a sharp distinction between hard and soft modes of governance impractical (Cross 2011; Den Boer 2014; Den Boer et al. 2008). On the contrary, empirical evidence suggests that we are observing a common trend towards a "diffusion of responsibilities, either inside or outside government, through the generalization of network structures" (Dupont 2004: 87).

In view of the influence of transgovernmental networks (TGNs) on state preferences and agenda-setting in international security cooperation what can be stated with regard to their influence on each other and the implementation of agreed collective action? Not much in their favour, it seems at first glance. Fägersten (2010, 2016) concludes that different bureaucratic cultures and interests often inhibit cooperation in intelligence-sharing. Likewise, for the realm of counterterrorism, Bures (2012) notes that a lack of trust, diverging bureaucratic channels and varying modes of working may cause counter-productive duplication and crowding in the field. However, relatively little research has been conducted on the concrete impact of these differentiated networks on security governance or policy outcomes at the EU level. It remains unclear what the causes and effects of the changing composition and conditions of security networks are. Are designed networks that follow supranationally prescribed institutionalisation more efficient or effective than spontaneously founded informal horizontal networks? What are the advantages of practical problem-solving and day-to-day cooperation for integrating intergovernmental arrangements into the EU's structure? Here again, it seems impractical to distinguish sharply between formal and informal cooperation, as the lines between both are increasingly blurred and both progressively occur within 'formal' institutions such as Europol (Carrapiço & Trauner 2013; Johnston & Shearing 2003; Wolff & Mounier 2012). Kahler (2009: 17), for example, lists three modes of networked governance that may evolve in parallel and interact with one another:

- "Governance through networks that emerge from state membership in formal intergovernmental organisations (Hafner-Burton & Montgomery 2009);
- Governance by transgovernmental networks, cross-border networks of government agencies (Eilstrup-Sangiovanni 2009);
- Governance that includes a role for private or NGO networks in particular issue areas (Cowhey & Mueller 2009)."

All three types can be found in many structures of EU internal security governance. For example, Europol itself has emerged as a consequence of state membership in the EC/EU, and numerous networks have since emerged from state membership in Europol. In addition, Europol embodies operational police networks and transgovernmental cooperation between interior ministries, taking place in fora like the Europol Management Board. Finally, there is a role for private and other non-state actors at Europol. The number of crime-fighting alliances with academia, think tanks, non-governmental organisations (NGOs) and corporations exemplify this, for example, in the area of cyber and financial crime including Internet and communications providers, financial institutes and banks.

Next to the emergence of informal, networked and horizontal forms of governance alongside the influence of subnational actors, the empirical reality of EU policymaking clearly captures the growing relevance of formal institutions and supranational actors in EU JHA. Similar to the asymmetrical diffusion and power of informal modes of governance across areas of internal security, formal institutions display varying degrees of influence in different issue areas. Block (2011) for instance claims that Council instruments had little or no effect on national policing practices and argues that the impact of institutions is directly related to whether instruments are developed on the basis of police rationality and input. By contrast, Friedrichs (2008) finds that institutions related to cooperation on terrorism are comparatively stronger than in the domain of drugs. Others have assessed the areas of money laundering and extradition (Herschinger et al. 2011), or have evaluated the importance of institutions in the AFSJ overall (Carrapiço & Trauner 2013; Kaunert 2011; Lavenex 2010). However, broader, cross-cutting explanations for the growing role of supranational actors are still largely missing.[4] Some evidence points to the role of common threats and spillover effects across policy areas (Friedrichs 2008; Monar 2011) or the functional utility of common institutions that help establish certainty about expectations, provide information about other states' behaviour (Herschinger & Jachtenfuchs 2012; Knelangen 2001, 2006), can address efficiency concerns and solve collective action problems (Herschinger et al. 2011; Mitsilegas et al. 2003).

Nonetheless, "institutional issues have been relatively neglected overall," especially the recently emerging role of EU agencies in the area of JHA (Kaunert et al. 2013: 274). More research is particularly needed on interest shapers and 'institutional dynamics' driving the emergence and further development of supranational actorness in internal security (ibid.). This includes a closer look at the relationship between formal and less hierarchical institutions as well as multi-level governance structures, for which few studies exist.[5]

Fifth, integration in the area of JHA has been anything but linear and seamless. In fact, state preferences in this policy domain seem to be highly asymmetrical and variable; they differ across states, issues and time in line with diverging degrees of cross-country interdependence. Interdependence in this context may be understood as the interconnectedness in the causes and effects of security threats and thereby in the governance of internal security. A large body of empirical research scrutinises government responses to similar problems across different countries and shows that interdependence varies and is issue-specific (Dahlke 2011b; Darley 2010; de Graaf 2010b; Leruth 2014; Virta 2013). Concerning terrorism and drugs for instance, state interests tend to vary significantly in line with the domestic situation and with regard to the preferred scope of cooperation and the degree of institutionalisation (Friedrichs 2008; cf. Herschinger et al. 2011). Nevertheless, a multitude of cooperation initiatives have been formed to tackle both topics. In the area of cybercrime, cross-country interdependence is quite high because this issue lacks a clear territorial basis and thus possesses the potential to equally affect all states (Carrapiço & Farrand 2018; Clemente 2013; Schjolberg 2014; van der Meulen et al. 2015). Additionally, cybercrime is comparatively less politicised, which would suggest an easy path towards integration. Yet, there is a comparative lack of EU cooperation arrangements in this policy area, and supranationalisation is evolving relatively slowly with the creation of the European Cybercrime Centre (EC3) only as recently as 2013. Statistics confirm that asymmetry clearly matters when it comes to internal security. Some states simply seem to be less affected by terrorism (Europol 2016b: 10–21), cybercrime (Europol 2016c: 5) or trafficking in human beings (Europol 2013: 24). Considering the asymmetric effects of security threats, it hardly comes as a surprise that cooperation preferences vary across Member States and policy areas. Notwithstanding the apparent importance of issue-specific interdependence, its effects on state integration preferences are not yet understood very well. Is there, for example, a difference between interconnectedness in common threats and common institutions? Institutional linkages between countries can certainly have an impact when European integration, institutions and cooperation arrangements themselves alter interdependence relationships and structural interconnectedness among Member States (Cross 2011; Dalferth 2008; Den Boer & Wiegand 2015). Yet, irrespective of the nature of interdependencies, countries often react differently to seemingly similar circumstances. Integration preferences within the EU are usually asymmetrical and variable across states, issues and time – especially when it comes to sovereignty-sensitive areas.

Before taking a closer look at the process and drivers behind state preferences on EU police cooperation, this book briefly illustrates why studying the integration of this area matters and how a theoretical integration perspective can help make sense of the empirical state of affairs. Or, put differently: this book applies theories of European integration to explain what is happening in practice in the AFSJ.

Applying Theories of European Integration to the Area of Freedom, Security and Justice

EU internal security governance and police cooperation have been changing in practice and are evolving increasingly. This can be seen in the on-going, parallel institutionalisation and informalisation of cooperation, and it is reflected in the divergence of preferences across states, issues and time. A large body of empirical accounts provides evidence to this end. Yet, integration dynamics are rarely made explicit or form the main object of analysis. On the contrary, the longstanding view persists that internal security and policing are predominantly intergovernmental, even in an EU context. This disregards the empirical evidence of integration in this field, albeit often in more flexible models and different forms than traditionally associated with European integration. Notwithstanding the recent trend to study the EU's governance of internal security in the context of European integration, many accounts still regard integration as the ultimate goal of security cooperation or assume that a 'supranationalisation' of internal security may be against the will of EU Member States. Occhipinti (2015: 258) asserts that states "may be trying to steer [cooperation] in an intergovernmental direction, but [that] they are doing so against a current that is gradually moving them in a supranational direction anyhow." This book argues that this is not always the case and that states often deliberately opt for degrees of supranationalisation and networked politics where it serves their interests and policy objectives in the area of internal security. Seen through the lens of differentiated rather than straightforward integration, flexible modes of governance and integration alongside newly emerging cooperation formats must be understood as conscious choices by Member States to manage complex interdependencies or institutional deadlock.

The EU as a System of Differentiated Integration

Depending on the state preferences and policy area in question, institutional choice and policy outcomes can vary considerably. They range from fully supranational solutions, partial delegation of power and authority to the creation of new bodies, the professionalisation of intergovernmental or even informal cooperation and the strengthening of soft and networked modes of governance outside or paralleling the EU framework. Leuffen et al. (2013) describe the EU as a system of differentiated integration in which centralisation and territorial expansion vary across policies. This model is known by many other names: a Europe at multiple speeds, variable geometry, or *à la carte* Europe. Conceptualising the EU in such a way acknowledges that it has simultaneously become more integrated and more differentiated in the course of its history. Accordingly, many definitions exist for the concept. Dyson and Sepos (2010: 4) define differentiated integration as "the process whereby European States, or sub-units, opt to move at different speeds and/or towards different objectives with regard to common policies, by adopting different formal and informal arrangements, whether inside or outside the EU treaty framework, and by assuming different rights and obligations." This definition arguably very well suits the EU internal security and police cooperation with its many different formal and informal structures for cooperation.

Differentiated integration understands the EU as a construct between state and international organisation that varies across policies. This resembles the new institutionalist perspective of the EU as "less than a federation, more than a regime" (Wallace 1983). Studies on differentiated integration ask: which policies are taken up by the European enterprise and when? Why does differentiation

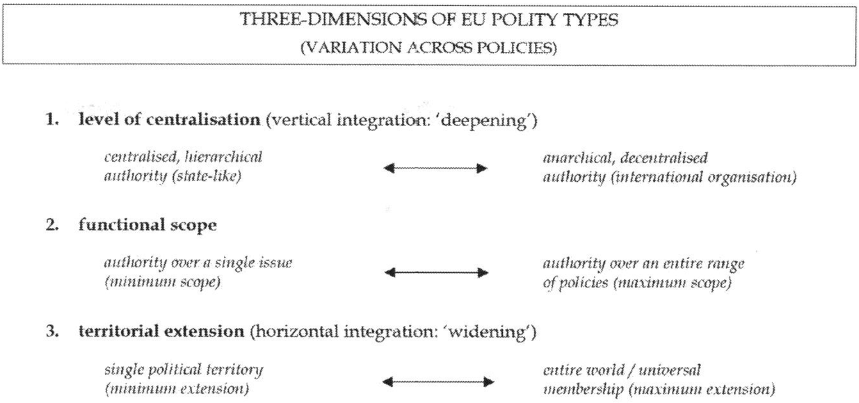

FIGURE 1.3 The EU as a Construct between State and International Organisation

Compiled by the author, based on Leuffen et al. (2013)

increase over time? How can we explain the temporal dynamics of European integration more generally? Leuffen et al. (2013) seek to answer these questions by applying a three-dimensional framework based on the premise that theories of European integration must explain both growth and differentiation in vertical, functional and horizontal integration (see Figure 1.3). These three dimensions of EU polity types – against which integration outcomes may be measured and compared across policy areas – are:

1. **The level of centralisation**, also known as vertical integration or 'deepening,' varies between centralised, hierarchical authority (resembling states) and a more anarchical, decentralised authority (resembling international organisations).
2. **The functional scope** can either be minimal (authority over a single issue), maximal (authority over an entire range of policies), or anything in between.
3. **The territorial extension**, variously known as horizontal integration or 'widening,' distinguishes between minimum territorial extension (a single political territory) and maximum territorial extension (universal membership covering the entire world).

Concerning vertical integration, state preferences and institutional outcomes may range from assigning the EU wide-reaching competence or even executive powers to limiting EU actors to a narrow, very limited mandate, a mere support role or none at all. With regard to the functional scope of EU cooperation, governments may favour arrangements that exclusively focus on single topics or a fixed number of issue areas or may promote a wider scope that allows the inclusion of all relevant policy questions in a given field. Finally, Leuffen et al. (2013: 15–18) distinguish between four types of horizontal differentiation that Member

States may advocate: (a) no differentiation, (b) external differentiation (when rules apply uniformly to EU Member States but vary for outside participants), (c) internal differentiation (variation in rule-application among EU Member States through opt-outs etc.) and (d) internal and external differentiation.

Many other models exist – over 30 in fact – that seek to conceptualise differentiated integration in the EU, ranging from the idea of a "two- or multiple-speed Europe" to the terms "avantgarde Europe" and "Europe à la carte" (Koenig 2015). However, most models agree on the categorical distinction between time, space and matter (cf. Stubb 1996; Holzinger & Schimmelfennig 2012). Differences between models arise mostly from the degree to which studies integrate normative and institutional factors into their theoretical framework.

This book adopts the differentiated integration approach developed by Leuffen et al. (2013). Their three-dimensional model is especially suited to evaluate preference formation and integration outcomes in EU police cooperation. First, it encompasses core assumptions of rationalism and is highly compatible with state-centric theories of European integration. This fits the area of JHA where decision-making is still predominantly intergovernmental. Second, differentiated integration theory accounts for multicausal explanations beyond intergovernmentalist tenets and is open to theory-synthesis. It studies the EU as a political system of its own rather than merely a construct built around national Member States (Leuffen et al. 2013: 10). And it brings a third element into the equation: EU cooperation as a conglomerate of different, often simultaneous and overlapping processes of integration and differentiation rather than a linear development. While many theories still regard integration as the end goal, a differentiated integration approach sees the EU as a system of differentiated integration in which centralisation, functional scope and territorial expansion vary across policies. This perspective thus best captures the political reality of the area of EU internal security and police cooperation. Its theoretical lens allows for a more in-depth qualitative assessment of European integration than single-theory-based frameworks. Additionally, differentiated integration theory incorporates flexible modes of governance and integration that seem particularly prevalent in the area of JHA. In fact, it departs from the assumption that "[d]ifferentiation is here to stay on the condition that exogenous and endogenous interdependence continue to grow" (Leuffen et al. 2015: 17). Differentiated integration conceptualises integration and differentiation outcomes both historically and politically: as governance tools for managing heterogeneity and institutional deadlock and to cope with uncertainty and risk (cf. Dyson & Sepos 2010).

This approach to differentiated integration situates state preferences across the levels of centralisation, functional scope and territorial extension – thereby allowing for wider inferences regarding institutional choice and integration outcomes. The multicausal model with its openness to theory synthesis practically lends itself to analysis and comparison of the influence of different explanatory factors from key theories of European integration. It places the different theories and their main tenets where they work best and connects different explanations across the divergent dimensions of European integration. For instance, Leuffen et al. (2013) argue that purely intergovernmental negotiations and unconstrained bargaining are most relevant at the beginning of the integration process and at low levels of centralisation, but that integration preferences generally become more endogenous and ideational as integration progresses; thereby, they synthesise liberal intergovernmentalist and constructivist explanations to complement not contradict one another. This book employs the framework by Leuffen et al. to assess the formation of state preferences on integration in the dynamic field of EU police cooperation.

Explaining EU Police Cooperation – But How?

While European Studies have long been an independent field of political science and international relations, a focus on the area of JHA has only recently emerged. Although empirical evidence demonstrates that the EU AFSJ has developed into "[...]one of the most dynamic and complex fields of European integration in recent years" (Leuffen et al. 2013: 243), it has received strikingly little attention from the theoretical literature on European integration. Presumably, it is often still considered a case of intergovernmentalism rather than part of larger integration processes in the EU.

EU internal security policy – particularly the evolution of the AFSJ into a crowded policy space – has only recently begun to be turned into a testing ground for traditional and newer theories of European integration. Some accounts underline the evolution "from weak community competences and largely horizontal or voluntary coordination mechanisms into an increasingly regularized or hierarchical field of 'supranational governance,' with a growing role of supranational institutions" (Bossong & Hegemann 2018: 23; cf. Kaunert et al. 2013). The other end of the spectrum comprises studies highlighting the prevalence of the Member States as principals in this EU policy domain (Kaunert & Léonard 2012; Monar 2003; Wolff 2015). However, theoretical explanations of European JHA integration have long transcended the classical intergovernmentalist-supranationalist divide. They have opened up to discussions of new, flexible modes of governance and cooperation that are emerging in this area. These include theoretical approaches to differentiated integration (Leuffen et al. 2013; Rittberger et al. 2014; Tekin 2015) as well as to networked governance and transgovernmental policy networks (Balzacq 2008; Bigo 2014; Kahler 2009; Lavenex 2010). They all show "the AFSJ as a hybrid area of EU activity that encompassed different decision-making modes and dynamics between institutions developing throughout time" (Maricut 2016: 241).

This book situates itself amidst these different theoretical debates and explanations of integration in the area of JHA. For its analysis of EU police cooperation and the drivers of state preferences, it comparatively assesses the main explanatory factors stipulated by rational-choice, state-centric theories and other theories of European integration. This undertaking is as much an attempt to identify commonalities and bridge the gap between different perspectives as it seeks to generate a holistic account that can most adequately explain integration preferences in EU police cooperation. To this end, the analysis draws primarily on liberal intergovernmentalism and new intergovernmentalism – which remain highly relevant, especially for the area of JHA – and, on the other end of the spectrum, neofunctionalism and social constructivism to capture and disentangle the complex dynamic shaping this policy domain. On the basis of a comprehensive study of the empirical and theoretical literature on JHA and police cooperation in the EU, three potentially most relevant explanatory factors have been identified: interdependence, politicisation and policy entrepreneurship.

Interdependencies

A number of theories highlight the influence of growing interconnectedness as key driver in the behaviour of EU Member States and their integration preferences. Among them are liberal intergovernmentalism and its recent adaptation new intergovernmentalism. Both understand European integration as a series of rational choices (Moravcsik 1998). However, liberal intergovernmentalism differs with regard to who makes these choices. It assumes that national leaders and governments sit in the driver's seat of decisions and processes of European integration (Moravcsik & Schimmelfennig 2009), thereby 'rescuing' the nation-state (Milward 1992). Consequently, national state preferences (particularly economic interests) lie at the heart of EU politics but are themselves shaped by issue-specific interdependencies of globalisation, as states are embedded in a domestic-transnational dichotomy (Moravcsik 1993). Policy outcomes are seen as the result of national state preferences and issue-specific interdependence and are shaped by problems of distribution and collective action.

Moravcsik (1998) divides the process leading to integration outcomes into three causal sequences (see Table 1.1). First, national preference formation is

TABLE 1.1 A Tripartite Framework of National Preference Formation

Sources of constraints and opportunities	*Causal sequences of international negotiation*	*Theoretical explanations*
1. Powerful domestic constituents	National preference formation	*Preferences* as set of specific policy goals and independent underlying national objectives
2. Relative power of each state	Interstate bargaining	Development of *strategies* for the realisation of preferences
3. The structure of international institutions	Institutional choice	Choice of institutional arrangements for securing *substantive agreements*

Source: Compiled by the author, based on Moravcsik (1998).

defined by pressure from domestic constituencies and underlying national long-term goals. Based on these independent variables, states define their preferences before entering negotiation. The second causal sequence consists of interstate bargaining or formal negotiation. Liberal intergovernmentalism assumes that the relative power of each state can best explain distributional outcomes. Third, institutional choices are made to secure achieved agreements. Which option is chosen depends on the structure of international institutions and whether existing institutions suffice to 'lock in' bargaining agreements, or states decide to adjust them or create new ones.

According to the liberal intergovernmentalist logic of Moravcsik and Nicolaïdis (1999), issue-specific interdependence shapes all stages and acts as fundamental determinant of national preferences; states act rational and respond to relatively stable issue-specific domestic-transnational pressures by seeking agreements that function most efficiently to realise these preferences. Asymmetrical interdependence may explain suboptimal bargaining outcomes, as some states might be more dependent on cooperation for realising their goals. Additionally, policy externalities might pressure states towards particular agreements. Institutional choices are made according to the same logic, depending on the need for credible commitments. This need is crucially shaped by the degree of issue-specific interdependence among all and each of the Member States.

To what extent then does interdependence drive integration preferences and decision-making in the area of internal security? How do issue-specific interdependencies become manifest in EU police cooperation? What does it look like when they shape state preferences? Liberal intergovernmentalism has been criticised and challenged by rival theories. Yet, it remains highly relevant for the field of European studies and explanations of EU integration (Kleine & Pollack 2018). And it practically lends itself to an analysis of the persistently intergovernmental area of EU police cooperation due to its focus on states as the main actors.

Liberal intergovernmentalism primarily focuses on economic interests as "the fundamental force underlying integration" (Moravcsik 1998: 15–16). This claim does not hold for the area of internal security and police cooperation, where different concerns matter as well if not more. Yet, collective action and distribution problems likewise impact outcomes in this policy domain. Not all EU Member States are similarly affected by common threats and therefore not equally incentivised to seek cooperation and common institutions to realise policy goals (Moravcsik & Nicolaïdis 1999: 61). In other words, some states may be 'more interdependent' than others, making them more eager to solve collective action problems through cooperation and integration.

Nevertheless, the focus of liberal intergovernmentalism on driving factors and preferences as exogenous omits the feedback loop between integration decisions and spill-over effects that might affect endogenous interdependence in the long run (Schimmelfennig 2015: 112; cf. Pierson 1996). External interdependencies comprise an interconnectedness in the causes and effects of security threats that produce negative externalities for states that act alone. Against it, internal interdependencies constitute spill-over effects from previous integration decisions; an interconnectedness in cooperation structures or institutions makes unilateral action difficult and ineffective and produces coordination problems. Member States thus develop a preference for integration when an "increase in exogenous or endogenous interdependence produces demand for more integration" (Leuffen et al. 2015: 9).

The recently emerging strand of new intergovernmentalism thus focuses on the institutional choice of Member States rather than the drivers of their preferences (Bickerton et al. 2015a-b; Puetter 2012). It recognises the on-going communitarisation of JHA policy – the shift towards supranational policy venues and their rules of decision-making – and attempts to reconcile it with the state-centric tenets of liberal intergovernmentalism. Seen through the lens of new intergovernmentalism, "Member States pursue more integration but stubbornly resist further supranationalism" (Puetter 2012: 168), resulting in an 'integration paradox': "integration without supranationalism" (Bickerton et al. 2015b: 703). An ever-growing increase in the activities of the EU since the Maastricht Treaty arguably collides with unaltered legal powers of the Union and "the absence of supranational decision-making" (ibid.: 704). This gap, new intergovernmentalism argues, is bridged by the pursuit and institutionalisation of enhanced policy-coordination among Member States by means of deliberation and consensus, and by the delegation of tasks to 'de novo' bodies rather than EU institutions. Integration without supranationalism is thus conceptualised as the result of (a)symmetrical interdependence in a particular issue area or at political and administrative level, which makes enhanced EU policy coordination necessary (Schout & Wolff 2016). Although new intergovernmentalism recognises the importance of the domestic context for the formation of state preferences, it argues that "problems in domestic preference formation have become standalone inputs into the European integration process" (Bickerton et al. 2015b: 714). Aggregated domestic interests are not exclusively seen as positive preconditions for European integration but can provide an impetus for integration as a means to solve national problems and constraints.

This angle conceptualises EU cooperation as negative rather than positive integration, shaped by domestic instead of transnational issues. It has been most prominently captured in the 'venue-shopping' approach. At the example of migration policy, Guiraudon (2000) demonstrates how governments deliberately move to European 'policy venues' to avoid national constraints. 'Europeanising' migration policy entails a more favourable institutional environment for policy officials with limited judicial scrutiny and less opposition from the national level (ibid.: 252 ff.). She illustrates how informal settings of transgovernmental cooperation opened up a new European policy space and created opportunities for the evolution of more institutionalised and "new organisational settings not previously available" (ibid.: 260–61). The EU level may offer an escape from national controls to Member States but likewise requires alternative strategies and resources to cope with its unique rules and actors and adjust to new relative bargaining and power positions (cf. Maricut 2016). Consequently, venue-shopping and the interplay among different policy venues and constituencies can develop a dynamic of its own, leading to unintended consequences and the blurring between high and low politics across policy areas and time.

In sum, intergovernmental, rational-choice European integration theories highlight the importance of issue-specific interdependence and domestic interests as drivers of state preferences. High interdependence and aggregated domestic interests (positive or negative) are argued to shape the behaviour of Member States, ultimately producing a convergence of preferences in favour of European integration. Applied to EU police cooperation, we can accordingly formulate the following hypothesis about the findings we should expect if these explanations were to hold:

> H1: The higher the interdependence in security issues, the more likely Member States are to favour EU police cooperation and integration.

Politicisation

Politicisation may be described as the process by which topics not previously in the eye of the public become the object of societal deliberation and public discourse (Hay 2007: 81; Zürn 2013: 19). This includes the salience of an issue, the degree of polarisation and the range of actors and audiences involved (de Wilde et al. 2018). Especially since Hooghe and Marks' (2009) well-known work on the politicisation of European integration and the growth of Euroscepticism over the past decade, many accounts have investigated the role of public and political contestation, and shown its rising importance in different EU policy domains (de Wilde et al. 2018; Grande & Kriesi 2016; Rauh & Zürn 2014). Even in the domain of JHA, a "dramatic increase in politicization and the involvement of top politicians" can be observed since the Lisbon Treaty (Bossong & Hegemann 2018: 23). As a consequence, postfunctionalism and its focus on EU politicisation constitutes the "most recent and arguably most fundamental challenge" to the theoretical explanations stipulated by liberal intergovernmentalism (Kleine & Pollack 2018: 1495). Postfunctionalist studies conceptualise politicisation as a constraint to European integration. They focus on its negative impact, for instance when societal deliberation transforms a public 'permissive consensus' into a 'constraining dissensus' (Hooghe & Marks 2009). The UK's 2016 Brexit referendum and withdrawal from the EU immediately come to mind. On the other hand, neofunctionalists highlight that public support, the 'permissive consensus,' can provide the backbone to early regional integration (Lindberg & Scheingold 1970; Schmitter 1969). Positive politicisation often helps to strengthen or even advance European integration (Diez Medrano 2003; Leupold 2015; Wonka 2015; Zaun 2018). Thousands of people all over Europe took to the streets to participate in pro-EU protests like the 'Pulse of Europe,' seeking to take a stand against Brexit, Eurosceptic and nationalist discourses.

Theories still largely focus on the postfunctionalist understanding of politicisation as a constraint to European integration, although most studies have likewise shown the difficulty of clearly categorising the effect of politicisation as either 'permissive consensus' or 'constraining dissensus,' and that politicisation in fact differs across topics and Member States (Börzel & Risse 2017; de Wilde et al. 2018; Hutter et al. 2016; Maricut, 2016). It can act as both driver or obstacle to preference convergence and European integration.

The current debate on politicisation in the EU is gradually evolving beyond the post-/neofunctionalist divide towards a more differentiated theoretical approach. State-centric theories of European integration likewise acknowledge the importance of politicisation and deliberation as shapers of state preferences amidst state-society relations and the domestic-European divide (Bickerton et al. 2015a; Leuffen et al. 2015; Moravcsik 1998). Policymakers deliberately engage in politicisation to maintain a 'permissive consensus' over the appropriateness of their policy choices (Boin et al. 2005: 92; Koenig-Archibugi 2004; Van Asselt & Renn 2011: 440). Publicly framing situations in one way or another often is an effective means for policymakers to manage expectations. Many contemporary theories of European integration thus address politicisation as an explanatory variable in its own right (Bickerton et al. 2015b; Puetter 2012). Schmidt (2018) observes how the 'new' theoretical approaches to EU governance emphasise ideational factors such as discourse and deliberation, and analytically focus on discursive institutionalism and constructivist ideas.

Member States can be both senders and receivers of politicisation. As political actors they are influenced and shaped by their environments. Governments respond to the saliency of an issue and public pressure. They base their actions on social norms and a 'logic of appropriateness' or follow a 'logic of consequentiality' that revolves around weighting possible consequences and practical results of particular policy options (March & Olsen 1989, 2006). Politicisation forms part of the structure in which political agents act. The public sphere and mass politicisation may act as drivers of state preferences and shapers of policy options. The public sphere encompasses constituencies, the media and other relevant civil society actors at domestic, European and international level. While these of course provide the socio-normative framework for policymakers, this book is more interested in how and when politicisation in the public sphere influences state preferences, including through discursive practices and active framing. If the public sphere is dissatisfied with a certain political action or lack thereof, intensifying public pressure could pose a 'constraining dissensus' to the authority and political standing of governments and thus influence their preferences (Boin & 't Hart 2003; Drabek 1994). With a view to assessing the impact of politicisation on the integration preferences of EU Member States, this book focuses on politicisation understood as increased salience and public debate of a topic rather than polarisation or deliberate conflict and social contestation. For the purposes of its analysis, it is less important who politicises rather than what the effects of politicisation are on state preferences.

While the state-society linkage in preference formation and politicisation is perhaps relatively uncontentious, the role of EU actors is less well-researched (Sandholtz & Stone Sweet 1998). Recently, EU institutions and agencies have themselves engaged in politicisation or become subject to public debate. Theoretical models that characterise the EU as "apolitical and/or technocratic" are no longer fully adequate; "Politicization has affected all EU actors' actions and interactions, making for a 'new' dynamic of EU governance that is more political in every way" (Schmidt 2018: 1548). In view of the large range of different audiences and principal-agent relationships at the EU level, supranational actors – arguably more so than Member States – seek arrangements that are acceptable to all. Framing and policy narratives vary widely depending on the issue area, topic and the audiences involved or represented. Consequently, EU actors often struggle between an active and a passive role in public debates, as well as between depoliticisation and politicisation respectively (Maricut 2016; Puetter 2012; Zaun 2018). This holds especially true with regard to JHA agencies like Europol, which often are purposefully created with a focus on operationalisation and soft modes of governance to avoid institutional constraints and political deliberation (Busuioc et al. 2011; Kaunert et al. 2013; Rittberger & Wonka 2012; Wolff & Schout 2013).

Regardless of 'who' politicises, different theoretical camps of European integration are increasingly recognising the impact of politicisation on state preferences. Schmidt (2018) convincingly shows how new approaches to intergovernmentalism, supranationalism and parliamentarism underline the relevance of 'ideas and discursive interactions.' Member States, the public sphere and EU actors interact as audiences and 'politicisers,' thereby creating politicisation around a particular issue. This can take different forms. When strong emotions are involved and politicise an EU topic, societal concerns and expectations must be managed across the perceived domestic-European dichotomy (Barnett & Sikkink 2008; Boin et al. 2005; Drabek 1994: 32; Grant & Keohane 2005). Although politicisation can be a deliberate strategy of public-political actors to reach certain goals and outcomes, it can likewise be the more random result of a biopolitical process among different societal actors and audiences through which the saliency of an issue grows. Similarly, politicisation may create a positive or negative societal basis for European integration depending on whether it favours or rejects EU collective action. Rather than being openly publicised, issues may also be 'depoliticised' when they are deliberately framed as technical or administrative matters rather than political questions.

Framing a topic or the EU in one way or another empowers different actors and can facilitate or inhibit public debate and ultimately European integration (Boswell et al. 2011; de Graaf 2015; Diez Medrano 2003; Leupold 2015). Guiraudon's (2000) venue-shopping approach exemplifies strategic depoliticisation by Member States. Shifting decision-making into more technical or informal policy venues avoids domestic, institutional or public constraints. Especially in the area of JHA, scholars have highlighted the importance of depoliticisation in the security discourse of both governments and EU actors (Bigo 2002;

Herschinger et al. 2013; Huysmans 2006; Rauh & Zürn 2014; Wolff 2015). Yet, the theoretical literature likewise acknowledges the limits of linking security to depoliticisation and has begun to study politicisation in this policy domain (Ehrhart et al. 2014; Hegemann & Kahl 2016, 2018; Rüger 2012). This book seeks to contribute to this debate by tracing the impact of issue-specific politicisation on state preferences throughout EU police cooperation.

Despite its depoliticisation focus, securitisation theory provides a suitable point for departure. Securitising a topic or policy area means framing it in terms of security, which often moves it into more operational, rational or technical policy venues where social and political contestation are less present and swift action can be taken. Securitisation approaches have gained prominence in studies of internal security policy and police cooperation since the Lisbon Treaty (Balzacq & Léonard 2013; Bigo 2014; Léonard & Kaunert 2011; Monar 2007). Assessing when, how and why issues are framed as a matter of security between Member States, EU actors and the public sphere may help to better explain state preferences and integration outcomes. Consequently, the interaction between securitisation and (de-)politicisation must be scrutinised carefully. Certain types of frames and policy narratives may be conducive to particular securitising moves and action at the EU level, while others might make securitisation more difficult by fostering a more differentiated, controversial or polarised debate.

CRISES AND SHOCKS

Crises and shocks present windows of opportunities to adjust existing frames. They "heighten the perceived need for action" and acceptance of related policy responses (Kaunert et al. 2013: 276). Many examples illustrate the deepening nexus between EU security policy and crisis management. Large-scale terrorist attacks on European soil have provided important momentum to Europeanisation in the area of counterterrorism and police cooperation (Bossong 2013; Bures 2018; Monar 2007). Politicisation scholars similarly observe how European crises may shape state preferences and integration outcomes because they "constitute exceptional moments of politicization" (Kriesi 2016: 34). External or internal occurrences cause significant shocks that create a sense of crisis or fear and foster the need for public leadership (Boin 2005; Kaunert et al. 2013). The crisis management literature emphasises that crises demand political responses, as they always entail elements of perceived threat, uncertainty and urgency (Boin et al. 2005). This is arguably nowhere truer than in the area of internal security and policing where shocks appear directly threatening to personal and national security, thus playing on emotions and the biopolitics of fear. The sense of urgency and uncertainty additionally opens the floodgates to framing in an attempt to manage the crisis and respond to public concerns (König 2015).

Crises and shocks may thus be described as 'politicising events' and can shape the interests and policy options of governments. Depending on the political and domestic context, Member States choose particular speech acts and frames in response to public pressure. In the face of the 2015 refugee and migration crisis, politicisation flared up across the EU in the form of highly polarised debates, including predominant security frames (Bourbeau 2013; Krzyżanowski et al. 2018). Many governments opted for national securitising moves that ran contrary to a common European course of action (Moreno-Lax 2018; Scipioni 2018).

At the same time, crises may open 'windows of opportunity' for preference convergence and positive integration outcomes. Following the theme 'never waste a good crisis,' Member States can make use of the perceived need for action to advance their policy goals. Crises may demonstrate insufficiently managed interdependencies in the EU and "magnify the importance of challenges associated with the spillover-enlargement effect" (Kaunert et al. 2013: 276). The influence of crises and shocks on state preferences is acknowledged across different theoretical camps, ranging all the way from intergovernmentalism to neo- and postfunctionalism (Bigo et al. 2015; Börzel & Risse 2017; Rittberger et al. 2017; Schimmelfennig 2017). In the area of JHA, crises do not only provide windows of opportunity for Member States, they have also increasingly become a means of securing public support and legitimacy for the EU. While polarised politicisation tends to hinder cooperation in the AFSJ (Maricut 2016), politicisation in crisis situations can help to overcome national reluctance and legitimise authority transfers to EU institutions or venues (Zaun 2018). Over the last years, terrorist attacks in France, Belgium, Germany and most recently Austria kick-started not only political activism but also the launch of numerous initiatives. These politicising events facilitated preference convergence and produced positive integration outcomes (Maricut 2016). In the aftermath of the 2015 Paris attacks, a European Counter Terrorism Centre (ECTC) was founded at Europol, and a range of additional measures is currently under development after the new EU Counter-Terrorism Agenda was published ahead of time following the terrorist attack in Vienna of November 2020.

In sum, theories of European integration have increasingly acknowledged the politicisation as an influence on state preferences and integration outcomes, including in EU JHA. Whereas domestic politicisation and salience of EU governance have traditionally been regarded as obstacles to integration, a recently emerging, 'new' dynamic of politicisation has yielded diverging preferences across Member States. This book scrutinises the role of politicisation on integration preferences in the domain of EU police cooperation. It does so by asking first, who politicises in each case and how, that is, what form of politicisation emerges, second, to what extent this draws on a sense of crisis and third, whether it is initiated deliberately or arises as the result of a less targeted, biopolitical process. Since the literature comprises three main, different understandings of politicisation and does not agree on its impact, the following competing hypotheses may be formulated as analytical starting point:

H2.1: The higher the politicisation in a given issue area, the more likely Member States are to favour EU police cooperation and integration.

H2.2: The higher the politicisation in a given issue area, the less likely Member States are to favour EU police cooperation and integration, and the more likely they are to prefer differentiation and decentralised, informal modes of cooperation.

H2.3: The higher the politicisation in a given issue area, the less likely Member States are to favour any police cooperation at the EU level.

Policy Entrepreneurship

The concept of 'policy entrepreneurs' from the sub- and supranational level is being increasingly applied to the area of JHA. Policy entrepreneurs can be described as actors employing their resources to shape policy processes and outcomes in order to further their own self-interests (Kingdon 2003). EU actors can be understood as maximisers of competence, agenda-setters and promoters of supranational policy venues (Guiraudon 2000; Pollack 1994; Sandholtz & Stone Sweet 1998; Zahariadis 2013). Rational-choice institutionalist, organisational and intergovernmentalist theories concede that state preferences may indeed be influenced through the strategic actions of supranational policy entrepreneurs and their integrative initiatives (Bickerton et al. 2015a-b; Kaunert et al. 2013; Pierson 1996). As integration evolves and the range of involved actors expands, Member States may gradually lose control over the process (Guiraudon 2000; Hall & Taylor 1996; Ikenberry 2001). While security is often argued to form a core state power and remain tightly in the hands of sovereign governments, policy entrepreneurs above and below the national level can undeniably play an important role and are driven by both rational self-interests and values.

THE SUPRANATIONAL LEVEL – INSTITUTIONS, PATH-DEPENDENCY AND CULTIVATED SPILL-OVERS

Rational-choice institutionalism acknowledges the role that institutions play in the determination of social and political outcomes. It is only one of various sub-branches of new institutionalism that evolved in the 1970s (Hall & Taylor 1996). Rational-choice institutionalism itself was originally developed with a view to the behaviour of the United States (US) Congress. This matters because it arose from a paradox that traditional rational-choice theory could not explain: the relative stability of congressional outcomes despite "the multiple preference-orderings of legislators and multidimensional character of issues" (ibid.). A similar paradox can be observed in EU internal security governance, where issues are likewise multidimensional, and preferences are not fixed and can vary greatly. Yet, institutional structures and generally, both informal and formal cooperation arrangements have continued to develop with relative stability.

Similar to liberal intergovernmentalism, rational-choice institutionalism attributes a key role to states as rational actors that use and design institutional structures deliberately and purposefully (Koremenos et al. 2001). However, it differs in the extent to which it recognises the role of institutions and international organisations, not only as an outcome but also potentially as an independent factor with the power to influence and shape state behaviour and preferences (cf. Hall & Taylor 1996; Ikenberry 2001). Institutions accordingly matter as both principal and agent. They are "humanly devised constraints that shape human interaction" (North 1990).

This classic 'calculus approach' to state behaviour assumes that states are the voluntary initiators of institutional design to ensure gains from cooperation. This assumption neglects the role of alternative causal factors and insights from group theory. Yet, proponents of institutionalism would argue that this 'neglect' is in fact another strength:

> [I]t matters less whether politics occurs within or among nations. What matters more is that politics occurs within a framework of mutually understood principles, norms, rules, or procedures—that is, within an institutional context. Institutionalism[...]can unify the analysis of politics and policy making at and across levels of analysis, contributing to the increasing transcendence of the traditional comparative-IR divide.
> *(Jupille & Caporaso 1999)*

Rational-choice institutionalism thus understands politics as a "series of collective action dilemmas" (Hall & Taylor 1996: 945) and institutions as "rational, negotiated responses to the problems international actors face" (Koremenos et al. 2001: 768). Regardless of whether they are seen as endogenous or exogenous to state preferences, institutions may be conceptualised as key shapers of integration outcomes because they present platforms for structuring the strategic state interaction of actors' preferences. They offer practical solutions to collective action and distribution problems arising from interdependence and the uncertainty about the behaviour of other states. Institutions may act as policy entrepreneurs and affect state preferences indirectly or directly. Kaunert et al. (2013: 277) call this the "institutional dynamics" that influence national positions and negotiation outcomes.

Indirectly, institutions impact Member States through spill-overs and path-dependency. In line with neofunctionalist tenets, they produce functional spill-overs within the same or different policy areas (Haas 1958; Lindberg & Scheingold 1970). The initial decision to create a common institution or charge a particular EU actor with a task or portfolio that was previously nationally administered can trigger a structural need for further institutionalisation and thus integration. In the policy domain of JHA, Kaunert et al. (2013: 276) term this the 'spillover-enlargement effect,' which they attribute to "the real and perceived criminal justice challenges presented by the Common Market and the Schengen area that have been magnified by the expectation of the widening membership of the EU." Additionally, EU institutions may have "shaping and constraining effects" on the Member States, thus leading to path-dependency (ibid.: 278). As the sunk costs and practical value of common institutions increase, it becomes progressively more uneconomical for governments to invest in or move to new policy venues. Neofunctionalists thus attribute integration preferences and preference convergence or variation States to levels of transnational interdependence and supranational capacity at a given point in time (Schimmelfennig 2017: 970).

Supranational institutions can also proactively assume a role as policy entrepreneurs to advance integration and make themselves indispensable (Zahariadis 2013). They may directly shape government preferences through cultivated spill-overs: the provision and promotion of integration initiatives (Niemann & Schmitter 2009). Supranational policy entrepreneurs offer and incentivise policy options that advance normative, institutional or policy settings in their favour, thereby often moving politics towards 'more EU.' Such entrepreneurship can take the soft form of promoting certain norms and practices or manifests itself in hard measures like making available earmarked funding for integration initiatives (Kaunert et al. 2013: 278). Cultivated spill-overs have recently become more frequent and important in the EU; studies especially demonstrate the role of the Commission (Bossong 2013; Kaunert 2010a-b; Niemann 2006; Zaun 2018). Borrowing from organisational theory, the achievement of a good reputation is a source of power for EU actors when they seek to influence state preferences and raise their own transactional authority (Waeraas & Maor 2015; cf. Carpenter & Krause 2012, 2014).

The shaping and constraining effects of institutions on state preferences are compatible with intergovernmental theoretical claims and strengthen them in two main ways. First, supranational policy entrepreneurs owe much of their role to interdependencies. In addition to issue-specific interdependence outside of the EU integration process (e.g. arising from globalisation), functional interdependence and institutional locking may push Member States to continue and expand the path of integration (Schmitter 2005: 268). The more states have invested in an institution or the more an institution has been able to establish itself, the more governments tend to depend on it. This internal or institutional (inter-)dependence might, on a second note, lead to a 'self-fulfilling prophecy.' As states seek to manage the interconnectedness in challenges via building common institutions, they become interconnected in power and capacity; once supranational actors become increasingly empowered as policy entrepreneurs, Member States lose some of the control over an integration dynamic that might seem more and more self-sustaining (Guiraudon 2000; Hall & Taylor 1996; Ikenberry 2001; Pierson 1996).

The interplay of supranational policy entrepreneurship and issue-specific interdependence seems vital in the context of European integration. Conceptualising interdependence as both exogenous and endogenous factor allows to complement the frequently criticised exogeneity-focused perspective of liberal intergovernmentalism and scrutinise the long-run 'feedback loop' between state preferences/integration decisions and institutional choice/spill-over effects. It could be argued that interconnectivity in causes and effects reflects exogenous interdependence, while interdependence in power and capacity often embodies a form of endogenous interdependence among Member States.

Supranational policy entrepreneurs, path-dependency and spill-overs are not classically associated with core state powers and policy areas like internal security. The expanding role and influence of EU actors in JHA provides evidence that supranational institutions can and do shape state preferences in this policy domain. If supranational policy entrepreneurs do indeed substantially affect integration outcomes in EU police cooperation, we should be able to make the following observation:

> H3: The higher the supranational policy entrepreneurship in a given issue area, the more likely Member States are to favour EU police cooperation and integration.

THE SUBNATIONAL LEVEL – POLICING CULTURES, EPISTEMIC COMMUNITIES AND BUREAUCRATIC RESISTANCE

Policy entrepreneurs may also be found at the (sub-)national level. Intergovernmentalist theories attribute domestic constituents a role in shaping state preferences and observe how domestic politics can drive European integration (Bickerton et al. 2015b; Moravcsik 1998). Functionalist studies similarly highlight the importance of the domestic political context for the formation of national preferences (Grande & Kriesi 2016; Hooghe & Marks 2009; Lindberg & Scheingold 1970). Finally, institutionalist and Europeanisation theories emphasise that the failure or success of integration initiatives hinges on the compatibility of new practices, norms and structures with local ones (Heritier & Knill 2000; March & Olsen 1995; Risse et al. 2001). The connection between the (sub-)national context, state preferences and European integration is thus relatively well-established in the theoretical literature.

At the same time, these accounts often focus rather broadly on the integration process in Member States, and on top-down and bottom-up approaches to explain how integration unfolds. They overwhelmingly either point to national and European political elites or grassroots movements and the lowest societal levels, with few studies in the middle ground. While various accounts have investigated the top-down effect of integration and tend to treat subnational bureaucratic and administrative actors as dependent variable, the explanatory power of subnational policy entrepreneurship in relation to states' integration decisions remains relatively little researched (Héritier et al. 2001; Wright 1994). This appears striking in the field of security and police where domestic actors are substantially involved at most stages of cooperation, begging the question when, why and how they independently shape state preferences and contribute to the success or failure of integration initiatives. Whereas the theoretical literature increasingly recognises the potential of the supranational level, particularly institutions, a similar body of studies has yet to emerge to investigate how subnational officials might act as policy entrepreneurs to constrain and influence the behaviour of Member States.

This book understands subnational policy entrepreneurship as the direct and deliberate intra- or intergovernmental policy advocacy by subnational actors like police officials and civil servants. Subnational policy entrepreneurship assumes that actors at the lower and local policy and implementation levels assume a (pro-)active role in driving the integration preferences of their national governments. This appears especially relevant in the area of JHA and police cooperation, where policymaking relies heavily on the expertise of subnational security professionals as well as law and order officials. Accordingly, domestic cultures, particularly police cultures, epistemic communities and bureaucratic resistance play important roles.

A growing theoretical discourse is acknowledging this dimension of institutional adaptation at the subnational level with regard to European integration. This includes intergovernmentalist approaches, which recognise domestic politics and national executives as inputs if not driving forces within preference formation and European institutional choice (Bickerton et al. 2015a; Moravcsik & Nicolaïdis, 1999; Moravcsik & Schimmelfennig 2009). Growing ideational convergence as well as intensifying "political and administrative interdependence" collide with the institutional diversity of Member States in different policy areas (Wolff 2015: 129). This renders cross-country institutional adaptation, if not further integration and formalisation, highly necessary. National executive officials often actively push for new cooperation and governance frameworks in the area of JHA. New intergovernmentalists argue that this leads to an inherent political tension between the functional need to further cooperate and the reluctance of Member States to delegate authority to supranational actors (Bickerton et al. 2015a-b). Institutionalisation or cooperation without supranationalisation therefore frequently occurs when *de novo* bodies are created and power is transferred to informal, horizontal and more flexible forms of governance. Such decisions in turn empower subnational actors as policy entrepreneurs.

Europeanisation accounts (Börzel 2002; Heritier & Knill 2000; Pollack 2019) likewise acknowledge the role of executive and administrative officials and emphasise the question of cultural compatibility or 'goodness of fit' between the supranational and domestic level (Olsen 1996; Risse et al. 2001). They observe how policy implementation varies depending on respective national bureaucratic and administrative structures. Mastenbroek and Kaeding (2006: 331) underline the importance of the "preferences or beliefs held by domestic political and administrative actors," which determine the "relationship between the *status quo* and the response to the EU."

Social constructivist and institutionalist accounts agree with this notion. They advocate sociocultural aspects of institutions and policymaking as independent variables that affect political convergence and regional integration outcomes (Hay 2008; Pollack 2019). Organisational theory likewise acknowledges the relevance of institutional adaptation, the "long-term substitution of existing practices and structures with new ones" (Olsen 1997: 159). Thus, integration preferences of Member States may not only be driven by rational cost-benefit calculations or institutional constraints at the international level but also by domestic cultures and customs that interact with and shape processes of institutional change and policy convergence. (Sub-)National administrative cultures and traditions clearly matter when it comes to explaining integration and differentiation processes. Domestic adaptation to EU cooperation and institutional change occurs gradually and varies depending on the distinct bureaucratic cultures and norms (Kickert & Meer 2011; March & Olsen 1989; Meyer-Sahling & Yesilkagit 2011).

The explanatory power of these cultures and traditions with regard to state preferences on European integration is not well-researched. Koenig-Archibugi (2004) shows the importance of political cultures, particularly understandings of sovereignty and authority, as an influence on Member State positions towards EU integration. In the area of JHA, domestic law and order officials play a role in the EU policy process and in the "emergence of a European 'homeland security' culture" (cf. Cross 2007; Fägersten 2010; Lavenex 2010; Wolff 2015: 141). New modes of governance have been emerging at European level that go beyond traditional, state-centric forms (Bossong & Hegemann 2018; Sperling & Webber 2014). The EU has therefore been described as "an ideal case of modern governance" (Kohler-Koch & Rittberger 2006), a phenomenon that can be found more and more in internal security as well.

Although formalisation, institutionalisation and supranational forms of governance have progressed significantly with regard to EU JHA since the Lisbon Treaty, soft modes of governance, informal horizontal networks as well as executive and administrative elites have similarly gained influence in this area (Bossong & Hegemann 2018; Guiraudon 2000; Kaunert & Léonard 2012; Lavenex & Wagner 2007). European studies and JHA research have taken a "public policy 'turn'" to explain the preferences of Member States and integration outcomes (Rhinard 2018: 42 ff.). They assess how executive and administrative officials influence preferences through their activities within epistemic communities, policy networks and advocacy coalitions. Epistemic communities may be described as a particular form of policy network with an emphasis on knowledge, or phrased more elaborately as "'a network of professionals with recognized expertise and competence in a particular domain and an authoritative claim to policy-relevant knowledge' within that domain or issue area" (Haas 1992: 3).

In EU internal security governance and police cooperation, law and order officials present an important example of such communities. Within domestic and transnational contexts they form knowledge-and expertise-based networks that are relevant to policymakers on multiple levels (Cross 2011, 2014; Wolff 2015). In recent years, policy and practitioners networks, especially cross-border networks of security professionals, have risen in prominence within European police cooperation (Balzacq 2008; Bigo 2014; Den Boer 2010; Dupont 2004; Huysmans 2006). Empirical studies clearly demonstrates the importance of horizontal TGNs among different national government (sub-)agencies and police authorities, while the theoretical literature has likewise increasingly picked up the concept of 'networked politics' (Börzel 1998; Den Boer et al. 2008; Kahler 2009; Rhodes 2008; Richardson 1996). Examples of the growing role, if not influence, of subnational officials and networks as policy entrepreneurs in the EU policy process range from proactive mobilisation around certain topics to indirect interest-shaping through bureaucratic resistance (Fägersten 2010; Hooghe & Marks 2001; Kaunert et al. 2013).

Studies of EU JHA overwhelmingly show the cumulative presence of TGNs and 'intensive transgovernmentalism' and often present both as functional responses to growing interdependence in this policy domain (Kahler 2009: 195). Accounts vary with regard to whether they assess TGNs as dependent structures and mere outcomes or as independent actors with the power to influence national preferences and international policy choices (Eilstrup-Sangiovanni 2009; Kahler 2009; Keck & Sikkink 1998). They also vary concerning why and when TGNs impact formal policymaking and cooperation at the EU level positively or negatively. On the 'active' end of the spectrum, subnational policy entrepreneurs are treated as independent drivers of state preferences and institutional choice in the area of EU police cooperation. Here, the self-interest and integration initiatives of knowledge-based policing networks drive national positions and EU policy outcomes (Boswell et al. 2011; Bures 2012; Den Boer 2010; Wolff 2015). Franko and Gundhus (2015) especially observe the "importance of physical action, excitement and informal connections, rather than legal regulatory frameworks and formal and technological connections." At the same time, they underline the persistence of "internal divisions, cultural differences and divided loyalties within what might at first appear as a unitary culture of transnational policing."

On the 'passive' end of the scope, subnational actors indirectly shape state preferences and integration outcomes in the form of bureaucratic resistance. Such resistance transcends the institutionalist notion of the 'inefficiency of history,' whereby institutions, national systems, structures and practices become progressively more robust towards changes as they evolve and time passes (Börzel 2002: 23). Bureaucratic resistance describes diverse domestic cultures and bureaucratic interests across Member States, and the "potential gap between decisions on policies or agencies and the actual outcomes" (Kaunert et al. 2013: 278). In areas such as JHA that fall within core state powers and predominantly intergovernmental modes of governance, policymaking tends to follow top-down channels and little leeway seems to exist for subnational influence.

Bureaucratic resistance to integration decisions arises when top-down decisions or high-level governmental preferences collide with the *status quo* of national executive and administrative officials that should ideally support and implement policy choices. Where domestic bureaucratic or policing cultures and traditions diverge too strongly, subnational actors passively or even deliberately resist and hinder the evolution of new cultures, networks and practices, including at European level (Kaunert et al. 2013). Similarly, (sub-)national executive and administrative structures are not easily transferred to the inter- or supranational level, irrespective of state preferences and integration decisions (ibid.; Fägersten 2010). This may be especially relevant in the area of EU police cooperation and internal security governance, where governments often opt for networked governance or policy outcomes that follow the agencification and operationalisation trend (Kassim & Le Galès 2010; Wolff 2015). EU police cooperation thus largely hinges on the domestic 'cultural' dimension and willingness of subnational actors to implement decisions. In conjunction with the growing role of security professionals at the EU level, this gives national executive and administrative officials considerable power in internal security governance. They may use this position to blur the lines between implementation and policymaking. Subnational actors can thus act as policy entrepreneurs to impact state preferences and advance or hinder integration.

In other words, subnational policy entrepreneurs matter with regard to shaping state preferences and integration in the field of EU police cooperation. This book conceptualises subnational policy entrepreneurs as local executive and administrative officials who act within some relation to the respective national governmental context and might form part of transnational advocacy coalitions, TGNs or epistemic communities relevant to EU police cooperation. Similar to supranational policy entrepreneurs, subnational actors can seek to influence state preferences – and thereby affect institutional choice – in a way that benefits their role in the policy process. This could take the shape of a negative or positive impetus towards integration. Subnational policy entrepreneurs might influence governments to favour informal, soft modes of governance, but they might just as well promote formalisation of cooperation or differentiated forms of integration where it suits their aims. Contrary to EU institutions, they can be expected to rather advocate outcomes that delegate power to local executive and administrative officials. If subnational policy entrepreneurs indeed drive state preferences in the area of EU police cooperation and the theoretical literature is correct, the following hypothesis should hold true:

> H4: The higher the subnational policy entrepreneurship in a given issue area, the less likely Member States are to favour EU police cooperation and integration, and the more likely they are to prefer differentiation and decentralised, informal modes of cooperation.

From Words to Action: EU Police Cooperation through Time

This book analyses which factors drive institutional choice and differentiated integration in the area of EU police cooperation. Concretely, it asks how and to what extent interdependence, politicisation and policy entrepreneurship shape the integration preferences of Member States. The relevance of this question derives, amongst others, from its timeliness. Internal security cooperation within the EU has evolved constantly since the 1970s and especially rapidly in the past decade, including a clear trend towards increasing institutionalisation. EU Member States demonstrate strong, albeit often varying, interests to work together on related issues. Additionally, differentiated integration has developed into a core characteristic of European integration and one of the main factors shaping the EU today.

Looking at the historic evolution of EU police cooperation, this book assesses how Member States form their preferences and make according institutional choices, thereby shaping differentiation or integration. Concretely, it aims at understanding how interdependence, politicisation and policy entrepreneurship play out in this policy domain to shape state preferences on the degree of vertical and horizontal integration as well as on the functional scope of policy areas. While it is rather uncontested *that* interdependence, politicisation and policy entrepreneurship play a role in integration outcomes, the extent to which they do so and the manner in which they shape the integration preferences of Member States is not yet well-understood. How exactly these explanatory factors influence state preferences and possibly function as causal mechanisms, as well as whether they can sufficiently account for preference formation on differentiated integration in the area of EU police cooperation is the object of study of the following chapters and this book's contribution to the theoretical literature on European integration.

The respective theory-grounded explanations (interdependence, politicisation and policy entrepreneurship) are compatible with state-centric understandings of EU policymaking and rational-design perspectives. The area of EU internal security is still largely an intergovernmental policy domain, and due to its sensitive nature and relevance for national security relies on rational decision-making in response to risk assessments and intelligence reports. Since states are *de facto* and *de jure* still in the driver's seat of EU internal security governance, this book focuses on the formation of national preferences of Member States, and how these in turn shape institutional choice and differentiated integration. The object of analysis is the Member State-level of EU police cooperation, that is, national governments embodied by high-ranking officials, executives and senior civil servants.

While Member States (or rather their preferences) lie at the centre of this book, a strict isolation or separation of analytical levels is not sensible. Moravcsik (1993: 482) himself advocates the importance of disassembling the process behind international policy outcomes. Any concrete explanations must depart from the processes shaping domestic state preferences. This book therefore treats the formation and evolution of state preferences within EU police cooperation as primarily dependent factors whilst bearing in mind that they may act as both determinant and outcome of the interaction between structure/polity, process/politics and function/policy (cf. Windhoff-Héritier 1983; Scharpf 1985). As integration progresses, state preferences can themselves play a role as determinants of institutional choice and processes of differentiated integration. Several scholars have stressed the importance of not only studying preferences as exogenous to European integration but also additionally considering processes of

TABLE 1.2 Drivers of State Preferences from a Structuration Perspective

Structural factors	Asymmetrical interdependence *Reluctance to integrate in areas of core state powers*
Contextual factors *'windows of opportunity'*	Politicisation *Crises and external shocks*
Agency	Supranational entrepreneurs *Prefer classical integration* (Sub)national policy entrepreneurs *Prefer differentiated, decentralised integration*
Assumptions about agents	Motivated by rational self-interest and/or by norms (e.g. European security cultures) that are empirically manifested into preferences

Source: Compiled by the author, based on Giddens (1986). The author would like to thank Adina Maricut-Akbik for suggesting this table.

preference endogenisation through the 'feedback loop' of spill-over effects across time (Pierson 1996; Schimmelfennig 2015). In the same manner, interdependence, politicisation and policy entrepreneurship may appear as both exogenous and endogenous factors to European integration. In other words, structure and agency are both important (see Table 1.2).

This means that factors may play out differently over time, impacting state preferences anew and yielding integration outcomes that diverge in their degrees of centralisation and territorial extension as well as the respective functional scope of cooperation (see Table 1.3). Therefore, the relative importance of each driving factor potentially varies across time and with regard to the three dimensions of differentiated integration.

This book's analysis is conducted through a qualitative causal case-study approach. It compares the processes around four institutional 'milestones' in the evolution of EU police cooperation since its inception in the 1970s until today (see Figure 1.4). In line with the 'waves' of EU internal security cooperation, each of the following chapters is dedicated to one of these milestones, substantive integration outcomes over time that changed the nature of internal security and especially police cooperation in the EU: (1) the creation of the Trevi Group in 1976 as an intergovernmental network between 12 Member States of the EEC; (2) the 1995 Europol Convention establishing the European Police Office; (3) the 2009 ECD which established Europol as official EU agency and (4) the 2016 Europol Regulation and the 2020 proposal for its revision, which represent the most recent changes in the organisation's legal framework and entail a number of further powers for EU actors.

These milestones all represent qualitative 'quantum leaps' of EU police cooperation. Yet, they display variation with regard to their contextual conditions and respective state preferences across the three dimensions of differentiated integration, thereby leading to divergence in the concrete institutional choices or integration outcomes. The case studies differ in their degree of centralisation

TABLE 1.3 Drivers of State Preferences and Theoretical Hypotheses

Issue-specific Interdependence	
H1:	The higher the interdependence in security issues, the more likely Member States are to favour EU police cooperation and integration.
Politicisation	
H2.1:	The higher the politicisation in a given issue area, the more likely Member States are to favour EU police cooperation and integration.
H2.2:	The higher the politicisation in a given issue area, the less likely Member States are to favour EU police cooperation and integration, and the more likely they are to prefer differentiation and decentralised, informal modes of cooperation.
H2.3:	The higher the politicisation in a given issue area, the less likely Member States are to favour any police cooperation at the EU level.
Policy Entrepreneurship	
Supranational	
H3:	The higher the supranational policy entrepreneurship in a given issue area, the more likely Member States are to favour EU police cooperation and integration.
Subnational	
H4:	The higher the subnational policy entrepreneurship in a given issue area, the less likely Member States are to favour EU police cooperation and integration, and the more likely they are to prefer differentiation and decentralised, informal modes of cooperation.

and territorial extension as well as in the functional scope of EU cooperation. European police cooperation in the 1970s comprised predominantly informal or semi-formalised arrangements including several transgovernmental counterterrorism networks and the intergovernmental Trevi Group. Instances of increasingly institutionalised, yet still highly decentralised cooperation only emerged around the 1990s, for example, through the Europol Convention. By contrast, the two more recent case studies on the Europol Council Decision and Regulation(s) of the past decade demonstrate institutional choices that move EU police cooperation towards stronger centralisation and a rapidly widening functional scope. Each case likewise contains examples of differentiation preferences. However, these were often not reflected in the ultimate institutional outcome because they had to give way to integration preferences. Yet, some instances of differentiation have increasingly emerged in parallel with integration structures, especially since the early 2000s. This development has led to the emergence of an interesting, ever closer relationship between formal and informal forms of governance in the area of EU police cooperation. Finally, the cases differ with regard to the Member States most relevant for each integration outcome. Whereas Germany, France and the UK mattered most for the creation of the 1970s Trevi Group, the establishment of Europol in the 1990s was most influenced by Italy, the UK and

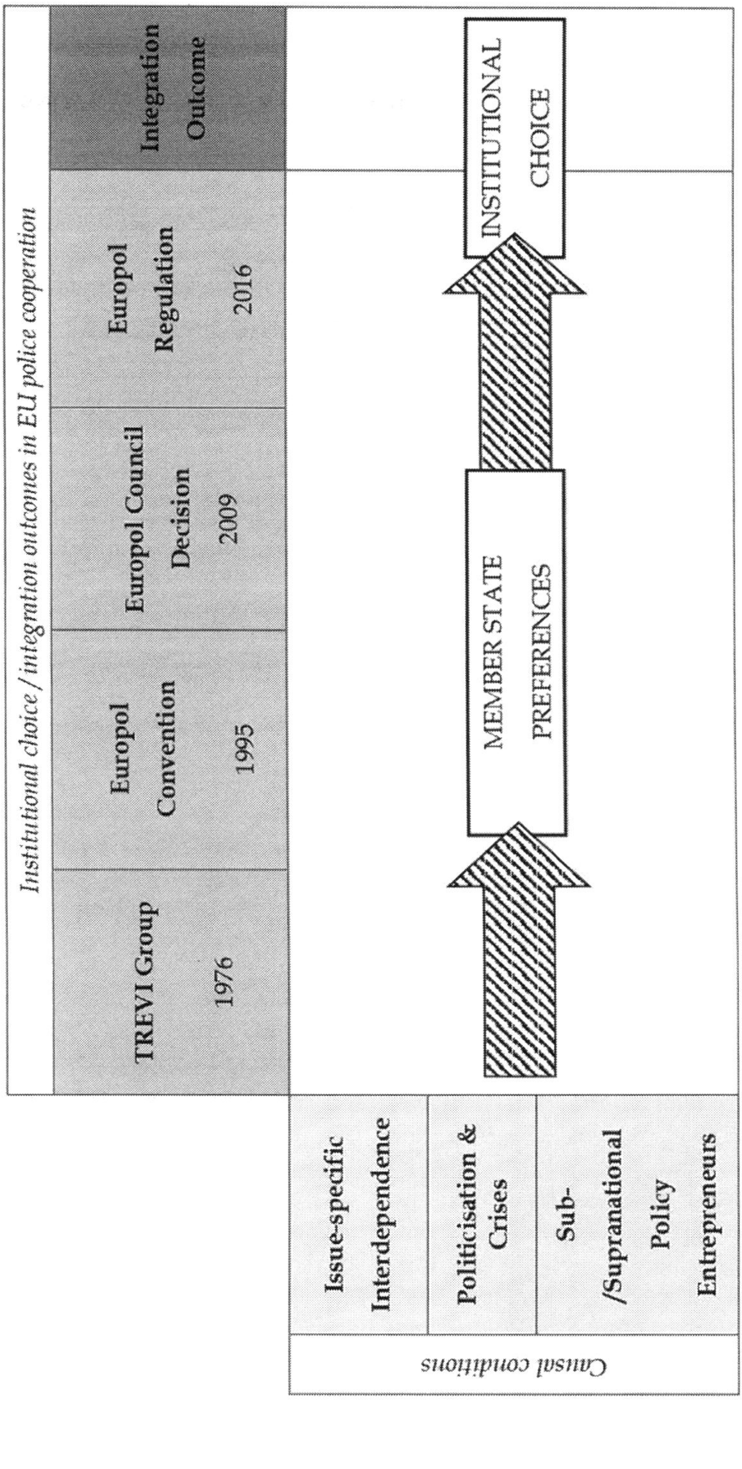

FIGURE 1.4 A Research Framework for the Institutional Evolution of EU Police Cooperation

Germany. From 2000 onwards, an increasing number of different Member States acted as initiators of EU police cooperation on different occasions, including in the transformation of Europol into an EU agency in 2009 and the adoption of the Europol Regulation in 2016.

To precisely identify 'key players,' the following chapters trace the causal process leading to the respective state preferences and integration outcomes in each case. Process-tracing presents an appropriate method to understand *how* interdependence, politicisation and policy entrepreneurship act as causal conditions to impact preference formation and ultimately the larger system of differentiated integration (Bennett & Checkel 2015; cf. Brady & Collier 2004; Caporaso 2009). Process-tracing allows opening up the black box in which these factors are active and scrutinising how exactly they operate via particular causal mechanisms in a causal process (Beach & Pedersen 2016; George & Bennett 2004; Ragin 1987; Seawright & Gerring 2008). Or, in the words of Frank Schimmelfennig (2015: 100): "[...]theory-testing analyses of European integration require process tracing for both theoretical and methodological reasons."

The techniques applied in the process-tracing analysis comprise qualitative content analysis and problem-centred interviews. Each chapter presents a causal case study of one institutional milestone of EU police cooperation. This entails an in-depth study of the process leading up to the specific preference and outcome and is done in a backward manner, departing from the particular outcome and then tracing the process backwards by identifying the most relevant Member States, their individual preferences, concrete underlying causal mechanisms and the original scope conditions. The primary focus lies on detecting the possible presence of the explanatory factors under scrutiny (interdependence, politicisation, policy entrepreneurship). If the explanatory factors act as causal conditions of EU police cooperation, they should be empirically observable in the form of entities or actors engaging in concrete activities that transmit causal forces from the scope condition to the integration outcome. It should be possible to trace the effects of interdependence, politicisation and policy entrepreneurship by observing particular causal mechanisms moving along causal forces ('mechanistic evidence') from the explanatory factors to pro-integration preferences and perhaps even positive integration outcomes (Beach & Pedersen 2016; Bennett & Checkel 2015). This in turn should provide evidence to either confirm or reject the theoretical hypotheses formulated for each driving factor (see Table 1.3).

For each chapter, the process was reconstructed through content analysis of primary and secondary sources that reveal information about national preferences. These include 'hard' primary sources such as policy documents and official government and EU documents, but also formal legal texts, political speeches and press statements. Archival research was conducted in national and EU archives in Brussels, Koblenz, London and Paris where over 400 archival sources on the chosen case studies were extracted. These comprised formerly undisclosed internal policy documents, communications, letters and briefings, mostly from national ministries of the interior or justice but also pertaining to other ministries, national government officials and EU institutions. Additionally, secondary sources were assessed wherever relevant, ranging from media and academic accounts to publicly available political and historic records. All documents were evaluated qualitatively through structured content analysis with an analytical focus on mentions of the explanatory factors, mechanistic evidence thereof or data falling within these categories (Gläser & Laudel 2010; Mayring 2010: 67 ff.).

For each category, a number of rules and criteria were defined that needed to be fulfilled for the respective explanatory factor to qualify as demonstrating a certain degree of presence and potential influence (see appendix for an overview of the criteria). If for instance an archival record recognised excessive demands on single governments and unilateral solutions in the area of policing, this was marked as evidence of 'high interdependence.' The causal mechanism at work here could for instance become manifest in functional pressure to cooperate in order to cope with increasingly interconnected threats.

In addition to archival documents, semi-structured, problem-centred interviews were conducted with high-level senior officials, executives and practitioners from the national and European level, as well as with security experts from the field of EU police cooperation and internal security. In total, 53 qualitative interviews were carried out between August 2017 and February 2022, including 14 women and 39 men (see Table 1.4). The results were summarised strategically in the form of comprehensive interview summaries. The findings were analysed qualitatively according to the same criteria applied to the archival document analysis. Where interviewees, for example, underlined the strong presence or involvement of supra- or subnational actors in the decision-making phase or policy process of an integration outcome, this was coded as 'high influence of supra-/subnational policy entrepreneurship.' The content summaries and preliminary results were continuously re-evaluated with regard to whether they were still authentic to the original interview data. Following this constant feedback loop in the data reduction and summary phase, the final conclusions from the interviews were comparatively analysed and checked against the findings and data extracted from the archival document analysis. All results were ultimately analysed in the context of the broader historic process and with regard to the evidence they provided for causal mechanisms at work, linking state preferences and integration outcomes with explanatory factors.

The combination of these techniques aims at methodological triangulation through the synthesis of findings from process observations, document analysis and interviews in each causal case study. Nevertheless, certain limitations remain. While archival research and document analysis may work rather well for the first two case studies – the Trevi Group of the 1970s and the inception of Europol in the 1990s – many more recent policy documents are not publicly available (yet). In turn, elite interviews may only be possible for the more recent case studies, as eye witnesses of the creation of TREVI are no longer available or not able to reliably reproduce a process that occurred 50 years ago.

TABLE 1.4 List of Elite Interviews

Interview No.	*Date*	*Affiliated Institution/Organisation*
1–5	August 2017	European Police Office
6	October 2017	European Commission
7	February 2018	European Drugs Unit/European Police Office
8–11		Participants at the European Police Congress, Berlin
12–13		European Commission, DG Migration and Home Affairs
14	March 2018	European Drugs Unit/European Police Office
15		European Commission, DG Migration and Home Affairs
16–20		Participants at the Security & Counter Terror Expo, London
21	April 2018	European Drugs Unit/European Police Office
22		State Office of Criminal Investigation Rhineland-Palatinate, Germany
23		Think Tank/Academia
24	May 2018	German Federal Criminal Police Office (BKA)
25–26		CYBERSEC European Cybersecurity Forum
27		Europol Management Board
28–29		European Police Office
30		Think Tank/Academia
31	June 2018	European Police Office
32	July 2018	European Police Office
33		General Secretariat of the Council of the EU, DG Justice and Home Affairs
34		European Commission, DG Migration and Home Affairs
35	August 2018	Europol National Unit
36–37		NATO Communications and Information Agency
38		Dutch Ministry of General Affairs
39		European Police Office
40	September 2018	German Federal Criminal Police Office (BKA)/ Federal Ministry of the Interior (BMI)
41	October 2018	Think Tank/Academia
42		Berlin Police Office
43–44		European Police Office
45–46	November 2018 & August 2019	European Vehicle and Driving License Information System (EUCARIS)
47–49	September 2021	Participants at the European Police Congress, Berlin
50–51	February 2022	European Police Office
52–53		European Commission

Therefore, this book places the methodological emphasis for the first case study (1970s) on archival document analysis rather than interviews, for the second case study (1990s) on both archival research and interviews, and for the remaining two cases (early 2000s) mostly on elite interviews supplementing the analysis of publicly available documents.

On the basis of the differentiated integration model put forward by Leuffen et al. (2013), the following chapters investigate the explanatory power of interdependence, politicisation and policy entrepreneurship as drivers of state preferences on European integration in the area of police cooperation. Each chapter traces the influence of these three factors on the formation of integration preferences across the three dimensions of differentiated integration: vertical, horizontal and functional scope. While the analytical focus lies on the impact on state preferences and the causal sequence of preference formation, the historic process-tracing approach of this book necessarily touches upon institutional choice and integration outcomes respectively.

Notes

1 The shift in power from the national to the supranational level.
2 Convention between the Kingdom of Belgium, the Federal Republic of Germany, the Kingdom of Spain, the French Republic, the Grand Duchy of Luxembourg, the Kingdom of the Netherlands and the Republic of Austria on the stepping up of cross-border cooperation, particularly in combating terrorism, cross-border crime and illegal migration (2005, May 27).
3 "core functions of sovereign government" (cf. Genschel & Jachtenfuchs, 2014: 1).
4 See for example Kirchner and Sperling (2007) with their liberal intergovernmentalist study on the evolution of EU institutions despite the persistence of strong state prerogatives in the area of security.
5 See for instance Müller (2015), who argues that TGNs increase in strength and importance for EU security cooperation, because they respond to and best govern the transnational network character of serious organised crime.

2

THE TREVI GROUP – BIRTHPLACE OF EUROPEAN POLICE COOPERATION

The first form of EU police cooperation was born in the 1970s with the creation of the Trevi Group. Initiated by Germany, France and the UK, the EC's Interior Ministers set up TREVI[1] as semi-formal platform to facilitate police cooperation on terrorism. Interdependencies arguably played a key role as necessary condition and starting point for the development of pro-cooperation positions. The process leading to the creation of the Trevi Group demonstrates the ambiguous impact of politicisation as both reinforcement and impediment to integration preferences. Finally, subnational policy entrepreneurship – primarily by domestic police officials – mattered as influencer and amplifier of national preferences, although the impact differed greatly across national security systems and cultures. Supranational policy entrepreneurs, by contrast, were completely absent from the preference formation of Germany, France and the UK; they only mattered as passive actors in the policy process. The influence of interdependence, politicisation and policy entrepreneurs additionally diverged across the three dimensions of differentiated integration. High interdependence acted as primary influence on positive state positions concerning vertical and horizontal integration. Subnational policy entrepreneurship and politicisation, by contrast, had the highest impact on state preferences regarding the functional scope of cooperation.

The Trevi Group was launched at a Council meeting of EEC interior ministers in June 1976. Although TREVI was designed as an intergovernmental group outside the official EC framework, it can be argued to constitute the first real attempt at developing a structure at European level (Fijnaut & Hermans 1987). It already comprised certain characteristics situating it between a mere state-driven body and the EC, and may be seen as the first step towards differentiated integration of EU police cooperation. Although its horizontal extension comprised all nine EC Member States, vertically, no 'deepening' took place. Yet, the launch of

DOI: 10.4324/9781003262176-3

TREVI created a certain degree of centralisation and formalisation of European police cooperation. It laid the foundation for future vertical integration, including through the Group's close association with the EC in its structure, regularity and ways of working. Nonetheless, TREVI's original functional scope was limited to a single issue area: counterterrorism.

The process leading to its establishment and marking its early years exhibited conflicting state preferences on the degree of (until then non-existent) integration in this issue area. Germany, France and the UK particularly shaped the policy process and were most vocal about their preferences on police cooperation across the three dimensions of differentiated integration: the envisioned level of centralisation, the functional scope and the territorial extension (see Figure 2.1). While Germany had a strong preference for a high level of centralisation, the UK and France vehemently opposed plans for a superimposed structure with authority of its own. Unsurprisingly, Germany was unable to assert its preference, and TREVI was established as an informal, strictly intergovernmental body for the exchange of information and best practices instead of binding political and operational cooperation. Initially, Germany and the UK advocated a range of internal security issues to be covered by European cooperation. However, France demonstrated an outspoken reluctance for TREVI to cover more than a single issue. When the UK eventually shifted its focus on the fight against terrorism, TREVI was launched with this topic as its single priority. Finally, on territorial extension, the three countries concurred; they aimed for universal membership, ideally via the United Nations (UN) or Interpol. Since this was not possible, Germany, France and the UK agreed on the framework of the Community for membership in the Trevi Group.

While the main focus of this book lies on the explanation of state preferences, the ultimate institutional choice – a cooperation format with inherently intergovernmental characteristics but a strong potential for differentiated integration – reflects an asymmetrical influence of different driving factors across countries. This asymmetry caused different degrees of integration pressure in each Member State, which translated into different preferences and bargaining positions in the negotiations. The choice to launch TREVI as a semi-formal cooperation format outside but strongly linked to the EC framework would present a stepping stone for deeper integration in the future, as the subsequent chapters demonstrate.

Sketching the TREVI Process: 1972–1976

First Steps towards a European Conference on Internal Security

The first vision for a common European approach dates back to the Summer Olympics of 1972 in Germany (see Figure 2.2). They were overshadowed by an attack from a Palestinian terrorist organisation on the Israeli team, which became known as the Munich Massacre (BMI 1973b: 3; Oberloskamp 2012). Eleven members of the Israeli Olympic team were taken hostage and killed after

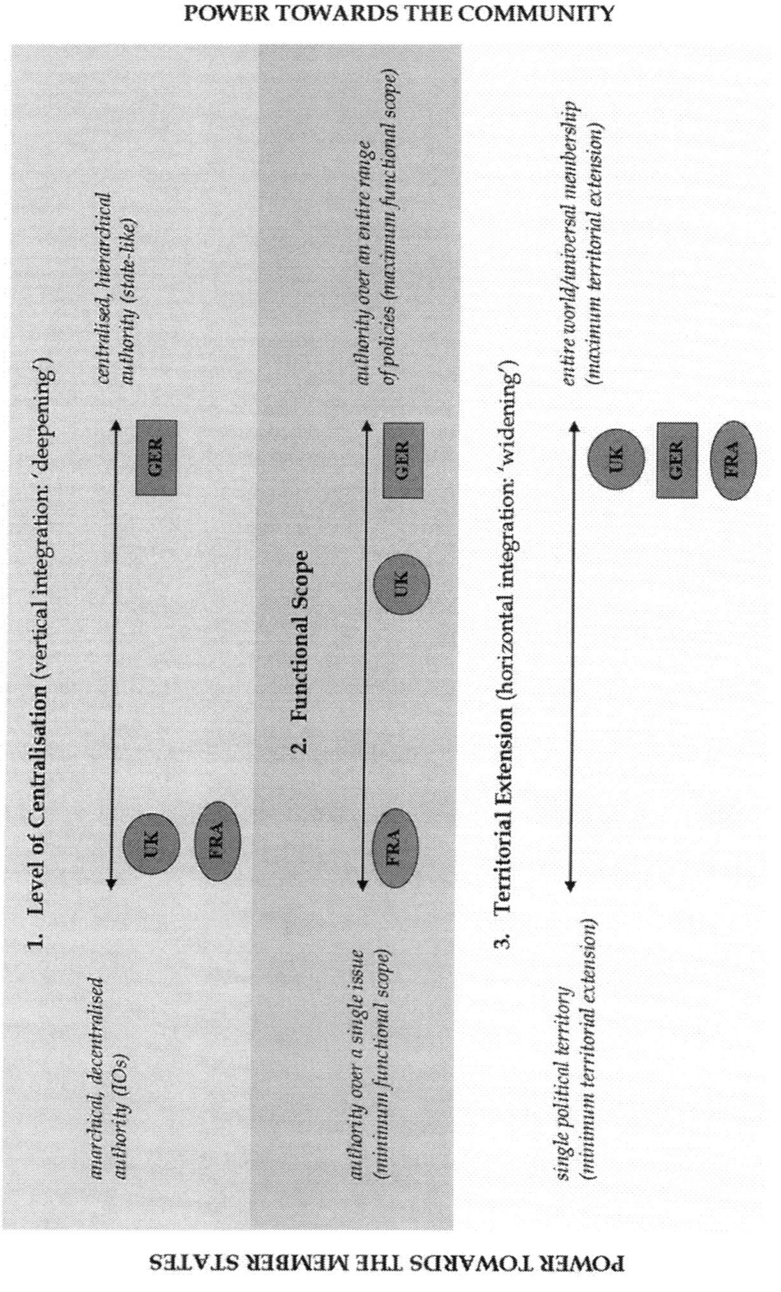

FIGURE 2.1 The Trevi Group: State Preferences on the Three Dimensions of Differentiated Integration

Compiled by the author, based on Leuffen et al. (2013)

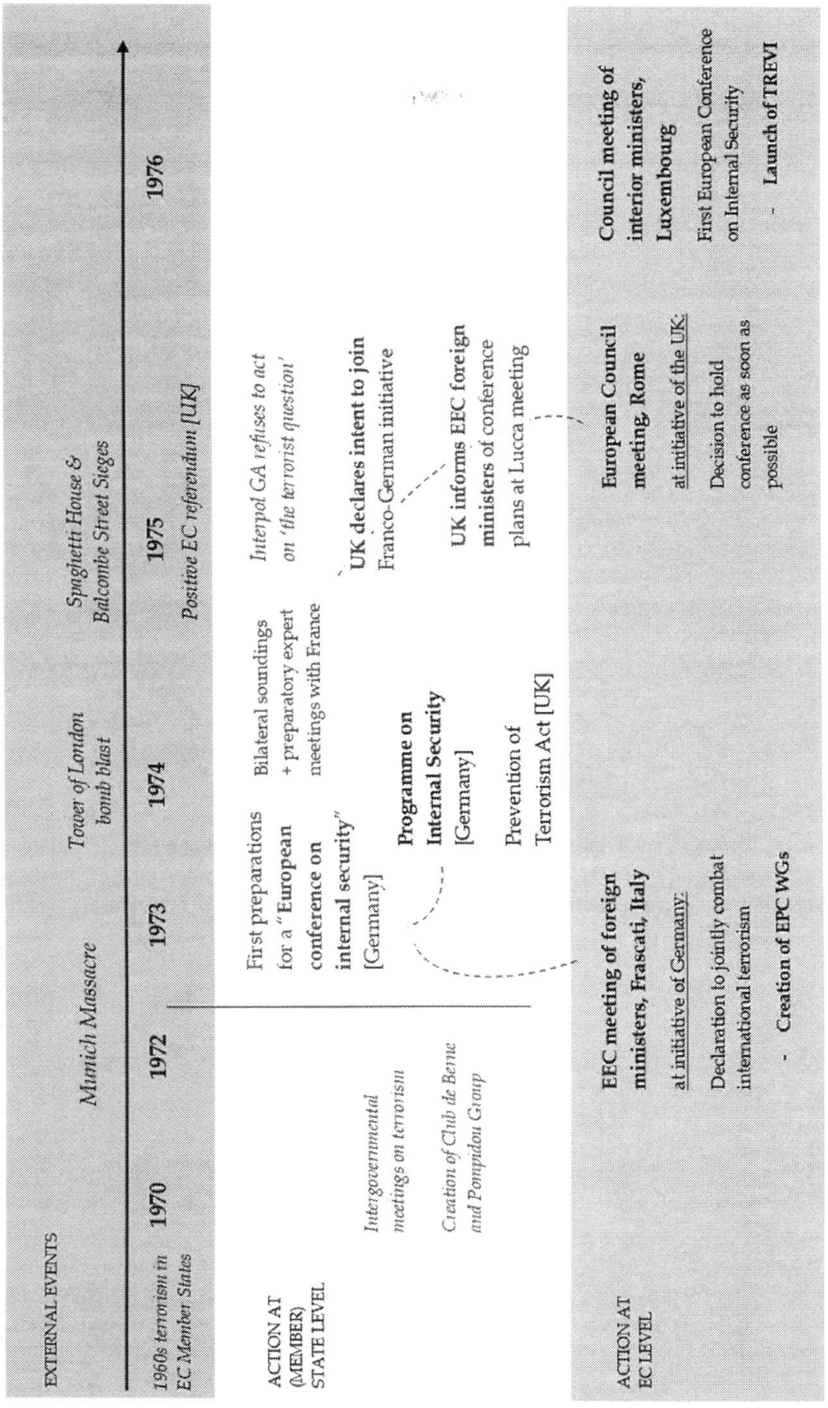

FIGURE 2.2 1970s European Police Cooperation and the Creation of TREVI

failed negotiations, alongside one German police officer and five terrorists. One week after the attack, German Foreign Minister Walter Scheel called for the collective fight against international terrorism at an EEC meeting in Frascati on 12 September 1972 (Friedrichs 2008: 47; BMI 1973b: 3). Consequently, three WGs were established under European Political Cooperation (EPC), a framework for Member States' cooperation in the area of foreign policy, and tasked to deal with questions related to terrorism and surveillance of foreign nationals (Merk 1973a). However, cooperation in this format never took off and already petered out a few months later (Streicher & Bracht 1975a).

Germany launched a new attempt at instigating European internal security cooperation in early 1973, this time outside the EPC format (see Figure 2.2). The impulse came from top political levels. Interior Minister Hans-Dietrich Genscher himself initiated the process towards a European conference on internal security (Streicher & Bracht 1975a). In the light of failed counterterrorism action in the EPC framework, Germany deliberately adopted a more flexible, piecemeal approach. Instead of informing all nine EEC Member States of its plans for a European conference on internal security, it first contacted France in 1974 to discuss ideas (BMI 1974b). First talks with senior officials at the French Ministry of the Interior (FMI) revealed a general willingness to further develop European cooperation (Merk 1974a). In view of the 'aggravated security situation in Western Europe' and the 'internationalisation of organised crime,' France endorsed the need for a European conference on internal security (ibid.: 2). Although both countries acknowledged the increase in international interdependencies and the subsequent need to strengthen interstate cooperation on internal security, they differed with regard to the scope and extent of such an endeavour. Germany favoured a new initiative among EEC Member States in the hope of prompting sustainable, long-term cooperation not only in the fight against organised crime or terrorism but also the entire area of internal security (BMI 1973b). This was to present a building block towards European integration on the whole (Merk 1973a; von Rottenburg 1973). By contrast, France made very clear that it was not prepared to create a new multilateral initiative. Several previous attempts to spur similar action at global level – at the UN or the CoE – had proved cumbersome and unsuccessful. Against this backdrop, France preferred the bilateral intensification of cooperation among EEC Member States (Merk 1974a-b).

A bilateral Franco-German WG on 'general questions of internal security' was established in September 1974. It can be regarded as a first step towards a European conference on internal security (see Figure 2.2; Merk 1974c). While this group's initially declared purpose was the improvement of Franco-German cooperation in the fight against transnational organised crime, Germany was keen on clearly situating these efforts within the larger context of preparations for a common EEC policy on internal security (ibid. 1974b). The results of the WG and bilateral cooperation should form the basis for discussions at the envisioned conference on internal security (ibid. 1974c). After a number of transgovernmental and ministerial meetings, the French and German Ministers of the Interior agreed on 22 August 1975 that the European conference would require thorough preparations of at least a year. They decided to announce their plans at a meeting of EEC Interior Ministers in October (Bracht 1975a; Streicher 1975).

The United Kingdom as a Motor of European Cooperation

The situation changed when the UK became involved one month later during a visit of Lord John Harris, British Minister of State for the Home Office (HO), at the German Federal Ministry of the Interior (BMI) in Bonn (Maihofer 1975; Streicher 1975a). A positive outcome of a referendum over British EEC membership had cleared the way for the UK to become proactive with regard to European police cooperation (Wall 2013: 589 f.). On 14 October 1975, Home Secretary Roy Jenkins suggested to the Prime Minister to initiate a meeting of Community Interior Ministers on "[...]expanding co-operation in the European Community on matters of common interest to Ministers of the Interior, particularly in the fields of counter-terrorism and of technical support for police operations" (Jenkins 1975). Foreign Secretary James Callaghan later described Jenkins' efforts as "explor[ing...] the possibilities for consultation and cooperation on a Community basis[...]" (Callaghan 1975b). Interestingly, at this point the UK was completely oblivious to the German efforts towards the same goal, and vice versa. Only during Lord Harris' visit in Bonn in October 1975 did Germany become aware of the British intentions.

Three points are worth noting with respect to the UK's vision for European police cooperation. First, the original impetus came from ministerial levels. The meeting that launched TREVI was suggested by the British Home Secretary himself. In coordination with the British Foreign and Commonwealth Office (FCO) and the Cabinet, he recommended to present the idea at highest political levels: through a formal proposal at the European Council. Second, the early British government preference demonstrates a strong Community emphasis and shows no reservations with regard to a gain of EEC competences or a loss of national sovereignty. On the contrary, HO documents demonstrate that, while home affairs had not traditionally been a Community policy area, "the Home Secretary believes that, in this field as in others, the tendency is likely to be, and should be, increasingly to shift the weight of effort from the Council to the Community, which is a tighter and more effective institution" (Armstrong 1975). Third and finally, it is worth underscoring the pace at which British plans for a meeting of EEC Interior Ministers were advanced after the positive referendum outcome. Not even half a year after the successful EEC membership referendum, Prime Minister Wilson gave his consent to officially move forward with the HO proposal. Meanwhile, intradepartmental coordination among the British ministries was already at full speed, and informal soundings had been undertaken with France and Germany (Callaghan 1975b; Jenkins 1975). Whereas the vision of the Franco-German WG was a well-prepared conference among the nine EEC Interior Ministers that would produce a substantial policy outcome in the form of concrete decisions, the UK prioritised a fast realisation with the aim of creating multilateral WGs and direct practical exchange rather than political decisions and long-term cooperation (Streicher & Bracht 1975a; von der Gablentz 1975). In October 1974, British Foreign Minister James Callaghan announced the proposal informally to the EEC Ministers at a gathering in Lucca, Italy (see Figure 2.2). The proposal was subsequently agreed as agenda item for the European Council meeting in Rome in December (FCO 1975c).

Thus pressured to act, Germany engaged with the UK in an attempt to shape the British initiative and approximate preferences. Germany strongly suggested to not organise the resulting cooperation within the EPC framework, as the UK had intended, because of the experience with the failed EPC WGs in 1972 (Bracht 1975a-b). The compromise that was ultimately struck foresaw that the responsible EEC Ministers, senior officials and experts would not meet within the EPC format but rather outside any formal EEC body. Nevertheless, intensified cooperation among Member States was to be conducted in close connection to the work of EEC bodies (von der Gablentz 1975). Concerning the timing of the conference, the UK wanted it to be held as soon as possible, preferably in early 1976. Germany and France preferred the conference to be organised towards the end of the year with more time available for preparatory work to clarify the details of the envisaged outcome and facilitate decision-making (Streicher 1975). Germany actively tried to change the British position accordingly in advance of the European Council meeting (Streicher & Bracht 1975a).

Nonetheless, the UK moved forward and introduced its initiative at the Rome meeting of the European Council, where agreement was struck and the proposal accepted (Streicher & Bracht 1975b). Consequently, Germany – in close coordination with France – conceded the earlier point in time for the conference. It was set to June 1976 and would be prepared by EEC senior officials at transgovernmental level. A major point of controversy, however, remained the targeted outcome of the ministerial meeting in June, that is, the institutional choice for this new cooperation format. While Germany had hoped for a substantial policy outcome and concrete decisions on long-term cooperation among EEC Member States, the UK envisaged practical police cooperation organised in WGs (Bracht 1975a; Streicher 1975;). In advance of the conference of EEC Interior Ministers, Germany began to lobby extensively for its pro-integration preference. Next to bi- and multilateral talks with other Member States, Germany formally put forward its alternative vision. A paper conceptualising possible topics and outcomes of the conference, effectively rivalling and far exceeding the scope of the British paper, was circulated to all EEC Members before the first preparatory meeting of EEC Officials on 20 February 1976 (Streicher 1976).

France, contrary to Germany, very much welcomed the British ideas for European police cooperation. French President Valéry Giscard d'Estaing believed in "[...]an independent and coherent Europe," and pursued the aim of closer cooperation to achieve a political European Union. Nevertheless, France favoured a model of decentralisation, including on the European level. When the UK presented its proposal at senior officials level in Paris, the French side agreed but saw the purpose of the ministerial meeting as "a cover [to some extent] for closer and less formal collaboration on a bilateral basis between[...the UK], and[...]some others (Germany, the Netherlands and Italy[...]" (Tomkins 1975a).

Preference Divergence and Strategic Differentiation

By early 1976, Germany had accepted that its comprehensive plans for European internal security cooperation would not be realisable right away. However, it was determined to lay the foundation for binding, long-term decisions and include as many elements of its original vision as possible. Previous internal discussions across various German ministries had aimed at accomplishing a full political European union in 1974 (AA 1974). Yet, a full union was not deemed realisable all at once. Therefore, a 'step-by-step approach' of differentiated integration was thought promising on the way forward (ibid.). Building on these internal discussions, the German preference in the beginning of 1976 included the aim in the long run for an international convention that would formalise cooperation and legally 'bind' Member States (Streicher & Bracht 1976). As the British preference for a rather loose and practically oriented cooperation format rendered the immediate achievement of this goal unlikely, Germany began to lobby multilaterally at the transgovernmental level of EEC officials who were tasked with the preparation of the ministerial meeting in June (ibid. 1975b). When neither far-reaching political decisions nor concrete, long-term commitment seemed feasible, Germany advocated the adoption of a political declaration of intent at the June conference, which it regarded as a first 'building block' (Bracht 1976a; Merk & Bracht 1976a; Streicher 1976).

Germany significantly shaped the working level preparations and was actively involved in drafting the outcome documents. By the time the nine EEC Interior Ministers met in Luxembourg on 29 June, officially marking the inception of the Trevi Group, Germany had succeeded in introducing core elements of its preference. While no political declaration of intent was achieved, substantial text sections from the German proposal were included in the resulting resolution and press statement (Bracht 1976b). This included the necessity for permanent cooperation on the entire area of internal security, and the intention to hold a follow-up ministerial conference (Merk 1976a: 1–3). Germany would continue to voice its preference for permanent, increasingly formalised cooperation at different working levels after the ministerial launch of the Trevi Group (Merk & Bracht 1976b). The outcome of the first meeting of TREVI remained much behind German expectations and ultimately reflected the British preference. It focussed on counterterrorism and practical police cooperation through the TREVI WGs rather than more comprehensive political decisions on general internal security. While Germany nonetheless considered the conference and inception of TREVI a success, even 'significant progress' (Merk 1976a: 3), it would have preferred farther-reaching measures to institutionalise cooperation – a goal it determinedly pursued on the level of the WGs (Bracht 1976b). At the same time, France would remain generally unwilling to advance the Community initiative, while the UK continued its reluctance to formalise TREVI but was in favour of expanding contacts and practical cooperation.

The Community and Terrorism: Interconnected in Causes and Effects?

A growing interdependence in internal security among EC Member States was became increasingly apparent in the 1970s, even before the Munich Massacre. On the one hand, a Europe-wide factual increase in the (cross-border) activities of criminal and terrorist groups called the existing domestic security infrastructures in question. On the other hand, the rising number of terrorist incidents across Member States was publicised and framed as peaking interconnectedness in the effects of security threats within the EC. While issue-specific interdependencies (mostly in the fight against terrorism) importantly shaped the British and German preferences, especially on vertical and horizontal integration, they were much less perceived by France and remained largely insignificant for its preference concerning TREVI.

Germany

The factual increase in domestic and cross-border activities of terrorism and organised crime provided a key impetus for Germany to favour European police cooperation. Interdependencies intensified in the late 1960s and throughout the 1970s. The German Federal Criminal Police Office (BKA) reported the growing transnationalisation of terrorism; domestic terrorist cells like the RAF took advantage of foreign networks and the emerging interdependencies through economic liberalisation within the EEC (Herold 1974, 1975b). While terrorists and criminals began to conceptualise the EEC as one single territory in which to act, Member States – the BKA argued – still acted in isolation and lacked a permanent system of cross-border cooperation and information exchange, a prerequisite for meeting the emerging security challenges (ibid.: 5).

This position likewise appeared in internal BMI documents, including bilateral discussions with the FCO (1975a; cf. BMI 1974a, 1975a-c). Following a meeting between Lord Harris from the British HO with German Federal Interior Minister Werner Maihofer in September 1975, one official noted:

> [...p]olice investigations had[...] revealed the extent of close links between terrorists in different countries and this was encouraging the Germans to seek close collaboration with governments and police forces of other states.
>
> *(Bullard 1975)*

At the same time, terrorism did not even amount to 1% of all recorded criminal acts in Germany, although the number of incidents had risen sharply by the second half of 1975 (ibid.). Regardless, the German government dedicated considerable attention to the matter. The perception of an emerging 'security deficit' and growing internal interdependencies shaped Germany's preference to this end. In view of the envisioned European customs union and internal market, the Standing Conference of State Interior Ministers (IMK) and the BKA repeatedly stressed the need to enhance international cooperation to offset the effects of these developments and effectively manage German internal security (BKA 1976b; Bochmann 1974; Herold 1974). While subnational levels largely focused on emphasising concrete issue-specific interdependencies in the area of internal security, the national level appeared to be primarily influenced by broader political interdependencies emerging within the EEC as part of the integration process.

What is more, German political elites were quite aware of the Cold War situation and tensions at the international level (cf. party manifestos[2]). German politics of the late 1960s and 1970s were marked by a strong emphasis on peace in Europe and the world. This likewise showed in domestic affairs. Intra-German relations and a possible reunification were closely associated with an enhancement of East-West relations and relations between EEC Member States in the context of ensuring their common security. In view of the unlikely achievement of quick, effective measures and sustainable cooperation on an international level, all main German parties regarded the political union of European Member States as desirable and necessary. Integration was seen as a crucial prerequisite and building block for the reunification of Germany and political integration of Europe (AA 1974, 1976; Merk 1976b). It is therefore hardly surprising that Germany developed a strong preference for security cooperation among EEC Member States. And it was of the opinion that the survival of the EEC and ultimately European integration depended on the leadership of Germany, the UK and France. As German Chancellor Helmut Schmidt stated: "without a good triangular relationship of this sort, the EEC would go down the drain" (Wright 1976: 2). This was uttered rather fittingly at a meeting with the British Prime Minister in Bonn on 30 June 1976, the day after EEC Interior Ministers had officially met within TREVI for the first time and thus launched European police cooperation.

The German preference for permanent cooperation in the policy domain of internal security and policing was shaped in part by (external) security interdependencies and in part by (internal) political interdependencies. Both external and internal cross-country linkages were soon cited together in internal government documents preparing the ministerial kick-off conference in June 1976 (BMI 1976b; Merk & Bracht 1976a). Both reinforced one another to favourably influence the German preference on integration. The emergence of international terrorism on the one hand as well as the provisions of the Rome Treaty – envisaging a passport union and the abolition of border controls – raised interdependence in the fight against organised crime and international terrorism, and exerted functional pressure on policymakers to act (Oberloskamp 2015: 221 ff.). While the IMK and police levels were already discussing practical security interdependence within the EEC around 1974, German national policymakers and senior government officials only began to acknowledge the growing transnational connections among terrorist groups from 1975 onwards (Merk 1973b; Merk & Bahners 1973). Initially, the German preference did not include a concept for comprehensive international cooperation because it was thought that terrorist groups employed rather temporary cross-border support to one another instead of a sophisticated transnational strategy (BMI 1975c: 1). In the wake of the Munich Massacre, this began to change. Internationally operating terrorists, it was argued, required closer European police cooperation (ibid.: 3).

France

In contrast to Germany, interdependencies were comparatively low in France. Although terror attacks had been increasing in numbers since the beginning of the 1970s, they remained relatively low and domestically focused until 1975. Only from the late 1970s and early 1980s onwards, far-left radical groups began to perpetrate large-scale attacks in France and systemically operate with similar groups in other Member States (FMI 1986; Lammert 2015). A situation assessment from the German BKA from August 1975 observes how information exchange between Member States only occurred if one or more countries were affected by 'a spectacular act of violence from the terrorists' (Herold 1975b). The document cites various incidents in France, including the murder of two policemen and an informant on 27 June 1975 by Ilitch Ramírez Sánchez, a Venezuelan terrorist known as 'Carlos the Jackal.' A few months later, Sánchez also orchestrated an attack on the Organisation of the Petroleum Exporting Countries (OPEC) in Vienna, known as the OPEC Siege. A terrorist group sympathetic to the Palestinian cause attacked a meeting of OPEC leaders and took more than 60 hostages, including the present ministers (FCO 1976c). Himself a Venezuelan national and member of the Popular Front for the Liberation of Palestine (PFLP), the case Sánchez strikingly demonstrated the increasing internationalisation of terrorism. It constituted one of multiple incidents that could potentially be seen as evidence for the growing interdependence in home affairs by French police officials and authorities.

Yet, incident and casualty numbers on French soil remained comparatively low in the beginning of the 1970s, and interdependence did not seem to matter much as driver of the French preference regarding European cooperation. On the contrary, the apparent lack of interdependence as a strong push or pull factor enabled France to assert that no new cooperation structures were needed. As a consequence, the French government adopted a position of 'avoiding' or 'denying' indicators of growing interconnectedness, thus hindering the institutionalisation of European police cooperation, as the Abu Daoud Affair showed. On 7 January 1977, the Palestinian Mohammad Daoud Oudeh, known as Abu Daoud, was arrested in Paris (Lammert 2017: 56 ff.). He was wanted in Germany and Israel in connection with the 1972 Munich Massacre, as he was suspected to have planned the attack. However, French authorities rejected the German arrest warrant and Israeli detention request, and released Abu Daoud. He left France without delay, travelling to Algeria (HO 1977a). Germany, the UK and other Community members regarded the case as a failure of European security cooperation that illustrated the need to institutionalise collective action (ibid.). The affair demonstrates how the absence of strong interdependence pressure in France interacted with political reasoning, possibly direct pressure from its Arab partners, to produce a state preference that was not aligned with Community efforts.

The United Kingdom

In the UK, cross-border interdependence only emerged rather late as an indirect driver of the British preference and did so largely because of input from police officials and the German government. By 1974, the UK had recognised the need to work together within the EEC in an increasingly "inter-dependent world" where certain "practical problems[...]concern[...]all[...]Community members" (Nairne 1974). Nonetheless, this aspect did not present the rationale behind or justification for the launch of TREVI. Compared to the international scale, crime rates in the UK were relatively low and not necessarily transnational (HO 1969). Although terrorist incidents spiralled in the early 1970s, the British outlook on terrorism largely remained domestic. Groups perpetrating attacks and bomb blasts in the UK were mostly nationally rooted, and interdependence primarily discussed with respect to Northern Ireland, for instance in relation to the IRA and controlling exports of explosives (Carr 1973). Ultimately, interdependencies would be actively framed as high and rising to create public pressure and legitimacy for political action (HO 1974b).

The tipping point in the British position can be found in the second half of 1975 in relation to several developments: the UK's successful EEC membership referendum from June, the Anglo-German information talks in September and two highly politicised terror attacks and hostage-takings. In the wake of the general elections in February 1974, the Eurosceptic Labour manifesto had promised not only a renegotiation of the UK's terms of entry but also a 'Consultative Referendum' on the latter (Labour Party 1974). Labour had pledged that "until the British people have voted, we shall stop further processes of integration" (ibid.). The referendum was held on 5 June 1975. With a turnout of 64.03%, the public voted in favour of continued EEC membership with a clear majority of 67.2% Yes-votes. This positive outcome presented somewhat of a game changer in the UK's attitude towards European cooperation. In a powerful portrayal of the process that shifted the UK's national preference *From Rejection to Referendum*, Wall (2013: 589 f.) demonstrates how Prime Minister Wilson strategically exploited the positive referendum to surmount Labour opposition against British EEC membership and active Community involvement. Internal government documents confirm the importance of the referendum as a turning point, paving the way for the UK to assert a pro-integration preference and realise deliberations on European security cooperation:

> Now that the referendum has confirmed British membership of the European Community, the Home Secretary has been considering the scope for a Home Office contribution to the involvement of Britain in the Community, and for giving Home Office interests and activities a specifically Community dimension.
>
> *(Armstrong 1975)*

In early September 1975, a bilateral meeting was held in Berlin to discuss international terrorism. The development of the HO proposal for a British internal security initiative was well underway and first soundings had been conducted with Germany and France. In the information talks, Germany emphasised the growing transnational connections of RAF terrorists – particularly with neighbouring European countries – and provided comprehensive data as evidence for the need to collaborate more closely across borders (BMI 1975b-c; FCO 1975a). British police levels likewise began to advocate a focus on terrorism in advance of the meeting of Community Ministers of the Interior (Wood 1975). This convergence of views was hardly coincidental, considering the extent to which the HO involved law enforcement officials in the preparation of the TREVI conference, including in high-level meetings (FCO 1975d). Additionally, the British police was in direct contact with foreign police officials, most notably from the German BKA (ibid.). Subnational actors thus contributed to the emergence of counterterrorism as a British priority and of interdependence as a 'buzz word' in relation to European police cooperation.

Two terror attacks ultimately placed terrorism on top of the political agenda. The so-called Spaghetti House Siege and Balcombe Street Siege of September and December 1975 were broadcasted via television and radio and instigated tremendous public interest and politicisation. The Spaghetti House Siege had been planned as an armed robbery of a restaurant in London but turned into a hostage-taking and quasi-terrorist incident when the robbery failed. The three black men responsible for the siege claimed to be activists of the radical US underground organisation Black Liberation Army, and demanded transportation and safe passage to Jamaica in exchange for the release of the hostages (Bourne 2011). After five days of negotiation, including the deployment of 400 police officers, all hostages were released and the gunmen sentenced to harsh prison sentences (BBC 1975). The Balcombe Street Siege a few months later was instigated by four IRA members who would afterwards be known as the 'Balcombe Street gang.' Following a number of bomb blasts and targeted assassinations of public figures in the preceding months, the four terrorists – who were part of a six-strong IRA Active Service Unit (ASU) – clashed with the police in central London (Moysey 2008). After a car chase, the gunmen forcibly gained access to a flat in Balcombe Street, taking the inhabitants hostage (Moysey 2008). Resembling the Spaghetti House Siege, the terrorists demanded a plane and safe passage, this time to Ireland, but eventually surrendered after six days of intense negotiations. Both incidents can be argued to have mattered directly for the British preference concerning European police cooperation. Not only did they powerfully and very publicly demonstrate the transnational links of terrorists operating in the UK, they also uncovered operational shortcomings that could supposedly only be remedied through cross-border cooperation. An official British note to the other Community members in advance of the first ministerial TREVI meeting cited both sieges as examples for the growing need to work together in the fight against international crime and terrorism, to exchange experiences and best practices and to better manage internal and external interdependencies (BMI 1976a).

By early 1976, growing interdependence in the fight against international terrorism presented the UK's key rationale for improving cooperation in the area of internal security. In advance of a ministerial EPC meeting in Luxembourg, the UK officially underlined that "[...i]nternational terrorism[...]cries out for concerted and effective international action" (Lance 1976). However, the focus of the British government lay on interdependence in the effects of terrorism rather than in its causes. It considered a "discussion on the underlying causes" of terrorism irrelevant, while the interconnectedness in effects supposedly created an "urgent need for international counter-measures as the only means of checking terrorism" (FCO 1976e). The UK thus preferred practical cooperation that could effectively mitigate these 'effects' and prevent terrorist attacks – a position that became embodied in the Trevi Group. Interdependence would only reinforce this British preference on European police cooperation. The envisioned passport union and possible abolition of internal frontiers gave rise to great anxiety about the security implications of such an endeavour, not only within the British Government but also other European Member States and their security services (Angel 1977; FCO 1977; HO 1977b).

Politicisation and Public Pressure as Drivers of Common Action

The Munich Massacre at the Olympic Summer Games in September 1972 initiated governmental deliberations on international security cooperation. It marked the culmination of a politicisation process of 'internal security' since the mid-1960s. Politicisation undoubtedly acted as an important driver of state preferences for European cooperation in Germany and the UK where public pressure to act was relatively high. While national public and political debates certainly reinforced one another reciprocally, the British and German pro-cooperation preferences may convincingly be argued to constitute a political reaction to high politicisation: the favoured policy options often presented securitising moves and venue-shopping – solving domestically manifested problems at European level

(Friedrichs 2008; Lammert 2015). By contrast, politicisation in France was comparatively low in the early 1970s. The French government preferred to avoid any publicity of its involvement in European police cooperation on the fight against terrorism. It is thus hardly surprising that France was initially reluctant towards the German and British plans for a new Community format to work together on issues of internal security and preferred a very limited scope for TREVI.

Germany: Securitising Terrorism

In Germany, the activities of radical left-wing groups, particularly the RAF, had shaped a societal and political climate of increasing anxiety and awareness regarding terrorism and public security threats since the 1960s (Pfahl-Traughber & Berndt 1999: 363 ff.). The topic frequently returned to the agenda of the German parliament, the *Bundestag*, which for instance debated the increase in public fear of crime, and the need to establish 'law and order' (Bundestag 1968a-c). While discussions among government and opposition parties initially revolved around rising crime rates and transnational criminals operating in Germany, considerable emphasis was progressively dedicated to left-wing terrorism and the threat it posed to the German state (ibid. 1970, 1972, 1975a). In 1972, Kai-Uwe von Hassel, President of the *Bundestag*, even called for the defence of the German democracy against radical forces (*Dokumentation 11/72*: I–III).

By 1972, all main German parties addressed the issue of internal security in their manifestos. The SPD even made 'security' one of its main topics in the election campaign of 1972. The German government policy of Willy Brandt between 1969 and 1974, with Hans-Dietrich Genscher as Minister of the Interior, conceived internal security as part of social policy and building a safe society (Brandt 1969). A number of policy measures were executed from 1970 onwards in response to various terrorist incidents, including RAF activities (Pfahl-Traughber & Berndt 1999: 364). These included a set of repressive, technology-focussed law enforcement reforms, initiated by high political levels and police officials, including BKA President Horst Herold himself (Weinhauer 2006). Among the most important measures were the 1970 'action programme for the modernisation and intensification of the fight against crime'[3] that Willy Brandt had already announced in his Government declaration in 1969, and the comprehensive federal programme on internal security[4] launched in 1972 and 1974 respectively. These efforts to centralise, modernise and better coordinate law enforcement across Germany and its federal states illustrate the politicisation of internal security in Germany and the emergence of a policy field through this security *dispositif* (Dahlke 2011a; Saupe 2010).

Against this backdrop of a tense public-political climate and an emerging securitisation discourse, the Munich Massacre happened on 5 September 1972. It triggered a public outcry and a – perhaps strikingly strong – political reaction (Dahlke 2006; Noelle & Neumann 1974). The German Federal Ministers Hans-Dietrich Genscher (Interior), Werner Maihofer (Special Tasks, Interior from

1974) and Walter Scheel (Foreign Affairs) were members of the crisis committee that handled the hostage situation under the lead of Bavaria's State Interior Minister Bruno Merk (cf. Dahlke 2006; Oberloskamp 2012). They were first-hand observers of the attack; Genscher even directly negotiated with the terrorists and offered himself in exchange for the hostages. There can be no doubt that this direct human experience at the front lines of the terrorist incident and the momentous failure of the negotiations that resulted in the death of all Israeli hostages, five terrorists and a German police officer must have affected how these politicians regarded terrorism and internal security. In this context, Genscher's proposal for a European conference on internal security from early 1973 seems more than mere timely coincidence.

While interdependence certainly mattered as well – after all, already in 1971 Genscher internally requested the development of a 'uniform security concept' to respond to the 'security deficit' arising from the removal of intra-European border controls – the Munich Massacre provided a whole new impetus to advance European cooperation (von Rottenburg 1974). The politicisation in its aftermath reinvigorated considerations about interconnectivity in the field of policing and the need for collective action.

Although the Munich attack certainly created pressure to act on policymakers, public interest faded shortly after. Nevertheless, the immediate German political reaction in the aftermath of the Munich Massacre, as well as a lasting sense of uncertainty about internal and public security threats in the 1970s laid the foundation for European police cooperation on terrorism and internal security (Dahlke 2006: 113–114; Oberloskamp 2017: 49–50). Building on Foreign Minister Scheel's call for an international approach to fighting terrorism and transnational organised crime, German subnational actors continued deliberation at working level and began to openly politicise internal security from 1973 onwards. The IMK and particularly its new Chairperson Heinz Schwarz, Interior Minister for Rhineland-Westphalia, actively lobbied for a European conference and the institutionalisation of EEC cooperation in the form of a European police office. Formal calls for action at the IMK, directed at the Federal Government and especially the Interior Minister, were instrumental in placing pressure on federal policymakers. Frequent media coverage and consistently high salience of related developments additionally generated political momentum (Bochmann 1974; Kölner Stadt-Anzeiger 1974; Landtag Rheinland-Pfalz 1974; Schwarz 1973b). While bilateral WG-level preparations for the EEC conference had been on-going with France since 1974, two further politicising events spurred German efforts for European police cooperation and contributed to a shift of its topical preference on counterterrorism: the kidnapping of politician Peter Lorenz by members of the 2 June Movement on 27 February 1975 (he was set free on 4 March in exchange for the release of five terrorists), and the West German Embassy Siege in Stockholm on 24 April 1975, when six RAF terrorists forcefully entered the German Embassy in Stockholm, taking twelve staff members hostage and killing two.

These incidents undoubtedly played a part, if not directly resulted, in a culmination of the security debate among political elites in Germany, and would likewise dominate the 1976 federal elections. In contrast to the aftermath of the 1972 Munich Massacre, the political debate in 1975 explicitly dealt with the international dimension of terrorism. Rather than merely raising the salience of terrorism and public pressure to act, these politicising events illustrated existing interdependencies and amplified functional pressure. In a speech before the German *Bundestag*, Chancellor Helmut Schmidt underlined the "international connections of terrorists and[...]their followers" (Bundestag 1975b: 10735(D)). He was echoed by Interior Minister Werner Maihofer, who stated: "We are obviously facing in this modern terrorism – and I believe we agree on this[...] – an international problem." (ibid.: 10749(B)).

It would be presumptuous to assume a direct correlation between the Lorenz kidnapping and Stockholm Embassy Siege on the one hand, and the renewed politicisation of German counterterrorism and internal security policy on the other. However, in 1975, a new momentum could be observed in the German preference for advancing international action that went beyond mere functional pressure from interdependence. The BMI swiftly advanced preparations for the European conference on internal security to enable it to be held as soon as possible (Bracht 1975a). Contrary to its original preference for a holistic approach to the entire domain of internal security, Germany now emphasised a topical focus on the fight against terrorism (Callaghan 1975a).

This shift illustrates how different drivers together shaped the German attitude and at times interacted. In September 1975, roughly half a year after the Lorenz kidnapping and the West German Embassy Siege, the British Minister of State for the HO, Lord Harris, reported from a visit to Bonn that Germany's Interior Minister had told him the terrorist situation in Germany were "quiet at present" but that "[p]olice investigations had[...]revealed the extent of close links between terrorists in different countries and this was encouraging the Germans to seek close collaboration with governments and police forces of other states" (Bullard 1975). This seems to suggest that Germany's preference, at the time, was primarily driven by interdependence-considerations rather than politicisation.

Nevertheless, politicisation played a part in laying the groundwork for the emerging German focus on terrorism in its European cooperation ambitions. Towards the end of 1974, the British Embassy in Bonn had observed that "[p]ublic discussion on the danger to the State presented by[...terrorism] has continued to run at a high level" (Powell 1974). Politicisation was fuelled further by the Lorenz kidnapping and the Stockholm Embassy Siege. The German Federal Government response was a political demonstration of control. The establishment of massive multi-level crisis committees was intended as a clear signal about a toughened stance on terrorism not only to the German public but also to other European governments (Henderson 1975a-b). The public and media sentiment in Germany at the time called for and supported this increasingly hard line, a political course that was consensually adopted by the government and the opposition.

However, the reappearing rhetoric of an existential threat was at no point factually justified. Terrorism comprised only a relatively small fraction of all recorded illicit activities in Germany (Bullard 1975). This demonstrates how vital politicisation was for the saliency of terrorism as a topic that seemingly required urgent political attention. By 1975, German policymakers were prepared to undertake any measures necessary. In a statement before the *Bundestag*, Chancellor Schmidt dramatically proclaimed that "everyone who wished to protect the *Rechtsstaat*[...] must be ready 'to go to the borders of what the *Rechtsstaat*[...]allowed'" (Henderson 1975b). This deliberate politicisation would develop more and more into securitisation over the next years, finally culminating in the *moral panic* of the 'German Autumn' in 1977 (de Graaf 2015; Lammert 2015).

The reciprocal politicisation among the public, the media and policymakers presented a significant driver of the German government preference for far-reaching (inter-)national action on terrorism. In 1976, coinciding with federal elections, Germany developed a remarkable activism on a number of different levels. Building on an initiative of German Federal Minister of Justice Hans-Jochen Vogel, Germany extensively lobbied for a European Convention on the Suppression of Terrorism (ECST). It was eventually adopted by the Council of Europe (CoE) and opened for signature on 27 January 1977 (HO 1975c; CoE 1977). Moreover, German Chancellor Schmidt himself pushed for an EEC Convention on the taking of hostages, drawing on the European Council's 1976 Declaration on Terrorism (d'A Collings 1976). The German initiatives illustrate the coexistence of interdependence and politicisation – often interacting, sometimes reinforcing one another – as explanatory factors for its preference. While politicisation undeniably drove the German campaign for international cooperation, the official discourse cited growing interdependence as main reason for collective action to generate momentum for cooperation. Terrorism, it was argued, no longer threatened only single states but in fact "the existence of normal international relations[...]", thereby creating "new international tensions" (FCO 1976e). However, "[...]Bonn knew very well that any [UN or global] initiative stood no chance of success" (ibid. 1976f). The same rhetoric can therefore be found in the German proposal for a political declaration at the European internal security conference on 29 June 1976, which likewise justified European police cooperation with the need to counter the transnational security deficit emerging from globalisation (Bracht 1976b; Merk & Bracht 1976a).

France: Preoccupation with Domestic Affairs and Depoliticisation

Politicisation was much lower and played a significantly less decisive and different role with respect to the French preference. Contrary to Germany with its vested interest in launching the European internal security conference as soon as possible, France was much more sceptical if not actively opposed to such an initiative. While France had been informally cooperating with Germany on counterterrorism and was not per se opposed to intensifying cooperation and expanding it to other EC Member States, it was strongly concerned about the implications for its relations with Arab states, should existing European cooperation arrangements become publicly known (AA 1973; BMI 1973b). Foreign policy considerations shaped the French preference to strictly avoid any politicisation of its role in Community action against terrorism; France even threatened to retract completely in case its participation should be made public, and thereby effectively blocked Germany's plans for a rapid realisation of TREVI (ibid.).

Contrary to Germany's high domestic politicisation over spiking RAF terrorism, in France neither left- nor right-wing terrorism were particularly debated in the beginning of the 1970s. Although attacks had been increasing, the escalation of violence remained below the levels experienced by Germany. French terrorist groups were not similarly perceived as a major threat to the French state and public safety (Requate & Zessin 2007). Between 1974 and 1985, France would experience around 358 terror incidents, whereas numbers were much higher in Germany (2,355) (Chalk 1996: 177). Interestingly, the sheer number of terror incidents in the UK (242), which would strongly pursue Community action on terrorism, remained even below the one of France (ibid.). This demonstrates that high levels of terror attacks and factual interdependence alone are no sufficient explanation for a state preference in favour of European cooperation. Otherwise, Italy should have developed a proactive position and outspoken preference for Community engagement in the fight against terrorism. In the mid-1970s, the UK experienced the highest number of terrorist incidents and the highest fatality rate in Western Europe (Chalk 1996: 44 ff. & 177). Europe-wide, the most devastating attacks with the largest number of casualties were committed by the IRA in the UK and *Euskadi Ta Askatasuna* (ETA) in Spain and parts of France (Oberloskamp 2017: 15). The nationally-oriented nature of the IRA and ETA carry no obvious relevance as demonstrators of cross-border interdependence. At the same time, their large-scale, very violent and well-politicised attacks mattered greatly as creators of salience and public anxiety, and thereby of pressure on policymakers to act.

As a consequence, politicisation in France grew tremendously in the late 1970s and the 1980s. Far left radical groups like *Action Directe* began to more systemically perpetrate attacks that were modelled on the strategies of other transnationally cooperating left-wing terrorist groups such as the German RAF and the Italian *Brigate Rosse* (BR) (FMI 1986; cf. Lammert 2015). Until then, the French media and public had been more preoccupied with internal political matters than transnational security threats. The French Minister of the Interior, Poniatowski, was facing increasingly serious public-political problems (Walden 1975). In addition to political criticism over his handling of the FMI and the police, he was widely unpopular "in the country as a whole" due to "his tough tactics on crime" (ibid.). Accordingly, Poniatowski – together with Pandraud, Director General of the National Police – deliberately pursued a course of depoliticisation and decentralisation "to distance the Minister from the success or failure of particular police operations" (Tomkins 1975a).

The absence of and strong French reluctance to any kind of politicisation of common European efforts in the fight against terrorism led Germany to tread carefully and first develop its proposal for TREVI in close bilateral contact with France. The German BMI was quite aware of the French preference for bilateral cooperation and its opposition to the creation of new multilateral structures (Merk 1974a-b). Although ministerial levels agreed on the political leadership roles of France and Germany in the context of European integration, the Franco-German WG focused exclusively on practical and bilateral cooperation, and remained under the radar of public attention (Ewart-Biggs 1974a-b; Wright 1976). When the UK informed France and Germany that it would announce its proposal for a summit of EEC Interior Ministers at the 1975 European Council meeting in Rome, France reiterated its stance against a "public emphasis on the problem of terrorism" (Tomkins 1975b). Although France regarded the politicisation of EC police cooperation as explicitly undesirable, President Giscard d'Estaing was an outspoken advocate of advancing the European project and keen on making his efforts and the role of France in this endeavour publicly known (ibid.). Since 1969, France had persistently pushed for the creation of a European passport union, including the "suppression of frontier controls" – a matter that somewhat ironically exerted even more pressure on Germany and the UK to pursue Community cooperation on home affairs to manage interdependencies arising from the abolition of border checks (ibid.; cf. Merk 1974a).

The United Kingdom: A Public Debate on Safety and Terrorism

Similar to Germany, the UK experienced a large-scale public debate over its security situation. Left-wing terrorist incidents – targeted assassinations and bomb blasts against military and civilian targets – caused extensive media coverage, for instance the IRA-perpetrated blasts in the Houses of Parliament and the Tower of London in 1974. This also sparked discussion at political level about "public safety and decline in respect for the law" (HO 1974a-b). In November 1974, Prime Minister Harold Wilson affirmed "our determination to track down and deal effectively with the criminals who are at the back of these abominable murders," he spoke in direct reaction to citizens' concerns over terrorist activities in the UK (Prime Minister's Office 1974). Terrorism would continue to disrupt public order and stir anxiety in the following years. The 1975 Spaghetti House and Balcombe Street Sieges are examples of particularly politicised (quasi-)terror incidents. The Spaghetti House Siege entailed massive public and media awareness. The highest political levels, including the Home Secretary himself, were involved and 400 police officers together with the media were engaged in managing the six-day hostage crisis ('1975'; Bourne 2011). The Balcombe Street Siege had a similar, if not greater, mass politicising effect. As the standoff between the ASU and the police protracted for days, it was widely broadcasted and closely followed by the public on radio and television (Mahoney 1976; Moysey 2008).

Against this backdrop, the British government passed emergency legislation. Under the Prevention of Terrorism Act, detentions spiked in 1975 and 1976 (Prime Minister's Office 1979). Political discussions were likewise becoming increasingly heated. Recurring debate on the possibility of reintroducing 'capital punishment' for terrorist offences demonstrated just how high emotions were running among the British public and policymakers. The Home Secretary himself had to defend his Government's supposed lack of tough responses to terrorism in Parliament more than once for (FCO 1975e). The "general anxiety about terrorism" eventually translated into "Ministerial concern that action should be taken to deal with it[...]"(Prior 1975). As IRA bomb campaigns and widespread debate on public safety continued despite a number of domestic countermeasures at legal, political and operational level, the HO accelerated the realisation of its plans for European cooperation. In the fall of 1975, the UK initiated bilateral soundings with France and Germany, which centred on the growing pressure on European governments to act on terrorism. As the HO and FCO developed the British proposal for a meeting of EC Interior Ministers, they were highly aware of the rising "pressure of public opinion" in most European countries (FCO 1975a: 3). The FCO considered it "unlikely that the public or the media in the Nine would understand[...]any show of reluctance on our part" regarding European cooperation; it "would be interpreted as a failure to even deal with one aspect of the international scourge of terrorism" (FCO 1976b). Politicisation of the UK's domestic security situation thus shaped the British preference in favour of European police cooperation. Even after the UK had successfully initiated the first TREVI meeting in the summer of 1976, public pressure and politicisation continued to matter. The FCO did not cease to reiterate that "domestic opinion[...]will require us to attempt, or support attempts, to get some positive [counterterrorism] initiative off the ground" (Fifoot 1976).

In view of the strong domestic public and media interest in counterterrorist measures, it appears striking that the British Government initially kept its proposal for TREVI off the public radar. Originally, the HO was very much concerned that information would leak to the public and media before British plans had been discussed with the other Member States. An interdepartmental consensus existed among the British Government to avoid any politicisation of the TREVI proposal. When the *Daily Telegraph* printed a small piece on the envisaged meeting of EEC Interior Ministers while informal soundings with Germany and France were still on-going in September 1975, the HO expressed great concern and together with the FCO attempted to identify the source of the leak to prevent further public debate (Peterson 1975). Perhaps also worth noting is the conclusion of the FCO that the "tone of the report, with its enthusiastic commendation of the police, suggests that it originated in either Home Office or police circles" (Brimelow 1975; Fretwell 1975). Although the leak and the suspicion of its source do not suffice as evidence, police officials did have a vested interest in spurring on British plans for EEC cooperation.

Against this backdrop of high domestic politicisation, Germany and the UK commenced intergovernmental preparations of the European internal security conference (FCO 1976a; Merk 1976a). The international politicisation of interdependencies in the area of counterterrorism strengthened their preferences in favour of EEC cooperation. Large-scale terrorist attacks with a transnational dimension seemed to publicly reveal a growing interconnectedness among European Member States and countries worldwide. Examples include the OPEC siege in December 1975 (FCO 1976c), or the week-long Entebbe hijacking of a passenger plane by two Palestinian and two German terrorists – an incident that changed the British attitude towards additional cooperation initiatives on terrorism. From a national position "of considerable caution" towards counterterrorism cooperation at the CoE or the UN, the UK began to increasingly support the latter as a consequence of the OPEC and Entebbe attacks (ibid. 1976d-e). The power of these major politicising events of international scale is captured in an FCO note: "the Heads of Government were anxious[...]to make a resounding declaration on terrorism quite irrespective of its particular content" (ibid. 1976d).

The Influence of Police Officials and Other Subnational Actors

Similar to politicisation, subnational actors played a significantly more important role in the pro-European preference formation of Germany and the UK than in the French one. In Germany, with its strong federal system, subnational actors and practitioners were involved closely in the decision-making, especially the IMK and the BKA. In the UK, police levels were not as visibly but substantially engaged with the British HO. They contributed to the public-political debate on European police cooperation and affected the topical focus of TREVI on counterterrorism. Law enforcement officials in France were likewise preoccupied with the fight against terrorism. Nevertheless, they remained focus on domestic or bilateral approaches, and thus did not act as a pro-European driver of the French government preference.

In contrast to subnational policy entrepreneurship, supranational advocacy was completely absent from the process of preference formation that brought about the Trevi Group. The European Commission for instance only mattered in the British preference formation because the UK wanted to exclude it from TREVI as much as possible to avoid a potential competence shift towards the Community. Neither the Commission nor other EU actors or institutions actively shaped state preferences in advance of the meeting of EC Interior Ministers and subsequent launch of the Trevi Group.

Germany

At first glance, the German impetus for an EEC conference on internal security came from the highest political levels. After the Munich Massacre in 1972,

Foreign Minister Scheel openly called for international action, and it was Interior Minister Genscher who first requested a strategic concept for European internal security cooperation in 1973. However, subnational actors significantly contributed to the emergence of this German preference for European police cooperation and the topical focus of the first meeting of the TREVI Ministers on 29 June 1976. Most prominently, State Interior Ministers and officials from the BKA contributed to the German pro-integration preference.

The IMK itself presented an institutionalisation of intra-German cooperation on home affairs among the Federal Lands (IMK 2017). Founded in 1954, it was introduced as political forum to formalise the working level cooperation that had already been taking place between regional officials and practitioners. Its views and debates are directly shared with the German Federal Minister of the Interior who is a permanent member of the IMK, albeit without voting right, and thus participates in all meeting. In its resolutions, the IMK may formally ask the Interior Minister or the Federal Government to take specific action, and may commission strategic reports and policy proposals. It provides substantial input for national policy- and decision-making on internal security. Through a number of WGs, the IMK effectively connects Federal Government levels with the German states (*Länder*), law enforcement authorities and the intelligence service (Lange 1999: 118–127).

As early as 1973, in the wake of the Munich Massacre, the IMK discussed ways forward in the fight against organised crime. It tasked its WG II (internal security matters) with the submission of proposals for improving international cooperation (IMK 1973a). Building on the results, the IMK formally asked the Minister to initiate a European conference and insisted on the inclusion of the IMK Chairperson in all related developments and decisions (ibid. 1973b; BMI 1973a). Preparatory discussions at subnational level soon revolved around possibilities for an institutionalisation of international cooperation. In January 1973, Heinz Schwarz, Interior Minister of Rhineland-Palatinate and IMK Chairperson at the time, pitched the idea of a European regional police office, a 'Europol' to complement Interpol, to Interpol officials at a meeting in Paris (Schwarz 1973a). The same year, Rhineland-Palatinate submitted a motion to discuss this 'European police' at the IMK, where state and federal representatives agreed on the potential benefit of such a body (ibid.). Interpol – due to the many different judicial conceptions of its members, particularly diverging definitions of 'terrorism' – was no longer perceived as a sufficient platform for managing security issues that affected the rapidly integrating European territories (ibid. 1973b).

Consequently, at its session on 15 February 1974, the IMK officially charged WG II with turning the proposals for the improvement of international cooperation into a working paper, which was to be presented at the European conference on internal security (Landtag Rheinland-Pfalz 1974). Additionally, the IMK adopted the final version of the 'Programme for Internal Security in the Federal Republic of Germany,' building on the earlier draft of 1972.[5] While the initial version had focussed on domestic issues of internal security, the 1974 programme included a significant European dimension with regard to maintaining German national security. The programme highlighted an increase in crime rates and in the transnational activities of criminals, political extremist and terrorist groups in Germany and other European states. It linked the need for European security cooperation to the European integration process: cooperation on internal security was seen as a precondition for achieving the 'European political union' that Member States sought to achieve in the 1980s. Concretely, the IMK Programme for Internal Security cited the foreseen abolition of internal border checks as expected to produce a 'security deficit' that must be remedied through measures at European level. The document exemplifies how far-reaching plans for EEC cooperation were at subnational level in early 1974. Amongst others, the document supported the ideas of a 'common European policy of internal security' and 'permanent, also institutionalised cooperation.'

The German Federal Lands were actively involved in domestic agenda-setting and policymaking through the IMK, and thus considerably shaped the German national preference early on. Strongly in favour of European security and police cooperation, the IMK additionally had a preference for far-reaching institutionalisation including the creation of a European police office. This preference eventually culminated in a formal request to the Federal Minister of the Interior at the IMK meetings of November 1973 and February 1974, to prepare and pursue plans for a European conference on internal security (IMK 1973b). This request was publicised in the media and reiterated by the IMK throughout 1974 (Bochmann 1974; Welt am Sonntag 1974). Related input prepared by the IMK's WG II had a strong operational orientation and a focus on law enforcement and security practitioners, which is unsurprising because WG II not only consists of the heads of corresponding departments from the regional interior ministries but also of the BKA President and the President of the German Police University (IMK 2017). Issue-specific interdependencies provided the core rationale justifying a growing need for European cooperation, particularly between national law enforcement authorities (Bochmann 1974: 1). Mirroring the securitisation discourse from the Internal Security Programme, the WG proposals that were adopted by the IMK in June 1974 insisted that enhanced European police cooperation and/or an amendment of police powers would have to form the precondition for the removal of border controls; otherwise, it would not be possible to sufficiently balance the resulting security deficit (ibid.: 2 ff.). Moreover, they likewise conceived EEC internal security cooperation as necessary building block towards 'the realisation of the targeted/aspired European political union' (ibid.: 1). The conclusions of the June 1974 IMK meeting illustrate how State Interior Ministers as well as senior policy and law enforcement officials acted as subnational policy entrepreneurs to favourably shape the German government preference on European security cooperation. Noteworthy are especially the framing of issue-specific interdependencies and the political discourse of an emerging security deficit.

Next to the IMK, the BKA shaped the German national preference. It was founded in 1951 as an executive agency of the BMI. From 1970 onwards, in response to the experience with radical political and terrorist groups, the BKA was significantly strengthened in its capacity as Germany's central, coordinating criminal police office (Dahlke 2011a). Its annually issued Police Crime Statistics indicated steadily rising crime rates since at least 1963, including an increase in the share of non-German offenders.[6] This seems to imply growing interdependencies in the fight against crime in an 'ever closer union' of EEC Member States around the 1970s. While it is difficult to provide similar numbers and statistics for terrorist offences, the general sentiment and public perception at the time perceived an apparent trend, thereby effectively politicising a growing 'insecurity.'

In 1974, the Federation of German Detectives (BDK, *Bund Deutscher Kriminalbeamter*), a trade union representing the BKA, held its international criminal police congress ('Kripo International 74') under the theme of 'European Community – including for the Criminal Police' (BDK 2015). Contributions to the final report of the conference included – yet again – reflections on realising a European police office (ibid.; cf. Fijnaut 2016: 19 ff.). Notwithstanding the overall sentiment that growing interdependencies and the threat of an emerging security deficit rendered international police cooperation indispensable, BKA President Horst Herold decidedly rejected the thought of establishing a 'Europol' (Knelangen 2001: 193). He was concerned about the potential duplication if not the undermining of cooperation structures already existent within Interpol. Therefore, he preferred the enhancement of European police cooperation through Interpol rather than the creation of a new one (Herold 1974). International security threats, Herold argued, required global cooperation beyond the borders of the EEC. Nevertheless, Herold was not able to assert himself on the national level, and the BKA's initial preference for a more global format of international security cooperation did not succeed in taking hold among the responsible government officials. Irrespective of Herold's statement at the BDK congress in April 1974, the German State Interior Ministers continued to press for a European conference on internal security, and German federal levels went ahead with according to preparations together with their French counterparts (Landtag Rheinland-Pfalz 1974; Merk 1974c).

Despite the top-down political decision, it was senior officials who substantially prepared the conference in terms of its content, thereby laying the foundations for the meeting of EEC Interior Ministers. The Franco-German WG drew heavily on papers and proposals devised by the IMK and especially its WG II (BMI 1974b: 1; Merk 1974b). Moreover, senior officials from French and German Interior Ministries as well as from law enforcement cooperated directly and closely in the run-up to the conference. This included the BKA. Following the failure of BKA President Herold to press for the pursuit of a global framework via Interpol, the BKA's position *vis-à-vis* an inherently European cooperation format changed. In a situation assessment at the request of Federal Minister of the Interior Werner Maihofer from August 1975, Herold highlighted the growing transnationalisation of terrorism and voiced frustrations over the lack of effective counterterrorism-efforts through Interpol (Herold 1975b). The report stressed the need to shift to bi- and multilateral European levels to counteract the emergence of transboundary terrorist networks within the EEC and prevent domestic cells like the RAF to take advantage of increasing Community interdependencies (ibid.: 3 ff.).

Similar BKA assessments continued to nourish the discourse of an arising security deficit: the discrepancies between national law enforcement capacities and transnationally operating terrorism. Herold himself strongly advocated the enhancement of cross-border information exchange and called for the modernisation of police technology and the institutionalisation of communication channels (Herold 1975a; Wittschen 1975; cf. Weinhauer 2006). Another formal report to the BMI from February 1976 drastically depicted the negative consequences of the abolition of internal border checks and emphasised that a 'supranational internal security structure' among EEC Member States was indispensable to compensate the risks emerging from this development (BKA 1976a: 9). In the accompanying letter, addressed to the State Interior Ministers and the Federal Minister of the Interior, Herold directly asked the IMK to ensure that the described security implications would be considered in the IMK's European WG (Herold 1976a).

Both the BKA and the IMK would remain closely involved in preference-shaping after the launch of TREVI at the ministerial meeting of 29 June 1976. They would provide substantial input to the TREVI WGs and have regular exchanges with the Federal Minister of the Interior (BKA 1976b; Bracht 1976c). The input from subnational levels was not only initiated by subnational actors themselves, but was also regularly sought and even requested by the BMI, including in the preparations for the European conference on internal security (Herold 1976b; Merk 1973b). The IMK and the BKA thus helped shape the German position in favour of permanently formalising, if not institutionalising, police cooperation among EEC Member States – a government preference that remained unchanged for decades, culminating in the creation of Europol in the 1990s.

France

In France, subnational policy entrepreneurship played a similar albeit less significant role. Senior law enforcement officials and civil servants were substantially involved in preparing the first ministerial TREVI meeting and shaped the preceding policy processes within the Franco-German WG (Ewart-Biggs 1974b; Tomkins 1975a). Nevertheless, the influence of subnational advocacy on the French integration preference derived primarily from German and British police representatives, who pushed their French colleagues to accept, if not favour, the establishment of the Trevi Group.

The involvement of French police levels emerged naturally from the distribution of competencies within the political system. The responsibility for the fight against international terrorism solely lay with the *Direction de la Surveillance du Territoire*, which served as domestic intelligence agency and formed part of the French National Police (Wittschen 1975). However, this actually hindered the early preparatory phase for the European internal security conference. At its first meeting in Paris in November 1974, the Franco-German WG was to discuss ways of fostering a common European attitude regarding political terrorism. However, France – represented mainly by intelligence officials – refused to do so because the topic was already scheduled for a meeting of the European Heads of intelligence agencies (Oberloskamp 2017: 65 f.). Interestingly, the proposal for this agenda item at the gathering of EC intelligence services had come from the German Federal Office for the Protection of the Constitution (BfV). Bureaucratic resistance and institutional competition thus cut across the scope of the Franco-German WG and effectively rivalled its work. In France, this continued even beyond the launch of TREVI. Subnational policy entrepreneurs continued to obstruct the development of European police cooperation. French police officials – mainly from the intelligence side of the National Police – lobbied for a highly limited functional scope of TREVI. It is thus not surprising that France vetoed a Dutch proposal for the inclusion of intelligence agencies into the Group shortly after the ministerial meeting in June 1976 (Tomkins 1975a).

Apart from the legally embedded involvement of the French police in any action by the FMI against international crime and terrorism, the very close and personal relationship between Poniatowski and the Director General of the National Police, Robert Pandraud, ensured a direct influence of law enforcement authorities on the French preference. The British FCO noted in September 1975 that "it is a very personal appointment," and that "Pandraud reported directly to, and took his instructions directly from, Poniatowski" (ibid.: 3). This mattered greatly in view of Poniatowski's personal convictions and his vulnerable political standing at the time. Having pledged to step up efforts to combat crime when he came into office in May 1974, Poniatowski relied on tough policing measures and was perceived to be "encouraging his police to be too easy on the draw" (Walden 1975: 2). In view of his tough crime-fighting strategy, harsh anti-Communist stance and a number of mismanaged operations, he came increasingly under public and political attack, and heavily relied on Pandraud for counsel. To "distance the Minister from the success or failure of particular police operations" Pandraud initiated a number of systemic changes in the national police (Tomkins 1975a). Although the French National Police possessed a direct channel – through its Director General - for input into FMI policy and preferences, this input remained largely limited to domestic security and internal political issues.

What is more, Poniatowski and Pandraud regarded the infrastructure of Interpol sufficient for multilateral police cooperation and did not want to undermine it with parallel channels (BMI 1978b; Solier 1978). The official FMI position similarly reflects this emphasis on decentralisation and low-profile policing to deal with internal security problems rather than bold political commitments to European cooperation. Police actors thus effectively shaped the French attitude towards TREVI and the national preference for practical problem-oriented strategies and rather informal cooperation in the fight against terrorism on a case-by-case basis (Merk 1976a). French subnational policy entrepreneurship affected a national preference that was preoccupied with the domestic situation and domestic remedies – much in contrast to Germany and the UK where sub-national levels actively pushed for a transnational approach to internal security governance and policing.

Although the French National Police without doubt exerted a certain influence on the French preference against the establishment of TREVI as a new multilateral cooperation framework, its role was not as vital as that of British and German subnational. In fact, sustained transnational pressure from Germany and the UK – particularly senior government and police officials at the level of intergovernmental WGs – contributed to the shift of the French national position towards accepting police cooperation through TREVI. Yet, transnational pro-integration advocacy by subnational actors in Germany and the UK failed to substantially impact the French preference. Other factors, such as political considerations about the potential impact on French relations with Arab states or the perceived absence of significant interdependencies, presumably continued to negatively shape its preference on European police cooperation and produced an overall sceptical attitude towards the Trevi Group. This attitude would sustain itself throughout the following decade. It would be visible in the French outspoken unwillingness and at times deliberate 'politique de blocage' (FMI 1978; Schneider 1979). On multiple occasions, France actively hindered police cooperation via TREVI as well as attempts at expanding the functional scope of the Group, and even requested its dissolution (BMI 1978b; FMI 1978; Solier 1978).

The United Kingdom

Similar to Germany, British police representatives exerted significant influence on the UK's preference concerning TREVI. Following the Home Secretary's proposal for a meeting of Community Ministers, law enforcement officials effected terrorism as the preferred British focus of EC cooperation (Wood 1975). Many of the rather technical and operations-focused elements in the British note to other Member States ahead of the first TREVI meeting originated from the police side of the HO and derived directly from needs arising at the front lines of policing (cf. BMI 1976a). British senior police officials were closely involved in the shaping of the TREVI proposal before its announcement at the European Council meeting in Rome. They were substantially included in the preparatory work for the ministerial meeting (Wood 1975). Already in the fall of 1975, Robert Armstrong, HO Deputy Under Secretary in charge of the Police Department, played a key role in the development and the drafting of the Home Secretary's proposal for a meeting of Interior Ministers (FCO 1975b; HO 1975b). Armstrong was personally responsible for the bilateral soundings with France, and directly met with his French counterpart, Pandraud, Director General of the French National Police (HO 1975a). Similar to Pandraud, Armstrong thus acted as a direct representative of British police interests and concerns, which –

through him – were able to shape both the British government position and the negotiations in advance of the first TREVI meeting.

British police officials were involved on various levels, including as formal points of contact in higher political fora or as direct, more informal cross-border contacts with other law enforcement authorities (FCO 1975d). Their widespread presence and input in the intergovernmental WGs preparing the ministerial TREVI meeting was reflected in the outcome documents and ultimately the TREVI structure. Both contained a significant amount of police terminology and a focus on practical problem-solving and concrete aspects of police work. The influence of British senior officials in the policy process can likewise be seen in the change of the German strategy following the British announcement of its proposal in December 1975. Since the UK's proposal had been conceived at the highest government levels, Germany deliberately shifted to the subnational level for asserting its preferences against the British position in a bottom-up manner (Streicher & Bracht 1975b).

British police actors exerted considerable pressure on the British Government. Examples include the October 1975 premature news leak of British plans for a conference of Community Interior Ministers that seems to have originated in HO police circles. Senior police officers were in frequent and direct contact with HO officials, including at the highest levels and exchanges between the Commissioner of the Metropolitan Police and the Home Secretary himself (Brimelow 1975; Fretwell 1975). Although the influence of police levels on the British preference regarding European police cooperation must not be overestimated, it is remarkable to what extent police representatives were involved in this rather political endeavour. Initially, the British Government's stated aim for TREVI had been a rather loose exchange of information and best practices on public order and safety (BMI 1976a). Yet, when the TREVI Ministers finally met in June 1976, the UK's proposal concentrated on practical, even operational support and cooperation regarding concrete terror attacks and other rather narrowly-defined areas of police work. Contrary to French domestic security actors, British subnational policy entrepreneurs positively shaped the British integration preference.

In sum, subnational policy entrepreneurship certainly mattered for both shaping and multiplying ministerial impulses. However, it only proactively emerged as a driver of national preferences in all three countries once the initial impulses had been provided at higher levels. The German IMK and BKA first became active in response to the initiative of the BMI and at the request of the Federal Minister himself. In France, police levels likewise became active only once they had officially been asked to become engaged, for example in the Franco-German WG or in the bilateral soundings initiated by Germany and the UK. In the UK, the Home Secretary provided the initial impulse, after which the police side of the HO was engaged and increasingly began to provide input and actively lobby for European cooperation on counterterrorism.

The growing importance and influence of police officials in the process leading to the creation of TREVI can likewise be seen in the strengthened powers of law enforcement across all three Member States. Especially Germany and the UK responded to subnational reform calls and passed or amended legislation aimed at allowing the police to better tackle terrorism, often through tough policing measures. In addition to the judicial increase in police powers at home, subnational policy entrepreneurs in France, Germany and the UK became more and more active across European borders. Next to transnational contacts between police officers, senior officials from the German BKA (and IMK), the British Metropolitan Police Service, and the French National Police were directly and proactively involved in the preparations for the first ministerial TREVI meeting. Their involvement went beyond mere participation, as demonstrated by the serious concerns of the German Ministry of Justice, which feared that the TREVI cooperation – if coordinated by the BMI and police officials – might lead German law enforcement authorities to become less accountable, and to act progressively outside the control of the German Public Prosecutor's Office (Oberloskamp 2015: 55 f.). While domestic police levels in France, Germany and the UK did not initiate state preferences in favour of European cooperation, they played a major part in maintaining and enhancing the momentum – often harnessing politicisation by pushing policymakers towards securitising moves – and thus crucially shaped national preferences on TREVI.

Institutional Choice in a Nutshell: State Preferences on the Three Dimensions of Differentiated Integration

In sum, high interdependence acted as necessary condition and starting point for the development of pro-integration preferences in support of European police cooperation. Asymmetrical interdependencies account for the ultimate institutional choice of the Trevi Group as an intergovernmental body with inherent characteristics of differentiated integration. Whereas Germany and the UK reacted to growing interdependence by seeking common action, first on a global then a Community level, France experienced comparatively lower levels of interconnectedness and did not initiate or support new forms of cooperation (see Table 2.1). The TREVI case further demonstrates that politicisation can act as both reinforcement and deterrence of preferences in favour of European cooperation, and that it often interacts with interdependence in its impact on governments. In Germany and the UK, public debates on the problem of terrorism emphasised existing international connections and thereby contributed to positive national positions concerning TREVI. A similar debate was largely absent in France where public discourse revolved around domestic issues (see Table 2.1). What is more, the French Government actively undertook efforts to avoid politicisation in relation to its counterterrorism policy to not fuel the internal political crisis around its Interior Minister, and not to burden diplomatic ties with its Arab partners. Only in view of external pressure from other EC governments, France conceded a new European cooperation framework. Finally, subnational policy entrepreneurship likewise mattered as influencer and

TABLE 2.1 Driving Factors across France, Germany and the UK

	Issue-specific interdependence	*Politicisation & Crises*	*Supranational policy entrepreneurship*	*Subnational policy entrepreneurship*
France	*H1 Confirmed* Comparatively **low** interdependence in terrorism: *preference for decentralisation.*	*H2.3 Confirmed* **High** domestic politicisation related to French police system/ low politicisation of international terrorism: *preference for decentralisation and no cooperation at the EU level.*	*No significant impact*	*No significant impact* (weak subnational advocacy)
Germany	*H1 Confirmed* **High and rising** interdependence in international terrorism: *preference for EU police cooperation and integration.*	*H2.1 Confirmed* **High** domestic politicisation related to RAF terrorism: *preference for EU police cooperation and integration.*	*No significant impact*	*H4 Rejected* **Strong** subnational advocacy (BKA, IMK) of far-reaching European cooperation: *preference for European police cooperation and (part-) formalisation.*
The UK	*H1 Confirmed* **High and rising** interdependence in international terrorism: *preference for EU police cooperation and integration.*	*H2.1 Confirmed* **High** domestic politicisation related to public safety and (IRA) terrorism: *preference for EU police cooperation and integration.*	*No significant impact*	*H4 Rejected* **Strong** subnational advocacy (police side of HO) of European cooperation: *preference for European police cooperation and part-centralisation.*

H1: The higher the interdependence in security issues, the more likely Member States are to favour EU police cooperation and integration.
H2.1/2.2: The higher the politicisation in a given issue area, the more/*less likely* Member States are to favour EU police cooperation and integration/*and the more likely they are to prefer differentiation and decentralised, informal modes of cooperation.*
H2.3: The higher the politicisation in a given issue area, the less likely Member States are to favour any police cooperation at the EU level.
H3: The higher the supranational policy entrepreneurship in a given issue area, the more likely Member States are to favour EU police cooperation and integration.
H4: The higher the subnational policy entrepreneurship in a given issue area, the less likely Member States are to favour EU police cooperation and integration, and the more likely they are to prefer differentiation and decentralised, informal modes of cooperation.

amplifier of national preferences on EU police cooperation, particularly regarding its functional scope. However, not all subnational actors had equal access to higher decision-making levels. The German IMK and the BKA were embedded in the German federal, subsidiary system that ensured the involvement and participation of subnational actors in internal security policy. Although the first impulse for initiating Community cooperation and the European conference had come from a minister, the IMK and the BKA significantly shaped the German preference in the negotiations thereafter. In the UK, the police side of the HO – with its close ties to the political side – similarly moulded the British preference with regard to TREVI and especially its focus on terrorism. In France, no such subnational lobbying in favour of European police cooperation was present (see Table 2.1). While close (personal) ties existed between the Interior Minister and the Director of the National Police, the top-down nature of the French political system allowed for little to no bottom-up input in this area. It remains questionable whether this would have been different, had the French police system been less centralised. A preoccupation of high-level policymakers with internal affairs and averting political scandal at home might likewise limited subnational policy entrepreneurship on international police cooperation.

In view of the political blockage of far-reaching integration, Member States deliberately adopted strategies of differentiated integration in the negotiation phase for TREVI's establishment. Asymmetries in the impact of driving factors can explain this phenomenon, as they yielded diverging preferences across these countries and on the three dimensions of differentiated integration. The respective strength of single drivers determined not only preference formation on vertical and horizontal integration, and the functional scope of European police cooperation, it also impacted the probability of preference di- or convergence among Member States. High interdependence acted as primary positive influence on state preferences concerning vertical and horizontal integration. Subnational policy entrepreneurship and politicisation, by contrast, had the highest impact on state preferences regarding the functional scope. While Germany's strong pro-integration preference on all three dimensions of differentiated integration was presumably the result of relatively high functional, public and political pressure in various areas of internal security, similar levels of interdependence, politicisation and subnational policy entrepreneurship in the UK remained mostly confined to the area of terrorism, and thus produced a strong integration preference only in this issue area. France, against it, experienced comparatively low levels of all three drivers. Consequently, it did not favour EC police cooperation at all. The final design of the Trevi Group with its inherent differentiated integration characteristics therefore reflected not preference convergence but compromise; the intergovernmental structure of varying degrees of differentiation or integration across multiple levels reflected the asymmetrical impacts of respective driving factors. The final institutional choice presented an effective means to realise the core substance of each preference. However, this differentiated integration approach to European police cooperation was not primarily shaped by the Eurosceptics to obstruct or delay integration. On the contrary, Germany and the UK deliberately employed it as a strategy to advance cooperation at the time and integration in the long run.

Notwithstanding final agreement on the targeted format, scope and membership for police cooperation – a loose intergovernmental format outside the EC framework with an initial focus on terrorism, and a geographical extension to all Member States – this did not solve the problem where to situate TREVI in relation to the Community framework once and for all. Growing internal interdependencies would drive Germany to proactively advocate the gradual extension of the Group's functional scope and its level of centralisation, and France to persistently exercise a 'politique de blocage.' Meanwhile, the British preference should remain rather ambiguous, torn between the benefits of Community cooperation and the risk of a competence shift in favour of the EC. The following chapters take a look at how preferences on these three dimensions of differentiated integration changed in the course of the further development of TREVI until the 1990s and ultimately enabled the step-by-step integration of European police cooperation until today. They illustrate how the Trevi Group and related cooperation structures increasingly gained practical and legal authority of their own and gradually evolved into a more independent body across all three levels.

Notes

1 Controversy persists over the origins of the name 'TREVI.' The most commonly accepted explanation is that it stands for "Terrorisme, Radicalisme, Extrémisme et Violence Internationale" (Terrorism, Radicalism, Extremism and International Violence) (Bigo 1996: 86–87; Knelangen 2001: 91). Others have argued it relates to the fountain 'Fontana di Trevi' in Rome where the Group was set up in 1975 (Aden 1998: 77; Fijnaut & Hermans 1987: 40). This supposedly plays on the names of the Group's founders, the Director-General of the Dutch Ministry of Justice A. J. Fonteijn and the Italian Minister Fontana (Anderson et al. 1995: 53).

2 CDU 1969–1973: Wahlprogramm der Christlich Demokratischen Partei Deutschlands. http://www.kas.de/wf/de/71.8940/
- CDU/CSU. (1972). Regierungs-Programm: 'Wir bauen den Fortschritt auf Stabilität'. http://www.kas.de/wf/de/71.8940/
- Wahlprogramm zur Bundestagswahl 1969 der Freien Demokratischen Partei: "Praktische Politik für Deutschland - Das Konzept der F.D.P.". Nürnberg.
- Wahlaufruf zur Bundestagswahl 1972 der Freien Demokratischen Partei: 'Vorfahrt für Vernunft'. Frankfurt am Main.
  Regierungsprogramm der Sozialdemokratischen Partei Deutschlands 1969: 'Erfolg, Stabilität, Reform'. Bonn.
- (1972) Wahlprogramm der SPD: 'Mit Willy Brandt für Frieden, Sicherheit und eine bessere Qualität des Lebens'. Dortmund.

3 Sofortprogramm zur Modernisierung und Intensivierung der Verbrechensbekämpfung

4 Schwerpunktprogramm Innere Sicherheit

5 (1972) *Programm für die Innere Sicherheit in der Bundesrepublik Deutschland Teil I*
- (1974) *Programm für die Innere Sicherheit in der Bundesrepublik Deutschland*

6 *Polizeiliche Kriminalstatistik (PKS) 1972.* Wiesbaden.
- *Polizeiliche Kriminalstatistik (PKS) 1976.* Wiesbaden.

3

INSTITUTIONAL BEGINNINGS

The Europol Drugs Unit and Early Europol

The Trevi Group had been around for almost a decade when discussions over the shape and organisation of European police cooperation re-emerged in the mid-1980s. This included the possible establishment of a permanent secretariat and the expansion of the Group's functional scope. From 1985 onwards, some even demanded the creation of a whole new organisation to structure the common fight against international terrorism and organised crime. At the time, the EC was undergoing rapid changes in different areas that caused a sense of loss of control over national security and raised functional pressure to work together. From formerly nine Member States the EC had grown to comprise twelve members by 1986. Further enlargement would follow in 1995, bringing the count to fifteen. The Schengen Agreement was signed in 1985 by five of ten Member States, which committed to abolishing internal borders. Not even a year later the Single European Act (SEA) was adopted and additionally lifted national restrictions within the Community. Through the SEA, Member States took concrete steps towards the completion of the internal market, and laid the foundation for a political and monetary union including a single European currency. Other events like the fall of the Berlin wall and the Iron Curtain in 1989 as well as the subsequent collapse of the Soviet Union further spurred the need to work together within an increasingly borderless, interconnected EC – a need that was perhaps fuelled even more by the Maastricht Treaty and its then unprecedented integration agenda that transformed the Community into a Union: today's EU.

Against this background it is perhaps unsurprising that the European Council at its meeting on 28–29 June 1991 in Luxembourg decided to expand cooperation on matters falling under the newly created JHA-pillar. This included the establishment of a Central European Criminal Investigation Office that would lead to the official launch of Europol in 1999. The process that led there was – as with the Trevi Group – neither easy nor straightforward. Contrary to the

DOI: 10.4324/9781003262176-4

previous chapter where three Member States were clearly most important and identifiable in the process towards the launch of TREVI, this was not the case with regard to the creation of Europol. With the exception of Germany, which continued to play a significant and proactive role, no single Member State consistently shaped the process. This chapter thus studies the various phases leading to the launch of Europol, each marking a new stage of progress or changing dynamics in European police cooperation (see Figure 3.1). The first phase began in the mid-1980s when Italy proposed the consolidation of different cooperation formats under the single structure of a European Criminal Intelligence Office. Although the initiative failed, Member States began to increasingly discuss the need to formally join forces in the fight against drugs and took important steps to improve European coordination. This first phase in the process towards Europol culminated in a British proposal for the foundation of National Drug Intelligence Units (NDIUs) as predecessors of a European Drug Intelligence Unit (EDIU). While the NDIUs were quickly realised, no agreement could be reached on an EDIU, and the discussion was postponed.

Around 1990, preferences and negotiation dynamics changed again, initiating the second phase towards a European police office. Building on the developments of the late 1980s and the UK's efforts, German Chancellor Helmut Kohl planted the seed for the actual creation of Europol at a European Council meeting in June 1991 where he introduced a far-reaching proposal for JHA cooperation in the EU. Despite the consensus that cooperation needed to be intensified, Member States could initially not agree on the details. The second phase was marked by negotiations on the scope and powers of the early Europol, as well as by preliminary arrangements like the launch of the Europol drugs unit (EDU) – an instance of differentiated integration to circumvent political deadlock.

The third phase completed the timeline of the inception of Europol: the signing of the Europol Convention in 1995 until the commencement of operational activities in 1999. It was marked by intense negotiations on the implementation of the Convention, including discussions on Europol's institutional set-up, legal competencies and powers. When Europol finally began operating on 1 July 1999, it was the product of nearly a full decade of bargaining and reconciliation of different national preferences, the same maximalist-minimalist positions shaping the negotiations on the Maastricht Treaty.

The 1980s: First Attempts towards a Central European Body

The Scalfaro Paper: An Italian Proposal for a Permanent European Secretariat

At the meeting of TREVI Ministers on 20 June 1985, Italy's Interior Minister Oscar Luigi Scalfaro proposed the creation of a new European body to centralise existing European cooperation formats (see Figure 3.1). The 'Scalfaro paper' foresaw the establishment of a permanent secretariat at European level

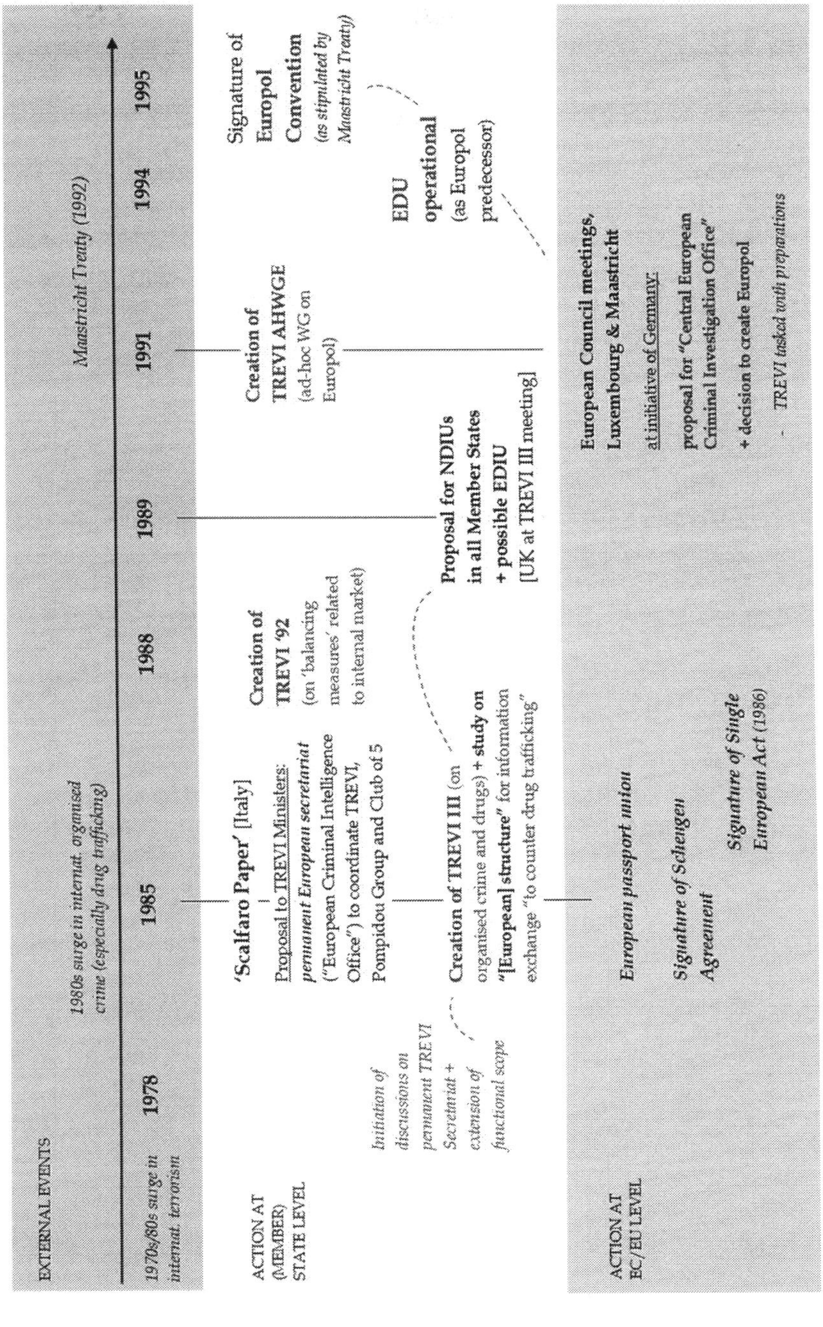

FIGURE 3.1 From TREVI to the Europol Drugs Unit and Europol Convention

to jointly coordinate the Trevi Group, the Pompidou Group and the Club of 5[1] (BMI 1985c). This entailed a central connection of national data bases and the coordination of joint investigation teams (JITs). The functional scope was envisioned rather wide, encompassing terrorism, transnational organised crime and drugs. In contrast to the Trevi Group's launch a decade earlier, the Scalfaro paper departed from a situation of rapidly expanding European cooperation. In view of advancing EC integration, Italy advocated the reconciliation of different, separate structures (ibid.: 1). This neatly illustrates the emerging relevance of spill-overs and path-dependency in a field of European cooperation that had not existed before the Trevi Group. Notwithstanding the overall 'maximalist' preference of Italy concerning European integration and the negotiation of the Maastricht Treaty, Italy had not been previously proactive in the area of police cooperation (Bruggeman 2016: 27). Around 1980, developments related to terrorism, drug trafficking and national police organisation produced considerable pressure on the Italian government to act.

TERRORISM AND DRUGS: GROWING TRANSNATIONAL LINKAGES

Since the late 1970s, Italy had been experiencing increasing terrorist activities similar to the ones that had so crucially motivated Germany and the UK in favour of establishing TREVI in 1976 (Hof 2015: 11 ff.; Requate & Zessin 2007: 437). BR were perpetrating more and more violent acts and assassinations from 1978 onwards and continued to shape the public debate and political securitisation discourse (Meade 1990: 183 ff.). In addition to intensifying cross-national links among domestic terrorist groups, the beginning of the 1980s marked a surge in international terrorism in Italy (BMI 1986).

These developments generated significant political and functional pressure on the Italian Government to act and favour a European solution. At the time, police cooperation with other Member States was not institutionalised in Italy. Accordingly, Italy showed a growing interest in TREVI and a common EC approach (BMI 1978c: 2). In 1978, it supported the proposal for a permanent TREVI Secretariat (BMI 1978a: 4). However, an agreement was postponed due to a lack of political will. Other Member States did not see the necessity for formalising and expanding cooperation. Many lacked similarly high levels of (inter-)dependence on European collective action, or regarded existing cooperation formats as sufficient (Boge & Schneider 1979; BMI 1978a). Contrary to Italy, Germany and the UK were highly active within TREVI. This lack of Member State support for the further centralisation of EC police cooperation would persist for almost another decade.

In addition to terrorism, drugs constituted another issue area in which European governments were increasingly interconnected. Since the late 1960s and early 1970s drugs had been emerging as a serious problem across European Member States (Busch 1999; Sheptycki 2000). They especially posed a problem in

Italy where they exemplified the transnational links of domestic criminal groups like the mafia. Yet, the Italian Government did not officially acknowledge drug abuse and drug crime as issues of concern until the mid-1970s (Friedrichs 2008: 144; Gardner 1979). By then, Italy was experiencing a massive surge in drug-related criminal activities that posed a considerable and direct threat to the government and its monopoly on the use of force. The Italian Mafia was incrementally professionalising its conduct and expanding its influence beyond the local and national confines (Arlacchi 1986).

Interdependence in the fight against drug trafficking and related crimes pushed Italy to develop a preference for international cooperation. A kind of international mafia entrepreneurship was evolving that capitalised on global market liberalisation and cross-border supply chains. Blurring the lines between licit and illicit economic activities, drug-related crime accumulated massive profits that financed transnational organised crime (ibid.). The Italian Mafia did not only horizontally widen its operational territory beyond national boundaries but it also began to vertically integrate different criminal areas (e.g. drugs and arms trafficking) to expand its economic power and political autonomy. Drugs were of fundamental importance for the rise of the Mafia as a serious contender of the state monopoly on violence. They enabled it to amass and (re-)invest an incomparable fortune and thus infiltrate almost every part of the sociopolitical and economic sphere. Unilaterally powerless in the face of this transnational threat, the Italian Government and law enforcement authorities began to pursue international cooperation in the struggle against global drug cartels. At first, this occurred on a bilateral basis, primarily with the US that possessed long standing experience in the investigation and pursuit of international drug trafficking (Friedrichs 2008: 144–147). In 1868, the European regional office of the US Federal Bureau of Narcotics (FBN) was located in Rome and transformed into the Bureau of Narcotics and Dangerous Drugs (BNDD) (Cusack 1974: 244 & 252). Following the US model, an Italian Central Drug Office was created in the mid-1970s in recognition of the "need for a centrali[s]ed coordinated unit" (Gardner 1979: 14). This 'Americanisation' of European drug enforcement similarly occurred in many other EC Member States, which began to acknowledge drugs as a significant problem of unprecedented scale.

A FUNCTIONAL NEED FOR CENTRALISATION

Most European countries were soon confronted with legal difficulties posed by their diverging national frameworks *vis-à-vis* the transnationally-oriented, semi-institutionalised and invasive American investigation methods (Friedrichs 2008: 134 ff.). This was especially true for Italy. Legal constitutional restraints and its security culture made it difficult for Italian policymakers and police officers to implement the innovative American techniques (Nadelmann 1993: 216 f.). Although Italy preferred a global approach to the fight against drug trafficking via Interpol, its decentralised system of security governance and internal compartmentalisation complicated cooperation, even among domestic agencies (Senato 1976: 18–23).

Italy's police system and internal security governance had been designed as a counter-trend to previous fascist structures (Hof 2011: 124 ff.). A strong inward-looking and nationally focussed legal culture in criminal matters as well as lack of political consensus impeded a strong Italian preference in favour of cross-border cooperation. Only from roughly 1978 onwards and in view of growing public anxiety did the Italian Government commence to perceive legal (constitutional) and systemic restraints to cross-border police cooperation as serious obstacle for its national security and police. The kidnapping and murder of Italy's former Prime Minister Aldo Moro shockingly illustrated the rise of terrorist violence and further radicalisation of the BR (Camera dei Deputati 1979). This opened the floodgates to a united political reaction to the activities of terrorist groups, including securitising moves such as comprehensive reforms and centralisation within the police system (Hof 2015: 12).

Politicisation and public pressure thus opened a window of opportunity for the shift of the Italian preference towards European police cooperation. While interdependence in the fight against terrorism and drugs was already exerting functional pressure to favour collective action, spiralling domestic salience can perhaps explain why Italy finally acted and proposed relatively ambitious institutionalisation and the integration of multiple initiatives within TREVI. An internal memo of the German BMI, evaluated Italy's initiative and its renewed efforts to intensify bilateral cooperation as primarily of "political and psychological importance" rather than an effective improvement of the existing security situation or cooperation arrangements (BMI 1985d). The EC thus presented a means of political venue-shopping for Italy to signal action and mitigate domestic anxiety.

A LACK OF INSTITUTIONAL ALTERNATIVES

A lack of cooperation alternatives at international level combined with rapidly rising interdependence moved Italy's preference towards a progressively pragmatic position acknowledging the benefits of a European approach. Global cooperation was still far from satisfactory in the 1980s. Interpol had neither been able to overcome the obstacles and deadlocks that had already frustrated EC Member States in the 1970s, nor had it sufficiently sped up procedures and improved its practical benefit (Fijnaut 1993: 11–12; Interviewees 7, 14 & 21). Although Italy had previously been hesitant and passive towards EEC initiatives in the fight against terrorism, it now began to embrace the European format.

Like many EC countries, Italy experienced a steady, albeit gradual rise in international organised crime and transnational activities of criminal groups around 1980 and explicitly voiced concerns about a loss of national control in the context of European integration (BMI 1982). The Scalfaro paper included similar arguments about the need to manage functional spill-overs of European integration.

The Italian proposal in 1985 came amidst an on-going discussion whether to expand the functional scope of the Trevi Group (see Figure 3.1; cf. BMI 1985b). In June 1985, the TREVI Ministers created a third WG (TREVI III) to deal with organised crime and drugs. The Scalfaro paper, against it, was not realised.

This seems counterintuitive in view of the shortcomings of Interpol and an emerging internationalisation of terrorist and criminal activities within the EC. Additionally, the rapidly expanding cooperation structures of TREVI, its various WGs across different levels, were becoming increasingly complex. External and internal interdependencies were high and rising across EC Member States, as was subnational policy entrepreneurship in favour of pragmatic professionalisation of existing cooperation networks (BMI 1986). Especially security and police authorities highlighted the benefit of a central body as envisioned in the Italian proposal. The German BKA expressed support for the Italian proposal and advocated the institutionalisation of cooperation on organised crime; it even demanded to go beyond the structure of a secretariat in the long run and create a European Criminal Police Office (Zachert 1985). The decision of European governments to not realise the Scalfaro paper demonstrates that the influence of subnational policy entrepreneurs remained limited.

INSUFFICIENT PREFERENCE CONVERGENCE?

Neither functional pressure to better structure cooperation nor subnational policy entrepreneurship sufficed to sway state preferences and unify police cooperation in 1985. The Scalfaro paper failed as a result of reluctance from other Member States and an overall lack of political will. Germany was concerned that the creation of yet a new body would lead to duplication and overlap. Instead, it advocated the expansion of the Trevi Group (BMI 1985b; Schreiber 1985). France was similarly sceptical with respect to Scalfaro's proposal and about its potential impact on national competencies if information exchange were centralised within a European secretariat (BMI 1985a). Most Member States preferred to focus on existing cooperation initiatives and fora rather than establishing additional ones. France naturally favoured Interpol, while the UK centred on TREVI and was opposed to any substantial formalisation (Anderson 1993b: 77–81; BMI 1983b). The lack of support for the Italian proposal seems striking in view of rising interdependence across all EC Member States, particularly the internationalisation of terrorism and organised crime and a well-established recognition of the drug problem.

A possible explanation could be the mismatch with state preferences on vertical integration. Interdependence pressure may have been high across most Member States and shaped their preferences in favour of European police cooperation, yet internal interdependence and spill-over effects had still not reached a sufficient threshold across Member States to turn the tide in support of deeper integration. Although TREVI had been in existence for almost a decade and was closely linked to the Community framework in practice, it remained formally outside the EC. TREVI had still not been able to establish itself as the main cooperation forum of European states. It certainly was a strong contender as unprecedented format that was quickly growing. However, in the mid-1980s, various countries (or single domestic agencies) still prioritised Interpol and bilateral networks for day-to-day cooperation. European governments lacked the political will to substantially change this running system and additionally questioned Italy's commitment. Even before the Scalfaro paper was presented at the meeting of TREVI Ministers in June 1985, other Member States were assessing the initiative as mere lip service and political venue-shopping intended to reassure the Italian public and politicians (BMI 1985d). Consequently, a proposal that could have presented a qualitative quantum leap in European police cooperation quickly faded into oblivion. However, it prepared the ground on which a British impulse for a European system of drug intelligence units would succeed a few years later.

The British Proposal for NDIUs as a Game Changer

Drugs continued to matter as an issue area that shaped the preferences of EEC Member States. In a WG meeting of TREVI III in April 1989, British Home Secretary Douglas Hurd proposed to create NDIUs in all Member States and assess the feasibility of establishing an EDIU at supranational level (see Figure 3.1). While some governments were surprised by the UK's initiative, and the discussion of an EDIU was postponed due to persisting scepticism, the proposal overall received strong support and led to the installation of drug intelligence units across the Community. With its European outlook, the British advance – similar to the Italian one before it – helped pave the way for a paradigm change in police cooperation. It enabled the eventual inception of a central European body to align national approaches. External interdependence in the area of drugs alongside internal interconnectivity within the Community acted as drivers of the British preference. Both were amplified by the politicisation and policy entrepreneurship from domestic police officials.

INTERNATIONAL COOPERATION ON DRUGS: STILL INSUFFCIENT

Since the 1960s, drugs had been emerging as an increasingly serious problem across most EC countries and drove states to strengthen cooperation. Yet, existing arrangements fell short of functional and operational needs. The so-called Pompidou Group had been founded in 1971 at the initiative of French President Georges Pompidou. It was strongly influenced by the American drug enforcement regime and the US preference for formalisation (Friedrichs 2008: 139–141). Similar to Italy, France had for a long time not prioritised this issue area, and had thereby become a notorious transit country and safe haven for international drug traffickers, very much to the annoyance of other countries. The US made a point of moving the European office of its BNDD from Rome to Paris to deal with this 'French Connection' (Friesendorf 2007: 37–78). The French media extensively reported on the spiralling domestic drug deaths and individual cases of overdose, and thus reinforced public pressure and the international 'naming and shaming' (Cusack 1974: 252; Gévaudan 1985: 45).

In this context, France launched the Pompidou Group in 1971. The group initially comprised all EC governments and the UK. It can be seen "as a French attempt at setting standards for a European approach to the drug problem" (Friedrichs 2008: 140). Although the group was intended to include operational and working levels, it never truly managed to move beyond high-level and strategic discussions. Next to the lack of operational and policy output, the integration into the CoE in 1980 and subsequent expansion of membership beyond the Community disqualified it as a possible central EC body (de Witte 1993: 96; Interviewee 7). Nevertheless, the Pompidou Group presented an important first advance on the path to European integration. It made formalisation and institutionalisation thinkable, and its deficiencies cleared the way for the development of alternative, improved European cooperation formats.

By the 1980s, a number of legal agreements had been successfully initiated at international level. The UN drug prohibition regime pursued repressive strategies and prioritised a crackdown on the supply side (Friedrichs 2008: 113 ff.). However, the UN regime remained insufficiently institutionalised due to strong opposition from some governments (FCO 1974). It also did not address the demand side and prevention aspects. However, European countries and law enforcement authorities increasingly sought to integrate normative-social strategies into their approaches to drug enforcement (European Council 1986: 12).

Interpol might have offered an institutional alternative for the European fight against drugs. The bulk of Interpol information exchange already centred on Europe. In 1981, Germany thus requested a European regional office at the Interpol GA (Interviewee 7; Pütter 1991). Although a Technical Committee for Cooperation in Europe was created, a European secretariat was not formally established until the mid-1980s and would only begin operating in 1987 (Baun 1987). Police cooperation via Interpol remained behind the political expectations and operational needs of European Member States, particularly in the areas of terrorism and drugs. This dissatisfaction became obvious through other European cooperation formats such as the Club de Berne and the Vienna Club, which began to deliberately schedule their reunions outside Interpol (Interviewee 7).

The lack of effective and comprehensive cooperation platforms in the fight against drugs, and the discontentment of national authorities formed crucial contextual determinants for the creation of a new Community structure. The inability of existing institutions to respond to rising functional and public pressure shaped the emergence of pro-integration preferences of European Member States.

THE COMMUNITY LEVEL AS A MEANS OF VENUE-SHOPPING

Rising national crime rates had become a salient topic among the UK's media and public since the late 1970s (Morgan 2014: 10 ff.). The progressive internationalisation of terrorism and reporting on the cross-national links of British terrorist groups fuelled public and political pressure on the government (BMI 1983a). From the 1980s onwards, British policymakers increasingly sought to counter politicisation through political and legislative securitising moves that signalled control (Anderson 1993a: 23 ff.). Part of this strategy was venue-shopping. The pursuit of international police cooperation presented a tactic to accommodate pressure to act on transnational problems. Similar to other European states, drugs were also emerging as a growing problem in the UK, both politically and in the public eye (MacGregor 1998). The unprecedented rise in domestic drug users and international drug connections shifted the British position from a sovereignty-focussed one to cautious support for international drug enforcement (Friedrichs 2008: 115–117; Morgan 2014: 24 ff.). While external interdependencies thus shaped the UK's preference in favour of extending the functional scope of European police cooperation, the UK maintained its nationalist attitude on vertical integration and continued to oppose any delegation of powers to a supranational body. Keen on preserving autonomy, it neither agreed with the demand-side orientation of other Member States nor did it initially support the institutionalisation attempt of the Pompidou Group (FCO 1974).

Internal interdependence would transform this anti-centralisation preference and lead the UK to propose the establishment of NDIUs and even a central EDIU in 1989 (see Figure 3.1). January 1985 marked the beginning of the European passport union and subsequent abolition of passport controls within the EC. In June, the Schengen Agreement was signed as a first step towards a common travel area without internal border checks. Moreover, the SEA of February 1986 would enter into force the following year. It targeted "an area without internal frontiers" and completion of the single market by 1992 (Section II, Art. 8a). All these developments heightened internal European interconnectedness. They confronted EC governments with potential collective action problems and thus created significant functional pressure to cooperate. Subsequently, Member States decided to expand TREVI's functional scope to drugs and organised crime, and to launch a study "with a view to the establishment of a [European] structure aimed at exchanging information to counter drug trafficking" (Europol 2016a: 25). Growing internal interdependencies and spill-over effects from European integration were beginning to effectuate an emerging paradigm-change in JHA cooperation.

This initiated a shift in domestic national security and policing cultures towards streamlining and rationalisation. The UK's police system and security governance had always been practically oriented, focussed on pragmatic cooperation and organised in an informal, flexible manner. Nonetheless, internal interdependencies and spill-over effects from EEC integration were suddenly creating a rising functional need to streamline and rationalise British policing. Law enforcement officials increasingly advocated centralisation as a means to benefit from innovative methods and best practices, and to better structure international police cooperation. The Metropolitan Police Services (MPS) of London began to serve as unofficial role model in the establishment of standardised policing tools within the UK and as the central point of contact beyond.

In the 1970s, subnational policy entrepreneurs instigated a systematic restructuring process. They demanded better integration of British internal security agencies and the centralisation of some tasks. A parliamentary report established that "virtually all forms of crime and all kinds of police-public relations now have transfrontier implications" (Anderson 1993a: 25). Subsequently, MPS Commissioner Sir Imbert lobbied for a 'British FBI' (Imbert 1989), while other police representatives even contemplated a possible 'Europolice' that could oversee the work of 'multinational operational units' (Gregory 1991: 154). Although these examples illustrate a wide acknowledgement at operational level of the need to rationalise and better structure police cooperation, political reluctance persisted (Busch 1995: 215 f.). The shift in the UK's security culture towards increasing centralisation was mostly the result of a functional necessity rather than of an integration-friendly political system and tradition. Notwithstanding strong subnational advocacy of vertical integration, the British Government continued to favour intergovernmental formats like TREVI to manage common threats (BMI 1983b).

A DRUG PROBLEM OF NEW MAGNITUDE: THE HEROIN EPIDEMIC OF THE 1980S AND 1990S

By the late-1980s, drug trafficking had not only emerged as one of the most serious security problems across the Community but it was also additionally interconnected with other crime areas (de Witte 1993: 96; Interviewees 7 & 21). Drug enforcement increasingly involved the policing of money laundering, fraud and arms trafficking. European integration gave rise to a European criminal area with inextricably intertwined security threats. The British proposal for the establishment of NDIUs and an EDIU came amidst this spiralling pressure and at a time when TREVI was starting to emerge as main cooperation platform (Interviewee 7; Knelangen 2001: 215). The extension of TREVI's functional scope from terrorism to organised crime and drugs had set a precedent, from which a certain path-dependency would follow. Additionally, the saliency of European security produced wide-spread public acceptance of international police cooperation as well as political and operational willingness to undertake necessary steps (Interviewee 7).

In 1986, the European Council expressed its concern about drug abuse and its dissatisfaction with existing international cooperation on the matter. It recommended to consider "ad hoc collaboration between the Member States and the Commission" (European Council 1986: 12). Already at this stage, the UK proactively sought to manage interdependencies and streamline national approaches and efforts at European level. It, for example, initiated the creation of an Ad-Hoc Group on Immigration (Bunyan 1997: 9), and proposed to install a central protected communications network across all Member States to improve coordination in the areas of drugs, illegal immigration and terrorism (Harrington 1985). Furthermore, the UK was concerned about the isolation of TREVI and aimed at better connecting it with other cooperation platforms (BMI 1986). A consensus was emerging sat the European Council and the Trevi Group that action needed to be taken to offset the adverse and potential security effects of the SEA and the Schengen Agreement (Bunyan 1997: 9 ff.). The 1988 European Council meeting in Rhodes thus requested the JHA Council to "step up its efforts," and initiated a 'Coordinators group on the free movement of persons' (ibid.: 12).

BEGINNING PATH-DEPENDENCY AND OPERATIONAL CALLS FOR CENTRALISATION

Against this backdrop, TREVI began to gain considerable political weight. In 1987, Member States had already decided to expanded its functional scope to drug trafficking and illicit drug use as well as hooliganism (Bunyan 1997: 11). Horizontally, the Group cooperated with third countries at operational level, thus expanding practical albeit not formal membership. Vertically, certain aspects of TREVI were institutionalised. Next to the implementation of a secure communications network, Member States agreed to create a "light administrative structure" for better coordination, "stress[ing] the need for an experimental and progressive phase" (ibid.). The creation of WG TREVI 1992 linked the Group even more to Community developments. TREVI '92 was tasked with the management of spill-over effects and balancing measures in relation the completion of the internal market (Busch 1995: 333 f.). It should "specifically consider the 'policing and security implications of the Single European Market' and[...]'compensate for the consequent losses to security and law enforcement' in the EC" (Bunyan 1997: 9).

In line with these developments – especially the cumulative focus on TREVI to cope with interdependencies – the UK proposed the creation of NDIUs and an EDIU in the spring of 1989. Although growing interdependencies had led the UK towards embracing the practical merits of structured Community cooperation, the idea for the Europe-wide creation of NDIUs and a central unit for coordination derived directly from British policing practice and the operational context. Since the 1980s, British security governance and policing methods had been undergoing a 'cultural' transformation, partially due to close cooperation with the US. British law enforcement and home affairs were gradually moving from a rather compartmentalised organisation to 'intelligent centralisation' (Busch 1995: 200–219). Drug policy and enforcement were streamlined, practices and structures rationalised – all in an attempt to better coordinate different actors at national level. Organisational and operational innovation based on the US model also entailed the structured collection of information and data, and subsequent consolidation in the hands of a central entity (MacGregor 1998). To spearhead the new integrated British approach to drug enforcement, an NDIU was created at the MPS in 1985 (South 1998: 96).

Implemented at national level, the new policing model yielded effective results and began to transform the UK's security culture and practices. From an operational perspective, it became evident quickly that a similar approach was sensible, even necessary, for European police cooperation (Interviewee 7; Knelangen 2001: 197–198). The intervention of British Home Secretary Douglas Hurd at the meeting of TREVI III may be regarded as an attempt to expand the UK's centralisation experience to the EC level. His proposal for the creation of NDIUs in all Member States, and an EDIU for coordination, originated from subnational policy entrepreneurship. Rather than an inherent normative desire to politically integrate, this step can be seen as a response to the deterritorialisation of national security and to functional spill-overs from Community integration. It was informed by the shift in British security culture towards practical rationalisation to better manage growing interdependence (Interviewees 7, 17 & 18).

As a result, a dichotomy evolved within the British preference. The practical need for intelligence-led centralisation of European cooperation collided with a strong political opposition to comprehensive institutionalisation at Community level. Whereas the UK's security and policing culture was developing towards more integration, its legal and political culture had a long-standing tradition of national sovereignty (Friedrichs 2008: 190). Police and policing were considered core state powers. This belief was engrained in the British "constitutional tradition[...as] an indispensable legal concept" and as a "principle of legal sovereignty in criminal law," and was embedded in the practice of British "executive law enforcement" (Anderson 1993a: 21). The UK's attitude is neatly illustrated by the British reaction to the German proposal for an 'FBI-like' European structure in 1988. When German Chancellor Helmut Kohl supposedly reiterated his intentions to create a 'European FBI' in a personal meeting with Prime Minister Margaret Thatcher, she is said to have responded: "Never ever." (Interviewee 21).

In the spring of 1989, only the proposal for NDIUs was adopted (Peek & Hoefman 1993). However, in December, the TREVI Ministers commissioned a study on "the need for the possible extension [of NDIUs] at European level" (Bunyan 1997: 36). An ad hoc WG on EDIU was established in 1990, followed by political agreement to actually realise such a structure one year later (Knelangen 2001: 199). In this vein, the UK's initiative substantially prepared the ground for the German proposal and realisation of Europol.

The 1990s: Starting Point for a European Police Office

Interdependence and spill-overs from Community developments had formed the British and Italian integration preferences. They likewise shaped the German proposal for the expansion of JHA cooperation and the establishment of a European police office (see 3.1). Since the 1970s and the creation of TREVI, Germany had aspired to integrate European police cooperation. Throughout the 1980s and 1990s, European interconnectivity in security threats and law enforcement grew further. Spill-over effects from previous integration decisions and other policy domains began to produce a functional need to integrate and reinforced the German historically 'Eurofriendly' position.

The German Historic Experience: Predisposing the National Preference to Eurofriendliness?

Germany's political system and its security and police culture in a way 'predisposed' it towards European cooperation. Germany had for a long time strongly interrelated its identity to the EEC. European integration – building common institutions and embedding legal norms – was regarded as the way forward in the political rehabilitation of Germany within the European and international community. By the 1980s, Germany had emerged as role model and driver of EC integration and linked its own fate to the deepening of Community ties (Interviewee 23). Its federal system with a power distribution across multiple levels presented an ideal test case for the EC, and in turn rendered Germany structurally compatible with European modes of governance and politically favourable towards them (Prime Minister's Office 1976; Interviewees 21–23).

This likewise applied to Germany's internal security governance. Since the 1970s, a restructuring process of the national police system had organised various competencies at the federal level. Reforms included the introduction of the BKA as central police coordination body at national level and to the outside (Lange 1999: 212 ff.). The modernisation of police work reinforced centralisation tendencies, as data collection and information management were streamlined. By the mid-1980s Germany was one of the leading countries in the computerisation and technical rationalisation of law enforcement activities (Busch et al. 1985: 115–146).

Growing Community Linkages: Connected in Threats and Institutions

Europol was the result of a top-down political initiative of the German Government (Interviewees 7, 14 & 21). Although the cooperation- and centralisation-friendly political system and security culture helped pave the way for Kohl's proposal, interdependencies and political spill-overs primarily shaped the German preference towards the creation of a Central European Criminal Investigation Office. In the mid-1980s, German and EC security governance became increasingly approximated. Germany already held an intrinsic preference for European integration and believed that domestic problems could only be solved at the European level. It is no coincidence that the structure and institutional set-up of both TREVI and Europol strongly resemble Germany's internal security architecture and political system (cf. Lange 1999: 170).

Moreover, functional spill-overs from the European single market affected Germany and required security authorities to adapt to new transnational threats (ibid: 201 ff.). Its central geographic location at the heart of Europe made Germany a transit country and especially susceptible to the effects of developments within its neighbouring countries and the EC. The internationalisation of organised crime in Germany illustrated these external interdependencies. It challenged German law enforcement with new practical problems and reinforced the need for transnational policing. Crime incidents had doubled over the course of 25 years (Rupprecht & Hellenthal 1994: 28–29). Especially in the fields of illegal migration and drugs, Germany was emerging as a hub of international trafficking as transit and distribution country within the EC (BMI 1983b; Interviewee 7).

In this light, Germany's support for the Belgian proposal for an expansion of TREVI's functional scope to organised crime in 1982 appears logical. Related internal discussions were initiated at the BMI in the same year (BMI 1982). At the meeting of the Stuttgart European Council in June 1983, Germany officially put its political weight behind advancing European integration in this area. In its 'Solemn Declaration on European Union,' the Council recognised the growth in activities of international organised crime and the rising interconnectedness among criminal groups. It highlighted the effects of cross-border crime at a time when national border controls were still in place, and called for enhanced JHA cooperation to offset negative consequences and a loss of national control in view of the SEA (cf. Siegele & Lümmen 1985).

Asymmetry as Driver of Avant-Garde Initiatives and Flexible Integration

Nevertheless, interdependencies were moving quicker than political measures. EC integration was not progressing fast enough for German policymakers. The asymmetrical effects of external threats and institutional linkages across Member States may explain why preference convergence in favour of integration was stalling at European level, and why Germany opted for a strategy of flexible integration. The negotiations on a common travel area and a European passport union had been moving at a sluggish pace since the 1970s. Chances of achieving an EC-wide agreement in line with German expectations seemed less than slim (Leuffen et al. 2013: 222 f.). Consequently, Germany opted for differentiated integration together with a group of likeminded Member States that were experiencing similarly high levels of interconnectedness and functional pressure. In July 1984, Germany and France signed the Saarbrücken Agreement. It stipulated the removal of border controls as well as far-reaching police and customs cooperation on drugs and illegal migration (Mitsilegas et al. 2003: 27 ff.). Not even one year later the Schengen Agreement extended the cooperation arrangement to the Benelux countries (Fijnaut 1992a). Although Germany would have preferred universal European membership, it purposefully chose flexible integration as a piecemeal strategy to European integration; the expansion to the rest of the Community was envisioned from the beginning (Monar 2001).

The 'political Schengen project' reinforced internal interdependencies among its members and within the Community as a whole. The German Government exerted considerable pressure to swiftly remove internal borders and frontier checks within the EEC (BMI 1985e). This high-level political pressure – paired with functional pressure from growing interconnectedness in threats and institutions – created a ripple effect at the domestic and European level and helped gradually shift state preferences on police cooperation towards the EC framework. By the mid-1980s, German police officials focused increasingly on the European level (Boge 1985: 38). TREVI had already been emerging as key cooperation body. The Schengen Agreement, the passport union and the SEA further strengthened the political prioritisation of the EC framework (Knelangen 2001: 194 f.). No suitable institutional alternatives rivalled the European format or TREVI. Interpol was still insufficient in the eyes of European governments and security authorities due to persistent confidentiality problems and trust issues (Interviewees 7, 14 & 21). In 1986, the International Police Association consequently discussed the creation of a 'European Interpol' as suitable alternative to offset the shortcomings of information exchange via Interpol and as "a joint cooperation mechanism" that would "allow for prompt and reliable answers" to transnational organised crime (Europol 2016a: 24; cf. Interviewee 14).

In this context, an important precedent was set for linking the Trevi Group to the emerging field of 'European' JHA. In June 1989, the TREVI Ministers tasked the Group with the preparation of countermeasures to safeguard the national security of EC Member States. To this end, they adopted the so-called 'Palma Document,' a working programme with according priorities and timelines (Bunyan 1997: 35). At a follow-up meeting in December, they formally acknowledged "the new requirements for cooperation arising out of the European construction and of the creation of a European area without internal frontiers" (ibid.).

These developments did not only illustrate a discursive change but they also would produce political spill-overs and expedite path-dependency and integration in this emerging European policy area. Already in late 1989, the TREVI Ministers adopted several balancing measures that had long been prepared by the Schengen signatories – a prime example of differentiated integration speeding up European integration as a whole (cf. Busch 1995: 333 f.). In a similar vein, TREVI Ministers built on the British proposal for NDIUs and an EDIU in their decision to "encourage[...]the creation of structures to centralise and co-ordinate information and to exchange intelligence" (Bunyan 1997: 36).

These developments and the political momentum at European level provided Germany with an opportunity to realise its longstanding preference on vertical integration: the comprehensive formalisation of European internal security governance. At the Hannover European Council in June 1988, German Chancellor Kohl called for an 'FBI-like' structure at European level (Anderson 1989: 30). In 1990, coinciding with the signature of the Convention implementing the Schengen Agreement, German Interior Minister Schäuble proposed a European Criminal Office as a central European police body to facilitate and coordinate information exchange (Schäuble 1990). These examples reflect the saliency of the early 'Europol thought' among political elites in Germany. In December 1990, Germany tied in with on-going Community deliberations regarding a possible EDIU. It introduced a graduated scheme for the creation and build-up of an EDIU at the TREVI experts meeting in

London. Very much in the spirit of differentiated integration, the German BMI saw the EDIU as a strategic "pre-stage for a European police unit with eventually executive powers for the effective fight against internationally oriented drug trafficking" (Busch 1995: 337).

Interestingly, from an operational perspective, no practical need seems to have existed for the further institutionalisation of European police cooperation. By the mid-1980s, German law enforcement and security authorities regarded cooperation with key EC partners and European Member States as well-established. The BKA described relations with the UK as "optimal" (Boeden 1984: 3); the BMI concluded that "no formal regulation" was necessary (Bischoff 1984). In a similar vein, the BfV did not see a need for further agreements and 'no obvious topic that would require discussion at ministerial level' (BfV 1984). The impetus for a German vertical integration preference thus did not come from subnational policy entrepreneurs. Police networks and the IMK had no noticeable influence. They would only be involved later, in the implementation of the Europol idea (Knelangen 2001: 206). When Germany officially proposed the creation of Europol at the European Council meeting of June 1991 – barely half a year after it had instigated the build-up of an EDIU – the initiative came as a surprise to German subnational levels and European Member States (Busch 1995: 145; European Council 1991a: 6). Kohl's federal government alone had devised the proposal. It was not previously discussed with the German *Länder*, although they had formally endorsed the thought of a European Criminal Police Office at the IMK meeting in May 1991 (Zachert 1992: 10–11).

Rapidly growing interdependence and spill-over effects informed this top-down German preference for creating a Central European Criminal Investigation Office. A series of events of Europe-wide significance reinforced this preference: the fall of the Berlin wall and the Iron curtain in 1989, the subsequent reunification of Germany in 1990 and the collapse of the Soviet Union in 1991. As a consequence, crime numbers rose suddenly and dramatically, not only in Germany but also in Central and Eastern Europe (Interviewee 7; cf. Rupprecht & Hellenthal 1994: 29). Especially Germany's reunification meant a 'significant overload' of its security authorities, in particular the BKA and BMI (ibid.). The German proposal for a 'Europol' may be argued to have been driven significantly by these developments.

Once the European Council had adopted Kohl's proposal, the TREVI Ministers were asked to prepare the details of this new European structure, and the AHWGE was founded to this end (Benyon et al. 1993: 160). In December 1991, the European Council decided to charge Europol initially with the coordination of information exchange in the area of drugs (European Council 1991b). This presented the official go-ahead for the creation of Europol. Following a suggestion from Germany, the TREVI Ministers agreed to merge discussions on EDIU and Europol and launched a two-step process towards Europol: the launch of the EDU (previously: EDIU), which would then be developed into Europol (Bunyan 1997: 40–41).

The Europol Convention as a Turning Point

Following the adoption of the German Europol proposal in 1991, EC Member States began to contemplate the institutional layout of this new body. "The initial proposal to establish Europol as a type of European FBI was extremely controversial in the political, professional and public domains. Lengthy discussions and negotiations took place in the TREVI WGs, the Council and its WGs, and the European Parliament before agreement was reached on the model, the structure, the tasks and the competences of Europol" (Storbeck 2016: 22). This process may be divided into two partially overlapping streams: (1) the focus on EDU as predecessor and drugs as initial issue area, and (2) the parallel negotiations on the Europol Convention until its adoption in 1995, and ensuing discussions over its implementation until Europol's commencement of activities in 1999. Both streams comprised differing state preferences on the three dimensions of differentiated integration. Internal interdependence, functional and political spill-overs as well as an emerging path-dependency mattered most as drivers of pro-integration preferences. Out of all Member States, Germany was the main driver behind the build-up of EDU and Europol. In the words of one European senior official: "without Germany this would have never happened" (Interviewee 21).

The Europol Drugs Unit

The British EDIU initiative presented the institutional basis for the establishment of EDU and eventually Europol. In June 1992, TREVI Ministers decided to merge the British and German proposals. The "European" Drug Intelligence Unit was renamed "Europol" Drugs Unit and was to form Europol's experimental predecessor. An EDU project group was subsequently launched under German leadership and began operating in September (Storbeck 2016: 21). The EDU took up activities in 1994. It marked a historic change in the pace and depth of European police cooperation and illustrated an emerging path-dependency in the area of JHA. Spill-overs from past cooperation shaped state integration preferences with regard to the horizontal extension and functional scope of EDU, while Community integration in other policy domains produced effects on vertical integration preferences.

The initial focus on drugs constituted a natural continuation of discussions within the EDIU (and TREVI) and thus the 'path of least resistance' for institutionalisation. In view of Germany's far-reaching vision for European police cooperation and Kohl's original plans for a European FBI, EDU might be regarded as deliberate strategy of differentiated integration to speed up the process. Although EDU was functionally and vertically limited, it presented a practical starting point for the German Europol thought.

Interdependence significantly shaped Germany's preference to this end. Drugs presented "the biggest problem" in Europe at the time (Interviewee 21). The largely ad-hoc informal character of cross-border police cooperation and its reliance on personal contacts continued to hinder national security and law enforcement authorities. Cooperation often evolved in line with bilateral relationships between individuals. In Germany, communication was better established with Turkish police authorities than with French ones (Interviewee 21; cf. Rupprecht 1993: 41). In addition to a lack of professionalised cooperation, steadily rising criminal interdependencies illustrated that "[...d]ifferences between police structures, legislation and judicial systems[... were] exploited and criminals ma[...d]e their haul on one side of the border and then cross[ed] over it to escape detection and prosecution" (de Witte 1993: 90).

While Germany's legal framework was relatively strict and drug enforcement rather effective, neighbouring countries with less rigid prosecution were increasingly emerging as safe havens for drug traffickers, from where drugs could easily be transported back into Germany (Interviewee 21; cf. Friedrichs 2008). The effects were felt Europe-wide. Drug cartels and criminal groups were strategically operating across borders, an argument that was likewise cited frequently in the EDU/Europol preparations (Knelangen 2001: 201). Interdependence in Germany was further heightened by its geographic location and especially the ramifications of the Schengen Convention, the SEA and the German reunification. Germany had become a popular hub as destination and transit country for drug traffickers (Interviewees 7 & 24). In 1991, the number of drug-related deaths in Germany reached an all-time peak with over 2,000 deaths (compared to 324 in 1985) (UNODC 2003: 118). Accordingly, the public and practitioners overwhelmingly worried that Member States, and the police in particular, were no longer in control of the crime and drug problem and failing to regain it (Interviewees 7, 14 & 21; cf. Busch 1999).

While drugs thus increasingly entered the radar of German (and European) policymakers, the final catalyst that drove Chancellor Helmut Kohl to propose a European FBI and then EDU was a highly personal one. Reportedly, a book on the transnational reach of the Italian Mafia and global drug cartels inspired Helmut Kohl to act (Interviewees 7 & 21). Following the read, he allegedly enquired of Interior Minister Schäuble to what extent this was a problem in Germany and Europe. Schäuble then tasked the BKA with a study. When the findings revealed extensive activity of transnational organised crime groups in Germany and thus emphasised significant interdependencies in the maintenance of internal security, Chancellor Helmut Kohl is said to first have demanded a European FBI (Interviewee 21). His focus – and the government's focus – on drugs was further fuelled by a white paper from the German Federal Intelligence Service (BND) from January 1992. The paper reported on the threat from international drug trafficking for Western nations, particularly emanating from the rising influence of drug cartels within democratic and political systems, and from the exploitation by criminal groups of open markets and transnational economic ties (BMI 1992; cf. Rauschgift 1992). The EDU Ministerial Agreement itself leaves no doubt as to the relevance of this factor; it underlined the "urgent problems posed by international illicit drug trafficking, associated money laundering and organised crime."

With a view to the vertical integration of police cooperation and particularly EDU, spill-overs from the context of European integration shaped state preferences. Since the 1970s, the increasing Europeanisation and internationalisation of policing structures and methods had prepared the ground for the idea of a 'Europol,' as had the advancing emphasis on the Trevi Group as "cornerstone for the ensuing development of police cooperation among EU Member States" (Europol 2016a: 25–26). This emerging path-dependency within EC police cooperation was reinforced in the 1990s. Changes in police cooperation were "a result of decisions made under the Maastricht and the Amsterdam Treaties and by the Tampere Council" (Storbeck 2016: 21). The TEU did not only transform the EC into today's EU but also created a "broad base[...]for JHA cooperation" (Bruggeman 2016: 27). Suddenly, Member States acknowledged as European "matters of common interest: police cooperation for the purposes of preventing and combating terrorism, unlawful drug trafficking and other serious forms of international crime," as well as "the organisation of a Union-wide system for exchanging information within a European Police Office" (Art. K.1, para. 9). Thereby, Europol had become formally linked to the EU's framework amidst the integration debate and negotiations following the Maastricht Treaty. Even the discussion and choice of the Europol headquarters (situated in The Hague) formed "part of a greater deal on the location of several EU institutions Europe-wide" (Storbeck 2016: 22).

Developments from other policy areas of European integration and instances of differentiated integration were becoming more and more tangible across Member States. The single market and the Schengen Agreement likewise heightened interdependence in JHA matters. Kaunert et al. (2013: 276) refer to this as the "spillover-enlargement effect:" the importance of EU enlargement as a push towards integration in the area of internal security. Not only did these developments heighten external interdependencies – the interconnectedness in threats among Community members – they also produced functional spill-overs from growing internal interdependence. Intensifying institutional linkages among Member States required and provided practical opportunities for cross-border police cooperation (Interviewee 7). In this context, differentiated integration initiatives like Schengen served as "pilot project[s] for police cooperation in the entire EC" (Busch 1995: 332).

The Ministerial Agreement on the establishment of the Europol Drugs Unit was signed in mid-1993. Information within EDU would initially continue to be exchanged via national systems. This presented a deliberate tactic of differentiated integration and strategic concession by Germany to facilitate the process towards Europol (Busch 1995: 339). When EDU began operating in January 1994 – with a mandate to assist national police forces in criminal investigations – police networks and subnational practitioners were highly sceptical if not opposed. They had not been included in the decision-making and regarded EDU as 'top-down political project' (Interviewees 7 & 14; cf. Europol 2016a: 14). Especially national criminal police offices and the German *Länder* objected to widening EDU's competencies, partially out of concerns that its inclusion in investigations and operational tasks might yield a loss of competencies on the part of national authorities (Interviewees 7, 14 & 21). Although the TREVI WG on Europol comprised senior officials from ministerial departments and law enforcement, representation was limited because of its small size (40 members) (Benyon et al. 1993: 160). Only with the creation of Europol would national police authorities start to be better represented at European level (cf. Anderson 1993a: 26).

EDU initially faced significant bureaucratic resistance across EU Member States – a factor that impeded a swift convergence of pro-integration preferences regarding Europol. National police officers were reluctant to share data via EDU, and officials of interior ministries insisted to exclude EDU from operational business (Interviewees 7 & 14). On the one hand, trust issues among different security authorities sustained this bureaucratic resistance to EDU, and by extension Europol for which negotiations were on-going. Turf wars and rivalries across countries and among national agencies further complicated the centralisation of European information exchange (Interviewee 14). On the other hand, criminal police offices in many larger EU countries already possessed extensive liaison networks and were not interested in pooling communication and analysis in a shared capacity at European level (Interviewees 7, 14 & 24). Consequently, the key task of the early EDU was to build a reputation and a clientele (Interviewees 7 & 21). Even before the Europol Convention was signed in 1995, its predecessor already had to prove the practical value of centralised EU police cooperation and stand out against established international structures such as Interpol and the Schengen Information System (SIS) (cf. Knelangen 2001: 217–219). This remained a critical challenge throughout the negotiations on Europol.

The Europol Convention

Similar to the EDU, interdependence alongside functional and political spillovers shaped the decision to establish Europol, and would continue to nurture path-dependency within European police cooperation. However, colliding state preferences protracted the process towards the final adoption of the Europol Convention. Originally, Germany had envisioned the completion of negotiations by December 1993 and had hoped for a timely launch of Europol. The German Government had aimed at creating Europol as a Community organisation, including independent operational powers within Member States (Interviewees 7 & 21; Knelangen 2001: 201). Instead, the Europol Convention was only adopted in 1995 and would come into force as late as 1998. It established Europol as intergovernmental organisation with a rather limited, relatively weak mandate. Differences in national security cultures, particularly bureaucratic reluctance, played an important part to this end and shaped state preferences in favour of an intergovernmental Europol that remained formally outside Community structures.

Official negotiations on Europol began in June 1992. The Europol project primarily constituted a European political "response to transnational crime" (Europol 2016a: 25). It illustrated the evolving (paradigm-)shift in the strategic priorities of many Member States and marked the culmination of a development towards new, European modes of governance in the area of internal security and policing. The consensus at the European Council to create a common institution reflected an emerging political commitment rather than mere operational police cooperation (Interviewees 7, 21 & 24). Whereas the Trevi Group had remained largely limited to counterterrorism, EDU and Europol focused on different and broader areas of organised crime as well. The mandates of EDU and Europol presented a political recognition of growing interdependencies. Additionally, Europol was the direct product of spill-overs and unintended consequences from European integration. Consequently, in June 1992, EU Member States agreed to draft a convention establishing Europol, thereby laying the foundation not only for a central coordinating body but also for deeper vertical integration.

The choice for a legal agreement in the form of an international convention broke with the rather ad-hoc, informal tradition of the Trevi Group that had previously characterised European police cooperation. This decision was not random at all but corresponded to formalisation trends at national, the EU and global level. At national level, security governance and law enforcement authorities increasingly embraced technical and operational rationalisation, which required a certain central professionalisation of information exchange (Busch 1995: 335 ff.). This applied especially to the management of common data bases, which included the SIS on which the Europol Information System (EIS) would be modelled years later (ibid.). At the EU level, a similar paradigm-change towards centralisation was evolving and can partially account for the formalisation preference with regard to Europol. The Maastricht Treaty established JHA as a pillar within the EU framework and framed Europol in the context of institutional consolidation and integration. Finally, a trend at global level to base cooperation on international treaties reinforced Member States' preferences in favour of a convention (Interviewee 21). There was a widespread belief that "harmoni[...s]ation through international treaty obligations and through harmoni[...s]ation of legal procedures[...was] a basic requirement for systematic police cooperation" (Anderson 1993a: 20). Therefore, the preference to professionalise European police cooperation through an intergovernmental convention was influenced not only by growing interdependence and functional spill-overs but also by political spill-overs and a comprehensive trend towards formalisation of international relations and policing methods. Europol thus reflects the "political rationale marking the shift from the ad hoc mechanisms developed from 1976 to the new Council of Justice and Home Affairs Ministers" (Bunyan 1997: 16).

The establishment of EDU and Europol has been described as an organic multidimensional process amidst evolving Community governance and cooperation

(Interviewees 7, 14 & 21). "There was no blueprint. Europol has grown historically. The build-up of the EDU often was like walking a tightrope" (Interviewee 7). The same verdict applies to the process that led to the Europol Convention. When the EDU began operating in January 1994, Member States still could not agree on important details of Europol, such as its functional scope and degree of centralisation. Spain aimed at an inclusion of terrorism in Europol's mandate, whereas the UK remained strongly opposed to this suggestion and preferred informal TREVI channels to deal with this matter (Busch 1995: 341; Europol 2016a: 81). Germany, by contrast, envisioned Europol to be involved in all areas of internal security, not only those related to terrorism or drug trafficking. It favoured a holistic inclusion of Europol at all levels. Against it, countries like Spain and Greece supported a narrow operational focus on specific cases and delinquencies rather than entire policy fields. On the extent of Europol's central powers, Germany had a well-known preference for deep vertical integration: Europol as quasi-autonomous EU institution. Ideally, the organisation would comprise its own, supranational personnel, independent competencies (also to act within Member States) and a strong legal basis (Knelangen 2001: 226 f.). Albeit not nearly as far-reaching, the Netherlands likewise favoured a fully integrated European police office (ibid.: 206). By contrast, France and especially the UK advocated a 'customers-oriented' approach. Backed by Italy and Spain, they preferred Europol as rather weak institution, mere agent and support tool of the Member States that should consist of national liaison officers as in the EDU. They envisioned no or very limited involvement of other EU institutions (e.g. the European Court of Justice (ECJ)) (Busch 1995: 341 f.).

THE ASYMMETRICAL EFFECTS OF DOMESTIC SECURITY AND POLICE CULTURES

The asymmetrical impact of driving factors can partially explain why national preferences on Europol diverged. Pressure from interdependence and politicisation was more present or stronger in some countries than in others. However, the most striking factor was national security and police culture. Political, professional and organisational differences mattered tremendously in defining the respective positions on Europol (Anderson 1993a: 31–35). They affected the performance of the EDU as well as the design and implementation of the Europol Convention. Preference formation and the ensuing bargaining process occurred mainly on the basis of domestic systems and whether these tended more towards intergovernmental or integrated modes of governance (Interviewee 14). Federal states like Germany and states with a tradition of interdepartmental coordination like the Netherlands were more open to the idea of shared powers and cooperation within a supranational framework, including a strong Europol at the heart of EU police cooperation (Bundesrat 1994: 19; Prime Minister's Office 1976). Against it, countries with a decentralised or compartmentalised police system and strong political sovereignty concerns mostly supported an intergovernmental legal basis for Europol. Among these were France, the UK and Belgium, which preferred a degree of vertical integration that left Member States in the driver's seat and little to no leeway for the development of autonomous powers and supranational authority (Knelangen 2001: 224 f.). In the negotiations on the Convention and the institutional design of Europol, these positions collided. Most important to the bargaining process were Germany, the UK and France, followed and reinforced by Spain, Italy and the Benelux countries.

The most important advocate for a strong role of Europol in EU police cooperation was Germany. It had initiated the Europol discussion and was the most active Member State during the negotiations on the Convention (Interviewee 21). German negotiators would travel back and forth to The Hague each week to ensure a direct say of German officials and counterbalance the input of more critical Member States (ibid.).

The German pro-integration preference on Europol seems to have been passed down from the top rather than *vice versa*. Similar to the initiative for Europol in 1991, the proposal for a Community agency with "investigative competences" derived from the highest political levels (Rupprecht 1993: 43 f.). Subnational policy entrepreneurship was only emerging and did not mould the German preference. Police representatives were only formally involved after the decision to create Europol had been taken at the highest political level, and representation was limited to few senior officials in the negotiation of the Convention. Although a certain 'European socialisation' arguably occurred among these officials, more operational police levels remained distant from political decision-making. They regarded Europol more sceptically, even opposed it (Interviewees 7 & 21). At the level of the *Länder*, the government's demand for a Europol with autonomous 'executive competences' was likewise met with considerable resistance, as sub-federal ministries feared a loss of powers on internal security policy (de Witte 1993: 44; Rupprecht 1993: 44). The IMK actively demanded the German Government to ensure the inclusion of the State Criminal Police Offices (LKAs) next to the BKA (Bundesrat 1994: 19; IMK 1995: 6). Additionally, the federal lands insisted on direct representation in the Europol negotiations, for example in the Trevi Group's AHWGE (Knelangen, 2001: 207 f.).

Notwithstanding the bureaucratic resistance of state governments and the police to stronger centralisation, they generally supported the idea of enhanced European police cooperation and a broad functional scope. Related discussions among police and state officials revolved around Germany as key transit country within Central Europe and the growing lack of national control in the fight against cross-border crime (Interviewee 7; Rupprecht 1991). Contrary to political arguments from the German Government of the need to advance EU integration, subnational representatives primarily emphasised functional spill-overs and rising interdependence. The Europol Convention reflects this two-sided input of political and police priorities and demonstrates the extent of the German influence on the final document. It reads somewhat like a laundry or shopping list catering to the needs and preferences of both politicians and law enforcement and reflects pressure from interdependence and spill-over effects alike (Interviewees 7, 29, 30 & 31). Article 2(2) lists as Europol's initial tasks high-profile crimes such as "unlawful drug trafficking, trafficking in nuclear and radioactive substances, illegal immigrant smuggling, trade in human beings" but also relatively low-profile offences like "motor vehicle crime." The annex presents an additional, rather long "[l]ist of other serious forms of international crime which Europol could deal with," thus illustrating both the wide response to and demand for European cooperation in different issue areas but also the political difficulty of including them all in Europol's functional scope.

This political difficulty derived largely from the asymmetrical effects of driving factors on state integration preferences. From the start, many governments were more open to flexible integration models than to extensive formalisation. In the Netherlands, high interdependence, strong public pressure and a cooperation-oriented security and police culture formed an ideal basis for a national preference in favour of EU police cooperation. Its decentralised police system with a strict separation between state and local levels was very well integrated procedurally through a culture of multi-level WGs and close cooperation with its immediate neighbours (Busch 1995: 181 ff.; Interviewee 30). Its Euro- and cooperation-friendly culture distinguished it crucially from France and others. Yet, when Germany proposed the establishment of Europol with investigative powers, Dutch subnational policy entrepreneurs resisted the superimposition of a central power at the EU level and shaped the Dutch preference accordingly. Albeit generally supportive of the Europol proposal, the Dutch Government was sceptical about the reconciliation of national systems and their considerable differences. The Netherlands did not feel comfortable with such a trailblazing quantum leap in Community cooperation because of the lack of precedent and the absence of organisational, legal and institutional preconditions (Peek & Hoefman 1993: 109 f.). Although the Netherlands preferred a low degree of vertical integration, they were highly interested in advancing European police cooperation. Especially the practical and financial benefits of a common capacity for information exchange mattered as influencers of the government position, maybe more so than in many bigger Member States. The Netherlands consequently supported the German Europol proposal, but lobbied for a step-by-step approach in the negotiations on the Europol Convention. The Dutch Council Presidency suggested to link up the EDIU and Europol proposals so as to create EDU as a "relay station" (ibid.: 110).

In the UK, national security culture and policing tradition likewise shaped its official negotiating position on the Europol Convention. While the UK was highly interested and involved in practical EU cooperation, it had no history of furthering European integration (Interviewee 23). Its political and legal sovereignty-focussed tradition predestined it to "almost always favour[...] inter-governmental cooperation rather than the pooling of sovereignty" (Anderson 1993a: 23). In advance of the Maastricht summit, Prime Minister Major had commented the Europol initiative:

> It is a classic case for intergovernmental co-operation between the countries of the Community rather than for co-operation within the framework of Community law. And it is an area where Governments, not the Commission, have expertise.
>
> *(Laursen & Vanhoonacker 1992: 427)*

In contrast to the central geographic location of Germany or the Netherlands, the peripheral and island status of the UK presumably made it less susceptible to growing Europe-wide interdependencies (Interviewee 7). Additionally, a deeply engrained decentralised law enforcement tradition with sometimes isolated bureaucratic cultures of different police entities made (sub-)national adaptation to formalised European cooperation a challenge. British law enforcement had always enjoyed a "considerable degree of independence from government control" (Anderson 1993a: 26) and demonstrated significant bureaucratic resistance against vertical integration via Europol (Interviewees 7 & 14). In view of well-established bi- and multilateral cooperation networks and informal contacts to EU and third countries, police officials saw little functional need to structure operational cooperation at European level and outright opposed an external oversight mechanism. Although police input into the British government position was arguably stronger than in Germany, it did not constitute a primary driver of the UK's preference. It may however well have reinforced the political doctrine of national sovereignty and the government's position in favour of minimum powers for Europol and an initially restricted functional scope. "[F]lexible and 'variable geometry' of cooperation[...was] seen by the British government and by British police officers as both desirable and inevitable" (Anderson 1993a: 25). This entailed a limited objective for Europol under the Convention, namely to "improve[...]the effectiveness and cooperation of the competent authorities in the Member States," a goal that would be achieved "progressively" (Art. 2(1) & (2)).

THE EUROPOL CONVENTION AS A COMPROMISE BETWEEN THE PREFERENCES OF GERMANY AND THE UNITED KINGDOM

The Convention presented a compromise between the German-favoured Europol as autonomous EU agency and the British preference for a weak body outside the Community framework. While deep vertical integration was still out of the question for the UK – as was the involvement of the ECJ – interdependencies and operational centralisation trends pushed the UK to favour European intergovernmental cooperation. Subnational interest shapers like the MPS promoted technological and methodological rationalisation of police work, and systemic centralisation tendencies contributed to the acceptance by British police circles of Europol as central coordination and support body. The collective organisational capacity, synergy effects and practical benefits of existing European cooperation formats had garnered subnational interest (Anderson 1993a: 37 f.). Particularly Schengen had facilitated police work through its central information system. The work conducted within the EDIU and later EDU project group was likewise proving the merits of common institutional structures for European police cooperation and especially data-sharing. Unsurprisingly, Article 3(1) of the Europol Convention stipulates as key task the facilitation of information exchange within the EU, including through the creation of a computerised data collection system. While the British Eurosceptical preference during the Europol negotiations was primarily shaped by its political system and doctrine of national sovereignty, technological trends in British policing and cultural changes in subnational policy entrepreneurship helped shift the government position towards favouring some degree of centralisation at European level. British law enforcement officials emphasised the functional need arising from interdependence on the one hand, and the practical benefits of pooled capacity on the other. Of course, a certain path-dependency deriving from TREVI and the British-initiated EDIU project additionally shaped the UK's preference in favour of intensifying European police cooperation.

The case of France, by contrast, illustrates how political denial, the national police and security culture, and a lack of path-dependency impeded a strong preference or active involvement in the Europol negotiations. While the interconnectedness of organised crime was undeniably growing in France as well, particularly with regard to drug trafficking and money laundering, policymakers for a long time refused to recognise, even outright denied the problem (Interviewee 30). Although the infamous 'French Connection' was eventually addressed by the government, French policymakers continued to reject the notion that organised crime was a central issue up to the 1990s (Anderson 1993b: 78). The matter of transnational criminal networks operating in France was politically downplayed as a primarily Italian problem (Interviewee 30).

At Community level, France adopted a rather reluctant, at times obstructive, stance (Busch 1995: 342). Its rather centralised political system and inward-looking governance culture created a rather Euroscpetical starting position (Interviewees 7 & 21; cf. Aden 1998). In 1991, it legally questioned "the constitutionality of the Schengen Agreement on the grounds it infringed national sovereignty" (Anderson 1993a: 23). Although the French Constitutional Court rejected the case, France saw similar problems with regard to Europol (Neumann 2012: 292). The majority of reservations on the draft Convention originated from France, with an emphasis on limiting the powers of Europol, since "a restriction on the sovereignty of Member States is unacceptable" (Council 1994: 67).

In contrast to Germany and the UK, where police actors were able to – at least partially – shape their governments' preferences, the French security and police tradition did not allow subnational policy entrepreneurship to the same extent. Not only was French law enforcement deeply embedded in a complex national legal and organisational culture that complicated international cooperation but it was also strongly influenced by domestic politics (Aden 1998). Notwithstanding decentralisation efforts since the 1970s, the police system remained tightly integrated with the government and bodies like the Gendarmerie continued to operate "under direct ministerial control" (Anderson 1993b: 55). Police officials often even adopted the government's political opinion and helped produce a "regular stream of politico-police scandals" (ibid.: 69). Consequently, public and political opinion regarding the police was highly ambiguous and divided.

The previous chapter already explored how the perception of the French police as embodiment of the state, and its repressive strategies towards public order formed a domestic environment that was preoccupied with internal discussion. This domestic 'seclusion' of law enforcement and the public-political influence on policing in France continued into the 1990s. Subnational policy entrepreneurship on Europol was accordingly weak if not completely absent. Contrary to Germany and the UK, French police structures were still largely compartmentalised. Internal coordination problems had not been systematically addressed. Despite the close integration of police and government, law enforcement was organised in a very hierarchical manner with a strict separation between different bodies and departments (ibid.: 64). Turf wars and bureaucratic rivalries within and among police authorities strongly conflicted with harmonisation and centralisation attempts, both at domestic and European level (Crozier 1964). This likewise hindered innovation. While Germany was at the forefront of systematic computerisation and technological rationalisation, French police officials still largely relied on analogous methods and personal contacts for information exchange (Anderson 1989: 88; Bigo 1996: 90).

Finally, a lack of path-dependency explains the French resistance to Europol. France had historically prioritised Interpol and been little enthusiastic about Community police cooperation (Interviewee 23). Whereas Germany and the UK were increasingly focusing on TREVI for police cooperation, the French political denial of the rise of transnational organised crime and its closed-off police culture contributed to a highly sceptical government position on the Trevi Group (BMI 1982). Considering its lack of investment in EU police cooperation, it is hardly surprising that France remained largely passive in the negotiations on the Europol Convention. It only showed an interest once Germany 'baited' France with Strasbourg as possible location for the Europol headquarters; the EDU project team was already situated there (Interviewee 21). Nonetheless, France never developed a preference in favour of EU cooperation or Europol. Despite pressure from growing interdependence, its political and police culture shaped a preference rejecting the integration ambitions of Germany and others.

STATE PREFERENCES ON EUROPOL: VENUE-SHOPPING OR INTEGRATION?

While interdependencies and national security cultures shaped state preferences across the EU, many governments neither developed strong pro- nor anti-integration preferences in the negotiations on the Convention. Although most countries exhibited a clear national position with regard to vertical integration – whether Europol was to be relatively weak or strong – the majority was undecided and passive with respect to organisational details and the functional scope. Germany, the UK and France largely dominated the bargaining process, which remained unstructured with ad-hoc and sometimes random input from different Member States (Interviewees 7 & 30). This explains the 'laundry list' character of the Europol Convention and is telling of the asymmetrical influence of driving factors on state preferences. Some governments primarily regarded Europol as an opportunity to manage national problems. This venue-shopping can be seen in the Spanish preference to include terrorism in Europol's functional scope, a priority that was mainly informed by the persisting domestic challenge posed by ETA rather than transnational criminal or terrorist pressures (Interviewee 30; Europol 2016a: 81). In the end, terrorism was included in the Convention among possible future tasks (Art. 2(1) & (2)).

The negotiation process on the Europol Convention illustrates how common driving factors across all Member States – rising interdependence and functional spill-over effects from market integration – shaped similar experiences. At the same time, the diverging security and policing traditions mattered tremendously in differentiating each national experience and preference. On the one hand, a need for the formalisation of cooperation, or at least for technical and organisational rationalisation, had emerged throughout the Community. As functional demands on national police and security authorities increased in line with growing interconnectedness, European cooperation became more and more attractive regardless of the official government position on EU integration. Interdependencies and spill-over effects thus ultimately convinced many Member States to favour Europol. Irrespective of preferences on vertical integration – which differed in accordance with the national systems – there was widespread recognition of the practical benefits of a common institution with shared capacity, pooled resources and operational synergies. The European Council similarly concluded: "[...c]ommon police institutions of the EC or of the EC Countries would[...]realize more efficiency and lower costs, even without executive power" (Bunyan 1997: 22–23).

In 1995, interdependence, functional spill-overs and an emerging path-dependency drove Member States to adopt the Europol Convention and subsequently establish Europol. Transnational criminal activities and the collapse of the Soviet Union gave rise to a new security paradigm among policymakers and practitioners: "[...w]ith regard to security strategy and the geography of crime,[...]the EU[...] should be seen as a single territory[...]. [...I]n terms of crime the EU states constitute a largely homogenous geographical area" (Rupprecht & Hellenthal 1994: 30). Functional spill-overs from the Schengen Convention and market integration further fuelled this trend. The abolition of internal borders produced a certain deterritorialisation of policing and internal security governance, and raised the scale of tasks and demands on national law enforcement. Member States, especially smaller ones, were not only increasingly interdependent with regard to transnational crime but also with respect to policing capacity (Interviewee 7).

Political spill-overs and path-dependency helped achieve a Europe-wide consensus about the need to rationalise police cooperation. Early institutionalisation initiatives at European level such as the Italian Scalfaro-paper and the British NDIU/EDIU proposal contributed to shifting state preferences towards Community cooperation and its ensuing formalisation. Especially the experience with the Trevi Group demonstrated the benefits of professionalisation and central coordination, against the shortcomings of informality and organisational isolation (BMI 1986). By the 1990s, TREVI had emerged as key cooperation format and had become linked to managing the security implications of the SEA. It was only logical to also task the Group with the creation of Europol.

By contrast, sub- and supranational policy entrepreneurship mattered little as drivers of state preferences in the Europol Convention negotiations. While subnational levels had varying input in the political decision-making process across Member States, they enhanced rather than shaped national positions. Against it, supranational actors were barely involved in the design and negotiation of the Convention (Interviewee 14). The European Parliament was not even consulted on the draft Convention (Bunyan 1997: 21). Although the Maastricht Treaty had given the European Commission a role in JHA, the latter had no formal right of initiation in the area of police cooperation (Interviewees 14 & 21; cf. Busch 1995: 340 f.). Consequently, the Europol Convention remained a project of the Member States. It had commenced at the highest political levels and was now gradually being expanded top-down.

Irrespective of the intergovernmental legal framework and situation outside the EU, the Convention marked an important step towards the formalisation and institutionalisation of European police cooperation. Its clear association with the EU – not only in geographic membership but also in relation to EU bodies – laid the foundation for further integration. This can already be seen in the process preceding the implementation and the beginning of activities at Europol. While the Commission's involvement remained limited, it gained the proverbial 'foot in the door' as a formal observer in the Europol Management Board (Art. 28(4); cf. Europol 2016a: 71).

Although a certain path-dependency was underway in EU police cooperation throughout the 1990s and shaped preferences on horizontal integration, political spill-over effects and binding commitments were not yet strong enough to positively impact Member States on vertical integration. Notwithstanding the gradual paradigm-shift towards a stronger focus on the EU in the area of JHA, "the Amsterdam negotiation was characterized by a 'maintaining national control trend'" "[...r]ather than [...]institutional spillover" (Devuyst 1998: 615). It is telling of the 'in-between' state at the time when Member States had recognised the benefits of EU police cooperation and were increasingly preferring the Union's institutional framework, but were simultaneously still reluctant towards deeper integration and sovereignty transfers.

GRAPPLING WITH BUREAUCRATIC RESISTANCE: THE EMERGENCE OF EUROPOL SALESMANSHIP

Subnational anti-integration advocacy exacerbated intergovernmental preferences even before Europol officially commenced activities in 1999. The early Europol faced considerable bureaucratic resistance from the police and security community. Whereas the original proposal had been devised by the highest political levels and decided at the European Council, the negotiation phase of the Convention and subsequent preparations for Europol's launch saw a gradual top-down inclusion of subnational officials from ministries and law enforcement. This growing role for domestic actors heightened the impact of bureaucratic resistance on state preferences and EU police cooperation as a whole. The top-down political nature of the Europol initiative collided with a police desire for operational autonomy (Interviewees 22 & 23). Europol's Management Board – comprising ministerial officials from the Member States – was tasked with drafting the implementing acts after the Convention entered into force in October 1998. Yet, "[...i]nitially, the chiefs of police in the Member States were highly sceptical about the need for the creation of a Management Board" (Storbeck 2016: 23). Law enforcement officials opposed further institutionalisation and resisted competency transfers to Europol. Not only did diverging domestic security cultures and policing systems produce "very different, heterogeneous interests" among the law enforcement community, trust among different authorities was a serious problem as well, and many larger criminal offices preferred their own cooperation networks (Interviewees 7, 14 & 29). Europol's main clients needed yet to be convinced to cooperate with and via Europol. Many police officials had barely even heard of the EDU or Europol, let alone knew either one existed (Interviewee 28). The Dutch head of police for instance first enquired about Europol in 1998 (Interviewee 30). At the time, many police officers openly deemed Europol "completely superfluous" (Interviewee 7).

The process preceding the commencement of Europol's activities as well as its early days in operation demonstrate that supranational policy entrepreneurship and politicisation mattered much more for the acceptance of the organisation than interdependence or spill-over effects. The first Europol representatives deliberately focussed on building a reputation and 'hawking' the organisation's services among national police officials (Interviewees 7, 21 & 30). The practical and analytical benefits of a central institution would help to build trust and interest. Similar to many smaller Member States, the Nordic countries for instance lacked extensive information and liaison networks of their own and were therefore intrigued by the possibilities of Europol (Interviewee 7). The functional merits of Europol thus presented a window of opportunity for supranational advocacy. Europol officials actively promoted the organisation as a means to solve domestic shortcomings or problems, similar to the 'laundry list' approach of the Europol Convention. Many law enforcement authorities used Europol for venue-shopping in single issue areas and gradually developed a pro-EU entrepreneurship.

The establishment of a Europol analysis project on outlaw motorcycle gangs originated from a Nordic initiative in response to the Great Nordic Biker War and particularly the *Hells Angels* (ibid.).

Next to the organisation's practical merit, Europol top officials and Member States' representatives in the Management Board harnessed the power of politicising events to shift state preferences. They for instance leveraged a migrant smuggling incident that was widely publicised for months to expand Europol's role in this area (Interviewee 7; cf. BBC 2000). The inclusion of trafficking in nuclear and radioactive substances among Europol's initial tasks reacted to widespread concern about the collapse of the Soviet Union rather than to factual interdependencies (Interviewee 7). Salience therefore facilitated supranational policy entrepreneurship and rendered governments willing to extend the functional scope of EU police cooperation (cf. Storbeck 2016: 22).

Europol's early days presented a tightrope walk between the concerns and interests of policymakers on the one hand, and those of practitioners, police officials and the public on the other. Although the creation of Europol constituted an unprecedented institutionalisation of police cooperation – and thereby an important step towards EU integration in the area of JHA – state preferences at the time were still shaped by political sovereignty concerns and bureaucratic resistance. Nevertheless, Europol's practical output and emerging entrepreneurship together with growing institutional binding and spill-overs were paving the way for the further development of the organisation. Whether Member States had intended for it to happen or not, Europol was quickly developing a dynamic of its own that would increasingly merge with the overall process of EU integration.

Institutional Choice in a Nutshell: State Preferences on the Three Dimensions of Differentiated Integration

Compared to the Trevi Group, the EDU and early Europol already presented significant steps towards EU integration in the field of police cooperation. While TREVI had gradually evolved into a more autonomous structure with growing practical authority and a slowly expanding functional scope by the late 1980s, it remained informal for the most part due to the lack of an explicit legal basis. Against it, Europol constituted an unprecedented level of integration because it marked a sudden change in the pace and quality of the institutionalisation of EU police cooperation. For the first time, Member States opted for an international binding agreement, which gave EU police cooperation a formal identity and legally committed them. Member States also agreed to expand Europol's tasks and competencies. Although its initial mandate remained relatively limited, its network did not. From the beginning, EDU and Europol were shaped by horizontal external differentiation, as cooperation with third countries formed a vital part of their day-to-day business.

The 1990s thus constituted a paradigm shift in European police cooperation. Interdependence, spill-overs and institutional path-dependency acted as primary drivers of state preferences to formalise existing, ad-hoc structures and associating them with the EU (see Table 3.1). They likewise shaped centralisation initiatives as well as the ultimate decision of Member States to institutionalise police cooperation through Europol. While interdependencies and functional spill-over effects undeniably shaped preferences in favour of horizontal integration and a large functional scope, national security cultures and police systems acted as intervening factors influencing government positions on the degree of vertical integration. Overall, domestic centralisation tendencies at operational levels favourably shaped attitudes in many Member States towards coordination and cooperation at European level, including the early thought of a Europol. Following its inception however, bureaucratic resistance from domestic officials often negatively affected vertical integration preferences and inhibited cooperation at Europol. Nevertheless, the influence of subnational policy entrepreneurs remained limited and ultimately succumbed to functional pressure from internal and external interdependence. Both pushed governments and subnational actors alike to prioritise Europol for addressing national problems, even if only as venue-shopping. Although European actors did not play a role at all in advance of the birth of Europol, the first signs of supranational policy entrepreneurship began to emerge in the late 1990s. For the first time in EU police cooperation, supranational actors like the European Commission leveraged politicisation and political spill-overs in an endeavour to promote integration at Europol. While national preferences were relatively easily reconcilable and largely converged on the horizontal and functional dimension, they differed considerably with regard to vertical integration, that is, the competencies and powers Europol should have.

The early phase of EDU and Europol constituted a tightrope walk in many ways. Due to a lack of trust among security authorities and bureaucratic resistance, governments preferred to strictly specify for EDU's legal framework that "transmission of personal information to non-Member States or to international organisations by the liaison officers will not take place."[2] Notwithstanding these *de jure* limitations on EDU's geographic extension, interdependencies beyond the EU drove a certain *de facto* external differentiation. Where national law enforcement authorities so required, EDU worked together with third countries on a case-by-case basis, including cooperation with Columbia on global drug trafficking or with Bulgaria on European vehicle theft (Interviewee 7). Unsurprisingly, the formal prohibition of cooperating with non-EU states was retracted by the Europol Convention, which recognised global interdependencies and the operational need for a wider geographic extension. When the Convention was adopted in 1995 and effectively absorbed EDU, cooperative relations of Europol with third states or bodies were explicitly allowed and encouraged (Art. 42). Internal and external differentiation would continue to matter in Europol's operational support activities and its day-to-day business throughout the 2000s. As an

TABLE 3.1 Driving Factors across Italy, the UK and Germany

	Issue-specific interdependence	*Politicisation & Crises*	*Supranational policy entrepreneurship*	*Subnational policy entrepreneurship*
Italy	*H1 Confirmed* **High and rising** interdependence in internat. terrorism and organised crime: *preference for EU police cooperation and integration.*	*H2.1 Confirmed* **High** domestic politicisation related to internat. (BR) terrorism: *preference for EU police cooperation and integration.*	*No significant impact*	*No significant impact* (weak subnational advocacy in favour of centralisation)
The UK	*H1 Confirmed* **High and rising** interdependence in internat. drug trafficking: *preference for EU police cooperation and integration.*	*H2.1 Confirmed* **High** domestic politicisation related to drug abuse and internat. terrorism: *preference for EU police cooperation and integration.*	*H3 Confirmed* **Growing political spill-overs** (from TREVI) and **functional spill-overs** (from European passport union, SEA and Schengen): *preference for EU police cooperation and integration.*	*H4 Rejected* **Strong** subnational advocacy (MPS) of restructuring European cooperation: *preference for European police cooperation and (part-)centralisation.*
Germany	*H1 Confirmed* **High and rising** interdependence in internat. drug trafficking: *preference for EU police cooperation and integration.*	*No significant impact*	*H3 Confirmed* **Growing political spill-overs** (from TREVI) and **functional spill-overs** (from European passport union, SEA and Schengen): *preference for EU police cooperation and integration.*	*No significant impact* (weak subnational advocacy in favour of centralisation)

H1: The higher the interdependence in security issues, the more likely Member States are to favour EU police cooperation and integration.

H2.1/2.2: The higher the politicisation in a given issue area, the more/*less likely* Member States are to favour EU police cooperation and integration/*and the more likely they are to prefer differentiation and decentralised, informal modes of cooperation.*

H2.3: The higher the politicisation in a given issue area, the less likely Member States are to favour any police cooperation at the EU level.

H3: The higher the supranational policy entrepreneurship in a given issue area, the more likely Member States are to favour EU police cooperation and integration.

H4: The higher the subnational policy entrepreneurship in a given issue area, the less likely Member States are to favour EU police cooperation and integration, and the more likely they are to prefer differentiation and decentralised, informal modes of cooperation.

organisation increasingly associated with the EU framework – and thereby more and more in between intergovernmental and supranational modes of governance – Europol would be critically shaped by avant-garde governments and smaller groups of like-minded Member States, as the following chapter demonstrates.

Notes

1 Comprising Austria, France, Germany, Italy and Switzerland.
2 Ministerial Agreement on the establishment of the Europol Drugs Unit, 2 June 1993.

4

EUROPEAN POLICE COOPERATION IN THE EARLY 2000s

Towards an EU Law Enforcement Agency

Europol as an intergovernmental organisation had barely taken up activities when the September 11 attacks claimed the lives of close to 3,000 people. September 11 is argued to have marked the transition to 'fourth wave' terrorism and subsequent transformation of counterterrorism approaches (Rapoport 2013). In the EU, "[t]he terrorist attacks in the United States in 2001, as well as the bombings in Madrid and London in 2004 and 2005, triggered another dynamic in the development of Europe's information management policies" (European Commission 2010b: 2). Governments increasingly preferred cooperation within European formats and frequently pushed for centralising and streamlining approaches in single issue areas of EU police cooperation (ibid.). In the early 2000s, a number of new priorities and cooperation initiatives emerged among EU Member States, including at Europol. Its functional scope was swiftly expanded to terrorism, euro counterfeiting and child pornography, and its supranational entrepreneurship was growing, particularly the role of Europol officials in national and EU policymaking. The ultimate demonstration, perhaps culmination, of this renewed momentum in EU police cooperation was the formal transformation of Europol into the EU's official law enforcement agency in 2009. Although the Europol Council Decision *de jure* left power in the hands of the Member States, it instigated a *de facto* shift of responsibility to Europol and the EU in various areas. The Council Decision constituted a qualitative change in the institutional character of Europol and EU police cooperation, and mirrored a broader shift of preferences towards an overall integration trend within JHA.

In this context, three observations stand out. First, shocks and crises seemed to have mattered greatly. In the early 2000s, spiralling saliency and public pressure in the aftermath of crises frequently led to positive integration decisions. More often than not, high politicisation made Member States more – not less – likely to favour cooperation at the EU level. Second, continuous pressure from

DOI: 10.4324/9781003262176-5

growing interdependence alongside functional and operational needs shaped state preferences pro integration. The developments of the early 2000s confirm the findings from the previous chapter. High interdependence in security issues and institutional linkages positively affected integration preferences. At the same time, the more asymmetrical these interdependencies were, the more likely Member States prioritised various cooperation formats, thus giving rise to internal and external differentiation as well as instances of differentiated integration. Third, supranational policy entrepreneurs increasingly mattered as influencers of integration preferences. While EU actors were gradually beginning to have an impact, political reputation and legacy at the EU level seem to have been of similar importance for state interests. Holding the Council Presidency favourably affected the legislative activities and integration preference of the responsible Member State. It partially explains the mushrooming of police cooperation initiatives, including at Europol. The 2000s demonstrate that governments shouldering the responsibilities of the Presidency were more likely to use their power for agenda-setting and initiating EU police cooperation.

United in Diversity? EUCARIS, Prüm and Other Instances of Flexible Integration

A number of initiatives outside Europol revitalised EU police cooperation in the early 2000s. The European Car and Driving License Information System (EUCARIS) and the Prüm network emerged outside the EU framework, then increasingly overlapped and were (partially) integrated. Both constitute cases of differentiated integration. Integration promoters like Germany and EU entrepreneurs such as the Commission acted strategically by allowing for differentiated and flexible models to advance integration in the long run. Strong subnational policy entrepreneurship and the absence or weakness of supranational entrepreneurs at early cooperation stages shaped state preferences in favour of informal avant-garde approaches and decentralisation. At later cooperation stages, functional pressure to formalise cooperation alongside a growing influence of supranational actors shifted Member States' positions towards EU integration. Ultimately, differentiated integration presented a strategy in the face of asymmetrical preferences rather than a preference itself or an end.

The Dutch Subnational Initiative for a European Car and Driving License Information System

EUCARIS is a decentralised information system that has been formally recognised by the EU and facilitates the exchange of vehicle and driving licence information and other transport-related data among European countries in the fight against vehicle-related crime. Having started in the mid-1990s as informal working arrangement between three Member States – then five and later even more – today it is an official, widely recognised information system with a continuously expanding base of users. It *de jure* overlaps with the EU landscape of information exchange and forms a *de facto* part of it. Its use is part-based on EU legislation, with a role for the Commission in the scrutiny of data protection, and extends to all Member States (although not all are formal signatories to all Protocols) plus a number of non-EU countries.

EUCARIS presents an example of differentiated integration in the evolution of European police cooperation. In the face of rising issue-specific interdependence, subnational policy entrepreneurship and the absence of supranational policy entrepreneurship best explain why Member States initially favoured differentiation over integration and chose an intergovernmental treaty between just a few governments instead of EU policy venues. As the relevance of supranational policy entrepreneurs in this issue area grew, EUCARIS became increasingly associated with the EU framework and was partially integrated.

MOVING CARS ALL OVER EUROPE: THE GROWING TRANSNATIONAL DIMENSION OF VEHICLE CRIME

Since the late 1980s, vehicle theft had become an increasing problem across Europe. Especially Central European countries were affected by Germany as key transit country and criminal hub for the import and export of stolen vehicles (Interviewees 24, 31, 45 & 46). Since the Schengen Agreement and the removal of border controls, vehicle crime and driving licence tourism were becoming a growing phenomenon across Member States (EUCARIS 2017b). As one practitioner put it: "a car stolen in Estonia can be used for a terror attack in Spain" (Interviewee 29). Vehicles from one country could be legally registered in another where the authorities had no record of foreign car theft. It was becoming a criminal trend to 'launder' stolen cars by exploiting differences in national systems and information gaps (Interviewee 46). Nevertheless, vehicle theft remained a secondary political issue. It primarily became manifest as relevant problem at the police level and in the daily practice of law enforcement. "Cars were being moved all over Europe," (Interviewee 30) "it became more and more important to check vehicles during import and export – the signal 'stolen' was/is very important information" (Interviewee 45).

In 1994, the Netherlands approached other Member States with a proposal to launch multilateral cooperation and share vehicle and driving licence information across borders (Interviewees 45 & 46). The initiative came from the subnational level: the Dutch Vehicles and Driving Licences Registration Authority (RDW). RDW Deputy Director Hans van der Bruggen contacted his counterparts in Belgium and Luxemburg about the preparation of a pilot project (Interviewees 45 & 46). The idea for professionalising cooperation was pitched at a scoping conference, where other European vehicle registration authorities confirmed they were experiencing similar problems. It was agreed that the Benelux countries should realise the pilot (Interviewee 46). The first step was a proof of concept to better exchange data on vehicles and driving licences among the national registration authorities of these three countries. This resulted in the establishment of enhanced albeit still informal cooperation and the development of a decentralised technical system to facilitate information-sharing (EUCARIS 2017b; Interviewee 45).

Three main factors explain the preference for a multilateral, informal format outside the EU framework among only a few Member States: asymmetric interdependence, subnational entrepreneurship and lack of institutional precedent at the EU level. First, an asymmetry in internal and external interdependencies among Member States influenced the Dutch preference for horizontal internal differentiation instead of EU-wide action (Interviewees 14 & 21). Cooperation among the security authorities of likeminded countries seemed more promising due to a perceived closer cultural proximity, shared policing experiences and traditions. Personal contacts and institutional ties were better established with some countries than with others, as was the case among the Benelux countries (Interviewees 14, 45 & 46). Additionally, external interdependence was higher with the Netherlands' immediate neighbours (Interviewee 24). Although other vehicle registration authorities were likewise experiencing problems with stolen cars and driving license fraud, not every country faced equal levels or regarded this as priority topic (Interviewee 46).

Second, subnational policy entrepreneurship explains short-term differentiation in the form of an avant-garde group to advance integration in the long run. Subnational officials at the RDW had an interest in circumventing political circles to get practical cooperation off the ground and yield results as fast as possible. Although the Dutch Ministry of Transport had been informed, the RDW preferred to directly contact other registration authorities and activate transnational networks to launch the conference and subsequent proof of concept. As one official phrased it: "You do not want to do things together with the ministry. It will take longer and there will be a lengthy legal process before anything can be done" (Interviewee 46). Differences in cultural ties and police capacity explain why subnational actors did not lobby for the creation of EUCARIS across all Member States. Experiences and institutional links varied among vehicle registration and law enforcement authorities. Some countries – including larger Member States – regarded their national resources and policing approaches as sufficient for dealing with cross-border vehicle theft (ibid.). It was thus seen as "easier to start with a few countries" (Interviewee 45). Hence, the Dutch preference to go ahead in the informal setting of an avant-garde group of transnational practitioners was informed by the entrepreneurship and functional need of subnational officials and their day-to-day experiences.

Third, not all Member States could be convinced to join the initiative from the start because EU legislative procedures did not yet account for this sort of cooperation. "It was brand-new; nothing like this had been done before" (Interviewee 46). No concepts were in place for European data exchange and no comparable efforts had previously been taken at the EU level; the Europol Convention had not even been signed yet. "EU legislation was not moving fast enough" (Interviewee 45). There was no precedent in JHA for formalising collective action at supranational level. Additionally, many of the countries with whom information-sharing was needed – primarily Eastern European and Balkan countries – were not part of the EU at the time (Interviewee 46). Consequently, the RDW deliberately opted for a cooperation format, a traditional intergovernmental setting that did not require EU membership.

THE IMPACT OF POLITICO-LEGAL CULTURES ON FORMALISATION PREFERENCES

Pursuing internal horizontal differentiation and avoiding vertical integration constituted a deliberate strategy of Dutch subnational officials to quickly achieve much-needed cooperation and practical results. The practical merit of an emerging central capacity soon drove other Member States to join the project, such as the UK and Sweden within two years after the launch (Interviewee 46). Yet, political rather than practical considerations – differences in legal traditions and political systems – ultimately shaped state preferences. France strictly opposed entering new multilateral treaties and was waiting for a Commission initiative instead (ibid.). In Germany, a legal tradition of formally embedding rules and norms trumped the interest of the German vehicle registration authority to participate. The latter was unable to assert itself *vis-à-vis* the German Ministry of Transport under whose political control it stood; "the Ministry was a breaking factor" (ibid.). German ministerial officials would not agree to becoming a part of this cooperation initiative unless it was formalised with an explicit legal base governing information exchange and especially data protection. Nevertheless, the increasing functional benefits and evolving magnitude of the cross-border data exchange eventually drove Germany to get involved.

Like Germany, the UK was caught in a preference dichotomy. Growing internal interdependencies created a need for cross-border cooperation, whereas political and sovereignty concerns informed a preference for strict formalisation. Both countries joined but actively pushed for legal formalisation (Interviewee 45). The British and German calls for a treaty appear to have been motivated primarily by their politico-legal cultures. In view of the rapidly expanding exchange of driving license and other personal data within the bounds of this cooperation arrangement, higher political levels in Germany and the UK aimed at safeguarding their sovereignty by ensuring adequate data protection (Interviewees 45 & 46).

The EUCARIS Treaty was signed in Luxembourg on 29 June 2000. Although it was not a legal instrument of the EU but a multilateral treaty between five Member States, it was clearly associated with EU data protection and privacy rules (EUCARIS 2017a). The latter clearly formed the foundation and baseline legislation for information exchange within EUCARIS (Art. 18, EUCARIS Treaty). Although this did not give the EU or the Commission an active role, it placed the protection of individuals and the processing of personal data under their responsibility. Article 24 even made compliance with EU Directive 95/46/EC on personal data a precondition for states wanting to accede to the Treaty.

Not only did this formal linkage to EU data protection law ensure the common standards that Germany and the UK had pushed for, but it also likewise catered to the practical need for professionalising cooperation that was becoming more complex. While the need to manage interconnectedness in vehicle-related crime had driven the original launch of cooperation, its professionalisation and beginning integration arguably responded to functional pressure arising from quickly intensifying interdependence in the day-to-day work of practitioners. It thus was not only governments who wanted a formal agreement and clear rules for sovereignty reasons, but also vehicle registration authorities who favoured some sort of institutionalisation to structure growing internal interdependence, preferably through the EU as single point of reference (Interviewees 45 & 46).

ASSOCIATING EUCARIS WITH EU POLICE COOPERATION

In 2000, vehicle crime represented a more and more visible and rapidly expanding criminal market across all EU Member States (Interviewees 24 & 31). Significant financial losses were becoming noticeable at the level of private corporations, especially insurance companies, and individuals. Beyond mere economic damage, stolen vehicles could potentially be used for terrorist purposes and thus posed a security threat (ibid.). Although EUCARIS had been started by vehicle registration authorities and ministries of transport within the EU's first pillar, the Treaty (Art. 9) targeted the transfer of information to police, customs, prosecution and national security authorities. Article 2(2) stipulated as one of the main purposes of EUCARIS "to assist in preventing, investigating and prosecuting offences against the laws of individual States in the field of driving licences, vehicle registration and other vehicle-related fraud and criminality." Although spill-over effects from other issue areas and cooperation developments certainly played a role, external and internal interdependencies acted as primary drivers of government preferences to expand the use of EUCARIS and increasingly integrate it as formal instrument of EU police cooperation.

While EUCARIS had already been operational as a technical platform since the 1990s, the legal and political process was only officially concluded much later (Interviewee 46). Following the Treaty's entry into force, horizontal external differentiation progressed quickly alongside (partial) integration of the information system into the EU framework. Functional pressure from heightened interdependence played a substantial role to this end. Other states could now officially apply for accession to the Treaty. Latvia and Slovakia acceded in 2010, followed by Romania in 2012 (Interviewee 45). This is not surprising in view of the high interconnectivity in criminal networks between Central European countries who were already members of EUCARIS and Eastern European states (Interviewees 29, 31 & 45). As more and more stolen cars were being moved from Eastern Europe to the EU and *vice versa*, the EUCARIS signatories approached Romania, Latvia, Estonia and Lithuania to exchange information shortly after the Treaty was concluded, even before the latter became EU members (Interviewees 24 & 45).

Other non-EU states likewise joined EUCARIS. Some are indirectly connected to the system today. Incorporating these countries was a logical step from a criminological point of view and a logical consequence of the practical needs arising from day-to-day cooperation. Not only were Switzerland, Norway and Iceland associated, but also the British dependencies of Gibraltar, Isle of Man and Jersey were themselves independently connected to EUCARIS (Interviewee 45). The move of the EUCARIS signatories towards external differentiation was thus driven by functional pressure from interdependence in vehicle-related crime and advocated by subnational practitioners. Spill-overs from other cooperation formats contributed to the widening of EUCARIS' membership, most prominently the Prüm network. Convincing the Prüm signatories to name EUCARIS as official data-sharing platform for all EU Member States can undoubtedly be called a breakthrough. It marks the formal connection of EUCARIS as first-pillar instrument to third pillar police cooperation (Interviewee 46).

Next to external differentiation, EUCARIS also embodied – still to date – internal horizontal differentiation (see Table 4.1). By 2012, 30 parties were connected to the information system (European Commission 2012d: 44). However, only 14 governments actually were formal members of EUCARIS, although the expansion process was on-going and remains so to date. Functional spill-over effects and an emerging supranational policy entrepreneurship produced ambivalent effects to this end. Accession today appears to be more difficult compared to the early 2000s when the EU data protection framework was not as advanced and the Commission had a much weaker role. The General Data Protection Regulation (GDPR) has made EU data protection and privacy rules much more stringent and their enforcement more rigid (Interviewee 45). Currently, it is up

TABLE 4.1 EUCARIS Cooperating Member States[1]

EUCARIS Treaty				*Prüm Council Decisions*	*Bilateral Agreements and National Legislation (Traffic Fines and Toll)*
			Participants		
Ratified	*Signed*	*To Accede*	*Associated*		
Germany Luxembourg The Netherlands United Kingdom Belgium Latvia Slovakia Romania	Finland	Estonia Hungary Lithuania Ireland Sweden Italy Norway Cyprus Czech Republic	Gibraltar Isle of Man Jersey Iceland Guernsey France	All EU Member States (+ Norway and Iceland) should participate. In 2019, only Italy and Ireland still have to connect.	Germany – The Netherlands France – Switzerland Switzerland – Germany Belgium – France Sweden – The Netherlands

Source: Compiled by the author, based on Interviewee 45.

to the Commission to take adequacy decisions on the protection level of personal data in non-EU countries wanting to accede to EUCARIS. If potential accession states do not manage to get on the Commission's so-called white list, they may not become formal parties to the information system.

MANAGING COORDINATION PROBLEMS: A ROLE FOR EU ACTORS

The increasing role for the EU in relation to cooperation on vehicle-related crime arose as a consequence of the functional need to regulate information exchange within EUCARIS and monitor compliance (Interviewees 45 & 46). Internal interdependence drove Member States to increasingly 'shop' for policy solutions at EU venues and associate intergovernmental cooperation with EU data protection legislation. They deliberately opted for an involvement of the EU to solve distribution problems related to information-sharing. Conferring power to the Union and its institutions was an unintended side effect as a consequence of parallel developments in the EU: spill-over effects from changes in the legal framework and other policy domains. Venue-shopping thus led to a loss of control (albeit relatively small) on the part of the Member States.

Initially, EU actors were not interested in promoting EUCARIS as a tool of EU cooperation. On the contrary, supranational policy entrepreneurship was largely absent in the early stages, and the Commission outright opposed the decentralised system. When Dutch negotiators approached the Commission before concluding the EUCARIS Treaty and offered it an official role in the technical system under development, Commission officials refused (Interviewee 46). Rather than taking an interest in the multilateral initiative, they pursued the creation of a new EU system that would centralise information exchange at the European Commission. This parallel development naturally collided with the preferences of the Member States who had signed the Treaty and led to an outright "war of opinion" between the Commission and EUCARIS signatories and users. Several practitioners underlined that they wanted to avoid waste and duplication where a functioning system existed that had been developed for almost ten years. "We wanted to prevent a new system from being made. The Commission was not very cooperative at the time, it was very self-interested and sought to make a new EU system for every topic instead of adapting existing systems" (Interviewee 46).

The historical turning point came in 2007 and the context of the Prüm Council Decisions that integrated the Prüm network into the EU framework and – more importantly – named EUCARIS the official information system for EU-wide cooperation within Prüm. Against the backdrop of overwhelming Member States' support for EUCARIS and its factual appointment as central data exchange platform in an EU context, the Commission finally abandoned its resistance and stopped to promote the development of a whole new system (ibid.). Institutional interdependencies and spill-over effects thus contributed to the prioritisation of EUCARIS over alternative cooperation channels.

In 2010, the Commission "agreed Member States could use the EUCARIS technology for the exchange of driving licences" based on other EU legislation (Interviewee 45). Since then, EU legislation has referenced EUCARIS as preferred cooperation mechanism for information-exchange on road transport undertakings. In 2012, Member States named EUCARIS the official platform to facilitate the cross-border exchange of information on road safety related traffic offences by legally linking it to the Cross-border Enforcement (CBE) Directive. Although these developments reinforced EUCARIS as an EU instrument, including EU-wide connection by 2013, they did not formally incorporate the EUCARIS Treaty into the EU legal framework. Most parties still used "the EUCARIS system based on various types of other legislation" (EReg 2017b). Complicated, often lengthy procedures inhibited day-to-day operations and produced a functional need to institutionally simplify and structure cooperation – a need that subnational officials continuously voiced in different venues (cf. European Parliament 2018). In 2012, the Commission proposed a regulation simplifying the transfer of motor vehicles registered in another Member State within the Single Market.[2] Had it been adopted, it could have consolidated the EUCARIS Treaty and other EU legislation as primary legal basis for governing related information exchange (Interviewee 46). However, Member States could not agree on all articles. A substantial step towards centralisation and integration thus failed at the political level despite pressure from policy entrepreneurs below and above the national level. In July 2018, the Commission formally withdrew its proposal. Nevertheless, the demand for better structuring cooperation continues to grow in line with internal linkages among authorities connected by EUCARIS. It is expected that a new proposal will be presented to the Member States in the next decade (European Parliament 2018).

THE EUCARIS PROTOCOL: DIFFERENTIATED INTEGRATION IN PROGRESS

In view of the failed draft regulation and steadily growing interdependence, EUCARIS signatories launched an alternative integration initiative in 2017. In the absence of a more flexible instrument, the EUCARIS Treaty needed to be amended to capture changing circumstances. Criminal markets continued to become more and more connected, and increasingly overlapped with other forms of crime. Subsequently, interdependence in the fight against vehicle-related crime was likewise high and generated a practical need to update cooperation structures (Interviewees 31 & 45). On 8 June 2017, the eight EUCARIS signatories thus signed a EUCARIS Protocol. The Protocol mirrors recent changes in EU regulation and legislation, which are finally "catching up" with the functional needs of practitioners (Interviewee 45). The Protocol widened the scope of the information system and opened it up for the use on legal bases other than the Treaty.

Paradoxically, the Protocol connects EUCARIS more closely with the EU, yet embeds differentiation and decentralisation. On the one hand, it strengthens the role of EU data protection law and its applicability to all data exchanges via EUCARIS (Art. 8 & 18). What is more, it strikes issues from the Treaty that are now covered by EU instruments, for example the aspect of document handling. On the other hand, the Protocol strikingly makes cooperation with Third Parties and thus external differentiation ever more important. Article 2(2) explicitly defines as the purpose of EUCARIS "to be at the disposal for Parties or Third Parties wishing to exchange data based on an EU legal act or any bilateral or multilateral agreement other than this Treaty." Furthermore, it broadens the applicability of EUCARIS considerably. Now the "system can be used for the cross-border exchange of all kinds of information based on other legislation than the EUCARIS Treaty itself" (EReg 2017a). Nonetheless, Member States are well aware that the format of a multilateral treaty is no longer very conducive. It remains "highly inflexible," and legally changing it could be "quite lengthy, sometimes several years" rather than months (Interviewee 46). The persisting state of dissatisfaction with the legal complexity of EUCARIS and its implications for operations and cooperation practice might yet open the floodgates to further integration.

While the integration process of EUCARIS continues today, it remains an instance of differentiated integration: an EU information system that is decentralised, yet part-based on supranational legislation and partially on other treaties and legislative acts. Its evolution since the 1990s demonstrates the strong influence of interdependence and policy entrepreneurship on state preferences. In reaction to intensifying cross-border links in vehicle-related crime, national registration authorities provided the impetus for practice-driven informal, multilateral cooperation where no precedent existed at the EU level. Asymmetrical interdependence and subnational policy entrepreneurship thus drove preferences on internal and external horizontal differentiation. The large initial influence of subnational policy entrepreneurs led to state preferences in favour of differentiation and decentralised, informal modes of cooperation. As one practitioner put it: differentiation is necessary, but "in the end you want a global exchange of data;" decentralisation is an appropriate model to circumvent a trust problem in the police pillar "where Member States like to keep data at the national level" (Interviewee 45). Although EUCARIS started as a technical platform in the realm of transportation and traffic, growing internal interdependence and an emerging EU policy advocacy motivated a vertical deepening of cooperation and widening of its functional scope (ibid.). The growing role of the EU, particularly the Commission, has become increasingly important in shaping state preferences on EUCARIS. As early as 2012, Member States underlined the significance of "the proper use of existing databases (e.g. EUCARIS); the need to improve Commission supervision and enforcement of existing EU legal instruments" (European Commission 2012d: 63). Yet, Member States still need to amend related legal instruments such as the Prüm Council Decision before police organisations will be able to make full use of vehicle-related information at the EU level. Whether and how this could be done and enable police authorities to fully employ EUCARIS, appears to be a question of political will in an otherwise relatively uncontroversial cooperation area. "On a technical level this is feasible very easily. It's the legislation that has still a way to go" (Interviewee 45). Supranational policy entrepreneurship and the extent to which it manages to influence state preferences could matter greatly for the future development of EUCARIS. The Commission, and a possible new proposal for a regulation, could emerge as important brokers in this regard.

The Prüm Treaty: A German Strategy towards Deeper Integration in Police Cooperation on Terrorism, Cross-Border Crime and Illegal Migration

In 2005, seven Member States signed the intergovernmental Prüm Treaty to enhance police cooperation on terrorism, cross-border crime and illegal migration. Five of them were likewise Schengen founding members, and four of them original signatories of EUCARIS (see Figure 4.1). Similar to EUCARIS, the Prüm network constitutes an example of differentiated integration. It resembles the Schengen process and has been described as "foundation for Europol" (Interviewee 30), but also as providing "no added value for Europol" (Interviewee 21). Some have termed Prüm a "clear political signal" for EU police cooperation (Interviewee 31), others a "significant countervailing political force" that "undermines the EU's ability to become an efficient policymaking body in the field of security" (Balzacq et al. 2006: 1 & 17). Functional pressure from rising interdependence alongside public-political pressure to react to a changing security landscape motivated Member States to launch Prüm as a new step in EU police cooperation. While integration preferences were heightened by these two factors, the ultimate differentiation decision – as was the case for EUCARIS – was driven by asymmetries, diverging operational needs and the lack of an institutional alternative at the EU level. Contrary to EUCARIS, Prüm presented a political, top-down initiative that lacked subnational policy entrepreneurship. Nonetheless, cultural differences in the security traditions and bureaucratic

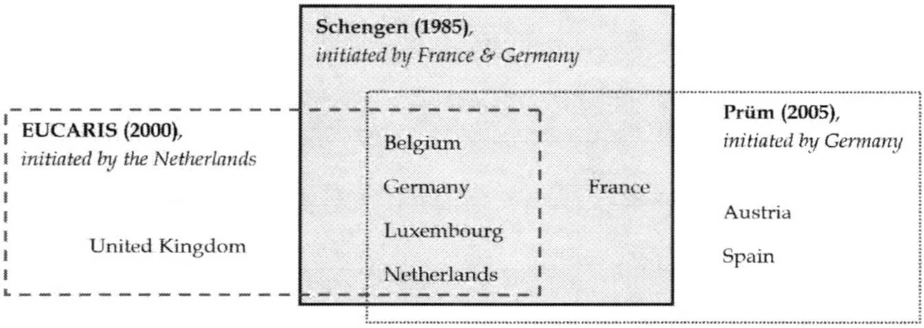

FIGURE 4.1 Mapping Flexible Cooperation Arrangements in the Early 2000s

resistance to an EU-wide approach shaped the institutional set-up and development of Prüm.

Around the turn of the millennium, intra-European interconnectedness in threats was experiencing another peak (Interviewee 30). Security and law enforcement officials were increasingly confronted with transnational criminal networks that challenged their day-to-day work and the viability of traditional policing methods and unilateral approaches (Interviewees 3 & 22). This was especially true for Germany and other countries at the heart of Europe (Interviewee 24). The growing number of bilateral police agreements initiated by Germany around that time bears testimony to this spiralling practical need. They include formal agreements with Switzerland (1999), Austria (2003) and the Netherlands (2005) (Schober 2017).

SEPTEMBER 11 AS A TURNING POINT

The expanding transnational dimension of crime and terrorism was perhaps most dramatically illustrated by the terror attacks of 9/11. They not only demonstrated growing interdependencies but also additionally generated politicisation in favour of more cooperation. September 11 has widely been acknowledged as 'game and paradigm changer' of security governance (Balzacq & Léonard 2013; Bures 2018; Monar, 2007). The attacks caused strong reactions across EU Member States. Especially Germany saw itself confronted with a need to review its security policies and cooperation arrangements. When it became known that the Al-Qaida attackers had been radicalised in Hamburg and had used Germany as safe haven for planning the attacks, this had a "fundamental psychological impact" (Interviewees 27, 30 & 32). Public and political pressure skyrocketed in Germany in the wake of 9/11 and marked an "enormous timestamp" for national security governance and policing (Henzler 2018). Numerous cooperation initiatives were launched at European and international level, including the Counter Terrorism Group (CTG) that connects all 27 EU Member States as well as Norway, Switzerland and the UK under the chairmanship of the Dutch intelligence agency. In Germany, a Joint Counter-Terrorism Centre (GTAZ) was finally created after plans for such a platform had existed since the 1990s (Interviewee 21).

SHORT-TERM DIFFERENTIATION AS DELIBERATE INTEGRATION STRATEGY

In February 2003, German Interior Minister Otto Schily proposed formalising police cooperation via a multilateral treaty to the Interior Ministers of France and the Benelux countries, Germany's close neighbours and the other original signatories of the Schengen Agreement (see Figure 4.1). Multiple expert meetings convened over the following months. However, France soon left the negotiation table due to constitutional and sovereignty concerns and was replaced by

Austria (National Council 2006: 3–4). After the details of the Prüm Convention were finalised in 2005, France and Spain joined the treaty at short notice (ibid.). Seven Member States signed it on 27 May. Although the Prüm Treaty constituted an intergovernmental treaty between a subgroup of EU Member States, its ultimate goal was the improvement of EU cooperation and inclusion into the supranational legal framework within three years (Art. 1(4)). Its signatories were "[e]ndeavouring, [...]to play a pioneering role in establishing the highest possible standard of cooperation" (Preamble). This begs the question why Germany did not pursue an EU-wide agreement in the first place. In view of its historic dedication to the EU and strong integration preference it appears striking that differentiation should be chosen in an area where interdependence was high and growing.

Two main factors shaped the German preference pro differentiation. First, a number of negative experiences with cooperation initiatives at the EU level influenced the decision of Otto Schily to advance cooperation via other channels. In the words of a senior German official: "I believe he was fed up with Europe" (Interviewee 40). Lengthy procedures, national reservations and the failure or deadlock of common projects clashed with an intensifying practical need to act on terrorism, transnational crime and illegal migration. A Swedish initiative for a European principle of data availability – information available to one should be available to all – was not going anywhere since its proposal after 9/11 (European Commission 2006b). The operational benefits of transferring the Schengen Agreement into the EU framework were likewise falling short of expectations (National Council 2006: 1). As was the second-generation Schengen Information System (SIS II); negotiations were protracted and the system was outdated even before it was adopted let alone operational (Interviewee 40).

Second, and perhaps most important for shaping the German preference towards differentiation, expediting police cooperation at the EU level was simply not feasible in the early 2000s. Similar to EUCARIS, no precedent existed at the EU level for the instigation of collective action that Germany envisioned. Institutional deadlock within the EU and a trust crisis among Member States additionally inhibited any attempt at further integration (Interviewees 10, 30, 33 & 40). Negotiations on the Constitutional Treaty were difficult and stagnant – complicated by public referendums in France and the Netherlands in 2005. Law enforcement and security authorities were reluctant to share data Europe-wide and continued to rely on their own networks (Interviewees 21 & 32). The practical experiences with the relatively young Europol and the Swedish initiative demonstrated the difficulties of ensuring EU-level information exchange. While the German-instigated Europol should have been the preferred option for furthering police cooperation, it "was not in a position to act "(Interviewee 32). Its mandate was still very much restricted and Europol lacked a practical track record and political standing. Additionally, differences between the legal frameworks of Member States, especially regarding data protection, posed substantial obstacles to reaching an EU-wide arrangement (Interviewee 24).

Notwithstanding Germany's overall preference for integration, deepening cooperation among all Member States simply was no realistic option and Europol no institutional alternative to a multilateral treaty outside the EU framework (National Council 2006: 1).

Despite these obstacles, Germany and its 'coalition of the willing' did not surrender ambitions for an extension of Prüm to all Member States. Internal horizontal differentiation presented a short-term strategy. Germany "had originally not been interested in a multilateral treaty;" it regarded the EU level as the most effective format to achieve quick practical results and deepen European police cooperation (Interviewee 30). Schily pushed for the swift completion of the draft Prüm Treaty with according resolve. Anecdotal evidence suggests he tore up a draft document on a flight to one of the experts meetings because it was "too unprogressive, lacked ambition and needed to be written from scratch" (Interviewee 40). The multilateral treaty, albeit seemingly advancing differentiation, presented a means for Germany to enhance European integration in the fight against terrorism, transnational crime and illegal migration in the long run; a "Europe of multiple speeds was practically necessary at the time" (Interviewee 29). Unsurprisingly, Prüm was deliberately modelled on the Schengen experience (Interviewees 24 & 33). Germany designed the Prüm Convention as a "laboratory for Europe," in which countries with higher homogeneity and capacities could go ahead, while others would be able to join later (Interviewees 29 & 40).

Prüm did not initially comprise enough countries to invoke the enhanced cooperation procedure specified by the EU treaties. With only seven interested parties, it fell two short of the required minimum of nine Member States (Art. 20 TEU; Art. 326-334 TFEU). Sovereignty concerns and the asymmetrical impact of driving factors explain why many governments remained hesitant or even opposed (Interviewee 27). Politically, JHA was not an established EU policy area yet; discussions about supranational competencies were on-going and emotions running high (Interviewees 3, 27 & 32). On the practical level, not all Member States experienced the same functional pressure to cooperate, as security threats, operational needs and capacities differed (Interviewees 14, 22, 27 & 44). Finally, enhanced cooperation had never been activated before and was regarded as a 'cumbersome and time-consuming' procedure (National Council 2006).

ASSIMILATING LEVELS OF INTERDEPENDENCE AND APPROXIMATION OF INTEGRATION PREFERENCES

An intensification of integration pressures and approximation between Prüm signatories and outside Member States ultimately produced a change of heart of the governments who had not originally signed the Convention. Finland, Slovenia and Hungary formally joined as early as 2007 (Interviewees 24, 29, 30 & 40). Intensifying external and internal interdependencies partially explain this shift. Additionally, the increasing impact of trailblazing effects, economic considerations and practical incentives account for the horizontal expansion of

Prüm. Although Member States still did not experience equal levels of interdependence, problems and patterns were becoming increasingly similar across all governments in the early 2000s, and relations between European security authorities more frequent in line with the rising internationalisation of security risks (Interviewees 14, 22 & 27). A semi-institutional interconnectedness between Prüm signatories and other Member States had been developing for some time and was gradually eroding bureaucratic resistance and generating a functional need to better structure cooperation.

The Prüm Convention provided a practical model to facilitate cross-border police cooperation (Interviewee 30). Similar to the Schengen experience, the initial 'heavy lifting' had already been done; a structure had been put in place and was being implemented. Around 2007, Prüm was no longer a vague idea but a concrete "ready-made product" (Interviewee 33). Joining Prüm offered clear operational benefits and relatively lower costs for any other parties. At the EU level, JHA ministers formally acknowledged that "[a]lready at this early stage,[... Prüm] has brought about noticeable operational success[, and...]amounts to a quantum leap in the cross-border sharing of information." (Council 2007a: 7). The network offered practical synergies alongside advantages from pooled capacity and central coordination. Economic considerations and cost-benefit calculations consequently played an important role as drivers of horizontal integration. While security cultures and norms had not yet significantly adapted to cooperating at the EU level, the first practical results from Prüm and the prospect of free-riding debatably motivated Finland, Slovenia and Hungary to join this cooperation format (Interviewees 27, 29 & 30). However, asymmetries in the level of interdependence persisted and explain why only a few smaller Member States opted to join Prüm; not all countries were as dependent on pooled capacity in combatting transnational threats. The UK, for example, already possessed a quite sophisticated DNA database (Interviewee 44). Smaller Member States tended to have less developed capabilities and more often favoured common police resources and systems (Interviewees 4, 21, 22 & 29). Thus, money mattered after all. The functional benefits of the Prüm network trumped national sovereignty concerns and bureaucratic resistance among non-signatories.

THE MADRID AND LONDON BOMBINGS AS WINDOWS OF OPPORTUNITY

Two terror attacks generated considerable politicisation and additionally shaped Member States' preferences in favour of joining Prüm. The bombings in Madrid and London in 2004 and 2005 exposed the shortcomings of unilateral policing and governance approaches. They sparked a public security crisis and fuelled expectations for political action in the EU (Interviewees 21, 22 & 40; European Commission 2010b). While 9/11 had undoubtedly initiated awareness of international (Islamist) terrorism and the need to adapt security policies and policing, the terror attacks in Madrid and London functioned as "actual catalysts for change and action in the EU," because they had been conducted on European soil and felt "closer to home" (Interviewee 40).

The Madrid train bombings of 11 March 2004 had been planned and executed by an Islamist terrorist cell with international connections within and outside Europe. Killing 191 people and injuring over 1,700, it was the deadliest attack in the history of Spain and the EU (SMJ 2006). A profound sense of crisis and shock was followed by a public-political realisation that international terrorism had arrived in Spain. In the face of this 'new' international terrorist threat, the Spanish government regarded the introduction of counter-measures indispensable (Proyecto 2005: 1418). The Madrid train bombings also caused a ripple effect beyond the national level. European heads of state or government called for immediate action and initiated a number of measures at the EU level (European Council 2004). In response to the attacks in Spain, they decided to advance the formalisation of information exchange between security agencies and especially police authorities by promoting data-sharing based on the principle of availability (Bunyan 2006b: 2).

One year after the attacks of 11 March (commonly known as 11-M), a similar incident occurred in the UK. On 7 July 2005, a group of Islamist terrorists committed a series of suicide attacks on public transport in London. With more than 50 dead and over 700 injured, the London bombings present the deadliest terrorist attacks in British history (HO 2006). Similar to 11-M, they evoked a strong emotional reaction among the public and policymakers, and a sense of crisis that needed to be managed. "Let no one be in doubt. The rules of the game have changed," announced Prime Minister Tony Blair a few weeks later (Wintour 2005). New counterterrorism legislation was introduced in October as "direct consequence" of the bombings (Cobain 2010). Although the proposals had been under development even before the attacks, the London bombings provided new momentum and political urgency (Clarke 2005; Interviewees 21, 33 & 40). The Terrorism Act 2006 was passed a few months later. At the EU level, the British Council Presidency proposed the introduction of a European Criminal Intelligence Model (ECIM) and the concept of intelligence-led policing for all Member States to fix the shortcomings of national security authorities and European information exchange (EUC 2008: 27; UK Presidency 2005).

The bombings in Madrid and London also brought EU cooperation on the radar of the public. In their aftermath, arguments of growing interdependence and a transnational necessity for cooperation, if not a stronger role for the EU, recurred in the media and political discourse (Bures 2018). These dual functions of the Madrid and London terror attacks – demonstrating interdependence and raising public-political pressure – can perhaps not be separated. Various interviewees pointed out that the "subjective perception of public security is just as important as a driver of governance" (Interviewee 22), and that it may indeed be less important whether politicised issues are "real" and the facts are true or the public and political sphere believe that they are (Interviewee 41). Following the Madrid and London bombings, narratives and discourse became more important as shapers of state preferences. The shortcomings of national security authorities were often framed as stemming from a 'new' kind of threat (Bures 2018; Interviewee 22). While the threat of international terrorism in Europe had arguably not changed significantly since 9/11, the public-political threat perception was skyrocketing (Interviewee 44).

THE PRÜM DECISIONS: INTEGRATING COOPERATION INTO THE EU FRAMEWORK

In this crisis climate, "not participating in Prüm, and by extension EU cooperation, was politically not feasible;" Member States could not justify it (Interviewee 27). Six more countries thus wished to accede: Italy, Portugal, Bulgaria, Romania, Greece and Sweden (Council 2007a: 8). With the exception of Greece, and together with the original signatories, they initiated the legal transfer of the network into the EU framework. On 15 February 2007, they "agreed on the integration[…] of the parts of the Prüm Treaty relating to police and judicial cooperation in criminal matters" (ibid.: 7). Seven countries had designed the Prüm Treaty. Not even two years later, heightened interdependence and politicisation drove a cohort of 15 Member States to support its inclusion into EU police cooperation.

This was to no small extent the result of German political efforts. With great resolve, the German Council Presidency pursued the integration of Prüm (Interviewee 30). In the words of one Council representative: "It clearly was a German political priority. The Germans were incredibly pushy and rushed to have the decisions done; there were even still mistakes in the draft. They had the manpower, the financial resources and generally a very good team behind it" (Interviewee 33). The transfer of Prüm into the EU legal framework was considered a potential "big hit" for the German Council Presidency and its political legacy (Interviewee 40). The suggestion stemmed from ministerial levels preparing the presidency around 2005. Unsatisfied with the "unambitious" envisioned priorities, the head of the responsible directorate proposed the inclusion of Prüm. This was met with hesitation, even outright bureaucratic resistance. German subnational officials signalled that it could be too early to integrate Prüm before the network was completely developed (ibid.). Nevertheless, the agenda was pushed through by the ministry.

In 2008, the Council of the EU hence adopted two decisions, known as the Prüm Decisions (2008/615/JHA & 2008/616/JHA). They not only integrated Prüm but also reinforced EUCARIS as central EU platform for exchanging car registration data (European Commission 2017c). Similar to dynamics at the early Europol, intensifying internal interdependence and subnational advocacy heightened pressure on governments to professionalise cooperation. Integration preferences were now increasingly shaped by the 'principle of viability:' an intensifying practical need to create synergies and use existing structures (Interviewee 29). Although Germany, as main initiator, had provided the lion's share of the financial means and political manpower to launch Prüm, growing operational needs and functional pressure to rationalise cooperation soon exceeded the resources that Germany alone could provide (ibid.). Integrating the Prüm Treaty into the EU framework not only solved coordination and collective action problems arising from the complexities of day-to-day cooperation practice, but it also offered a common budgetary and reference framework.

Other (Differentiated) Integration Initiatives and the Role of the Council Presidency

The case of Prüm introduces an interesting new element: political legacy and the expectations or opportunities created by holding the Council presidency. The theoretical literature already offers convincing evidence for the relationship between EU Presidency and legislative proposals in the Council (Tallberg 2003; Thomson, R. 2008; Warntjen 2007). While more research is required to confirm this hypothesis for the area of JHA and EU police cooperation, other integration initiatives of the early 2000s provide empirical evidence.

Holding the EU presidency in 1999, Finland proposed a Council decision (2000/642/JHA) to enhance cooperation among national Financial Intelligence Units (FIUs) that was adopted in 2000. The Dutch Presidency built on the initiative in 2004. It transferred a multilateral pilot project for professionalising FIU cooperation to the EU level and eventually extend it to all Member States (Amicelle & Chaudieu 2018: 656). Another milestone of EU police cooperation resulted from British advocacy one year later. In the second half of 2005, the British Council Presidency's proposal of an ECIM ultimately led to closer integration and introduced regular EU threat assessments and the EU Policy Cycle for organised and serious international crime (Interviewees 21 & 33; UK Presidency 2005). Based on British policing needs and the UK's National Intelligence Model, the ECIM was initially met with reluctance by other Member States. They could not see the practical added value of the model and regarded intelligence-led policing as "slightly counter-cultural" (EUC 2008: 27). The set-up phase was accordingly shouldered by a smaller group of Member States and followed a gradual, step-by-step professionalisation process. "We couldn't do everything with everybody," one Council official argued (Interviewee 33). The avant-garde group approach yielded good results that ultimately convinced other Member States.

Another example can be found in the establishment of Asset Recovery Offices (AROs) across the EU to facilitate "the tracing and identification of proceeds of crime" (Council Decision 2007/845/JHA). Austria provided the impetus during its presidency in 2006 and received support from the succeeding Finnish Presidency. Similar to the Prüm case and the German Presidency's ambition to transfer an instance of differentiated integration to the EU framework, the Austrian Presidency sought to build on and part-integrate an intergovernmental arrangement that had been launched by a subgroup of six Member States in 2004. This arrangement was CARIN, the Camden Assets Recovery Inter-Agency Network, originally initiated by Austria, Germany, the Benelux countries, Ireland and the UK (ESC 2006; Mühl 2011). Council Decision 2007/845/JHA formally recognised CARIN in 2007 and obliged all Member States to establish EU national AROs. It provided Europol with a coordination role through a Europol Criminal Assets Bureau (ECAB) as central contact point (Van Berkel 2017). A final example is the French Council Presidency of 2008. France employed the EU as a venue for the realisation of its new national security strategy by proposing to create a European Cyber Crime Platform (ECCP). The proposal was adopted in the same year and tasked Europol with the ECCP's development and coordination in the common fight against cybercrime (EUC 2010: 125; White Paper 2008). Holding the Council presidency arguably mattered as a positive influence on integration preferences, both in the form of political expectations and as a means of venue-shopping.

All these examples exhibit the impact of politicisation on the legislative activity of Member States. Politics and public visibility mattered in all cases. External crises and shocks provided important impulses to Council presidencies. In the aftermath of 11-M in 2004, Spain instigated the Advance Passenger Information System (APIS). In 2008, Belgium pushed for the adoption of a European Criminal Records Information System (ECRIS), following the case of serial killer Michel Fourniret and subsequent politicisation regarding the failure of domestic authorities. Although he had been sentenced and imprisoned for murder multiple times in France, Belgian officials had no knowledge of his criminal record when he moved to Belgium around 1990 (European Commission 2017b; Muller 2018). Looking back on the previous chapters, Germany likewise held the Council presidency when it first contacted France to discuss its proposal for a European conference on internal security in the beginning of 1974. Similarly, the British initiative in 1975 that paved the way for the establishment of TREVI came ahead of the UK's Presidency in the Council. Although the German-instigated creation of Europol did not coincide with the German Presidency, the final signature of the Europol Convention was most actively advanced by Germany during its Council presidency in the second half of 1994. While the presidency might itself constitute a driver of pro-integration preferences, for instance through the creation of public expectations and pressure to leave a political legacy, further research should investigate whether this is indeed the case. The Council presidency may just as well present a contextual determinant, window of opportunity or 'enabling factor' by as obvious venue for the policy choices targeting EU collective action.

In sum, the early 2000s confirm that issue-specific interdependence acts as important driver of integration preferences. At the same time, asymmetries played a crucial role for state differentiation preferences. Second, the above cases provide evidence towards the positive influence of politicisation and crises. In the aftermath of terrorist attacks on European soil, Member States reacted positively to growing salience and public-political expectations. Third, asymmetries drove differentiation. The asymmetrical effects of interdependence and politicisation across Member States hindered preference convergence let alone integration. Asymmetrical trust relationships and operational needs among police authorities additionally shaped the initial pursuit of enhanced rather than EU-wide cooperation. As time progressed, this paved the way for integration. Fourth, supranational policy entrepreneurship evolved alongside cooperation. Initially, no precedent existed for EU actors in this policy domain. Only as cooperation (and integration) proceeded, EU policy venues and actors established their role and legitimacy, and opened up new issue areas to the influence of supranational advocacy.

The Europol Council Decision: Transferring Intergovernmental Cooperation to the EU Framework

Europol had only been in operation for seven years when discussions emerged on its practical future and legal framework in early 2006. By then, respective Council presidencies had already initiated three amending protocols to the Convention to improve Europol's operational functioning and to changing threats and needs (see Figure 4.2). Nevertheless, these legal instruments were cumbersome and inflexible, and not a single one had entered into force yet (European Commission 2006a: 2). "[A]ttempts by the Council to address Europol's requirements[...]were complicated by the years' long ratification process required for any change to the intergovernmental legal basis" (Europol 2016a: 52). By contrast, the ECD was negotiated and adopted rather swiftly. A proposal was on the table at the end of 2006, adopted by the Member States not even two and a half years later in April 2009, and became formally applicable on 1 January 2010, transforming Europol into the EU's official law enforcement agency.

The ECD constituted a "delicate balance between continuity and change" (ibid.: 53). The most important changes included:

1. a significant expansion of Europol's functional scope to all areas of serious transnational organised crime (Art. 4, Council Decision 2009/371/JHA);
2. a gain of powers, including the right to "suggest the setting up of joint investigation teams" and participate in JITs (Art. 5.1(d) & 6), and act as central office for combating euro counterfeiting (Art. 5.5);
3. new, strengthened roles for subnational actors through the creation of Europol National Units (ENUs) (Art. 8) and for supranational actors through the integration into EU JHA (Art. 42).

The ECD altered Europol's rigid governance structure. Whereas decisions in the Europol Management Board had previously been taken unanimously, the ECD stipulated a two-thirds majority procedure (Art. 37). Although devising a strategy for Europol remained a task of the Board, "the initiative for defining the strategy" *de facto* shifted to Europol itself, and thus provided Europol with further

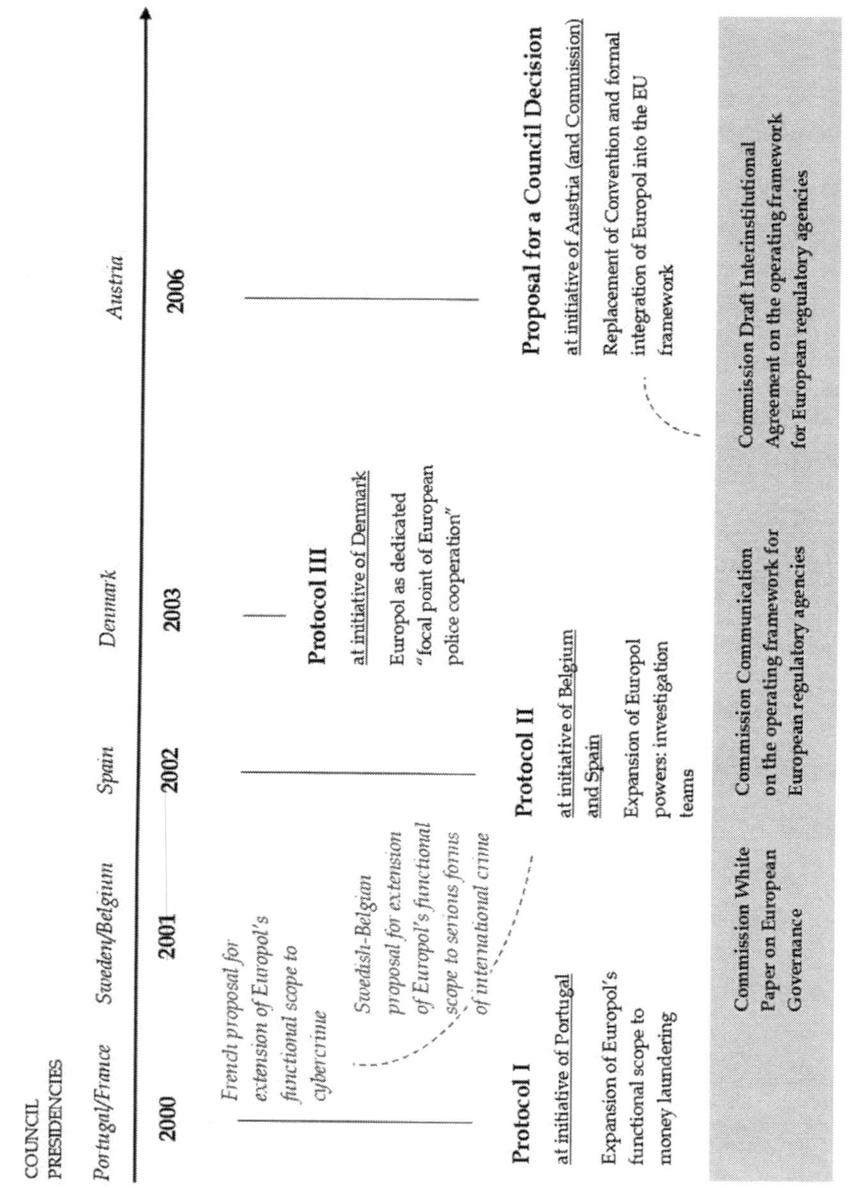

FIGURE 4.2 A Legal Chronology of Europol: from the Convention to the Council Decision

agenda-setting powers (Europol 2016a: 54). The ECD not only marked the formal transition of Europol from an intergovernmental to an EU organisation, but it also paved the way for a gradual shift of power in EU police cooperation away from the Member States and towards Europol and the EU. All interviewees underlined the great importance of Europol's integration into the EU framework as well as the subsequent momentum and leeway this gave to Europol and its institutional development. In the words of one enthusiastic official: "In retrospect, it is unbelievable what all has been achieved. It is an amazing success story" (Interviewee 30).

In this 'success story,' three factors seem to have mattered most as drivers of state preferences on transforming Europol into an EU agency. First, interdependencies presented the most significant influence on vertical integration preferences. As Member States were increasingly becoming interconnected not only in threats but also in emerging structures of police cooperation, collective action problems intensified. Lack of trust, bureaucratic resistance and diverging goals between political and practitioners' levels all undermined the operational benefit of the early Europol. EU governments thus opted for further centralisation in an attempt to fix shortcomings and more effectively structure police cooperation. Second, spill-over effects shaped state preferences to integrate. Earlier integration decisions (mainly the creation of TREVI and Europol) were producing functional spill-overs and pressure to formalise evolving cooperation as it became more and more complex. Additionally, political spill-overs – most notably from the Lisbon Treaty – influenced Member States to increasingly favour the EU level for problem-solving. Next to an emerging path-dependency due to the 'shaping and constraining effects' of Europol as a common institution (Kaunert et al. 2013: 278), cultivated spill-overs and supranational entrepreneurship drove governments to transform Europol into an EU agency. Finally, politicisation favourably impacted the preferences of Member States. Multiple crises provided public-political pressure at domestic and the EU level. While these might not have been primary drivers, they created important additional momentum and opened windows of opportunity for integration.

Fixing the Convention: Amending Protocols I, II and III

Europol had taken up its activities in July 1999, while "a fledgling organisational structure was still being developed" (Europol 2016a: 49). An evaluation report from February 2000 criticised the organisational fragmentation in Europol's governance and the inflexibility of its mandate and legal basis. The report also found "[l]ack of commitment, poor feedback, insufficient support and different expectations" among Member States and their police authorities as well as "differing and sometimes conflicting priorities at the political and law enforcement levels with respect to what Europol should do and how" (ibid.). These shortcomings alongside an insufficiently established practical track record produced a dangerous mix that undermined, perhaps even threatened, not only the operational benefit of the young organisation but also its institutional development and EU police cooperation as a whole (Interviewees 7, 9, 21, 22, 29, 35 & 41). In many areas, collective action problems and information asymmetries persisted – issues that the creation of Europol should have alleviated.

Whereas most Member States were relatively satisfied with Europol's operational output in the area of drug trafficking, it fell short of expectations in other areas. In line with globalisation and increasing transnational economic activity, money laundering was becoming a global problem and had "assumed vast proportions throughout the world" (Karamanou 2000: 11). This interconnectedness was even higher in the EU and intensified around 2000. The single market had been completed, the Schengen *acquis* was integrated and growing, and financial flows across countries were increasing in quantity and complexity ahead of the realisation of an economic and monetary union. While the euro was only launched in its physical form on 1 January 2002, it had already been released as 'book money' in 1999, and presented an alternative means of payment next to national currencies (European Commission n.d.). In July 2000, the Portuguese Council Presidency proposed to include money laundering among the issue areas falling under Europol's responsibility.[3] The initiative was uncontentious and adopted as amending Protocol I to the Europol Convention in November (see Figure 4.2).

Against the backdrop of these developments, counterfeiting of money and forgery of other means of payment was increasing as well (Interviewees 1, 21 & 24). Although euro counterfeiting was "no significant problem" in police work at the time (Interviewee 21), the introduction of the Euro alongside the internal and financial market produced spill-over effects, including new opportunities for criminal activities and profits, for example through drug trafficking and cybercrime (Interviewees 7, 31 & 38; Carrapiço & Farrand 2018). The capacity to deal with these effects differed greatly across Member States. Whereas larger countries often possessed sufficient resources to combat euro counterfeiting, many small ones lacked similar means to do so. In the euro area, cooperation became a prerequisite to prevent single countries from becoming safe havens for counterfeiters and money launderers (Interviewees 21 & 30). Growing economic and capacity interdependencies as well as criminal interdependencies thus produced functional pressure to counteract the considerable threat of spiking financial losses in all Member States.

PROTOCOL I: DEALING WITH INTERDEPENDENCE IN THE FIGHT AGAINST MONEY LAUNDERING

Taking action against money laundering and euro counterfeiting at the EU level also constituted a political question. It was "politically quite attractive, because it was very well saleable and something politicians could do for the public stage" (Interviewee 21). Furthermore, nominating a central contact point presented a political necessity to coordinate action within the EU but especially with outside partners, third countries such as the US, who needed to know whom to approach for cooperation on money laundering and payment fraud (Interviewees 24 & 31). Political spill-overs and an emerging path-dependency soon shifted the attention of national policymakers to Europol as the obvious choice as central contact point at the EU level and to the outside. It was well-connected to European structures and presented a direct channel to respective law enforcement authorities. In contrast to Interpol, Europol was also better institutionalised through the Europol Convention and its evolving governance framework (Interviewees 21 & 30). Although Protocol I had formally inserted money laundering into the list of Europol's competencies, Europol was only named the central office for euro counterfeiting in 2005, following the initiative of five Member States (2005/511/JHA). Protocol I presented a first step in this direction. It helped to establish Europol as official actor in one more issue area of EU police cooperation and strengthened its profile as central cooperation body at subnational and operational levels (Interviewee 31). Protocol I foreshadowed the emerging influence of supranational policy entrepreneurship and perhaps helped pave the way for the ECD. Notwithstanding the quick, uncontentious adoption of the Protocol, the European Parliament criticised the legal instrument for its inflexibility:

> It is regrettable that the procedure for the entry into force of the protocol is based on the same procedure applying to the original Europol Convention, i.e. it must also be adopted by the 'last' Member State. This procedure will delay the adoptions of the Protocol at EU level.
>
> *(Karamanou 2000: 12)*

The Parliament would continue to push for the adoption of an EU legal instrument. Already in 2001, the Council had discussed "the possibility to replace the Europol Convention by a Council Decision" (European Commission 2006a: 3). Yet, it decided to wait for the outcome of the Constitutional Treaty and to instead opt for additional protocols as interim solution.

PROTOCOLS II AND III: FROM VENUE-SHOPPING TO EUROPOL AS EU FOCAL POINT

Not long after the Portuguese initiative in July 2000, even before Protocol I was adopted, the French Council Presidency presented a proposal for the extension of Europol's functional scope to "computer crime" (French Presidency 2000). Like money laundering, this issue area was strongly affected by globalisation. The intensifying internationalisation and digitisation of markets, interactions and social structures affected both public and private spheres (Niemeier 2007). This 'structural change' not only increased cross-national interconnectedness among countries, but it also rendered national borders and conventional, unilateral governance instruments less important, even obsolete (Interviewees 1, 22, 24 & 29).

This created substantial new opportunities for criminals and terrorists. At the beginning of the 2000s, the "transnational dimension of criminal issues was increasingly empirically proven and perceived as a problem" (Interviewee 30).

Thanks to the Internet, different criminal areas and groups were becoming more interconnected (Interviewees 21, 22, 28 & 29). New criminal markets, methods and types of crime were forming online. Whereas police officials initially regarded the Internet merely as a new channel for criminal activity, it soon became evident that "cyber was here to stay" (Interviewee 35). When cyber or high-tech crime first emerged as a separate form of crime, it presented a primarily economic rather than security concern. Similar to money laundering, cybercrime – especially, illicit activities related to non-physical means of payment and online transactions – presented very real financial threats (ibid.). Law enforcement officers increasingly recognised and voiced that security governance needed to become similarly connected across borders to counter this trend (Interviewee 27). Yet, police cooperation at the time was still rather limited and practically focussed on "the old topics stemming from the 90s" like drugs, mafia style groups and vehicle crime (Interviewee 35).

In view of spiralling external interdependencies that exploited growing institutional connections among Member States, the French Council Presidency suggested an extension of Europol's functional scope in October 2000. The importance of emerging criminal areas as a driver to this end can be seen in the overhaul of the French proposal just a few months later. The subsequent Council presidencies of Sweden and Belgium presented an even more ambitious proposal to widen Europol's mandate to deal with all other forms of transnational crime that had been listed in the annex to its Convention. In March 2001, the Council adopted a formal proposal (2001/C 176/05), which expanded EU police cooperation to include a whole array of (more than twenty!) new and emerging forms of crime, including counterfeiting and product piracy, forgery of money and means of payment, organised robbery, kidnapping, illicit trafficking of a variety of objects and computer crime.

This not only presents a remarkable development of Europol's functional scope, but it also constitutes a quantum leap in the integration of this newly created institution of EU police cooperation. At this early stage of Europol, the sudden 'Euromania' of its Member States, their preference to cooperate at supranational level and the quick expansion of Europol's responsibilities primarily responded to the rapid growth of interdependencies of criminal structures across borders and issue areas. As integration and time progressed, these would be increasingly complemented by additional driving forces that made 'deeper' (rather than merely 'functional' or 'wider') integration seemingly indispensable.

One of these drivers was politicisation, which became powerfully visible in late 2001. Politicisation in the aftermath of 9/11 not only generated direct pressure on policymakers to act, but it also presented a window of opportunity for supranational policy entrepreneurship in the area of counterterrorism. The September 11 attacks placed international terrorism on the radar of countries around the world as "politically largest problem," and marked the arrival of

Islamist terrorism as a topic in Europe (Interviewee 21). September 11 "changed everything" (Interviewee 27). It determined the focus and development of EU police cooperation over the following years (Interviewees 8, 22, 24, 27 & 32). High emotions and a public sense of crisis created a political climate that was conducive to EU action and advocacy. To Member States, supranational policy venues offered a convenient escape from and practical solution to domestic public pressure. Against this backdrop, Europol's Director Jürgen Storbeck was able to stress that "something needed to be done at EU level" and initiate the creation of an according WG at Europol (Interviewee 7; cf. Europol 2001: 11).

In the second half of 2001, the Belgian Presidency – jointly with Spain, which succeeded it in 2002 – proposed to expand Europol's powers through a second protocol to the Convention. The initiative was presented at the Council in February 2002 and adopted in November, effectively empowering Europol officials "to participate in a support capacity in joint investigation teams" and "to ask the competent authorities of the Member States concerned to conduct or coordinate investigations in specific cases" (2002/C 312/01). Albeit not quite an instance of vertical integration, Protocol II presented a significant step towards strengthening Europol's powers and its role within EU police cooperation. Discussions on a third amending protocol were initiated by the Danish Council Presidency in July 2003. Protocol III was adopted in November, making Europol "focal point of European police cooperation" (2004/C 2/01).

The amending Protocols to the Europol Convention provide evidence that holding the Council Presidency matters for integration preferences and initiatives. Between 2000 and 2003, all six presidencies proactively furthered EU police cooperation via Europol and beyond. The Spanish Presidency, for example, likewise initiated the creation of a "European network for the protection of public figures" and a European Institute of Police Studies.[4] Across this time, none of the other drivers – interdependence, politicisation or policy entrepreneurship – rose significantly in order to sufficiently explain the sudden activism of these countries. It might be argued, however, that the office particularly exposed the respective governments to the influence of supranational entrepreneurship and cultivated spillovers as well as to politicisation, public scrutiny and pressure to act (at the EU level).

The legal adaptation of Europol's mandate in the early 2000s was generally regarded as necessary and welcomed by the EU as a whole. Nevertheless, the choice of amending protocols was strongly criticised as insufficient and inflexible across different levels. In a report on the Third Protocol, the European Parliament re-emphasised its "concern at the instrument chosen," and reiterated its "recommendation to the Council on the future development of Europol and its automatic incorporation into the institutional system of the European Union" (von Boetticher 2003: 6):

> It is regrettable that a more flexible instrument[...]was not chosen, for example a decision[...]. This is particularly regrettable because Europol has a key role with respect to cooperation between Member States' authorities in the field of cross-border crime investigation.

Replacing the Convention: The Europol Council Decision

The choice of legal instruments – patching up shortcomings of the Convention through amending protocols – demonstrates that governments sought to strike a balance "between the intergovernmental nature of Europol and the EU framework," yet were eager to defend national sovereignty and "preserve their primacy in the governance of Europol" (Europol 2016a: 18 & 53). In 2006, the Austrian Council Presidency launched discussions on the future of Europol and potentially replacing the Convention (European Commission 2006a: 3). In 2009, Member States adopted the ECD. This change of preferences is best explained by significant practical shortcomings of the Convention and the influence of politicisation and supranational policy entrepreneurship.

Despite the amending protocols, the intergovernmental legal framework remained insufficient to improve EU police cooperation. The narrow legal definition of Europol's mandate prevented support to law enforcement authorities in cases where the cross-border character could not be clearly established (Interviewee 21). To receive operational support from Europol, police officials had to succumb to rigid and lengthy cooperation procedures (Interviewee 40). Europol's legal framework was unable to respond to the swiftly changing needs of a growing organisation. "The financial regulation was a catastrophe, the staff regulations were not satisfying either, and the headquarters building was not suited and soon too small" (Interviewee 21).

As the Europol Convention had been a top-down political project of governments rather than police authorities, early EU police cooperation lacked a trust basis and was hindered by domestic bureaucratic resistance (Interviewees 21 & 29). Although law enforcement officials were requesting a larger role and more substantial input, they largely remained the 'recipients' of initiatives from above (Interviewee 44). With limited opportunity for policy entrepreneurship in the development of Europol, subnational actors remained sceptical, even reluctant to cooperate via Europol and share information. Despite the establishment of a central body and formal channels for cooperation, different national security cultures and policing traditions did not automatically adapt to these new modes of working and jointly fighting cross-national phenomena (Interviewees 21, 22, 29 & 30). EU police cooperation in the early 2000s – although intended to balance asymmetrical interdependencies in criminal issue areas – incorporated structural asymmetries between law enforcement authorities. Institutional and informal linkages among domestic police officials and authorities varied across countries, as did the degree of domestic adaptation to cooperation via Europol and the evolving supranational policy domain of JHA. The structural-legal change in EU police cooperation that had been superimposed onto national officials through the Europol Convention was in many cases quicker than the practical and cultural adaptation, which lagged behind. Many police authorities were unwilling or unable to cooperate. The first French contribution to Europol's EU Organised Crime & Threat Assessment (OCTA) comprised several hundred pages of uncoordinated information submitted by different national security actors (Interviewee 21). Europol's first three annual organised crime reports did not even include contributions from Italy (ibid.), and the proposal for an EU Policy Cycle was met with outright resistance from Dutch law enforcement officials (Interviewee 30). This domestic bureaucratic resistance to EU police cooperation and Europol would only be overcome slowly in line with a gradual socialisation process among national police authorities. The ECD and Europol would prove important means to this end.

Similar to the integration obstacles surfacing at Europol, structural shortcomings from the Maastricht Treaty were becoming increasingly visible in practice in the form of "rather cumbersome decision routes in the Third Pillar;" "new structures were simply superimposed on those already in place" (European Commission 1995). Most JHA priorities at European level were arguably driven politically rather than through functional pressure from interdependence (Interviewees 9 & 24). Despite the original impetus behind Europol as a top-down initiative of senior policymakers, its rapidly expanding role under the Convention presented somewhat of a "baby that nobody wanted" (Interviewee 30). Member States sought to strictly limit and control what the organisation could and should do (Interviewee 40). The failure of the Constitutional Treaty in mid-2005 debatably marked the peak of this trust crisis. It illustrated that European constituencies were dissatisfied with the institutional reality of the Union (Interviewees 29, 30 & 34). A consensus was thus emerging among practitioners, policy- and decision-makers about the growing need to fundamentally restructure the EU (Interviewees 1, 29, 30 & 33). Two years later, the Lisbon Treaty was signed. It gave the EU legal personality, dissolved the former pillar structure and integrated JHA into the consolidated Union framework. These structural changes marked a shift in state preferences towards integration and opened the floodgates to supranational entrepreneurship in EU police cooperation.

FUNCTIONAL AND PUBLIC PRESSURE AS JOINT INFLUENCES ON INTEGRATION PREFERENCES

While public-political reform expectations perhaps paved the way, growing interdependencies and politicising events together shaped Member States' positions in favour of a new legal framework for Europol. Although the Convention had created an institutional structure for EU police cooperation, structural deficiencies made cooperation via Europol "the exception rather than the rule" (Interviewee 35). Vertical integration of EU police cooperation presented a means to solve collective action and coordination problems.

Multiple crises illustrated this need and made shortcomings in the common fight against crime and terrorism publicly visible. September 11 constituted the first one of these paradigm-shattering crisis moments. Through 9/11, Islamist and international terrorism only really "arrived in the EU" (Interviewee 27). The attacks gave Europol a window of opportunity to offer its unique services, as single point of contact for cross-checking the names and personal data of terrorist suspects who were often registered in different national databases under multiple alias or variations in spelling (Storbeck 2001). The attacks marked a temporary peak in the involvement of Europol and its role in information exchange and data analysis (Interviewee 21). Although Europol was granted an increase in human and financial resources dedicated to counterterrorism, bureaucratic reluctance prevented any significant institutional consequences. Notwithstanding the post-9/11 "internationalisation of terrorism" and counterterrorism strategies in the Western hemisphere, Islamist terrorism still seemed relatively far away from the EU. The focus remained mostly on groups and possible targets in the US (Interviewees 10 & 35).

This would only change in 2005, after two more crises had reinforced the public salience and political momentum of EU police cooperation. The 11-M attacks of March 2004 presented the first incident of international terrorism on European soil and shook EU Member States. Not only did they motivate a number of Spanish initiatives at European level and the creation of the EU Counter-Terrorism Coordinator (CTC) (European Council 2004: 14), but they also prompted public calls to improve EU police cooperation (Interviewee 21). Accordingly, European governments were eager to signal action and control to their constituencies by committing themselves to "to ensur[...ing] that the optimum and most effective use is made of existing EU bodies, in particular Europol and Eurojust, to promote cooperation in the fight against terrorism" (ibid.: 6). Although this did not immediately alter the powers and standing of Europol, it reactivated the momentum garnered from 9/11 and heightened the salience of EU police cooperation. The sense of crisis after 11-M arguably created a ripple effect that helped shift state preferences towards deeper integration.

The London bombings of July 2005 reinforced this momentum and perpetuated the 'crisis mode.' They instigated the gradual shift in EU police cooperation "from retrospective learning to preventive policing, and from Europol as a passive to a (pro-)active actor" (Interviewee 21). The London attacks presented a game changer in various regards. First, they powerfully illustrated cross-border interdependencies in the fight against terrorism within the EU. British government officials repeatedly emphasised the rapidly expanding international links of criminal and terrorist groups, and public discourse framed the bombings as a direct consequence of coordination and collective action problems among different security authorities (Bures 2018; Interviewees 22 & 44). Second, the attacks fuelled the sense of crisis produced by 11-M and reinforced public pressure to react to the security shortcomings. The London bombings thereby provoked a significant qualitative leap in data exchange and information-sharing via Europol (Interviewees 3, 10, 15 & 27). The combination of publicly exposed interdependencies in the area of counterterrorism and heightened politicisation provided a window of opportunity for Europol to prove its value and become substantially involved in national investigations of this scale. In the aftermath of the July bombings, Europol's Director proactively offered the organisation's services to the UK. British officials not only accepted the offer, but they also welcomed Europol's support in the investigations and were eager to openly harness Europol in the analysis and assessment of related data (Interviewee 21).

The combination of high interdependence and politicisation drove Member States to turn to Europol as a solution for collective action problems. As one interviewee phrased it: "policymaking in the area of internal security usually needs a good crisis" (Interviewee 33). The terror attacks in Madrid and London instigated a process that eventually led to the adoption of the ECD less than three years later on 6 April 2009. This process was largely a matter of step-by-step legitimisation of Europol as relevant player within EU police cooperation and "certainly a question of using the right crisis" (Interviewee 33).

MOVING PREFERENCES TOWARDS A COUNCIL DECISION: PATH-DEPENDENCY, SPILL-OVER EFFECTS AND SUPRANATIONAL ENTREPRENEURSHIP

Europol, and in fact the whole of EU police cooperation benefited from the politicisation of a single issue area. The public psychological effect of the terrorist attacks mattered perhaps more as a catalyst of pro-integration preferences than actual interdependencies (Interviewees 21, 35, 38 & 44). In the words of one official: "Terrorism is a bizarre thing, it's a high-profile area. It goes up and down. Organised crime is never politicised. Cyber isn't, corruption isn't. These areas rarely trigger the same public reaction, although they are often statistically the much bigger threat" (Interviewee 33). In the aftermath of each terror attack, available resources and momentum for EU police cooperation skyrocketed. Yet, they quickly faded away again and data submission to Europol declined as public attention abated (Interviewee 35). Politicisation alone can therefore not explain why Member States moved towards favouring long-term, vertical integration. Neither politicisation nor functional pressure suffices as accounts for the adoption of the ECD and the far-reaching institutional and legal changes it initiated.

The missing link is provided by path-dependency, spill-over effects and the supranational entrepreneurship that arose in the early 2000s. First, EU police cooperation was increasingly influenced towards deeper integration by the path-dependency of emerging supranational structures and policy venues. Functional pressure to continue and expand cooperation at Europol followed the general paradigm shift in the early 2000s, away from intergovernmental treaties and conventions towards EU legal instruments and the creation of agencies as tools for administration, regulation and execution (Interviewees 14 & 29). The Lisbon Treaty demonstrates the spirit at the time of expanding the EU's functional scope and competences. It responded to growing public and political expectations at national and the EU level to follow the path of common institutions and collective action in Europe (Interviewees 27 & 29).

Second, the growing practical and institutional interconnectedness between national police authorities produced a functional need to further structure and regulate cooperation. Linkages in one area created functional spill-overs to other issue areas; cooperation in the fight against terrorism often also made cooperation on drugs and arms trafficking necessary. While cooperation between law enforcement officials frequently began as information-sharing on a case-by-case basis, the practical benefits soon produced a demand for additional cooperation, for instance the exchange of best practices and the initiation of common training programmes.

Third, state preferences on EU police cooperation were shaped by cultivated spill-overs and supranational policy entrepreneurship. Although different EU actors played an important part in promoting the integration of Europol into the EU's institutional structure, the European Commission and Europol arguably developed the most significant supranational advocacy. While the Commission very actively promoted deeper integration, Europol mainly impacted government positions through the 'shaping and constraining effects' of being a common institution (Kaunert et al. 2013: 278). Their political weight and entrepreneurship *vis-à-vis* the Member States grew continuously in line with their practical track record, organisational reputation and standing.

THE EUROPEAN COMMISSION

At the beginning of the 2000s, neither Europol nor the Commission had developed a real say in the government-driven design of police cooperation (Interviewees 21, 23 & 30). Nevertheless, both organisations were making the most of their limited influence and sought to expand it. The European Commission ensured its own institutional relevance and paved the way for the ECD through its uniformity agenda for EU agencies and corporate governance (Interviewees 29 & 33). As early as 2001, a White Paper on European Governance (COM/2001/428 final) laid down the cornerstones for institutional reform of the Union (see Figure 4.2). Barely one year later, a Commission Communication on the operating framework for European regulatory agencies initiated the process of judicial streamlining within a more coherent policy framework for all relevant EU bodies (COM/2002/718). Finally, a draft Interinstitutional Agreement on the operating framework for European regulatory agencies was presented to the Member States and adopted in 2005 (COM/2005/59).

By then, Commission advocacy began to overlap with and amplify Europol's entrepreneurship. A formal cooperation agreement between the two had been signed in early 2003 and now facilitated further contacts. Franco Frattini, the European Commissioner for Justice, Freedom and Security, frequently liaised directly with Europol's Director. In this way, the Commission not only developed substantial knowledge on the state of play of EU police cooperation, but it also publicly promoted Europol and its organisational needs (Interviewees 21 & 23).

As one official phrased it: "the role of the Commission has changed tremendously since 2004, and they do drive now" (Interviewee 33).

The proposal for a Council decision to replace the Europol Convention was an original suggestion from the European Commission in the context of its uniformity agenda (see Figure 4.2; Interviewees 14, 21 & 29). In 2006, the Commission strongly criticised the stubborn *status quo* of EU police cooperation despite persisting shortcomings: "none of these instruments [the Protocols] have entered into force yet, due to the fact that not all Member States have ratified them.[...E]ven after the entry into force of the three Protocols, further improvements to Europol's functioning are still desirable" (European Commission 2006a: 2). The Commission especially underlined two driving factors that exposed shortcomings and thus supposedly called for further integration. First, it emphasised growing functional pressure from external interdependencies: the need to respond to "the emergence or increase of new security threats such as terrorism, which pose new challenges to Europol and require novel approaches" (ibid.). Second, the Commission pointed to internal interconnectivity and the functional need to exchange information, which made "it necessary to further adapt Europol's legal framework" (ibid.). This adaptation, it advocated, should take the shape of a Council decision that would transform the organisation into an EU agency, thereby placing it under the scrutiny of the Commission among others.

When the Austrian Presidency presented this idea in 2006 and Member States began to discuss possibilities, the Commission played a major part in overcoming governmental reluctance and designing the ECD (Interviewees 14, 21 & 29). A first draft was devised by the Commission in the same year. This presumably provided the Commission with a first-mover advantage and enabled it to set the general tone of the decision and influence the scope of its content and institutional design (Interviewee 31). In contrast to the Member States, the Commission was able to present a uniform position and 'united front' in the negotiations on the ECD. Although EU members preferred to keep EU police cooperation an intergovernmental affair and feared that placing Europol under the umbrella of the Union would lead to more bureaucracy and less national flexibility and control (Interviewees 14 & 21), they agreed more far-reaching changes were needed to cope with the shortcomings of the Convention. However, Member States were divided on how this should be accomplished, whether or not a new legal framework was necessary and if so, what this should look like (Interviewees 29 & 31). This provided an opening for the Commission to influence the debate and state preferences.

To this end, the European Commission harnessed functional and public integration pressure. By the early 2000s, many European governments had already significantly invested into Europol or were committing themselves to working together with other law enforcement agencies via the organisation. The growing and divergent needs of domestic police authorities not only created an argument to widen the functional scope and capacity of Europol, a vertical adaptation of the governance framework offered a way to better coordinate and manage collective action problems. Parallel developments at the EU level intensified institutional linkages and shifted the standard policy venue, if not the power itself, towards supranational structures. The Commission's uniformity initiative and the Lisbon Treaty helped shift state preferences towards more rather than less EU (Interviewees 27 & 29). The public-political momentum of various terror attacks helped further supranational entrepreneurship and shape state preferences towards convergence, for example in favour of an EU Action Plan, a "minimum definition of terrorism" and the launch of an EU counterterrorism strategy (Bures 2018: 158–159).

The European Commission continuously fuelled the trend towards EU collective action in the JHA domain and lobbied for more centralisation or at least coordination at supranational level. As discussions on the ECD progressed, it published a communication sketching 'the way forward,' a future agenda for the role and governance of EU agencies (COM/2008/135 final). When the ECD was adopted in 2009, it not only transformed Europol into a decentralised EU agency, but it also attributed a formal role to the Commission in the governance and strategic guidance of Europol. Through the ECD, the Commission obtained a permanent seat on Europol's Management Board, a role in its budget supervision and financial planning, and as a default, Commission decisions would apply to Europol by analogy. The European Commission's emerging supranational entrepreneurship is thus reflected in the ECD and its subsequent changes in Europol's legal framework and governance structure.

EUROPOL

Next to the Commission, Europol increasingly developed a policy entrepreneurship in the early 2000s in response to a window of opportunity and political expectations at the EU level (Interviewees 24 & 27). After 9/11, the organisation began to take a proactive role in EU police cooperation rather than only acting as an agent of the Member States. For the first time, discussions at Europol revolved around what it could actively offer to governments and police authorities, and Europol officials approached relevant actors with initiatives and proposals (Interviewees 24 & 30). At the Council, Europol officials successfully lobbied for establishing the organisation as central coordination body and point of contact within Europe and to the outside (Interviewee 30). This pattern of harnessing crisis momentum to establish and expand its role could likewise be observed in the aftermath of the attacks in Madrid and London in 2004 and 2005. Without having been charged to do so by the Member States, Europol immediately offered its services to the affected authorities and proactively assumed a support role (Interviewee 40).

Nonetheless, Europol's entrepreneurship evolved gradually and was strongly focused on establishing its legitimacy as an actor in EU police cooperation. This partially presented a response to bureaucratic resistance from governments and law enforcement authorities. When the organisation commenced operations in 1999, it was neither well-known nor interesting to national and local police officials (Interviewees 21, 22, 27 & 32). "Especially in the early years, [...]Europol was not considered a particularly good career move" (Groenleer 2009: 291). Some national systems, like the French one, offered better benefits and professional prospects than Europol was able to provide for moving to the supranational level (Interviewee 7). Many national police bodies boycotted Europol outright or indirectly: the flow of information from Europol to the domestic level was often curbed, and vacancy notices did not always reach potential applicants because senior law enforcement officers were concerned it might lead to brain drain (Jeffreys-Jones 2007). Additionally, staff seconded to Europol often had slimmer career prospects when returning to their national police force; if they wanted a future in their own domestic system, they often had to leave Europol prematurely and return to their original positions (Interviewee 24). Consequently, the development of some sort of entrepreneurship was essential for Europol's institutional survival. By raising its public profile and proactively offering its services, the organisation could reassure police authorities that European and national policing were complimentary rather than a zero-sum game.

In a way, Europol's pro-integration entrepreneurship was a response to the different security cultures and policing mentalities of the Member States (Interviewees 21, 22, 27 & 32). Lack of trust remained one of the key problems among national officials and agencies involved in EU police cooperation (Interviewees 2, 7 & 29). Already at the domestic level, coordination between single police entities was a challenge. Institutional rivalries and turf wars often hindered or prevented effective police cooperation (Interviewee 27). When the Netherlands began to reform and part-centralise their police system in the late 1990s, this was met with strong reluctance from different local entities. One official involved in the process remarked: "one of the regional police chiefs told me I was taking away his most beautiful daughter. They were not pleased, there was a lot of competition" (Interviewee 32). This competition also extended beyond the national context. Security officials were often reluctant to share and exchange information with Europol, afraid of losing control and sceptical of other security and policing traditions. Germany, for example, strictly separated law enforcement and intelligence. By contrast, in the French and the British systems, police and general interior affairs were relatively integrated (Interviewees 14, 21 & 22). While British and German law enforcement authorities attached great importance to prevention, this did not constitute a priority in France and was not even included among the tasks of the Spanish police (Interviewees 22 & 27). These cultural differences presented significant obstacles to cooperation via Europol in the early 2000s. Police officials had so far mostly worked together on a bilateral and case-by-case basis and were not used, even opposed, to this new institutionalised form of cooperation and general information-sharing via the EU level.

Europol officials launched an EU-wide public relations offensive in an attempt to build an organisational reputation, make its positive practical track record more visible and promote itself as coordination and socialisation platform to national police authorities. Representatives from Europol travelled to Member States to introduce the organisation and advertise its services, sometimes tailor-made to the criminal problems faced by a country or authority – a process that one interviewee described as "building a clientele for Europol" (Interviewee 7). At the EU level, Europol officials repeatedly voiced concerns about the shortcomings and restrictions of the Convention to their supranational counterparts in other EU institutions. Especially from 2004 onwards, Europol closely liaised with the Commission to emphasise the need for a new legal framework to the Council and to each Presidency (Interviewee 21).

Intensive networking and public relations work constituted key elements of Europol's strategy to build a positive public image. Senior officials and representatives of its management exploited every possible opportunity to raise the organisations profile through the media, visiting international conferences, reaching out to governments directly and speaking with national and local practitioners (Interviewee 7). Although Europol staff were initially hesitant about being able to force Member States to step up involvement and support of the organisation, the management's strategy of 'power through public pressure' paid off eventually (Interviewee 21). In the wake of 9/11, Europol's advocacy contributed to the establishment of a counterterrorism task force at the agency (Europol 2001: 11). Harnessing the political momentum, it could offer an additional venue to national policymakers for collective action and signalling control. Its entrepreneurship likewise surged in the aftermath of the Madrid and London bombings. Europol not only directly approached the affected governments with an offer for support, but it also managed to achieve a substantial increase in information exchange and the establishment of an EU First Response Network at Europol (Interviewees 21 & 40). While the crisis momentum of terror attacks can only temporarily provide opportunities for policy entrepreneurship, Europol was able to maintain and further develop its advocacy beyond these politicising events. Its continuous involvement with the Member States and other EU actors resulted in the right of the Europol Director to participate in Council meetings, a concession that had been achieved against the will of the Commission (ibid.).

Europol additionally generated functional pressure on policymakers to further integrate in the area of EU police cooperation. Through a growing array of services and unique products, the organisation gradually convinced EU governments and national police authorities of its practical merit and legitimacy. Its growing portfolio of cross-national tools, resources and solutions was increasingly relevant to domestic police officials. "Europol became progressively interesting to national and local levels because of its practical track record. This started slowly at the beginning of the 2000s and then changed enormously and the demand skyrocketed" (Interviewee 32). Between 2000 and 2009, the use of Europol by Member States and third parties increased steadily and significantly (see Figure 4.3). Through developing a public, corporate profile, an organisational reputation and practical track record, Europol had succeeded in promoting

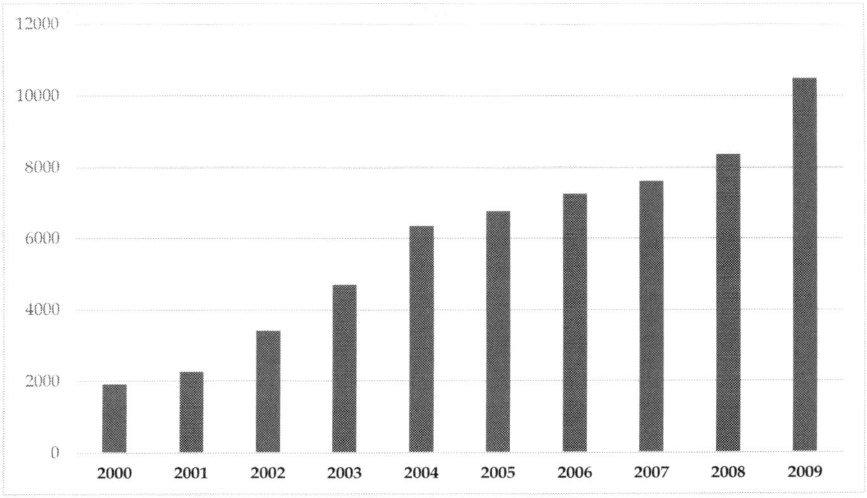

FIGURES 4.3 New Cases Initiated at Europol (2000–2009) by Member States, ENUs, Non-European Union States and International Organisations

Compiled by the author, based on Europol Annual Reports

itself as key platform for EU police cooperation. Its entrepreneurship was presumably so successful because it proved its value and justified its existence not only as coordination platform and agent, but also as proactive initiator and broker. Additionally, Europol acted as socialisation platform for domestic police authorities, which successfully built trust and overcame bureaucratic resistance. Its organisational entrepreneurship and reputation raised its public image beyond the EU and thus created a boomerang effect: the more non-EU countries and entities contacted Europol and began to cooperate via the organisation, the more its legitimacy was reinforced and the more functional pressure was exerted on Member States to likewise pursue and intensify cooperation through Europol (Interviewee 21). As one interviewee formulated it: "That's the nice thing about the EU, once initial resistance and obstacles have been overcome, the process continues on its own. It was the case for Prüm, and it was the case for Europol" (Interviewee 40). Spill-over effects thus played a part in rendering Europol's supranational entrepreneurship so successful.

The emergence of Europol's policy entrepreneurship is perhaps best described as 'self-fulfilling prophecy' (Interviewees 7, 9, 21 & 30). Talking about Europol as a semi-autonomous actor – a justified entity in its own right within EU police cooperation – consistently enhanced the organisation's reputation and legitimacy, which in turn fed into the image of Europol as the core of European policing. The more its officials promoted Europol and its services, and the more the latter were used by domestic law enforcement officers, the more demand was generated for further services and involvement. This snowball effect gradually but continuously raised the profile of Europol as an agent as well as its legitimacy as initiator and principal with the power to shape state preferences.

By the time the Council was discussing the ECD, Europol had built a solid practical track record and a clientele network beyond its original mandate. Although the organisation did not exert as much or as direct influence on governments as the European Commission, its continuous advocacy and role within EU police cooperation contributed to shaping state preferences in favour of integrating Europol into the EU framework. This influence would only continue to grow in line with its institutional development and professionalisation (Interviewee 32).

Institutional Choice in a Nutshell: State Preferences on the Three Dimensions of Differentiated Integration

In the early 2000s, a number of developments motivated Member States to further integrate EU police cooperation. Compared to previous integration initiatives, the ECD constitutes an unprecedented leap in the integration of EU police cooperation, possibly still the most significant one to date. Transforming Europol into an EU agency substantially increased vertical integration by giving the Union and its institutions a formal role in the development and oversight of the organisation. Member States' preferences to this end were primarily driven by interdependencies and supranational policy entrepreneurship. The ECD presents the culmination of a process that had been started in the early 2000s and quickly expanded the number of issue areas in Europol's mandate.

This chapter has identified three factors that seem to have mattered most as drivers of integration preferences: issue-specific interdependence, supranational policy entrepreneurship and politicisation in the wake of security crises. The above cases confirm the liberal intergovernmentalist hypothesis that high and growing interdependence drives governments to prioritise EU cooperation and integration. Rising (external) interdependence in the areas of vehicle-related crime, terrorism and illegal migration played an essential part in the establishment and ultimate (part-)integration of EUCARIS and Prüm into the EU's institutional framework. Similarly, increasing interdependence in money laundering, cybercrime and other areas of transnational organised crime shaped state preferences towards furthering Europol's role. Second, the emerging structures of EU police cooperation were intensifying internal or institutional interdependencies between domestic authorities. With the creation of EUCARIS, Prüm and Europol, cross-border cooperation grew rapidly and produced a practical need for further professionalisation. In all three cases, subnational officials and practitioners themselves favoured some degree of institutionalisation, resulting in the appointment of the EU as single reference point for data protection regarding EUCARIS, the adoption of the Prüm Council Decisions, and the establishment of Europol as the EU's official and central hub for police cooperation.

The early 2000s confirm the findings from the chapters on TREVI and the EDU. External issue-specific interdependencies provided the initial impetus for the inception of cooperation among EU law enforcement authorities. In the early integration stage, a certain (semi-)institutional interconnectedness quickly emerged among cooperating Member States and produced functional pressure to formalise cooperation. The EU framework and Europol presented effective means to solve collective action and coordination problems. However, the more asymmetrical these interdependencies were, the more likely Member States with high levels of interdependence strategically prioritised flexible integration.

From 2000 onwards, path-dependency, spill-over effects and supranational policy entrepreneurship began to increasingly shape the preferences of Member States. This presents a striking change compared to TREVI and the EDU, where supranational actors had no or only very limited influence. Earlier integration decisions were now creating functional pressure on governments to continue and expand EU police cooperation. Not only did the sunk costs of establishing Europol and investing in common action among European law enforcement officials generate a certain path-dependency, parallel developments related to the evolution of the EU made further integration among European law enforcement authorities indispensable. EU actors proactively promoted supranational settings and venues for the further development of EU police cooperation. A large range of integration initiatives illustrates this trend, particularly by the European Commission and Europol itself. These include the progressive association of EUCARIS with the EU framework and the uniformity of governance related to EU agencies that eventually led to the integration of Europol through the ECD. In response to supranational policy entrepreneurship, numerous instances of differentiation were transferred to the EU framework and central coordination placed in supranational hands. Europol and the Commission thus increasingly built a 'clientele' among the Member States and their law enforcement authorities.

Finally, politicisation in the wake of security crises mattered significantly as 'window of opportunity' for the influence of interdependence and supranational entrepreneurship on state preferences. September 11, 11-M and the London bombings created important political momentum. Each terror attack generated a public debate on the state of affairs in European police cooperation that allowed the European Commission and Europol to promote themselves. Although politicisation and a sense of crisis and urgency cannot alone explain why Member States opted for deeper integration, they had a vital and positive impact on state preferences in the early 2000s. This chapter shows that politicisation in conjunction with one of the other factors constitutes a sufficient condition for pro-integration preferences. Especially the combination of high interdependence and politicisation produced integration preferences with a sustainable and long-term effect in the area of EU police cooperation. Where public pressure reinforced functional pressure as causal mechanism, Member States prioritised substantial integration. This pattern can be observed throughout the 2000s. What is more, various instances of initial differentiation exhibited a striking lack of politicisation and public pressure. Their ultimate integration into the EU framework coincided with increasing salience or crisis momentum.

In sum, integration preferences on EU police cooperation were primarily driven by growing interdependencies and supranational policy entrepreneurship in the early 2000s. Politicisation acted as sufficient condition in conjunction with one or both of these driving factors. This seems to confirm the neofunctionalist tenet that cross-national interdependence and supranational entrepreneurship primarily drive the integration preferences of Member States. Depending on the relative (or asymmetrical) strength of both, they influence preference convergence or variation. The analysis of EU police cooperation between 2000 and 2009 additionally supports new intergovernmentalist tenets that distinguish between early and later stages of integration and claim that Member States might lose control of the process. Although EU governments opted for enhancing Europol's role, they did not originally intend to integrate it into the supranational framework. The more issue areas and powers Member States delegated to the agency, the more path-dependency and spill-overs they created that increasingly justified Europol as an actor. The early 2000s demonstrate how unintended consequences of initial cooperation decisions shaped future integration. Contrary to the decades before, state preferences on EU police cooperation were impacted by previous integration steps and the "long-run 'feedback loop' between state preferences and institutional choice" (Bickerton et al. 2015a: 707).

Studying the processes leading to EUCARIS, Prüm and the adoption of the ECD confirms that a "mixture of ideational convergence[...and] institutional diversity[...]help us understand the intensification of integration" in EU police cooperation (Bickerton et al. 2015b: 709). Diverging domestic security cultures, bureaucratic traditions and institutional environments complicated early-stage cooperation. Europol increasingly acted as socialisation platform for European police officials and played an important role in building trust among Member States' authorities. The behaviour of Europol and the European Commission in the early 2000s might provide evidence for the claim that "supranational institutions are not hard-wired to seek ever-closer union[...and that they] act strategically: when faced with a favourable environment for entrepreneurialism they may well take advantage of it[...]" (ibid.: 712).

If the findings of this chapter are to hold, the development of Europol after 2009 should be able to demonstrate a continuity and increase of spill-over effects as well as supranational entrepreneurship in the formation of state preferences. Additionally, a further decrease of domestic bureaucratic resistance and differentiation initiatives should be observable as the integration of EU police cooperation advances.

Notes

1 This table provides a non-exhaustive overview. The totality of cooperating states also derives from other legal bases.
2 Draft Regulation COM/2012/0164 final.
3 Council doc. 2001/C 176/05.
4 Council docs. 2002/C 42/08 and /10.

5

SNOWBALLING INTO THE FUTURE? THE EUROPOL REGULATION AND BEYOND

When the ECD transformed Europol into the EU's official law enforcement agency on 1 January 2010, it marked an unprecedented step in the integration of EU police cooperation. Barely six years later, in May 2016, Member States adopted the Europol Regulation, which rendered the ECD obsolete. The Regulation empowered the EU in various regards. Not only did it alter the general voting rules in Europol's Management Board from two-thirds to simple majority for most decisions, but it also strengthened Europol's standing by widening its analytical capacity and allowing it to ask Member States to initiate criminal investigations and operational cooperation. The Regulation additionally introduced formal roles in the agency's governance for a Joint Parliamentary Scrutiny Group (JPSG) and the European Data Protection Supervisor (EDPS). It thus marks the peak of integration dynamics in EU police cooperation to date, including a revised proposal from 2020, which has further strengthened Europol and its legal framework.

While rising interdependencies and intensifying spill-over effects had already been important enhancers of integration preferences around 2000, they likewise shaped state preferences on Europol after 2010. Internal and external interdependence among European police authorities deepened further, through cooperation structures but also in the fight against common threats, and a steadily growing nexus between different areas of crime and terrorism. Thanks to Europol's new status as EU agency, the organisation had gained a constant foothold as actor in EU police cooperation and was increasingly emancipating itself. It continued to benefit substantially from processes that Member States had set in motion in the early 2000s, particularly spill-over effects from the Lisbon Treaty. Supranational policy entrepreneurship likewise continued to play a role and increase significantly. Politicising events – especially the crisis momentum from terror attacks – provided windows of opportunity for EU actors to shape state preferences in

DOI: 10.4324/9781003262176-6

favour of integration. Although politicisation did not act as independent driving factor, it was frequently present in a set of jointly sufficient conditions that influenced governments to pursue EU action.

A Centre Approach on the Path to an Ever More Sophisticated EU Actor

Following its transformation into an EU agency in 2010, Europol quickly sought to promote and establish itself as centre of law enforcement expertise with a focus on criminal analysis. Four dedicated centres were launched at the agency between 2013 and 2020: the EC3, the ECTC, the European Migrant Smuggling Centre (EMSC), and the European Financial and Economic Crime Centre (EFECC). They all represented reactions to rising interdependence in these issue areas as well as supranational policy entrepreneurship in the wake of politicising events. Globalisation and digitisation acted as key transformers of governments' preferences. However, the extent to which they were able to effectuate integration at Europol differed across issue areas. Only in the cyber security domain, functional pressure from growing interdependence was the primary driver of state preferences, and the EC3 accordingly an operationally-informed integration initiative. By contrast, governmental preferences to launch the ECTC and the EMSC were strongly shaped by public pressure and post-crisis politicisation, while the EFECC was the result of the combined influence of functional and political pressure. The establishment of Europol's operational centres demonstrates that high interdependence may independently act as sufficient condition for pro-integration preferences, while politicisation acts as a multiplier and usually forms part of a set of sufficient conditions.

The European Cybercrime Centre

Europol had begun to develop a capacity on cybercrime long before the EC3 commenced operations (see Figure 5.1). In 2002, its mandate was first extended to this issue area and a High Tech Crime Centre (HTCC) was launched at Europol, although the centre remained very small with only four officials until 2010 (EUC 2010: 124). The EC3 was launched in January 2013 as one of five strategic objectives defined by the 2010 EU Internal Security Strategy (ISS). It officially made Europol the EU's central hub for the fight against cybercrime. Europol' activities within the EC3 were to cover a broad range of topics, including cybercrime by organised criminal groups, online child sexual abuse and cyberattacks (European Commission 2012b: 4). The creation of the EC3 was primarily driven by interdependencies and supranational policy entrepreneurship. Politicisation only played a complementary role as enabler of the former two. The process illustrates how these driving factors gradually and jointly built political momentum, and shifted state preferences towards vertical integration in the cyber domain.

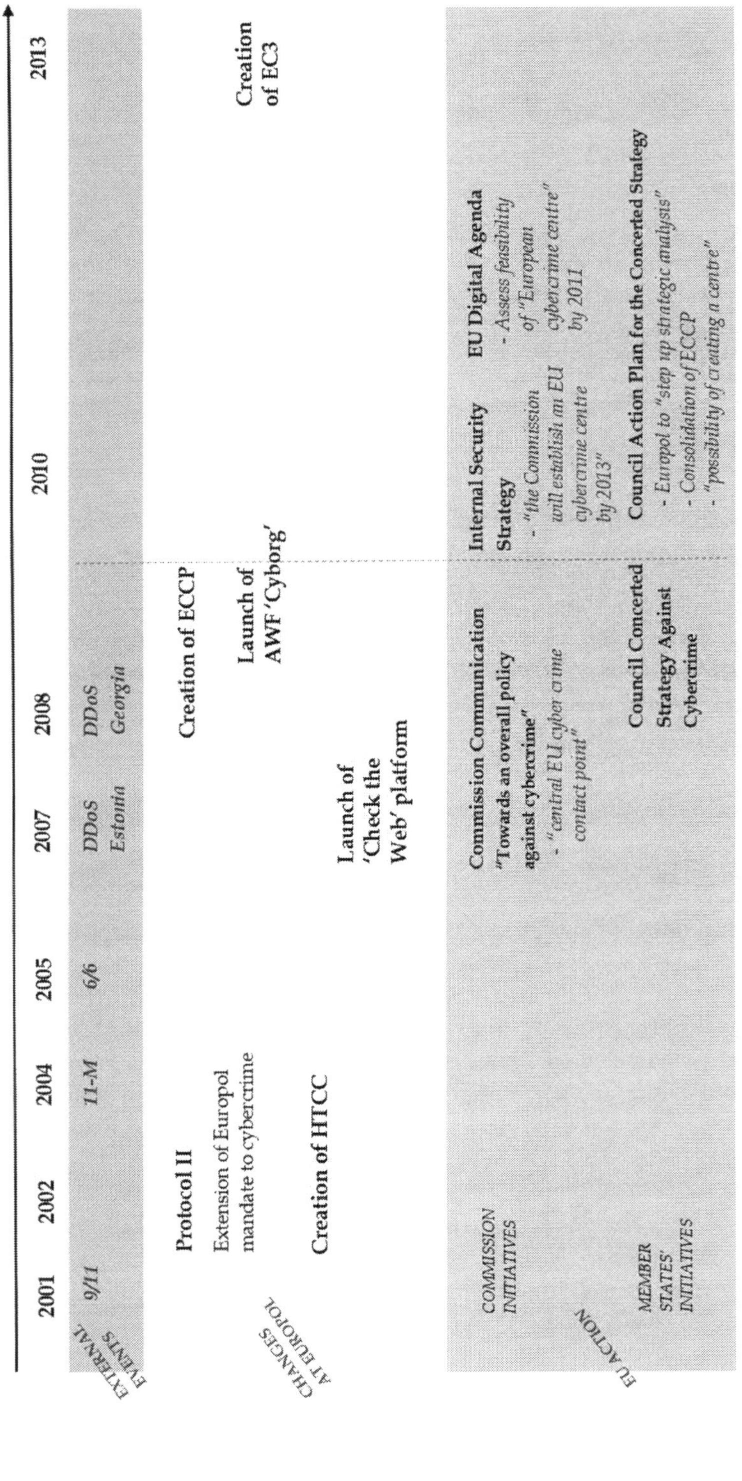

FIGURE 5.1 A Chronology of Europol's European Cybercrime Centre (EC3)

INTERDEPENDENCIES: THE IMPACT OF GLOBALISATION AND THE INTERNET

Growing internal and external interdependencies in cyberspace were key drivers to this end. International police cooperation on cyber security was becoming increasingly important (Interviewees 32, 35, 36 & 39; Maaßen 2018). The interplay and interconnectedness among humans, physical systems, technology, and cyberspace were growing, with an unprecedented intensity and professionalisation of emerging networks (Interviewees 11, 32 & 37). As a consequence, territorial delimitations were becoming superfluous in many regards; new forms of crime and illicit activities online were exploiting this space outside conventional forms of governance. As one interviewee stated: "The Internet and especially the Internet of Things have expanded the attack surface of nation-states everywhere. They have completely transformed the business model of criminals. Everything is cyber nowadays: terrorism, drug trafficking, money laundering and so on" (Interviewee 28). The day-to-day operations of domestic police officials demonstrated the rapid emergence of cyber across almost all criminal issue areas, and its cross-country magnitude as 'borderless crime' (Interviewees 36–39).

Increasing interdependencies had a massive impact on police work and by extension on the preferences of Member States. Traditional unilateral or informal models could no longer effectively combat quickly evolving "forms of crime that did and could not exist thirty years ago" (Interviewee 35). In the cyber realm, countries and law enforcement authorities faced the same security threats and challenges posed by illicit actors (Interviewee 37). The growing digital and global interconnectedness additionally facilitated an increase in the complexity and sophistication of other types of crime. Transnational organised crime benefited tremendously from the rise of the Internet and mobile communications technology. Whereas criminal activities in the late 1990s had still been carried out by hierarchical, territory-based groups relying mostly on analogue means, from the turn of the millennium they were becoming increasingly international, resembling global supply chains in their transactional, network-based structures (Interviewees 13, 25, 26 & 44). The Internet significantly extended the scope of illicit activities. Requiring comparatively low-cost, low-tech means on the one hand, and lacking robust law enforcement and governance structures, the Internet made cybercrime available to everybody at any time (Interviewee 28).

Internal interdependencies were likewise rising and exerted functional pressure on EU Member States to step up police cooperation. Emerging EU structures and systems were becoming a potential target to malicious cyber activities. Somewhat ironically, the professionalisation and digitisation of central cooperation tools originally intended to strengthen EU police cooperation were now coming back to haunt practitioners by expanding the attack surface to the EU level (Interviewees 16 & 20).

POLITICISATION: LEARNING FROM CRISIS EVENTS

Politicisation ultimately triggered states to act on their preferences. A series of politicising events illustrated just how interconnected countries were becoming, and how exposed to threats from cyberspace (see Figure 5.1). The September 11 attacks of 2001 first brought cyber on the radar of security authorities in Europe and the US. The involvement and deliberate use of the Internet in the planning, organisation and execution of this terror attack raised the salience of cyberspace among practitioners (Interviewees 27 & 35). The 2004 Madrid and 2005 London bombings further fuelled political momentum. They made European security authorities drastically aware of the opportunities cyberspace offered to terrorists, not only criminals, as well as the chances for networking and cooperation between both. The Internet clearly acted as multiplier of radical and extremist content. Recruitment and radicalisation were no longer reliant on mouth-to-mouth propaganda but freely accessible and diffused online (Interviewee 28; Maaßen 2018).

The 11-M and 6/6 attacks politicised cyber security 'by proxy' and generated functional spill-over effects (cf. Carrapiço & Farrand 2018). Fighting terrorism and organised crime at the EU level more and more required combatting cybercrime as well. Post-crisis momentum and functional spill-overs helped turn cyber into a field of its own and into a priority for EU police cooperation (Interviewees 27 & 35). This can be seen in a number of governmental integration initiatives in the early 2000s. In the aftermath of the Madrid bombings in 2004, European heads of state or government agreed to develop a strategy and action plan to combat radicalisation and recruitment to terrorism (Council 2005c: 1). The strategy was adopted one year later and included measures to counter terrorist use of the Internet (ibid. 2005a). It stressed the importance of collective action at the EU level and highlighted the role of the European Commission. Following the 2005 London bombings, the Commission "announced its intention to explore possibilities of tackling of content used to radicalise individuals for terrorism on the Internet" (ibid. 2007b: 2). At the national level, Member States launched the 'Check the Web' project at Europol in May 2007 (see Figure 5.1). 'Check the Web' was established as central information portal and technical platform for the collection and storage of data related to Islamist terrorist propaganda and radical content online (Europol 2012d). The original proposal had come from the German subnational level, an initiative by the German BKA (Bundestag 2015a: 1). The project was first discussed multilaterally outside the EU framework within the G6-format in the spring of 2006 (Interviewees 35 & 40). Germany deliberately launched the platform as a smaller pilot with only a few Member States because domestic capacities related to cyber security varied across countries (Interviewees 25 & 26). It was considered easier and more efficient to adopt a flexible approach with an avant-garde group of states and circumvent formal intergovernmental or EU channels. The establishment of 'Check the Web' thus strongly resembles the creation of Prüm and especially EUCARIS. Both likewise originated from the subnational level and initial differentiation was similarly driven by practitioners' interest to quickly achieve operational results. In the case of 'Check the Web,' asymmetrical capacities and strong subnational policy entrepreneurship played a crucial role in shaping state preferences in favour of (initial) differentiation.

Comparable to Prüm and EUCARIS, politicisation helped shift preferences towards integration and led to the formal transfer of 'Check the Web' to Europol. The political momentum generated by 6/6 as well as expectations related to the Council Presidency that Germany assumed in January 2007 generated significant public pressure on German policymakers to act. The same logic of political legacy that influenced Germany to propose the integration of the Prüm Treaty into the EU framework also applied to the issue area of cyber. 'Check the Web' was subsequently established at Europol in May 2007. Although the German Council Presidency initially organised the expert meetings, this responsibility was soon transferred to Europol (Council 2007b: 5). This not only formally widened the agency's functional scope and advanced horizontal integration by extending cooperation to all Member States, but it also gave Europol a key coordination role and thus strengthened vertical integration.

While the Madrid and London bombings generated the political momentum to integrate 'Check the Web' at Europol, pro-integration preferences were shaped primarily by high and skyrocketing interdependencies in the area of cyber. At the Council meeting of 22–23 May 2007 Member States discussed the launch of the project and measures to counter terrorist use of the Internet:

> It is hardly possible for one individual member state to cover all suspicious terrorism related activities on the Internet. [...]In all of this work the activities of the various actors (Member States, Commission, Europol, SitCen, et al.) have to be coordinated in a targeted way.
>
> *(Council 2007b: 3)*

Two other crises demonstrated this growing functional pressure to cooperate and thus impacted integration preferences: the cyberattacks against Estonia and Georgia. On 27 April 2007, a series of Distributed-Denial-of-Service (DDoS) attacks targeted Estonia's critical infrastructure. The attacks continued through 18 May, "shut[ting] down the websites of all government ministries, two major banks, and several political parties[...as well as affecting] the parliamentary email server" (Herzog 2011: 51). Like most other EU Member States, Estonia's critical infrastructure relied increasingly on the Internet and electronic forms of communication and information processing. The cyberattacks were able to take down a large share of online services and significantly disrupt the day-to-day business of government officials and ordinary citizens alike (Interviewees 25 & 26).

The unprecedented attacks demonstrated the pitfalls of digitisation: cyberspace as entry point to the electronically interconnected national infrastructures of entire countries. While 9/11, 11-M and 6/6 had only politicised cyber by proxy, the cyberattacks on Estonia directly illustrated the emerging threat from cyberspace and cyberterrorism. Cyberterrorism may be defined as "the use of computer network tools to shut down critical national infrastructures[...]or to coerce or intimidate a government or civilian population" (Lewis 2002: 1). Globalisation and digitisation "enabled transnational groups—such as the Russian diaspora—to avenge their grievances by threatening the sovereignty of nation-states in cyberspace" (Herzog 2011: 49). Indeed, most malicious traffic that hit Estonia between 27 April and 18 May 2007 had come from other countries, and directions for targeting Estonian websites had been distributed online (Ottis 2008: 164). While the cyberattacks on Estonia served as "a wake-up call" for European governments, they did not affect more critical systems and infrastructure, and failed to completely halt public and political everyday life (Interviewees 25 & 26). Nonetheless, the attacks practically demonstrated the caveats of digital interconnectedness and the potential of cyberspace for abuse by criminal and terrorist groups. They reinforced Member States' determination to better cooperate on cyber matters and created an opening for Germany's proposal to launch 'Check the Web' at Europol.

The cyberattacks against Georgia presented the final political flashpoint in the series of politicising events that shaped state preferences in favour of further integration. Beginning on 20 July 2008, Georgian servers were flooded with malicious traffic (Korns & Kastenberg 2009: 60ff.). A second, considerably larger round of DDoS attacks followed only a few weeks later in August. The initial wave was mainly directed towards websites of Georgia's government and media, whereas later ones targeted the servers of banks, corporations and public institutions (Interviewees 18 & 25; Shakarian et al. 2013: 24). A large number of servers were shut down by the attacks and continued to disrupt government activities and communication throughout August (Hart 2008). The attacks paralysed Georgia's banking system for multiple days, and thus had an economic impact as well (Corbin 2009; Shakarian et al. 2013: 27). As a result, the country was increasingly cut off electronically and isolated from the outside world. Yet, similar to the Estonian cyberattacks, the result could have been much worse had it not been for "Georgia's limited Internet infrastructure" (Markoff 2008).

The 2008 DDoS attacks against Georgia have been described as "the birth of true, operational cyber warfare[...and] the most significant development ever seen in the field of information security or cyber conflict studies" (Thomson 2008). Whereas the July attacks had still been widely considered cybercrime, strong evidence suggested that Russia might have been involved in the August wave, which would make it an act of war (White 2018: 9). The peak of the DDoS attacks against Georgia in August 2008 coincided timely with physical Russian military action as part of the Russian-Georgian war (Korns & Kastenberg 2009: 60). The malicious traffic hitting Georgian servers came from outside the country and the malicious software could be traced back to hosting services in Russia (Shakarian et al. 2013: 28f.). The cyberattacks are now widely regarded as a targeted cyberoperation within Russia's information warfare against Georgia in the context of the Russian-Georgian war. It presents the first case of hybrid warfare, employing both cyberspace and conventional methods alongside each other (ibid.: 24ff.).

The 2008 DDoS attacks had a tremendous psychological impact on governments, especially in Europe and the US. They demonstrated how digital interdependencies could threaten the security of entire nation-states and how the Internet was widening the attack surface. It extended the number of potential attackers from hierarchical, criminal groups to potentially every individual online. "The cyberattacks of the Russia-Georgia War provide empirical evidence of the extent to which cyberspace empowers third-party non-state actors in modern conflict" (White 2018: 5). Although the attacks can still not be clearly attributed to the Russian government, evidence strongly suggests the involvement of Russia-based non-state actors (EUC 2010: 11; Nazario 2009). This included criminal groups, professional hackers and ordinary citizens. Although the malicious traffic was directed at Georgia, global interdependencies made every country or entity with digital ties to Georgia a potential target. The emergency transfer of Georgian government websites to the servers of an American web-hosting enterprise suddenly extended the list of targets to the US (White 2018: 9–10). Similarly, the transfer of Foreign Ministry web content from Georgia to Google servers in the US heightened the potential for spill-over attacks on American entities (Korns & Kastenberg 2009: 67).

The cyberattacks against Estonia and Georgia constituted a wake-up call to governments in the EU. They drastically raised the salience of cyber as an issue area and underlined the need for international cooperation in view of globalisation and digital interconnectedness (Interviewees 36–39). Contrary to the crisis momentum generated in the aftermath of 9/11, 11-M and 6/6, politicisation following the cyberattacks against Estonia and Georgia was largely of a political nature. Rather than producing public pressure among European constituencies, the incidents triggered political pressure at EU and international level to prevent similar attacks in the future. "The attacks in Estonia and Georgia changed everything. Now cyber is high on the political agenda everywhere" (Interviewee 38). This seems to confirm the asymmetrical effect of politicisation and the public eye. Although fields like cyber may well become politicised by proxy, that is, in conjunction with other, more 'high-profile' issue areas like terrorism, and thus rise in salience among practitioners and government officials, they seem to be less likely to become politicised independently or among individuals and civil society. Perhaps this is best explained by the lack of a clear attribution of legal responsibility for protecting individuals in cyberspace and the limited visibility of cybercrime and cyberterrorism as well as their consequences in the everyday lives of citizens (Interviewee 33). In contrast to physical attacks like the Madrid and London bombings, the cyberattacks on Estonia and Georgia exhibited a danger to the functioning and sovereignty of nation-states rather than the immediate safety of national citizens. Additionally, the extent of the DDoS incidents was mostly visible to security practitioners and officials instead of the general public.

The DDoS attacks generated significant political momentum at the national and the EU level and shifted state preferences further towards integration. Newly developed National Cyber Security Strategies (NCSS) formally recognised the growing transnational dimension in this issue area (Interviewees 21, 22, 24, 27 & 35). Various Member States for the first time included cyber security and defence as priority areas in their national security strategies, including European and international elements. In June 2008, France pursued action in this area at the EU level (Interviewees 28 & 31; cf. EUC 2010: 125). Perhaps unsurprisingly coinciding with the French Council Presidency in the second half of 2008, France presented a proposal and tasked Europol with the creation of the ECCP, a "platform for reporting offences noted on the Internet" and asked it to "coordinate [the] European response to Internet-related crime" (Quillé 2009: 6).

EMERGING SUPRANATIONAL POLICY ENTREPRENEURSHIP IN THE CYBER REALM

Supranational policy entrepreneurs benefited tremendously from the political momentum from the attacks against Estonia and Georgia (see Figure 5.1). Europol not only acted on the invitation of the French Council Presidency to establish the ECCP, the agency proactively "proposed to open a dedicated [Analysis Work File] AWF" to support domestic authorities in combatting cybercrime by organised groups (ibid.: 7). AWFs constitute formal projects at Europol in direct support of investigations into related criminal cases in the Member States. This enables "Europol specialists[...to] prioritise resources" and assume a proactive, central role in the cross-national analysis of related data and the coordination of information exchange and operational cooperation (Europol n.d.-b). Opening the AWF 'Cyborg' at Europol widened its involvement beyond the mere development and hosting of the ECCP technical platform to a proactive analytical role. In addition to Europol, the European Commission leveraged the political momentum to push state preferences towards EU cooperation on cyber matters. Following the adoption of Council Directive 2008/114/EC in December 2008, by which Member States committed to evaluate further action to protect European critical (cyber) infrastructure, the Commission presented an EU strategy and action plan to the Council in 2009 (European Commission 2009b). The Commission suggested to prioritise the establishment of Computer Emergency Response Teams (CERTs) in all Member States and proposed several actions at the EU level. In the light of the incidents in Estonia and Georgia, the initiative was positively received and adopted as initial "framework for coordination and cooperation 'to engage Member States, the private sector and civil society'" (EUC 2010: 19).

Despite the positive momentum in favour of EU collective action in the fight against threats from cyberspace, not every European government developed a strong pro-integration preference. The UK did not include in its NCSS "a single reference to the EU by name" (ibid.: 17). The national approach to cyber security quickly came under fire as British practitioners and political elites increasingly debated global interdependencies. An in-depth inquiry was initiated in October 2009 to assess the potential role for the EU in the protection against cyberattacks. The final report unsurprisingly underlined the transnational character of cyberspace and the Internet, and stressed the need to strengthen the international outlook in the UK's NCSS. Nonetheless, the EU was only seen as "second best" option, since external interdependencies were global in nature (ibid.: 17). Resembling the initiation of the Trevi Groupin the 1970s, British policymakers preferred universal membership in the common fight against cybercrime and other cyber-related threats. "[T...]he Internet operates as a global phenomenon and does not recognise borders," noted a Government statement (ibid.).

Internal interdependence and path-dependency ultimately trumped the global interconnectedness in threats and swayed the British preference towards the EU format. Again resembling the TREVI case, cooperation structures at international level were weak at best, often informal and ad hoc. They did not constitute an actual institutional alternative to the rather well-established EU format. Although the North Atlantic Treaty Organisation (NATO) seemed like an obvious choice, persisting disagreement over common definitions and technical standards rendered the prospect of effective cooperation difficult, even unlikely (Interviewees 16 & 35–37). Institutional interdependencies within the EU were relatively higher and formal cooperation structures already in place. Cybercrime had been incorporated into Europol's areas of competence in 2002 and a number of related projects had been successfully launched at the organisation by 2009, including the HTCC, 'Check the Web,' the ECCP and the AWF 'Cyborg' (see Figure 5.1). Member States were increasingly internally interlinked and relied on each other's response, defence and resilience capacities (Krings 2018; Münch 2018).

High intra-EU interconnectivity alongside the lack of global institutional alternatives in the cyber domain account for the horizontal shift of the British preference towards EU police cooperation. Institutional linkages and path-dependency potentially explain why Member States ultimately opted for deeper integration, including the creation of the EC3. A lack of formalised cooperation produced significant collective action problems in the day-to-day work of EU practitioners and generated functional pressure to integrate. Whereas the ultimate responsibility for cyber security continued to lie with national governments, the majority of cyber incidents were local manifestations of global phenomena. Insufficient cross-border coordination and diverging domestic strategies challenged police officials when combatting online threats. Different understandings of cyber security and asymmetrical cyber capacities complicated cooperation. Although most European NCSS included "general cyber crime and espionage type of threats," they varied considerably concerning what constituted a threat, how to define cyber security, and the extent to which they emphasised cooperation at EU and international level (Luiijf et al. 2013: 5). Perhaps even more importantly, Member States varied greatly in their dependence on the Internet and their cyber security and defence capabilities (Interviewees 7, 18, 19, 25 & 26). In an ever more connected landscape of the EU information systems and electronically interlinked national infrastructures, the potential attack surface of a single country was *de facto* extended to all Member States; a weak cyber security capacity in one country posed a risk to all. The British inquiry accordingly concluded that this policy domain presented "a legitimate area for the EU to be concerned about, and that it had some role to play[...] as bringing the Member States with less developed systems for handling cyber-attacks up to the level of the most advanced" (EUC 2010: 15–16). By 2010, the need for international police cooperation on cyber issues had become an undisputed reality among politicians and law enforcement officials. Despite "an exponential growth [of cyber security risks] over the past decade, [...]the ability to adapt to and counter these risks[...was] lagging behind" (Interviewee 37).

EU actors exploited this political momentum. Around 2010, supranational policy entrepreneurship was additionally enabled by political spill-overs. Integration decisions of the Member States from the late 1990s and early 2000s were beginning to show effect and facilitate cultivated spill-overs as an influence on state preferences. The ECD had granted Europol a new organisational self-concept (Interviewees 5, 10 & 30). It could now promote its services from a completely different point of departure as the EU's official law enforcement agency. Functional and public pressure further opened the floodgates to supranational policy entrepreneurship. They were strategically leveraged by EU actors in the promotion of vertical integration. Policymakers were faced with public pressure to demonstrate strength and take action on the one hand, and with functional pressure to manage intensifying collective action problems in practice. It was politically difficult to justify a national course of action (Interviewees 14, 21 & 27). Supranational actors were able to capitalise on this situation. Europol continued to reiterate the emergence of new forms of crime due to the "increasing 'technicalisation'" everywhere, and the growing danger of virtual organised crime groups and 'high-tech crime' to develop "into a principal criminal threat" (EUC 2010: 124). It repeatedly stressed the need for intra-EU harmonisation of cyber capabilities: "There is clear asymmetrical development; some MS [Member States] are forging ahead with great advances in certain areas, whilst other MS lag behind in terms of technology" (EUC 2010: 16).

The Commission likewise played a major role in advocating the EU as primary venue for police cooperation on cybercrime. Following the DDoS attacks against Estonia in 2007, the European Commission published a communication setting out steps "Towards a general policy on the fight against cybercrime" (European Commission 2007). Although the document acknowledged the legal limitations of the EU's competence in this intergovernmental policy domain, it listed a number of possible measures and asked governments to include the Commission and pursue EU action alongside national measures (ibid.: 9). Most importantly, the Commission alluded to the possible creation of a "central EU cyber crime contact point," the first formal mention of what would eventually become the EC3. Yet, supranational entrepreneurs would only be able to generate enough momentum in 2010 to shift state preferences accordingly.

While no single politicising event sparked the launch of the EC3, EU actors leveraged the aggregate political momentum that had built progressively since 2000. By harnessing both functional pressure from practical interdependencies and public concerns in relation to cyber security and organised crime, Europol and especially the Commission managed to develop a sustainable entrepreneurship and influence Member States' preferences (Interviewees 12, 13 & 31). Amidst a series of cyberattacks by hacker groups like Anonymous and LulzSec in 2011 that showcased the vulnerability of increasing electronic interconnectedness, the European Commission stressed to Member States that: "[...t]he threat is very much a real one. The number of cyber attacks in the world is on the rise and the cost of cybercrime is skyrocketing" (Malmström 2011: 1). Commission and Europol officials coordinated closely to raise the salience of this topic and build awareness among EU governments about business opportunities for criminals, "crime as a service" that was easily accessible online (Interviewees 17, 19, 24 & 28). By highlighting the financial losses and societal costs associated with cybercrime, supranational entrepreneurs were drawing the attention of Member States to the physical effects of digital causes. As a consequence, it was becoming "extremely rare that one ha[...d] to discuss the necessity of international cooperation with police officials and national authorities" (Interviewee 35).

The cyberattacks against Estonia and Georgia finally acted as multiplier of pressure on Member States to further integrate (Interviewees 23, 26, 34 & 35). Heightened salience in the aftermath of the attacks drew attention to existing interdependencies and re-emphasised functional pressure to cooperate. Moreover, politicisation among the media, practitioners and civil society generated public pressure, which EU actors harnessed. One practitioner described this as "a PR [public relations] effect reinforced by common sense arguments: there has to be tangible progress, it needs to be quick and publicly visible, and it's simply more efficient to do it at EU level. So the EU steps in" (Interviewee 28). The JHA Council Conclusions from 27–28 November 2008 exemplify this phenomenon. Member States built on the Commission's suggestions for a general cybercrime policy and adopted a concerted work strategy, in which they formally acknowledged the "continual increase in offences observed on the Internet which are increasingly transnational," and asked the Commission to support EU governments in the assessment of practical measures (Council 2008: 1).

Against this backdrop, the Commission exerted considerable influence on the EU ISS that was adopted by the Member States in February 2010 (see Figure 5.1). It listed cybercrime as one of the "main crime-related risks and threats facing Europe today" and made it a formal priority within the EU ASFJ (Council 2010a: 2). The Strategy as a whole reflected the pro-EU discourse of the Commission, Europol and other supranational actors (Interviewees 12, 13 & 15). Cyber security was framed as common challenge for the EU and European police cooperation rather than single Member States or authorities, cybercrime as a "cross-border, anonymous threat to our information systems and[...] many additional challenges for law-enforcement agencies" (ibid.: 14). To advance integration-friendly discourse and strengthen path-dependency and supranational entrepreneurship within EU police cooperation, the European Commission increasingly harnessed Europol's practical track record and positive reputation. While Europol also sought to proactively raise its profile around 2010, it was itself becoming a "tool for raising the visibility of EU policy-making in JHA" (Interviewee 35).

In view of heightened political pressure to adapt national preferences to a more transnational approach, a gradual paradigm shift emerged in EU police cooperation to follow and reinforce common institutions and herald "an age of EU agencies" (Interviewee 14). This can be seen in the common Action Plan to implement the concerted strategy to combat cybercrime that was adopted in April 2010 (see Figure 5.1). In this plan, the Council of the EU asked Europol to "step up strategic analysis on cyber crime," and invited both Europol and the Commission to support Member States in the "consolidation, [...]revision and, if necessary, the updating of the functions assigned to Europol's European Cybercrime Platform" (Council 2010b: 2). Most importantly, European governments finally took up the Commission's idea of a "central EU cyber crime contact point" (European Commission 2007: 9). In 2010, the Council tasked the Commission to conduct "a feasibility study on the possibility of creating a centre" and to "consider, in particular, the aim, scope and possible financing of the centre and whether it should be located at Europol" (Council 2010b: 4). Member States thus not only recognised the Commission and Europol as key entities of EU police cooperation but also *de facto* legitimised them as actors in their own right. The 2010 Action Plan may therefore be regarded as critical moment in the development of a supranational mandate on cybercrime. It acted as catalyst for the creation of the EC3 by reinforcing the ISS as well as the roles of the European Commission, Europol and other EU actors.

THE EUROPEAN COMMISSION

The European Commission progressively produced cultivated spill-overs related to cyber security. Its EU Digital Agenda from August 2010 directly reacted to the Action Plan in various regards (European Commission 2010b). It urged Member States to jointly counter "the rise of new forms of crime – 'cybercrime'" (:5) and to "[...s]et up or adapt national alert platforms to the Europol cybercrime platform" (:18). The Digital Agenda not only formally acknowledged the ECCP as central tool, but it also for the first time proposed the establishment of a European cybercrime centre (ibid.: 18). To implement the ISS, it boldly announced: "By 2013, the EU will establish, within existing structures, a cybercrime centre,[... which] should become the focal point in Europe's fight against cybercrime" (European Commission 2010c: 9). This formal declaration perfectly embodies the evolving self-confidence of the European Commission and is remarkable for two main reasons. First, it by far exceeded the task given to the Commission by the Member States in their Action Plan on cybercrime from April 2010. They had merely invited the Commission to "draw up a feasibility study on the possibility of creating a centre" and assess "the aim, scope and possible financing of the centre and whether it should be located at Europol" (Council 2010b: 4). The Commission's November Communication reflected a very different understanding and listed the creation of a European cybercrime centre as a definite rather than possible action. Second, the Commission declared ownership for the initiative rather than presenting itself as mere agent. Perhaps even more striking, an accompanying memo to the document deviated significantly and read, "the *Commission* will establish an EU cybercrime centre by 2013" (European Commission 2010a). The Commission's discourse and proposed actions testified to its evolving organisational emancipation and self-confidence as actor within cyber security.

In its promotion of the EU as main policy venue for police cooperation on cyberspace, the European Commission increasingly employed a strategy of deliberate politicisation. It began to harness and fuel public pressure to shape state preferences in favour of strengthening common institutions like Europol. Various interviewees emphasised the importance of this recently emerging, supranationally driven politicisation of police cooperation and JHA (Interviewees 6, 12, 15, 23 & 33). As one senior official phrased it: "politicisation has become a tool of legitimisation for the EU in the area of JHA" (Interviewee 27). Although no new phenomenon, as the trend had already begun in the 2000s, the European Commission's narratives and discursive strategies reached a "whole new quality and dimension" from 2010 onwards (Interviewee 23). Whereas previous pro-EU discourse had remained relatively vague, underlining the general need to cooperate on a level above the national one in view of globalisation and digitisation, it was now becoming much more concrete (Interviewees 6, 32 & 35). Emerging cyber threats were explicitly framed as collective action problems and complemented by securitisation narratives stressing the necessity to move from standalone intergovernmental solutions to integrated 'one-stop shop' solutions at the EU level (Interviewees 16, 18, 23, 28 & 44).

Supranational politicisation of police cooperation on cyber matters additionally harnessed public pressure. Rationality-focused arguments revolving around the functional need to integrate were more and more supplemented by arguments about the growing public demand for EU action. The Commission deliberately "instrumentalised public opinion polls to push EU involvement" in JHA (Interviewee 27). It began to fortify its integration initiatives by citing Eurobarometer reports and polls about the attitudes of European citizens towards security (Interviewees 6, 12, 15, 23 & 33). The long-standing public opinion across Member States was consistently high in favour of EU action. EU decision-making in the fight against organised crime – rather than unilaterally agreed approaches – had been receiving almost constantly above 60% public support among European citizens until 2010 (see Figure 5.2). The European

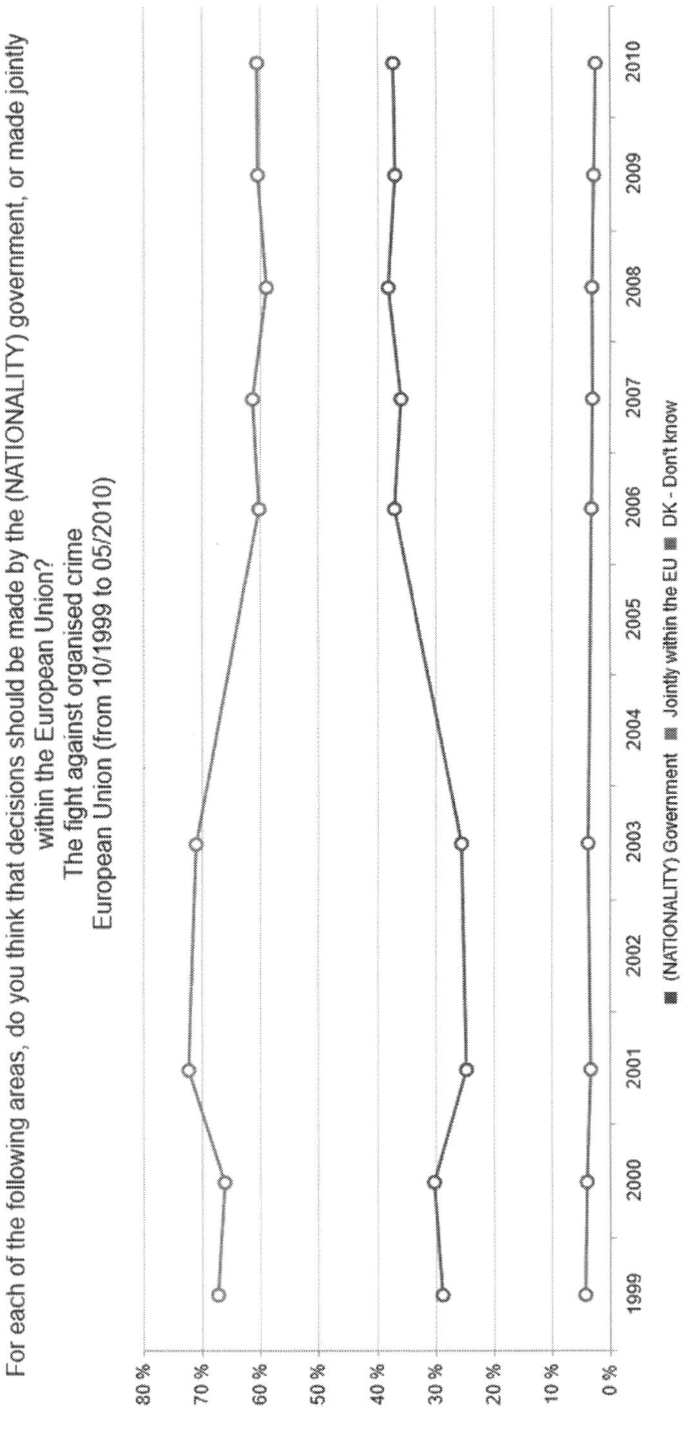

FIGURE 5.2 Public Support for EU Action in the Fight against Organised Crime (1999–2010)

Compiled by the author, based on European Commission (2019), Eurobarometer Interactive

Commission could and did rely on these numbers to strengthen its legitimacy as an actor. Its proposed implementing actions for the ISS were accordingly justified: "Four out of five Europeans want more action at EU level against organised crime and terrorism" (European Commission 2010c: 2).

EUROPOL, COMMON SENSE ARGUMENTS AND PUBLIC PRESSURE

Supranational actors likewise leveraged public pressure to favourably shape state preferences in the discussions on the creation of a European cybercrime centre. The Commission emphasised the relevance and effect of threats from cyberspace on everyday life. Once again relying on Eurobarometer data, it stressed that more than 50% of European citizens were openly concerned about cyber security (European Commission 2012a). Officials from the European Commission and Europol continuously underlined the negative effects of cybercrime for private individuals and companies on the one hand and of isolated counter strategies and policies within the EU. Both asserted, networked security and integrated crime-fighting approaches were adamantly needed to protect citizens in cyberspace and required central actors to coordinate this process at the EU level (Interviewees 12 & 19):

> [T...]here has never been any attempt to link together these policies in a coherent and comprehensive strategy. [T...]here is now a unique opportunity to take a more strategic approach, and to identify and exploit synergies between the various activities.
>
> *(European Commission 2010a)*

To this end, the Commission saw a central role for itself and did not shy away from formulating this in the according Communication (ibid. 2010c).

When the fate of the EC3 was decided in 2012, path-dependency and the economic benefits of a central capacity at the EU level amplified the effects of supranational entrepreneurship. An independent feasibility study had been conducted by RAND Europe for the European Commission. It considered four main scenarios: "[...m]aintaining the status quo[, ...an] ECC owned by Europol[, ...an] ECC hosted but not owned by Europol[, ...and a] virtual ECC" (Robinson et al. 2012: 2). Maintaining the *status quo* in the fight against cybercrime was not an option, as "[...c]ybercriminals can leverage poor co-operation between different countries – this is especially true for those countries that 'export' cybercrime." (ibid.). While the remaining three options – a centre owned by Europol, only hosted by Europol or the creation of a virtual one – were comparable in terms of costs, the report found that "there were major differences in institutional complexity and the organisational parameters between the different options" (ibid.: 3). In view of the various levels and actors involved in combatting cybercrime, the experts recommended to choose "a model that places it [the centre] in the middle of a broad capability to tackle cybercrime, exploiting the strengths of each organisation that possesses existing competencies, skills and knowledge" and that this did "not necessarily mean setting up a wholly new organisation" (ibid.). The feasibility study thus recommended the launch of an EC3 at Europol (ibid.: 4).

Europol offered the advantages of an emerging central capacity and economies of scale. Since the extension of its mandate to cybercrime in 2002, its competence and involvement in this issue area had grown steadily (see Figure 5.1). Platforms like the HTCC, the ECCP and 'Check the Web' had been launched and Europol's analytical capabilities had been boosted through the creation of AWF 'Cyborg.' By 2012, Europol had been operational for over a decade and managed to build a clientele and organisational reputation and establish a positive track record among European practitioners and policymakers (Interviewees 24, 28, 34 & 35). Member States recognised the practical merit of the agency and the functional need to build on existing EU structures. Political spill-overs and path-dependency thus acted as enablers of supranational policy entrepreneurship in the cyber domain. EU actors now deliberately harnessed functional and public pressure as well as the practical demand for their unique services to generate input legitimacy on the one hand, and showcased their good track record in practice to strengthen output legitimacy.

Against this backdrop, the European Commission proposed the creation of the EC3 as "part of Europol and[...]focal point in the fight against cybercrime in the EU" in March 2012 (European Commission 2012b: 3). It was politically "not feasible to oppose" this proposal (Interviewee 27). The political climate required Member States to show a willingness to cooperate at the EU level and strengthen common institutions. Although senior officials agreed that Europol was and remained "an agency *in support* of the Member States" (Interviewee 28), it had become a credible player in its own right and increasingly acted as 'policy consultant' for domestic decision- and policymakers (Interviewees 12, 33 & 34; Santos Vara 2018: 454). Even before the EC3 launch officially made Europol the EU's central hub for the fight against cybercrime, "Europol[... had] become a driver or at least a very good political advisor" (Interviewee 33). In early June, the JHA Council adopted the Commission's proposal to launch the EC3 at Europol. By accepting to establish it as "focal point in the fight against cybercrime in the EU" (European Commission, 2012c: 3), and tasking the Commission and Europol to take the lead in the development of the EC3, Member States *de facto* transferred power to the supranational level and advanced vertical integration. Barely one month later, on 1 July 2012, an EC3 implementation team commenced work at Europol, enabling the centre to be launched by January 2013 (Europol 2014b).

The European Counter Terrorism Centre

Member States had involved Europol in the field of counterterrorism since at least 2000 (see Figure 5.3). Even before 9/11, an AWF ('Hydra') on Islamist terrorism was opened at Europol (Europol 2009: 10). A counterterrorism task force

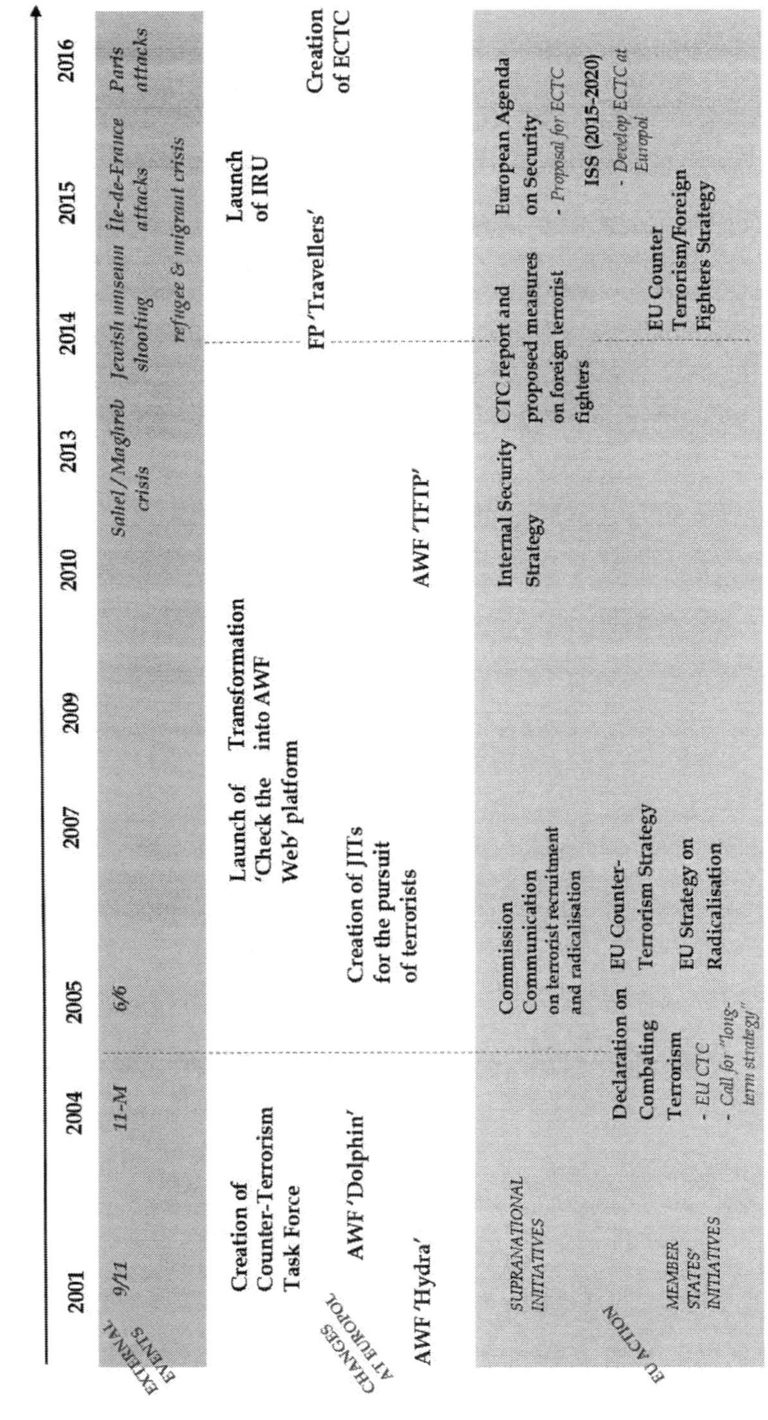

FIGURE 5.3 A Chronology of Europol's European Counter Terrorism Centre (ECTC)

commenced operations shortly after, following the initiative from Europol's Director Jürgen Storbeck and Gilles de Kerchove, JHA Director at the EU Council General Secretariat, who would later be appointed EU CTC (EUC 2008: 154; Europol 2001: 11). In September 2003, AWF 'Dolphin' was opened at the agency to collect data and provide operational support on non-Islamist extremist terrorist organisations threatening the EU (Europol 2009: 10). Europol staff initially encountered strong reluctance from European governments and national security officials, who were unwilling to share information and cooperate via Europol in this area (Interviewees 21 & 29). This would change and result in the launch of the ECTC in January 2016 as an unprecedented step towards integration. Not only did the centre formalise EU police cooperation on terrorism and consolidate existing functions and projects, but it also centralised information exchange and operational coordination at Europol. Member States thus opted for giving the organisation a key role as main broker and hub of expertise in the EU's fight against terrorism. Their preference for cementing and widening Europol's mandate in this policy domain was primarily influenced by politicisation and supranational entrepreneurship. The creation of the ECTC was achieved as a result of public and political pressure generated by terror attacks and harnessed by EU actors.

2004–2006: TERROR ATTACKS AS WINDOWS OF OPPORTUNITY FOR EU ADVOCACY

The 11-M attacks in 2004 significantly raised the salience of counterterrorism among policymakers and the public. They acted as window of opportunity for supranational entrepreneurship in this strongly intergovernmental policy domain. In the aftermath of the attack, the Commission prepared a communication on "Prevention, preparedness and response to terrorist attacks" (European Commission 2004). This communication fed into the meeting of European heads of state or government on 25 March. Their Declaration on Combating Terrorism (see Figure 5.3) called for "the development of an EU long-term strategy" and created the position of an EU CTC to "co-ordinate the work of the Council in combating terrorism and[...]maintain an overview of all the instruments at the Union's disposal with a view to regular reporting to the Council and effective follow-up of Council decisions" (European Council 2004: 3 & 14). The CTC would soon assume a role beyond mere coordination and initiate the creation of the ECTC at Europol.

First, however, the London bombings further politicised counterterrorism policy at European level and enabled supranational entrepreneurs to influence state preferences in favour of additional integration. Shortly after the attacks, the European Commission published another communication in September 2005, this time on terrorist recruitment and radicalisation (European Commission 2005). Rather than limiting itself to recommendations, the Commission "announced its intention to explore possibilities of tackling of content used to radicalise individuals for terrorism on the Internet in order to address the factors conducive to violent radicalization" (Council 2007: 2). The EU Strategy for Combating Radicalisation and Recruitment reiterated this need for action at the EU level (ibid. 2005a). In the same month, the Council adopted an EU Counter-Terrorism Strategy on the basis of proposals from the British Council Presidency and the CTC (ibid. 2005b). The Strategy exhibits a first substantial shift of Member States' preferences towards EU police cooperation and more supranational involvement in the area of counterterrorism. While the London bombings undeniably provided the political momentum for governments to adopt the Strategy, Member States highlighted that rising interconnectedness required collective action:

> The European Union is an area of increasing openness and an area in which the internal and external aspects of security are intimately linked. It is an area of increasing interdependence, [...]an environment which terrorists abuse to pursue their objectives. In this context concerted and collective European action, in the spirit of solidarity, is indispensable to combat terrorism.
>
> *(ibid.: 6)*

The Strategy acknowledged the important role of the Commission in the development of measures and stressed the need to "move from ad-hoc to systematic police co-operation," "in particular through Europol" (ibid.: 8 & 13). Not only did this strengthen EU policy venues for police cooperation on counterterrorism, but it also gave EU actors an active role. Europol could for example be involved in the creation of JITs for cross-border investigations related to terrorism (ibid.: 13).

Similar to the process leading to the EC3, politicisation presented windows of opportunity for supranational advocacy. Many of the measures adopted by the European or JHA Council in the aftermath of the Madrid and London bombings originated from proposals of the European Commission and the newly established CTC. On the one hand, both impacted state preferences as 'enablers' of collective action by soft power means; they actively advertised venue-shopping (Interviewees 9 & 12). EU actors emphasised the prospect of central resources and funding being made available for domestic activities as well as the possibility to outsource certain administrative tasks and benefit from pooled technical expertise. Additionally, the Commission and the CTC exerted influence and lobbied for more EU involvement through agenda-setting and shaping discussions (ibid.).

EU actors harnessed politicisation and public pressure to further their entrepreneurship and make themselves indispensable (Interviewees 23 & 27). Similar to the fight against cybercrime, supranational actors could rely on steady, high public support for EU action. Since 2001, more than 70% of EU citizens across all Member States were supporting joint EU decision-making in the fight against international terrorism (see Figure 5.4). The relatively uncontested role for the

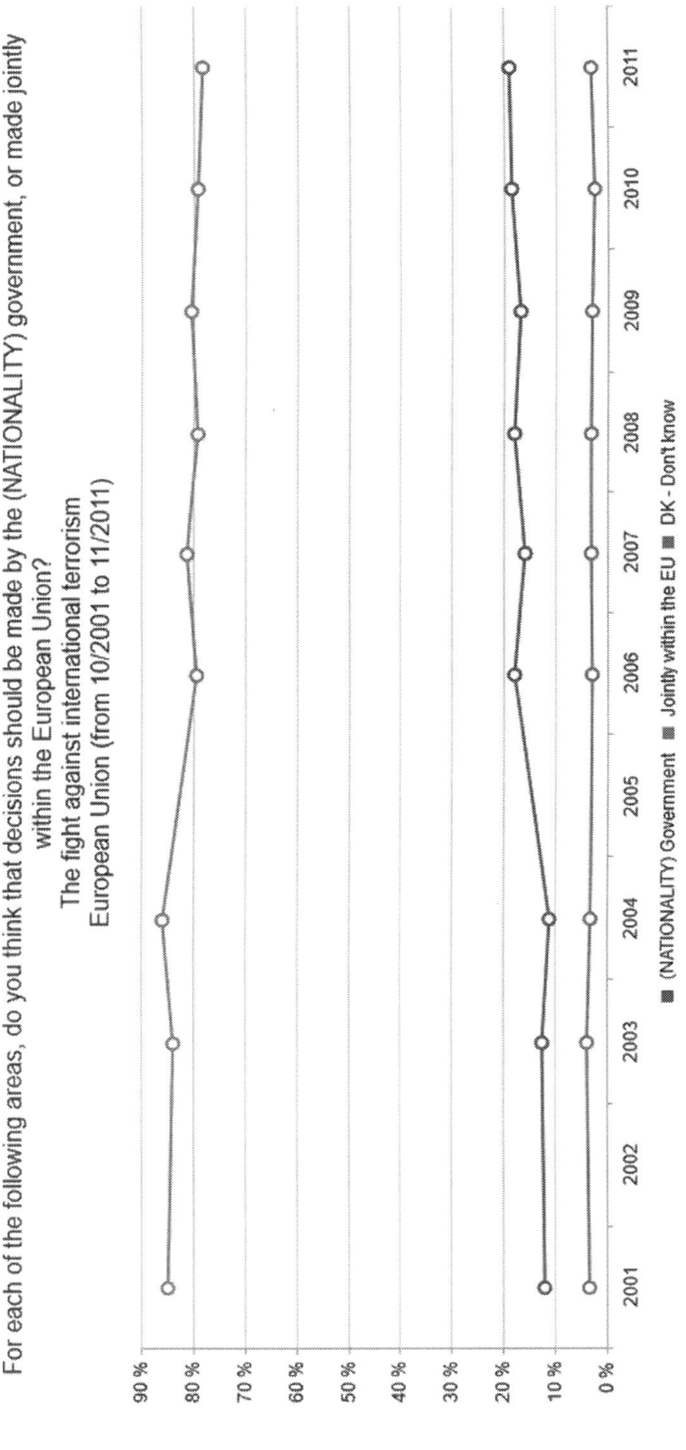

FIGURE 5.4 Public Support for EU Action in the Fight against International Terrorism (2001–2011)

Compiled by the author, based on European Commission (2019), Eurobarometer Interactive

EU in this area together with the post-crisis momentum following the terror attacks in Madrid and London possibly facilitated the impact on EU governments of supranational policy entrepreneurs. Arguing against proposals for EU collective action in the immediate aftermath of the attacks was politically hardly feasible for policymakers (Interviewee 27). The Commission and the CTC were able to exploit this public pressure and leverage salience to increase their own visibility and influence in this policy area.

Supranational policy entrepreneurs particularly underlined functional pressure from interdependencies in their promotion of Europol as main cooperation venue. Commission officials pushed for an expansion of Europol's competencies as part of a broader strategy to boost EU cooperation formats in JHA. "If Member States saw 'Europol is here,' this would also send the message: 'The EU is here,' and by extension that meant the Commission" (Interviewee 35). The Commission's announcement from 2005 to explore potential measures against online radicalisation was realised in May 2007 on grounds of functional pressure. In the respective Council conclusions Member States recognised the need for collective action at the EU level: "It is hardly possible for one individual member state to cover all suspicious terrorism related activities on the Internet" (Council 2007: 3). Next to external interdependencies, rising internal interconnectedness pushed preferences towards the EU level: "In all of this work the activities of the various actors (Member States, Commission, Europol, [...]et al.) have to be coordinated in a targeted way" (ibid.). A first step was the launch of the 'Check the Web' platform at Europol.

THE ROLE OF INSTITUTIONAL INTERDEPENDENCIES AND SPILL-OVER EFFECTS

Europol's entrepreneurship began to substantially impact state preferences from 2009 onwards. Functional spill-overs enabled the agency to develop an increasingly relevant advocacy role in counterterrorism and produce cultivated spill-overs. The ECD formally recognised Europol as key actor, as did the Member States' decision to launch the EC3. These developments were now producing spill-over effects on the domain of counterterrorism. The expansion of Europol's functional scope, including a mandate for cyber security and terrorism, and its strengthened *de jure* powers as central hub for police cooperation in the EU opened the floodgates to cultivated spill-overs and a *de facto* role for Europol in shaping state preferences. Tracking illicit activities online and collecting information on Islamist terrorist propaganda on the Internet through 'Check the Web' almost naturally required similar and follow-up tasks at Europol in the area of counterterrorism. Europol was able to convince Member States of the functional need to adapt existing projects and expand its mandate accordingly. By 2009, it was increasingly seen as sophisticated actor in its own right by European governments and security authorities; its solid practical track record and positive reputation progressively allowed the agency to assert itself as policy entrepreneur and negotiate with Member States at eye level (Interviewees 1, 14, 31 & 35).

Consequently, in 2009, Europol initiated the transformation of 'Check the Web' from mere technical platform into an AWF (Bundestag 2015b). Similar to the issue area of cybercrime where Europol's advocacy in relation to the HTCC and the ECCP had yielded the creation of AWF 'Cyborg,' the opening of AWF 'Check the Web' created a central role for Europol. Instead of merely hosting a technical portal where Member States could collect and store data related to Islamist terrorist propaganda and radical content online, the organisation now gained an operational role in countering terrorist abuse of the Internet. Europol's success in initiating the creation of AWF 'Check the Web' not only exhibited the emerging new self-conception of Europol as a policy entrepreneur of EU police cooperation, but it also paved the way for embedding more projects and eventually the ECTC in the agency (see Figure 5.3). Following the 2010 EU ISS – which identified terrorism as one main security challenge – a Focal Point (FP) was opened at Europol. Previously AWFs, FPs allow Europol to collect and process data on specific criminal offences for the purpose of analysis. This particular FP gave Europol a key role in coordinating the exchange of financial messaging data between the EU and the US as part of the Terrorist Finance Tracking Programme (TFTP) (Council 2010a: 13).

Europol's growing entrepreneurship not only extended to the higher political levels in the Member States. Through its growing relevance as central actor of EU police cooperation, it directly interacted with police officers and practitioners at subnational level, who significantly boosted Europol's analytical involvement and operational support functions. The adoption of a new AWF concept in August 2011 exemplifies how domestic police authorities enabled further organisational emancipation and marked a new level of maturity and sophistication in Europol's 'actorness' and entrepreneurship within EU police cooperation (Interviewees 5 & 31). In late 2010, the Heads of Europol National Units (HENUs) – representing national law enforcement authorities and domestic police levels – initiated a discussion on the structure of Europol's analytical work (Europol 2012b: 4). The impetus for reform thus came from subnational actors. Yet, it had been prepared by Europol officials who had continuously lobbied for a more coherent, strategic support role for themselves (Interviewees 11, 18, 19, 24 & 31). Following the HENUs' decision to develop a new AWF concept in January 2011, a WG produced a concept that was adopted in August. It merged Europol's existing more than 20 AWFs into only two, one on serious and organised crime (AWF SOC) and one on counter-terrorism (AWF CT). Additionally, the new concept introduced the possibility to create FPs and Target Groups (TGs) within each AWF. While AWFs presented the main systems to process information on concrete criminal issue areas and to provide operational support, FPs could be opened within each AWF to "focus[...] on a certain phenomenon from a commodity based, thematic or regional angle" and centrally coordinate EU police cooperation on the topic (Europol 2012b: 5). Finally, TPs could be opened at any time as "operational project with a dedicated

Europol team to support an international criminal investigation or criminal intelligence operation against a specific target" (ibid.: 7).

This step is remarkable for two reasons. First, the possibilities under the new AWF concept for Europol to structure and expand its analytical capacity were completely novel and had been single-handedly conceived by Europol staff and the HENUs. As the agency itself acknowledged, "[e...]ven though Europol's legal framework does not explicitly foresee Focal Points or Target Groups these definitions developed in consultation with the HENUs form a reasonable and legitimate implementation of the term 'analysis project' in the sense of the ECD" (Europol 2012b: 4). Second, the new AWF concept significantly strengthened and extended Europol's role and powers in the initiation of analytical work and operational support in the Member States. Not only did it allow Europol and other EU bodies to initiate FPs, the decision to open the latter was placed in the hands of Europol, in consultation with the Member States (ibid.: 6). In contrast to the procedure for opening an AWF, FPs no longer required a feasibility study and allowed Europol to immediately receive operational information. The introduction of FPs thus constituted a permanent 'workaround' to lengthy legal procedures and was intended to practically facilitate "targeted information gathering;" "whenever M[ember] S[tates] are confronted with a new crime phenomenon, they may simply send their information to Europol, knowing it will already be processed and assessed by the relevant experts" (ibid.).

The new AWF concept empowered Europol alone to decide upon opening a TP, although Member States could make suggestions (ibid.: 7). This arguably constituted a significant gain in power for Europol because the opening mechanism effectively bypassed national levels in the approval of specific operational and analytical activities at Europol (Interviewee 39). Europol was now able to independently set operational priorities, allocate resources and develop its expertise. Some might even argue that "by gathering information before punishable offences have even been committed, Europol is assuming powers that come close to those of an intelligence service" (Bundestag 2012: 1).

The adoption of the new AWF concept in 2011 arguably exhibited vertical integration at Europol 'from below,' and illustrates the effects of Europol entrepreneurship on domestic police officials. Until 2010, the gradual emergence of Europol as "the backbone" of EU police cooperation was primarily driven by political actors 'from above,' at the initiative of national governments or EU actors (see Figures 5.1 and 5.3). The previous chapters have demonstrated how subnational actors frequently shaped state preferences in favour of differentiation rather than integration. However, around 2010, subnational policy entrepreneurship evolved more and more towards integration initiatives. Although bureaucratic resistance remained a problem in many areas of EU police cooperation, especially in counterterrorism, Europol's practical track record was beginning to generate more demand from operational levels (Interviewees 15, 22 & 24). Particularly among the HENUs – positioned between Europol and national police authorities – Europol was gaining acceptance and was increasingly acting as socialisation platform rather than mere coordination mechanism (Interviewees 18 & 19). As one Europol representative phrased it: "we have a limited role but we can make a difference by identifying operational issues to Member States. It just takes time, especially in low-profile crime areas. But there is a rapidly growing demand" (Interviewee 32). The new AWF concept demonstrates how Europol simultaneously benefitted from and deliberately fuelled an emerging paradigm shift among police officials from unilateral solutions to common solutions at the EU level (Interviewees 22 & 23; Münch 2018). It exhibits how Europol officials directly lobbied subnational actors to acknowledge it as 'one-stop shop' and central cooperation mechanism (Interviewees 14, 23 & 40). To this end, the agency strategically leveraged functional pressure and operational needs at the sub-state level to promote vertical integration among the HENUs.

2013–2015: CUMULATIVE CRISIS MOMENTUM AS FINAL TURNING POINT

Notwithstanding the growing opportunities for supranational entrepreneurship around 2010, Member States only really succumbed to public and political pressure for an ECTC from 2013 onwards (see Figure 5.3). Politicisation and policy advocacy from the CTC, Europol and the Commission formed key drivers to this end. Similar to the early 2000s, a series of crises presented windows of opportunity by generating public and functional pressure to improve EU police cooperation.

In 2013, the first one of these 'crises' formed in the Sahel and Maghreb regions and drove European governments to discuss measures at the EU level. Against the backdrop of the armed conflict in Mali since early 2012, Member States were beginning to feel the impact of "trans-national jihadism and cross-border migration" (Boserup & Martinez 2018). This culminated on 16 January 2013 when a group of 32 militants with links to Al-Qaeda crossed into Northern Algeria from Mali and attacked a joint venture gas plant between Algerian and foreign companies near In Amenas ('Algeria Hostage Crisis' 2013). For three days, the gunmen held over 800 workers hostage, including 130 foreign nationals, until they were finally freed by Algerian security forces (Borger et al. 2013). In the process, 40 hostages were killed. The kidnapping's "scale and degree of violence led French Defence Minister Jean-Yves Le Drian to describe the militant action as an 'act of war'" (Græger & Lindgren 2018: 197).

In the wake of the In Amenas hostage crisis, supranational actors were able to strategically position themselves as policy initiators. Member States were concerned about "the implications of the Sahel/Maghreb (crisis in Mali, In Amenas) on EU internal security," particularly the issue of foreign terrorist fighters travelling from the EU to Islamist hotspots in these regions (CTC 2014: 6). Accordingly, they tasked the CTC with preparing countermeasures at the EU level. The result was an extensive report comprising a list of 22 measures that were adopted by the JHA Council at its meeting on 28 June 2013 (Council

2014b: 8). These included actions towards the assessment, prevention, detection and pursuit of (returning) foreign fighters (ibid. 2013: 5). The proposals reflect significant supranational entrepreneurship and promotion of EU fora and integration. They also illustrate the emerging role of the CTC as increasingly influential "political, strategic, and operational guide" of the Member States (Busch & Monroy 2017: 2). "In his recommendations he constantly call[...ed] for more competences and capacities," including for Europol as central intelligence and coordination hub in the fight against terrorism (ibid.). As a result of the CTC's report, FP 'Travellers' was opened at Europol in April 2014 to work on foreign fighters and related terrorist networks (Avramopoulos 2015).

Three more politicising events amplified public and functional pressure on Member States. They marked a peak of politicisation and supranational entrepreneurship in the counterterrorism domain. The terror attacks in Brussels and Paris in 2014 and 2015 triggered a final shift of state preferences (see Figure 5.3). They presented opportunities for the CTC, the Commission and Europol to frame Islamist terrorism as common challenge and shape political action (Interviewees 35, 43 & 44). On 24 May 2014, a French national murdered four people at the Jewish museum in Brussels. The attacker, Mehdi Nemmouche, had previously fought in Syria for the so-called Islamic State of Iraq and Syria (ISIS). The Brussels Jewish museum shooting therefore had a particular psychological impact as "Europe's first terror attack by an Islamist fighter returning from the war in Syria" ('Brussels Jewish museum shooter' 2019; cf. CEP 2017). The attack triggered political action among Member States and EU actors. A subgroup of EU governments most affected by the foreign fighters phenomenon – led by Belgium – stepped up the exchange of information and best practices to enhance cooperation throughout 2013 and 2014 (Council 2014b: 4). At the EU level, the European Council reaffirmed the conclusions adopted on the basis of the CTC's report in June 2013. It called for the swift implementation of the package of measures, emphasising that the "rise of the Islamic State of Iraq and the Levant [ISIL...]is a major threat to European security and that determined action to stem the flow of foreign fighters from Europe is needed" (ibid. 2014c: 1). The Council of the EU reiterated this call in October. It underscored the need to improve information-sharing and strengthen Europol, particularly cooperation through FP 'Travellers.' These calls were complemented roughly one week later by the EU counterterrorism/foreign fighters strategy that focussed on Syria and Iraq and cooperation with third countries (Council 2015b). Similar to many of the on-going discussions and proposals it was based on drafts of the CTC and the Commission.

Public pressure and political momentum remained high even half a year after the Brussels shooting and continued to fuel a multi-level policy debate among EU actors and Member States how to best cope with the threat from Islamist terrorism. Amidst this process, a second terror attack hit Europe and caused the salience of EU counterterrorism policy to skyrocket even further (see Figure 5.3). Between 7–9 January 2015, 17 people were killed in a series of attacks across Île-de-France and Paris ('French Terror Attacks' 2015). These included the shooting of 12 at the headquarters of the French satirical magazine *Charlie Hebdo*, the murder of a policewoman in a Paris suburb and a hostage situation at a Jewish supermarket in which the attacker murdered four of the 19 victims. The terror attacks were finally brought to a close following a major manhunt in which the perpetrators were shot dead ('Charlie Hebdo Attack' 2015). They had been French nationals of Algerian and Malian descent with ties to the MENA region and radical Islamist circles ('2015 Charlie Hebdo Attack' 2018), and were known to security authorities by criminal record, including arrest for attempted travel to Syria and Iraq (Chrisafis 2015). Al-Qaeda in the Arabian Peninsula claimed responsibility for the Charlie Hebdo attack, while the third attacker claimed to be pledged to ISIS (Meichtry et al. 2015). He likewise declared to have coordinated with the gunmen who had committed the Charlie Hebdo shooting (CEP 2017a).

THE COUNTER-TERRORISM COORDINATOR'S PROPOSAL FOR AN ECTC

Europol directly benefited from the EU CTC's visibility and involvement in the aftermath of the January 2015 Paris attacks (Farnung 2018). The attacks sparked significant public shock among citizens and policymakers. In France, around 3.7 million people participated in a march against terrorism, and the slogan 'Je Suis Charlie' became a symbol of global solidarity (Devichand 2016). A number of initiatives were proposed by EU actors in the following weeks and months, and adopted by the Member States for the most part (see Figure 5.3). The CTC proposed a range of measures at the EU level, including action to prevent radicalisation online and to improve information exchange on counterterrorism (CTC 2015). Citing the example of the UK's Counter-Terrorism Internet Referral Unit (CTIRU), the CTC suggested to step up the role of the EU and especially Europol in monitoring and flagging terrorist and extremist content online (Interviewee 28). In a similar vein, the CTC proposed, "Europol's Check the Web project could be beefed up to allow for monitoring and analysis of social media communication on the internet" (ibid.: 3). Unsurprisingly perhaps, he received direct support from the UK, which placed the possibility of an EU Internet Referral Unit (IRU) on the agenda of the informal Council meeting in Riga on 29 January (Interviewee 28). Additional agenda items included some of the CTC's other proposals. Among these was – arguably the first explicit mention of – the "creation of a European Counter-terrorism Centre at Europol, [which] like the European Cybercrime Centre (EC3), would allow Europol to translate existing capabilities into operational impact quickly" (CTC 2015: 7).

The impact of the CTC's entrepreneurship did not only become manifest in changes at Europol, but it also was already reflected in the Riga joint statement of JHA ministers. The document formally acknowledged growing interdependencies and the "multidimensional threat involving different areas of crime." This adoption of pro-integration or securitisation narratives and show of political action mirrored a shift in governmental preferences towards EU police cooperation (Interviewees 21, 38 & 43). While the Riga joint statement acknowledged the terror attacks as evidence for the interconnectedness of Member States in the fight against terrorism, the sudden shift in preferences was primarily driven by post-crisis politicisation, spiralling salience and public pressure. Interdependence in the fight against international terrorism had arguably been consistently high for years; "the threat had always been there" (Interviewee 44). Yet, the degree of interdependence in the fight against terrorism varied across Member States and strong asymmetries in this issue area prevented a universal shift and convergence of national positions towards EU police cooperation. Functional pressure was thus not able to single-handedly move state preferences towards integration in counterterrorism. Politicising events like the Paris terror attacks ultimately corroborated this need across Member States. They powerfully illustrated existing linkages and produced widespread public and political preferences for EU integration as necessary means to countering international terrorism.

In the light of crisis politicisation and supranational policy entrepreneurship, JHA ministers decided to expand EU action on foreign terrorist fighters, particularly through Europol's FP 'Travellers.' They agreed to assess the development of "Internet referral capabilities, also through Check-the-web,[...] within Europol" (Riga Joint Statement 2015). The Riga conclusions were reiterated by European heads of state or government on 12 February. They echoed the need to strengthen collective action at the EU level and called for "specific counter-terrorism measures" (European Council & Council 2018). Consequently, on 12 March 2015, the JHA Council formally asked Europol to "develop the 'Check the Web' project into an EU Internet Referral Unit (EU IRU)" (Council 2015c: 4). European ministers thereby directly acted on the January proposal of the CTC (Bundestag 2015b). In justifying the creation of an EU IRU, they applied many of the same security and threat narratives that EU actors had employed to securitise cybercrime policy (Bebe 2015). Their decision to mandate Europol with the development of the IRU not only provided the agency with a lead role in designing the degree of centralisation and functional scope but also with an opportunity to shape state preferences. Member States had *de facto* recognised the organisation as sophisticated actor that could initiate policy changes and mould EU police cooperation (Interviewees 35 & 44; cf. Europol 2015a). The CTC's report additionally shaped the decision of JHA ministers to make EU information exchange and operational cooperation a top priority in the fight against terrorism (Council 2015c). They invited Europol to prepare suggestions for the improved use of its platforms and services (ibid.: 6). Although the Council acted on the CTC's proposal for an EU IRU, the idea of an ECTC was initially nowhere to be found in the declarations and conclusions of EU governments. Especially Germany opposed the establishment of a counterterrorism centre at Europol (Haber 2015: 2). Only later, the 2016 Berlin Christmas market attack would change this preference, and Germany – driven by police officials at the

BKA – would even explore the possible expansion of Europol's ECTC (Busch & Monroy 2017: 4).

CONVINCING THE MEMBER STATES: THE COMMISSION AND EU ADVOCACY

Supranational policy entrepreneurship ultimately shifted state preferences towards the launch of an ECTC at Europol. The proposal was tabled again in April 2015 in the context of the Commission's 'European Agenda on Security,' which prepared the ground for the renewal of the EU ISS (European Commission 2015b: 13). While the Commission could only advise Member States to create such a centre, it strongly leveraged public and functional pressure to this end. The mere act of formally including the proposal in the security agenda created pressure on national governments. The Commission explicitly underlined that "[c...]itizens and Member States expect the EU's support in fighting terrorism and radicalisation and facilitating coordination and cooperation between relevant authorities" (ibid.; cf. Figure 5.4). Moreover, it highlighted the need to further integrate in view of growing institutional links and interdependencies. Europol, the Commission emphasised, had become a key venue for EU police cooperation on terrorism and could help improve its effectiveness and efficiency:

> [B...]ringing together its anti-terrorism law enforcement capabilities, pooling resources and maximising the use of already existing structures, services and tools [...would] achiev[...e] economies of scale [that...] could be brought together as a European Counter-Terrorism Centre within Europol.
>
> *(ibid.)*

Concretely, the European Commission suggested to bring together the FPs 'Travellers' and 'TFTP' as well as the newly created EU IRU. Through its 'European Agenda on Security,' the Commission was able to assert itself and the CTC's proposals, and thereby ultimately shift state preferences in favour of an ECTC within Europol. This reflects the considerable growth of the Commission's role as a policy initiator and agenda-setter in JHA over the past decade (Interviewees 6, 15, 23 & 33). Particularly since the ECD, Commission entrepreneurship within EU police cooperation had evolved and grown in line with its influence *vis-à-vis* the Member States. By 2015, the European Commission had established itself as key player and legitimate principal in the area of internal security. Its proposals within the 'European Agenda on Security' reflect this organisational self-confidence. Not only did they mirror the Commission's "integration-friendliness" in a rather intergovernmental policy domain, but they also likewise demonstrated the institution's growing influence on state preferences (Interviewee 15). The European Commission was in a favourable position to initiate policy and shape preferences on EU police cooperation in high-profile areas of internal security; Member States could not afford to simply dismiss its proposals, and had to at least argue why not to adopt Commission initiatives (Interviewee 14).

Unsurprisingly, elements of Commission entrepreneurship and its security agenda increasingly showed in government positions (European Commission 2015b: 5; see Figure 5.3). The Commission's reiteration of the CTC's proposal for an ECTC was finally embraced by the Member States. In June and July 2015, the JHA Council even facilitated further pro-EU input by tasking a number of integration-friendly actors with the implementation of the EU ISS and particularly the ECTC. Work was carried out at mixed intergovernmental and the EU levels on the one hand, and supranational levels on the other. Both lobbied for deeper integration. This included the Council's Standing Committee on Operational Cooperation on Internal Security (COSI), which comprises senior officials from national interior ministries and Commission representatives and allows for the participation of Europol observers. Additionally, Member States attributed a central role to the Council's Working Party on Terrorism (TWP), a body focused on the operational aspects of EU police cooperation and thus complementing COSI's strategic and policy guidance (Luxembourg Presidency 2015: 11 & 35). Consisting of national experts, the TWP liaises with the CTC and Europol (Council 2018). These mixed intergovernmental and supranational settings had arguably produced political spill-overs and now increasingly acted as pro-EU socialisation platforms; a majority of officials working at these levels were united in the belief that EU collective action was indispensable in most areas of police cooperation (Interviewees 3, 31 & 33–35).

This belief was reiterated by EU actors in the implementation of the EU ISS (2015–2020) and the development of the ECTC. Particularly the Commission, the EU CTC and Europol influenced state preferences in the process. The CTC for instance worked closely together with the Council Presidency and helped shape the JHA Council's agenda and conclusions (Europol 2015c). On the basis of his reports and input, the Member States charged supranational actors as well as mixed policy venues consisting of (sub-)national and the EU levels with the development of the ECTC (Interviewees 5, 10 & 15). This benefitted Europol as well, which was tasked with a central role (Europol 2015c: 3–4). In contrast to the Commission and the CTC's often highly visible and public entrepreneurship, Europol primarily used the working level and mixed intergovernmental-supranational channels to promote itself and advance deeper integration. Its influence in the development of the ECTC was considerable, particularly through its input at COSI and the TWP on the one hand, and its reports to the Council and cooperation with the Commission and the CTC on the other. By 2015, Europol had expanded its role from mere provider of operational and analytical support to strategic and political adviser of the Member States. This 'function creep' allowed it to shape state preferences through pro-EU lobbyism as well as concrete policy input. One senior official summarised this development as follows: "We're now having discussions with and at Europol that were unthinkable ten years ago when Europol was still in a situation where it had to beg to be involved. Now Member States come to Europol to discuss prioritisation and Europol has to decide for which areas it can offer in-depth support" (Interviewee 35).

Although the process towards the launch of the ECTC at Europol was well underway, the Paris attacks of 13 November 2015 additionally strengthened supranational entrepreneurship and public pressure to accelerate integration (see Figure 5.3). An "unprecedented wave of terror attacks," for which ISIL claimed responsibility, killed more than 100 people and injured over 350 in the French capital (Europol 2015c: 4). Although the series of coordinated attacks exhibited a new degree of sophistication that took security officials by surprise, it did not mark a quantitative increase in the threat across Europe (Interviewees 43 & 44). Contrary to public perception, the terror incident of 13 November was not unprecedented in its scale of violence. Interdependencies among Member States arguably remained at a similar level. Yet, politicisation in the aftermath of the Paris attacks shifted state preferences towards collective action and further integration of EU police cooperation on counterterrorism. Previous terror attacks and politicising events had already generated a growing sense of security crisis and loss of control among the public and policymakers (Interviewees 23, 24, 30 & 32). The Paris attacks of late 2015 – as second-largest terror incident since 11-M with an accordingly high media coverage and widespread psychological effect – finally tipped the scale with regard to state preferences (Interviewees 13, 14, 19 & 44). It possibly mattered less at the time whether interdependencies and external threats were 'real' but rather that European politicians as well as the media and public believed they were and called for swift action (Interviewees 41 & 42). And they did. Some even claim that the attacks of November 2015 changed the "status quo in the European security paradigm" (Brisard 2015: 5).

EU actors yet again harnessed the salience and post-crisis momentum to impact the positions of Member States in favour of integration. Amidst significant public pressure to demonstrate action and control, supranational entrepreneurs presented EU police cooperation as effective solution to do just this: solve practical coordination problems in the fight against terrorism (Interviewees 24, 27 & 35). Their proposals for dealing with these threats at the EU level *de facto* provided an effective means of venue-shopping for policymakers in the management of citizens' concerns and domestic shortcomings (Interviewees 27 & 44). The CTC and the Luxembourg Presidency jointly prepared a note detailing measures to enhance counterterrorism capabilities at the EU level (Presidency & CTC 2015). This note formed the basis for an extraordinary COSI meeting as well as an emergency Council meeting (Europol 2015c: 4). The conclusions of both reflected and reiterated the points contained in the CTC's note, most importantly the need to cooperate with and via Europol on counterterrorism and increase information-sharing and exchange through the agency. This included the swift launch of the ECTC and rapid connection of national authorities to the centre (Presidency & CTC 2015: 3). Additional calls to further boost Europol – provide it with "adequate resources," expand its functional scope within counterterrorism and its access to common databases – were likewise echoed by the Member States and would later help shift their preferences in favour of a new legal framework for the agency, namely the Europol Regulation (cf. Jones 2015).

The European Commission similarly leveraged the post-crisis momentum from the Paris attacks and called on Member States to react to the functional integration pressure this terror incident had supposedly exhibited (cf. Bigo et al. 2015). It stressed the need to advance existing structures and accelerate the adoption and implementation of integration initiatives. This included Europol's ECTC and EC3 but also other EU instruments such as Prüm (ibid.: 5). Finally, the Paris attacks provided an opportunity for advocacy by Europol itself. A Europol report submitted on 17 November – a mere four days after the terrorist attacks – framed the incident from a securitisation angle. It emphasised the "[c…] lear international dimension in the planning and coordinating of attacks, involving a network (not group of lone actors)" and the high probability and serious threat of more attacks. Europol thus underlined the need for collective action at the EU level and positioned itself as key player and central cooperation venue (Europol 2015c: 13f.). In the light of substantial supranational entrepreneurship and high politicisation, the JHA Council on 20 November 2015 committed itself to strengthening "the EU response to terrorism" (European Council & Council 2018). Member States decided to improve law enforcement cooperation and information exchange, and launch the ECTC at Europol on 1 January 2016 (Council 2015a).

The European Migrant Smuggling Centre

Only one month later, the EMSC was launched at Europol in February 2016. Rather than mere coincidence, the close temporal proximity of the two centres was a result of similar driving forces (see Figure 5.5). The same terror attacks that had generated public pressure to cooperate on counterterrorism likewise highlighted the need to cooperate on migrant smuggling, which was reinforced by the crisis in the Sahel and Maghreb region and the 2015 refugee and migrant crisis. Additionally, supranational policy entrepreneurship mattered greatly for swaying state preferences towards the EU level in the fight against facilitated irregular migration and trafficking in human beings (THB). Especially the European Commission and Europol acted as pro-EU lobbyists and were able to influence state preferences accordingly. While interdependencies were present and rising as well – a trend that was featured prominently by politicising events and policy entrepreneurs – they did not act as primary driver of state preferences in the case of the EMSC.

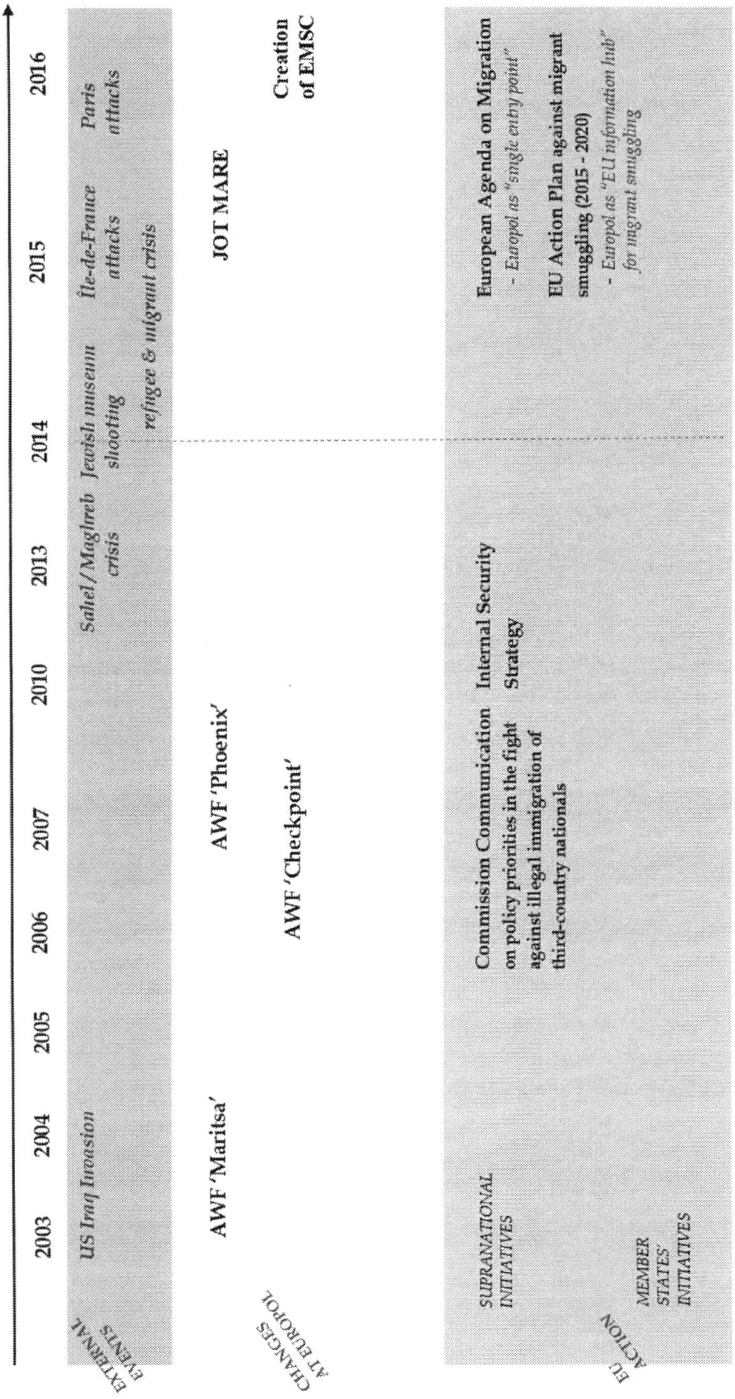

FIGURE 5.5 A Chronology of Europol's European Migrant Smuggling Centre (EMSC)

PAVING THE WAY FOR VERTICAL INTEGRATION: FIRST OPERATIONAL IMPULSES FROM THE PRACTITIONER LEVEL

Preventing and fighting illegal migrant smuggling and THB had already formed part of Europol's initial tasks under the Europol Convention (Art. 1(2)) in the 1990s. Nevertheless, strengthening Europol's powers and widening its involvement in this issue area was not necessarily a priority for EU Member States in the early 2000s. Before the 2015 refugee and migrant crisis finally provided the necessary impetus for integration in this policy domain, policy entrepreneurship paved the way.

A first intensification of EU police cooperation via Europol was the direct result of subnational policy entrepreneurship (Interviewees 4, 6 & 12). In 2002, national police officials lobbied the European Commission to "empower" Europol in the common fight against illegal facilitated immigration and THB (European Commission 2002: 32). The EU Police Chiefs Operational Task Force had only been launched a few years earlier to "exchange, in co-operation with Europol, experience, best practices and information on current trends in cross-border crime and contribute to the planning of operative actions" (European Council 1999). The task force quickly developed a life of its own and was increasingly able to consolidate its informal entrepreneurship with the operational development of EU police cooperation (Bunyan 2006a; Van Buuren 2012). In March 2001, the police chiefs suggested to strengthen Europol's role by expanding its involvement and giving it "more operative powers" (European Commission 2002: 32). These proposals were directly included in the Commission's 2002 comprehensive plan to combat illegal immigration and THB. A common AFSJ, both asserted, similarly produced a common crime area with new opportunities for criminal groups (Interviewee 22). Growing interconnectedness therefore required better coordination at the EU level in related issue areas (ibid.: 26). Supra- and subnational policy entrepreneurship thus effectively leveraged functional pressure and reinforced one another to enhance EU police cooperation.

Although this did not immediately effectuate deeper integration, it initiated a gradual shift of state preferences and prepared the ground for future changes. To this end, subnational policy entrepreneurs instigated the first *de facto* centralisation tendencies at Europol: the opening of AWF 'Maritsa' on THB from and through Bulgaria (see Figure 5.5; Europol 2012c: 1). The analytical project team with designated experts was launched in 2003. It followed directly from the EU Police Chiefs Task Force action plan on preventing and combating THB, which likewise concentrated on Bulgarian networks, victims and perpetrators (Dingelstad-Frankova 2013: 9). The particularly intense criminal interconnectedness with Bulgaria in this issue area may explain why preferences formed in favour of launching AWF 'Maritsa' with its rather narrow focus. Issue-specific interdependencies thus shaped the police chiefs' preference in favour of collective action at the EU level, while persisting asymmetries explain the topical diversity and venue-shopping approach within subnational policy entrepreneurship. The task force's agenda and action plans reflected a wide range of issues, including general criminal developments as well as very narrow threats and trends challenging only a few if not single Member States. This 'shopping list' seems contrary to the simultaneous emphasis on the functional need to develop Europol as a means for coherent, effective action. It reflects asymmetrical interdependence pressure at domestic operational levels. In preparation of the 2004 Eastern enlargement round, Austria, Germany and Finland initiated action plans under the theme of illegal immigration at the task force's meeting of May 2003 (Bunyan 2006: 5). All three countries shared borders with the future new members and expected to experience the highest levels of interdependence.

Notwithstanding the limitation of centring on Bulgarian-based networks, the AWF constituted the first formal focal point of Europol's analytical and operational support activities in the area of THB and illegal immigration. Although subnational policy entrepreneurship remained overall informal and neither involved political levels nor directly impacted state preferences, the bottom-up process that led to the opening of 'Maritsa' may be argued to have presented a first institutional stepping stone for further integration at Europol. Within a few years, the mere existence of the AWF would itself generate further demand for enhancing EU police cooperation. In this vein, the venue-shopping of subnational actors – concretely, domestic police chiefs – produced a political spill-over effect on governments.

NURTURING PATH-DEPENDENCY: SUPRANATIONAL POLICY ENTREPRENEURS

Supranational policy entrepreneurs harnessed both spill-over effects and functional pressure as entry point for influencing shape state preferences in favour of integration. In view of the 2004 Eastern enlargement round, EU representatives reiterated heightened criminal interdependencies and the practical need to enhance police cooperation (Interviewees 29 & 30). Europol itself stressed the "growing problem of illegal immigration in the Member States" (Europol 2004: 11). Public-political discussions at national level likewise reflected this widespread discourse of potentially importing crime into the EU (Interviewees 29 & 30). Rather than impeding integration, politicisation and public pressure thus moved state preferences towards favouring EU policy venues in response to related security risks (Interviewees 14 & 21). In 2004, Member States accordingly named (facilitated) illegal immigration and THB one of five Europol crime priority areas (Europol 2004: 6).

Despite high politicisation, the Eastern enlargement round did not substantially impact state preferences. It failed to generate sufficient political momentum for deeper integration in EU police cooperation on illicit immigration and THB. Domestic practitioners were simply "not concerned enough" (Interviewee 7). Police cooperation arrangements had been in place for some time, including through Europol and AWF 'Maritsa,' and transition arrangements for the integration of the new EU members additionally softened the effect of the horizontal widening (Interviewees 14, 22 & 29–31). Salt and Almeida (2006: 169) likewise conclude: "the issues raised by irregular migration, especially migrant trafficking and human smuggling, have risen on the political agenda[...], however, the rhetoric has run ahead of the research. There is a fundamental lack of hard evidence relating to most aspects of the problem." Indeed, the issue area experienced "relative stability" since 2000; "available data in irregular migration flows d[id...] not support the view that irregular migration is on the increase" (ibid.: 171). This seems to confirm that politicisation alone may not suffice to affect government preferences, but rather that politicisation – as complementary driving factor present in a set of conditions – acts as relative enabler or enhancer of interdependence and policy entrepreneurship.

This mechanism can likewise be observed in 2006, when a sufficient level of politicisation interacted with rising interdependence and was leveraged by supranational policy entrepreneurs to shift state preferences towards action via Europol. Two AWFs would be opened at the agency: one on facilitated illegal immigration and one on THB (see Figure 5.5). In 2006, the armed conflicts in Afghanistan and Iraq reached a new level that impacted the EU (Interviewees 21 & 31). Although violence had been gradually escalating since 2004, the number of refugees leaving both countries skyrocketed from 2006 onwards (see Figure 5.6). Refugees from Afghanistan and Iraq amounted to almost half of all refugees worldwide, leading to an according peak in asylum applications and irregular border-crossings (Amr &

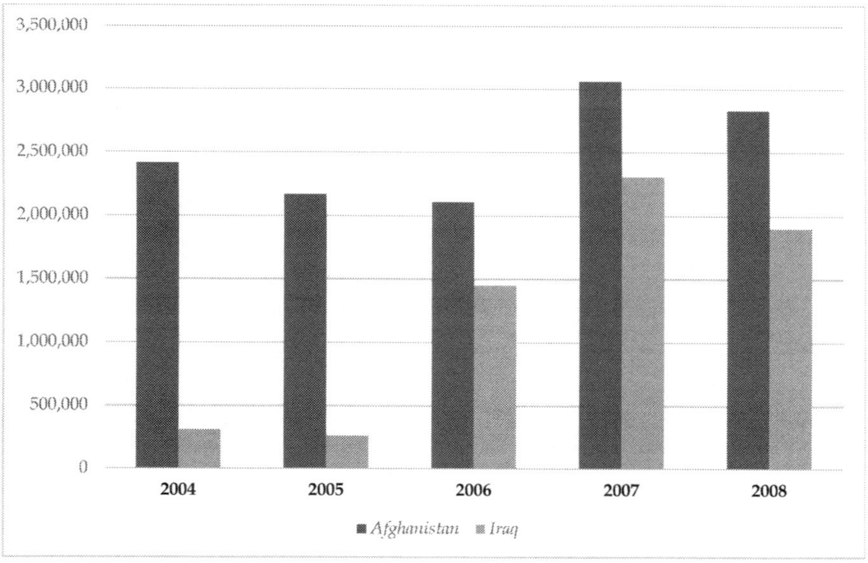

FIGURE 5.6 Global Refugees from Afghanistan and Iraq (2004–2008)

Compiled by the author, based on UNHCR Refugee population statistics database (n.d.)

Ferris 2009: 6; Parusel & Schneider 2011: 10). While the increase in violence became most noticeably manifest in the number of refugees leaving Iraq, Afghanistan's security situation likewise deteriorated significantly due to the Taliban resurgence and spiking attacks (CFR n.d.; Ferris 2009: 23). Notwithstanding the spiralling salience and refugee numbers in relation to the wars in Afghanistan and Iraq, the actual impact at the EU level was relatively small compared to many other asylum and destination countries (Koser & Schmeidl 2009: 10; UNHCR n.d.). Yet, between 2004 and 2007, Afghanistan and Iraq were consistently among the top countries of origin of refugees coming to the EU. Particularly in Denmark, Germany, the Netherlands, Sweden and the UK – the main destination countries in the EU – Afghan and Iraqi refugees remained high on the political radar and featured continuously among the top three or top five origin countries.

Supranational actors harnessed this political momentum. In early 2006, the European Commission prepared a communication on policy priorities regarding illegal immigration of third-country nationals. This document built on the AFSJ priorities that Member States had adopted through The Hague Programme in November 2004, but also stressed the growing need to react to "mounting migratory pressure at the EU's external borders" (European Commission 2006: 2). Notwithstanding existing arrangements with neighbouring and Balkan countries, the Commission advocated the improvement of cooperation via Europol and the enhancement of Europol's coordination role in the fight against facilitated illegal immigration and THB (ibid.: 11). Europol itself likewise actively promoted its services in this context, both at practitioners' and governmental levels (Interviewees 3, 21 & 29). As a consequence, AWF 'Checkpoint' was opened at Europol in October and focused on facilitated illegal immigration into and within EU Member States, with an initial emphasis on Iraq and Afghanistan as countries of origin (Europol 2009: 10).

Growing interdependencies in this issue area, repeatedly voiced by supranational actors, also instigated the revision of AWF 'Maritsa' (Interviewees 3, 7, 14 & 21). Its narrow focus on Bulgarian trafficking networks "seemed no longer suitable and fit for purpose" (Dingelstad-Frankova 2013: 10). Subsequently, in June 2007, the Member States launched AWF 'Phoenix' at Europol, which targeted THB more generally and allowed for the involvement of the agency concerning any related "forms of criminality[...] affecting at least two Member States of the European Union by Organised Crime Groups as well as any associated criminal activities[...] uncovered in the course of the investigation into these criminal networks" (Europol 2009: 10). Furthermore, Europol joined the Commission's group of experts on THB (ibid. 2012c: 1).

Although a discourse of growing interdependence framed EU police cooperation as necessary response to a rising functional need, politicisation and supranational policy entrepreneurship primarily drove state preferences towards integration. The number of 'apprehended aliens' – especially irregular migrants coming to the EU from Iraq and Afghanistan – rose sharply between 2005 and 2007 (European Commission 2009a: 29ff.). Yet, the overall impact on the EU arguably remained relatively small; the wars in Afghanistan and Iraq did not significantly alter Member States' interdependence in the fight against facilitated illegal immigration and THB (Interviewees 14, 22 & 29–31). The military interventions in the region would have presented a much more pressing opportunity to address persisting drug trafficking networks that likewise operated in the EU (ibid.). However, this aspect did not raise similar salience or public pressure and lacked supranational advocacy. It was therefore unable to push Member States towards action at the EU level (Interviewees 10, 21 & 29). Instead, the strategic leverage of politicisation by supranational policy entrepreneurs in the area of illegal migration and THB shifted state preferences towards further strengthening Europol through AWFs 'Checkpoint' and 'Phoenix.'

BUREAUCRATIC RESISTANCE AND LACK OF TRUST AS PERSISTENT OBSTACLES TO INTEGRATION

Nevertheless, the relevance of these developments should not be overstated. EU police cooperation remained far from perfect. Not only was participating in AWFs not mandatory for Member States, but also bureaucratic resistance continued to hinder information exchange and cooperation via Europol (EUC 2008: 24 & 34). Despite a gradually emerging acceptance at political level, even preference, of Europol as central policy venue, domestic security officials and practitioners at the operational levels often lagged behind (Interviewees 14, 22, 32 & 33; cf. Irrera 2018; Ziercke 2018). This likewise held true for the domain of illegal immigration and THB, where Europol had not previously played a substantial or systematic role. Only with the opening of the AWFs, the agency officially positioned itself as coordinator and actor in this issue area. It was just beginning to function as socialisation platform. One interviewee observed: "Europol was still in a situation where it had to beg to be involved" (Interviewee 35). In a similar vein, Augustin Diaz de Mera, Member of the European Parliament and rapporteur for the draft ECD, concluded: "It is not a problem of the Member States, but rather of their special services not being able to trust each other as much as they should. The key is trust" (EUC 2008: 24).

In addition to lack of trust, bureaucratic resistance derived from a lack of path-dependency; no precedent existed for Europol involvement in this issue area. The organisation was still working on raising its visibility and building a positive track record as the "only restricted level for the [systematic] sharing of confidential information between European law enforcement agencies" (ibid.: 35). In contrast to national policymakers, many police officers were yet to be convinced of the practical benefit of engaging Europol in cross-national cases instead of using their own networks. Many practitioners feared that submitting data to the agency would merely produce additional bureaucratic effort and yield few or unsatisfactory results. It was considered quicker to continue a known and reliable *modus operandi* – that prioritised national cases – instead of investing in a new external and unfamiliar mechanism whose merit was unclear (Interviewees

21, 24 & 27). This would change as more and more Member States joined AWFs at Europol and the more tangible analytical output and operational support by the agency became as a result (Interviewees 32 & 35).

Policy entrepreneurship and politicisation provided the ultimate impetus that shifted state preferences towards establishing the EMSC. After numbers of irregular migration to the EU had risen in 2006 and 2007, they abated again in the following years. This decline was rarely reflected in public discourse. On the contrary, "based on media reports alone, one has the impression that Europe's borders are increasingly porous" (Morehouse & Blomfield 2011: 14). Irrespective of the decline in absolute numbers related to irregular migration, interdependencies in the fight against THB remained high and continued to exert functional pressure on Member States to cooperate. In July 2012, Europol concluded:

> Trafficking in human beings (THB) remains a serious problem in the EU. It is likely that every single EU Member States is affected by THB in one form or another with a number of Member States clearly favoured by traffickers as the main 'market places'.
>
> *(Europol 2012b: 1)*

The agency stressed that interdependencies were changing in two main ways. First, they were growing quantitatively within the EU as a consequence of the borderless Schengen Area, the AFSJ and recent EU enlargement rounds (ibid.: 2ff.). Second, they were evolving qualitatively, as criminal networks were becoming more sophisticated and closely intertwined across Member States (ibid.: 5). In the light of these changes, Europol argued, EU governments needed to widen crime-fighting and policing to transnational and particularly European approaches, including the systematic involvement of Europol (ibid.: 7). Nonetheless, Europol's advocacy could not substantially mitigate bureaucratic resistance from subnational practitioners or lack of trust among Member States. The levels of public and functional pressure did possibly not yet suffice to provoke a shift of state preferences towards further integration steps within EU police cooperation.

THE 2014–2015 REFUGEE AND MIGRANT CRISIS AS CRITICAL MOMENT

The refugee and migrant crisis presented a watershed moment in this context (see Figure 5.5). The years 2014 and 2015 constituted historic peaks in the number of refugees worldwide and travelling to the EU since World War II (AFP 2015). Not only has it therefore been called the EU's "greatest challenge since the debt crisis" (Park 2015), at the height of the crisis in August 2015, German chancellor Angela Merkel stated that "[...t]he issue of asylum could be the next major European project, in which we show whether we are really able to take joint action" (AFP 2015). Over the course of 2014 and 2015, the number of third-country asylum seekers alone rose sharply from 431,100 in 2013 to

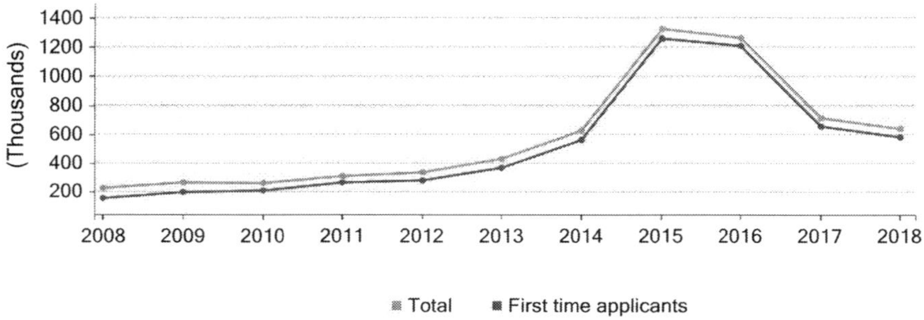

FIGURE 5.7 Asylum Applications (Non-EU) in the EU-28 Member States (2008–2018)

(Eurostat n.d.)

1,322,800 (see Figure 5.7). The number of illicit border crossings into the EU likewise skyrocketed (see Figures 5.8 and 5.9). While the refugee and migrant crisis in the EU exhibited rising interdependencies and produced functional pressure on European governments to cooperate, politicisation mattered even more as driver of state preferences.

The increase in arrivals to the EU was highly politicised in all EU Member States and received significant press coverage. A number of common patterns may be identified. First, all public debate reflected "high levels of public anxiety about immigration and asylum across Europe" (Berry et al. 2016: 4). Second, mass media played an important role as agenda-setter and framer of the crisis and public opinion. While press coverage overall framed the arrival of refugees and migrants as mostly negative, some incidents were reported with great empathy and sparked declarations of solidarity, such as the appearance on the Turkish shore of the lifeless body of a three-year-old Syrian refugee who had drowned while his family attempted to cross the Mediterranean Sea (ibid.: 5). Both negative and positive media reports contributed to building public pressure and a sense of crisis, urgency and the need to act – be it in order to protect 'Fortress

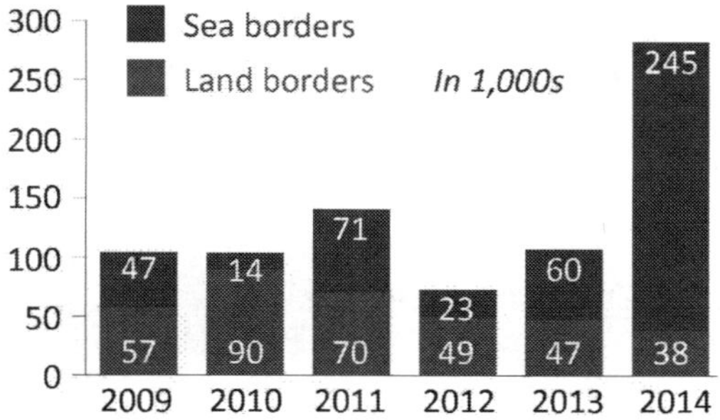

FIGURE 5.8 Illegal Border Crossings into the EU by Third-Country Citizens

(Sabbati & Poptcheva 2015: 1)

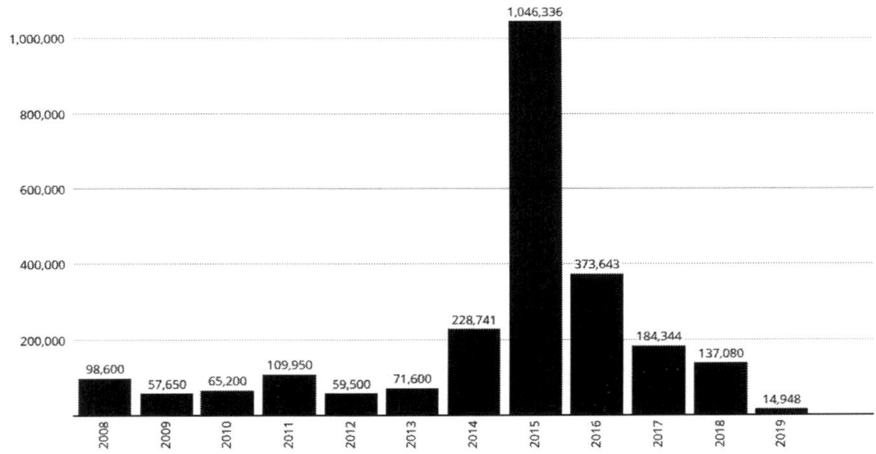

FIGURE 5.9 Total Irregular Arrivals to the EU (2008–2019)
(Council 2019a)

Europe' or to save lives. Third, the EU – rather than national levels – was consistently regarded and highlighted as main policy venue for collective action and crisis management (ibid.: 10). Fourth, and perhaps most important in the context of shifting state preferences in favour of launching the EMSC at Europol, from early 2015 onwards, the refugee and migrant crisis was increasingly framed in terms of security threats to the EU, particularly migrant smuggling (ibid.: 9-11). The shift across European countries towards securitisation frames presented not only a reaction to rising interdependence in the fight against facilitated illegal immigration, but it was also a political reaction of domestic policymakers to public anxiety, and an attempt at blame-shifting by EU political elites on migrant smugglers (ibid.: 11). Ironically perhaps, populism and politicisation thus boosted the involvement of the EU in the management of the refugee and migrant crisis. As Member States sought ways of responding to growing public pressure, they favoured strengthening Europol and EU police cooperation as a means of venue-shopping (Interviewees 32, 33 & 34).

Public pressure, political momentum and securitisation frames were exacerbated by the terror attacks of 2015 (see Figure 5.5). The Paris attacks of January and November 2015 not only illustrated interdependencies in the EU's fight against terrorism, but they also likewise provided (or were framed as) evidence for a growing crime-terror or asylum-terror nexus amidst the on-going refugee crisis: links between facilitated irregular migration and terrorism (Interviewees 14, 15 & 22; cf. Rekawek et al. 2018: 8). Crisis politicisation after the Paris attacks and unrelenting migratory flows into the EU together boosted the level of public pressure experienced by national policymakers. The salience and framing of migrant smuggling as a threat to European security quickly became the focal point of public and political debates concerning the on-going refugee and migrant crisis (Berry et al. 2016). Some even claim:

> The refugee crisis in Europe c[ould...] no longer be understood as separate from the crisis of terrorism after the Paris attacks on 13 November 2015. In fact, the two crises were never really separate in the nationalist imaginary to begin with. [...W]hat was only implicit in the European response to the Syrian refugees has now become explicit in the response to the tragic attacks in Paris: that migration is understood to be a form of barbarian warfare that threatens the European Union.
>
> *(Nail 2016)*

The joint effect of these crises pushed Member States to prioritise the issue areas of migrant smuggling and THB. Although migration had been on the EU's agenda for a while, it only now became a "hot topic" among national governments (Interviewees 33 & 34). Growing salience and public pressure thus constituted the main impulse for Member States to promote collective action at the EU level and employ securitisation frames in the management of the refugee and migrant crisis. Rather than driven by operational input from police levels, this shift in preferences presented a political reaction to public fear (Interviewees 14 & 15). On 12 February 2015, the European Council decided to strengthen the EU approach on foreign fighters and terrorist travellers, and on the prevention of security impacts from external crises and conflicts (European Council 2015a).

TIPPING THE SCALES: EUROPOL'S GROWING ACTORNESS

Politicisation opened a window of opportunity for renewed supranational policy entrepreneurship. In 2015, EU actors began to increasingly harness public pressure to impact state preferences towards deeper integration (Interviewees 2, 5, 10, 33 & 34). Especially Europol developed a strong pro-EU entrepreneurship. In March 2015, the Joint Operational Team (JOT) MARE had been launched at Europol to fight facilitated illegal migration to the EU via the Mediterranean Sea (Europol 2016b). The initial participating countries were France, Germany, Italy, Spain and the UK – all among the top ten destination countries within the EU, where functional and public pressure were arguably relatively high ('Migration to Europe in charts' 2018; Schröder 2015: 2). Although not even ten people coordinated JOT MARE at Europol at first, it presented a stepping stone for enhancing Europol's involvement and thereby further integration of EU police cooperation in this issue area (EUC 2015: 72).

Rather than utilising public anxiety over the migration-terror nexus, Europol's policy entrepreneurship harnessed politicisation of growing criminal threats in relation to irregular immigration. Amidst the unfolding refugee and migrant crisis in 2014, it reported instances in various Member States, where irregular migrants or criminal groups had developed links with terrorist groups. Nevertheless, Europol commented very hesitantly on the extent and long-term sustainability of such cooperation (Europol 2014a: 13 & 22). Instead, the agency highlighted the functional need to respond jointly to the unprecedented increase in the number of irregular immigrants arriving to the EU (Interviewees 14, 24, 27 & 35). It stressed the growth of this number by 332% from 2013 to 2014 and underlined the parallel rise in use of smuggling services by many illegal immigrants after their entry of the EU (Europol 2015b: 13).

Additionally, Europol tied in with functional pressure and the shadow of the future if policymakers did not support European solutions to the refugee and migrant crisis. Europol officials repeatedly stressed the "profound impact" of the refugee and migrant crisis on "Europe's criminal landscape" (Europol 2016d: 2). Europol officials particularly highlighted the negative economic and security effects in relation to the emergence of sophisticated migrant-smuggling networks that operated across borders within the EU and were making significant profits from their criminal enterprises (ibid.; Interviewees 27 & 35). They emphasised that every single Member State was to some extent affected by migrant smuggling to and within the EU (see Figure 5.10). Out of more than one million

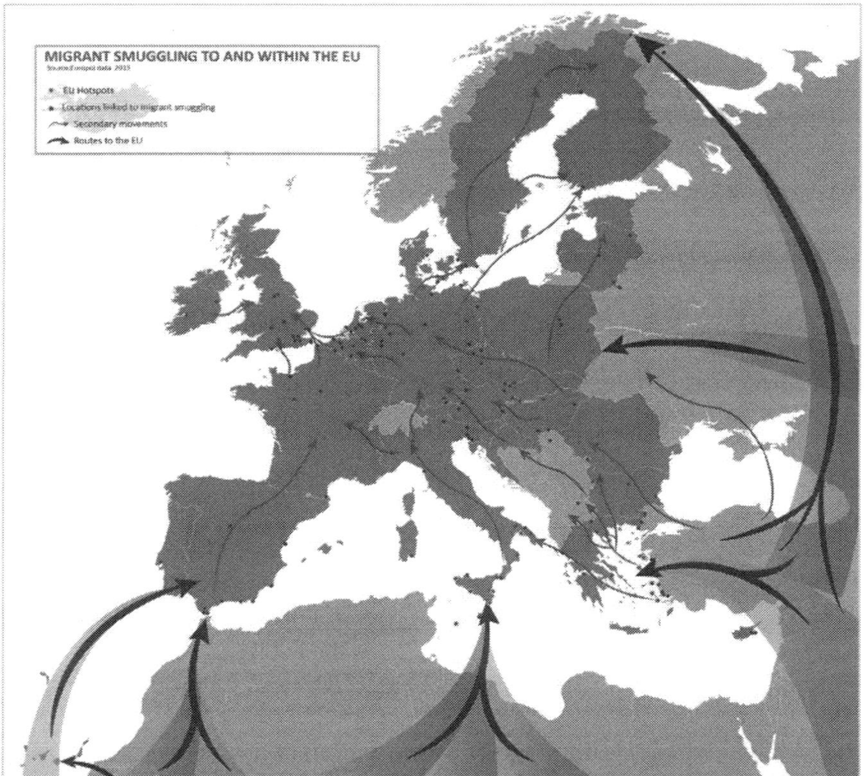

FIGURE 5.10 Migrant Smuggling to and within the EU

(Europol n.d.-a)

migrants arriving to the EU in 2015, over 90% had employed smuggling services, a trend and criminal market that Europol claimed was only going to continue in 2016 (Europol 2016d: 2). The agency presented and promoted itself as 'suitable remedy' (Interviewee 15). Its central position at the heart of police cooperation as well as its emerging capacities within the AWFs and JOT MARE arguably made it the ideal policy venue to counter rising internal and external interdependencies (Interviewees 24, 27 & 35). National policymakers could not very easily refute this "common sense argument" in the midst of on-going crisis politicisation and calls from subnational police officials for improving efficiency in cross-national cooperation and information exchange (Interviewees 34, 42 & 43). On the contrary, prioritising supranational policy venues allowed Member States to explain governance failures as a result of collective action problems at the EU level. National governments and Europol alike thus framed Europol as effective solution for domestic problems and security threats (ibid.).

Combined politicisation and supranational policy entrepreneurship consequently drove European governments to adopt securitisation measures at the EU level. While reinforcing internal and external borders marked the initial phase of collective action in 2014, from 2015 onwards Member States increasingly focused on common police action to target migrant smugglers and human traffickers. At a European Council meeting on 23 April 2015, European heads of state or government recognised the urgent need to respond to the refugee and migrant crisis and committed themselves to "strengthen [...]presence at sea, to fight the traffickers, to prevent illegal migration flows and to reinforce internal solidarity and responsibility" (European Council 2015b). They concretely highlighted the role of Europol and encouraged active engagement by the agency and the European Commission.

Against this backdrop, the European Commission presented its Agenda on Migration in May. In line with the general political and media discourse, the Commission emphasised the "need for swift and determined action in response to the human tragedy in the whole of the Mediterranean" (European Commission 2015c: 3). It harnessed existing securitisation frames by stressing that the fight against migrant smuggling should be a key priority for the Member States. Europol, the Agenda stipulated, "will immediately strengthen its recently established joint maritime information operation (JOT MARE) – and its focal point on migrant smuggling" (ibid.: 3f.). Europol would be transformed into a "single entry point for inter-agency cooperation on smuggling" (ibid.). Similar to the EC3 and the ECTC, the first mention of such a central contact point – the predecessor of the EMSC – was proposed by an EU actor, the Commission. Its EU action plan against migrant smuggling reiterated this endeavour. Although the document did not yet explicitly mention the idea of establishing an according centre at Europol, it stressed the need to develop Europol into an "EU information hub for migrant smuggling" (European Commission 2015d).

Europol strategically built on the Commission's entrepreneurship to promote its services and EU police cooperation. Appearing before the UK's House of Lords in August 2015, Europol Director Rob Wainwright stated that, to sustainably combat migrant smuggling, "Europol's role[...] may be instrumental" (EUC 2015: 78). In his view the organisation's resources and competencies required significant boosting, including the creation of 25 new posts at Europol until 2017 – a demand repeated to the Council, the European Commission and the European Parliament (ibid.: 79ff.). The relevance of Europol's direct advocacy in front of the British House of Lords should not be underestimated. The UK had been the main initiator of JOT MARE in March 2015.

As a result of supranational policy entrepreneurship, Member States accepted the proposal to merge Europol's analytical projects in this issue area within a new-to-be-launched centre (Interviewees 6, 31, 32 & 43). Even before the Paris attacks of 13 November, 2015, the JHA Council had invited Europol to "accelerate the establishment of the European Migrant Smuggling Centre (EMSC) to strengthen its capacity to support Member States in better preventing and fighting against migrant smuggling" (Council 2015b: 5). While state preferences had already shifted towards prioritising integration in this field, and the decision to create the EMSC at Europol had already been taken, politicisation following the terrorist attacks in Paris boosted the preferences of Member States to this end (Interviewees 22, 27 & 40). The EMSC was subsequently launched at Europol in February 2016, one month after the creation of the ECTC (Europol 2016d: 14).

The European Financial and Economic Crime Centre

Following the creation of the EC3 in 2013 and the ECTC and EMSC in early 2016, the EFECC was created at Europol on 05 June 2020 to better support Member States in the fight against financial and economic crime, centralise EU police cooperation in this issue area and promote the systematic use of financial investigations. Similar to the launch of the other centres at Europol, it was the culmination and consolidation of a number of developments (see Figure 5.11). Although the EU had been officially involved in the fight against financial crime and money laundering since 1991, the competence to act in criminal matters initially lay with the Member States alone. As a consequence, "money [was flowing...]easily across borders, but information about money movements[... did] not" (Mouzakiti 2020: 353). The first attempt at institutionalising cooperation and information exchange captures this structural discrepancy. Tracking financial flows and investigating suspicious transactions "was not assigned to the 'traditional' policing sector, but [to] special agencies[...]. These 'new policing' institutions became known as[...]FIUs[...and were situated] between the reporting and law enforcement sectors" (ibid.). The decentralised nature of FIUs in the EU posed a considerable challenge, as tremendous amounts of data that needed to be processed and analysed. Eventually integrating them into Europol's structure made sense for various reasons.

Since Europol's very beginnings, financial and economic crime had formed part of its mandate. Even the very narrow functional scope of the EDU – tasked with the fight against drug trafficking – already included "associated money

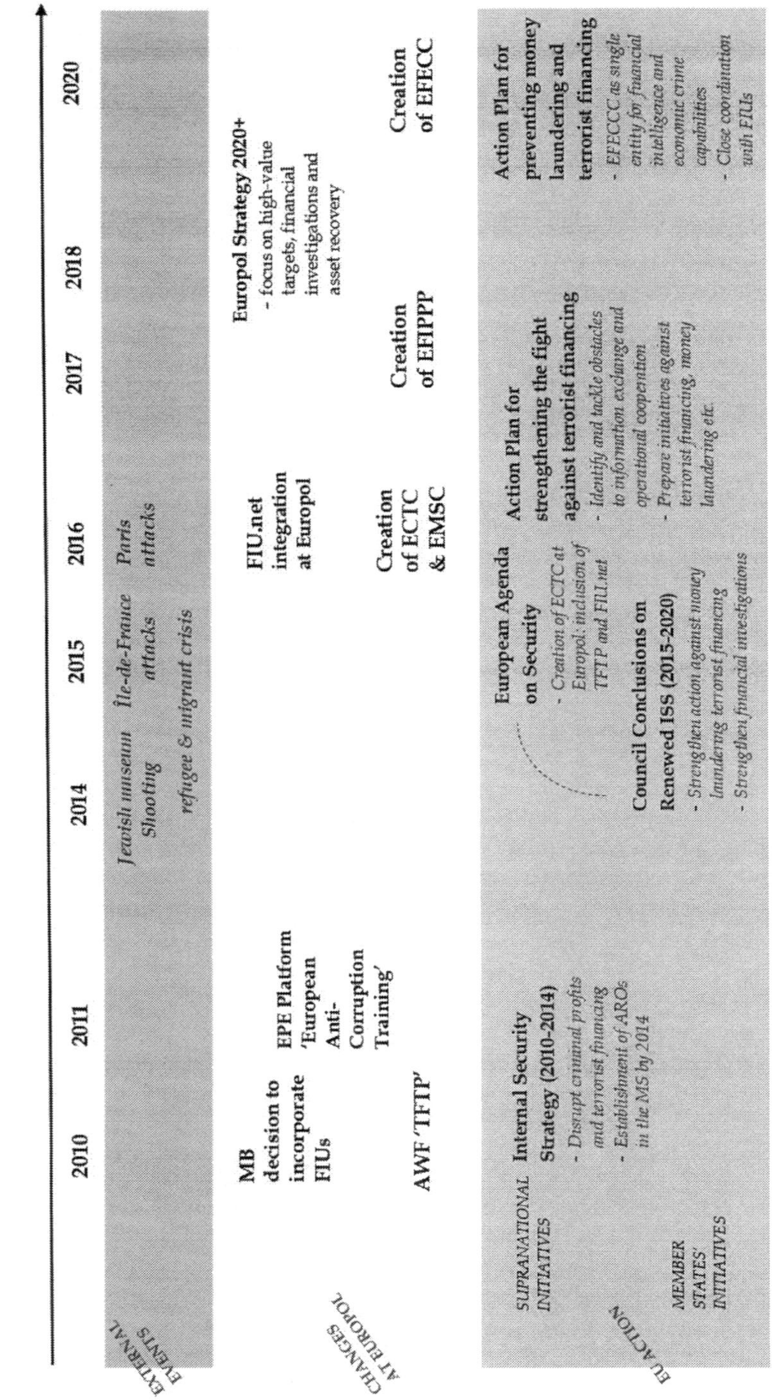

FIGURE 5.11 A Chronology of Europol's European Financial and Economic Crime Centre (EFECC)

laundering activities." The Europol Convention continued and expanded Europol's mandate in this area. Although the initial issue areas specified under Europol's objective did not explicitly include financial or economic crime, the Convention declared Europol competent to deal with "illegal money-laundering activities in connection with these forms of crime or specific manifestations thereof" (Art. 2(3)(1)). Additionally, the annex listed swindling and fraud, racketeering and extortion, counterfeiting and product piracy, forgery of money and means of payment, and corruption. National law enforcement authorities were initially hesitant to make use of Europol for support in these issue areas or in financial investigations. Not only was its involvement in this issue area not yet established and related services still under development, but also the agency itself was brand-new with no known track record among officials in the Member States. The Europol Annual Report 1999 bears testimony to the early scepticism of practitioners:

> In accordance with the advice received from the Heads of National Units, Europol reserved resources to support criminal investigations in the area of money laundering by providing expertise at request. However, no request was received from competent services in the Member States.
>
> *(Europol 2000: 16)*

Instead of operational support, the agency thus focused on activities related to information-exchange and training as well as on the provision of strategic and analytical products. It engaged substantively in outreach and communication activities to raise its profile among practitioners (Interviewee 50). The early Europol relied heavily on the demand and support from Member States, as it did not have a standing clientele. In 1999, it received "essential support" from the Member States in the development of its activities in the newly mandated field of forgery of money and other means of payment. The annual report explicitly mentions the crucial role of Seconded National Experts (SNEs) from "France, Germany, Italy and Spain[...in] enabling the initiation of the preparative phase of the Euro Project within Europol" (Europol 2000: 17). The launch of the euro and the establishment of the eurozone – the monetary union of (initially) 11 Member States – created interdependencies that now needed to be managed. This may explain why EU governments were very willing to support Europol in the development of its role. They had a vested interest to improve cross-border cooperation. Especially larger and economically stronger Member States were eager to offset the negative effects of a common European currency and monetary policy. They feared to have the most to lose from euro counterfeiting and related financial crime. As a consequence, they were overall favourable towards strengthening Europol and EU police cooperation in this issue area.

In 2000, the Council extended Europol's mandate to money laundering in general. Spiralling case numbers and costs associated with financial crime were shaping state preferences accordingly. Growing financial and economic interdependencies and spill-overs from other issue areas created functional pressure to improve cooperation. A 'money laundering protocol' was drawn up to amend the Convention accordingly. In the following years, 9/11 and other terrorist attacks additionally moved the financing of terrorism on top of the political agenda and made it a priority at European level and within Europol's support activities (Europol 2003: 18). Europol became increasingly involved in developing tools and concepts to improve analysis and operational cooperation on a wide range of related topics, including suspicious financial transactions, money laundering and bank fraud. To this end, various AWFs were opened at Europol's operational department:

- AWF 'SUSTRANS' in November 2001 to deal with "criminal organisations involved in money laundering activities and related offences;"
- AWF 'TERMINAL' in April 2003 to target "networks consisting of individuals involved in fraudulent activities related to payment card fraud;"
- AWF 'SOYA' in March 2005 to target "criminal groups involved in the production and uttering of counterfeiting currency, specifically the Euro" (Europol 2009: 10).

The extended list of forms of crime falling within Europol's competence – including the emerging priority area of financial and economic crime – was carried over into the Council Decision. When the ECD was adopted in 2009, it formally named Europol the EU's "Central Office for combating euro counterfeiting" (Art. 5(5)). This in turn gave it the right to suggest measures to improve coordination and empowered it to support – also financially – national investigations of euro counterfeiting.

Shortly after the ECD had entered into force on 1 January 2010, Europol's MB decided to incorporate FIUs into Europol (see Figure 5.11). This likewise entailed integrating FIU.net into the agency – the decentralised computer network used by European FIUs – and establishing Europol's Secure Information Exchange Network Application (SIENA) as standard communication tool (Europol 2016a: 101–102). To Member States, this decision presented a practical fix for the problems associated with cross-border information exchange in this area and the large amounts of data processed by FIUs. At the time, European FIUs shared a common mandate and objective and may very well have been willing to cooperate, yet their structural set-up differed significantly across Member States. Rather than a coherent set of entities, EU governments had developed their FIUs under different models, comprising "administrative, police, judicial and 'hybrid' authorities" (Mouzakiti 2020: 354).

Placing Europol at the centre of this decentralised network and embedding it as central host of FIU.net was intended to solve collective action problems and manage complex interdependencies (Interviewee 50). Moreover, the incorporation of FIUs into Europol had an important – perhaps unintended – effect on the evolving role of Europol in the fight against financial crime. It set a precedent for the build-up and institutional involvement of Europol – and in fact the EU – in this domain. Formally tasking the agency with hosting and managing FIU.net and establishing its communication application as main tool not only placed Europol at the centre of information exchange and financial intelligence cooperation in the EU, but it also established Europol as a key actor and set it up for a potential role in the institutional continuity of EU police cooperation in this area. Already in August 2010, following the conclusion of the EU-US TFTP, Europol presented the logical choice as central point of contact for the EU. A dedicated AWF was opened in its operational department and further strengthened the agency's role as main hub of coordination and information exchange (see Figure 5.11).

The decision to give Europol a formal role in relation to the TFTP linked its activities in the fight against financial crime and money laundering to the fight against terrorism. This link-up matters because the high-profile area of counter-terrorism may politicise other issue areas by proxy and can by extension advance collective action or integration on other topics (e.g. cyber). This would likewise be the case in relation to financial crime and the ultimate decision to launch EFECC at Europol.

However, politicisation alone did not effectuate the creation of such a centre at Europol. Growing interdependencies were generating an operational demand to institutionalise cooperation (Interviewees 31 & 50). In December 2010, one fifth of the content in the EIS was connected to forgery of money, which constituted the third largest crime area within Europol's system at the time (Europol 2011: 12). Concerning information exchange via SIENA, 37% of all new cases were related to fraud and swindling, the forgery of money or other fraudulent means of payment (ibid.: 13).

The prominence of money and financial flows in relation to criminal activities or illegal purposes was likewise reflected in the 2010 EU ISS. Tracking financial flows and cutting off criminal profits or terrorist funding presented key themes in the EU objectives defined by the European Commission. Still under the impression from the terrorist attacks in Madrid and London in 2004 and 2005, the Strategy emphasised the importance of better identifying and disrupting financial transactions and assets supporting terrorist activities in the Member States. To this end, the Commission intended to strengthen action at the EU level, especially information exchange and the development of "a policy for the EU to extract and analyse financial messaging data held on its own territory" (European Commission 2010d: 8). The ISS 2010 highlighted the relevance of better understanding and stopping criminal sources of income and particularly strengthening law enforcement cooperation (ibid.: 4–5). Concretely, it obliged Member States to finally implement Council Decision 2007/845/JHA and establish AROs by 2014 (ibid.: 6). The impetus for this Decision had likewise originated from the Madrid and London attacks. Similar to the Prüm framework, it sought to part-integrate the existing intergovernmental network CARIN into the EU framework. Europol was named central contact point and a coordination unit was established at the agency, the ECAB (Van Berkel 2017). Notwithstanding the prominence of financial crime, terrorist financing and illicit profits in the ISS 2010, the responsibility for taking related action and measures was primarily placed on the Member States and the European Commission.

Europol continued to be involved closely yet largely informally. Although its legal framework allowed the agency to deal with related forms of crime, and it had been given a formal role as central point of contact for the recovery of criminal assets and in relation to US-EU cooperation on terrorist financing (AWF 'TFTP'), Europol lacked a single, consolidated mandate for this area. Its different roles and activities within various networks and on multiple topics remained overall disconnected. In practice, Europol acted as coordinator, exchange platform and trainer for aspects of anti-money laundering (AML), combatting financial and economic crime or countering the financing of terrorism (CFT). However, its activities and involvement continued to grow separately from one another and evolved at different speeds, mainly driven by operational demand from Member States and law enforcement authorities (Interviewees 24, 31 & 39). In 2011, Europol had for instance established an online platform for 'European Anti-Corruption Training' as part of the Europol Platform for Experts (EPE) and was preparing the launch of an additional platform for 'Money counterfeiting and payment card fraud (PaySafe)' as well as the integration into EPE of the existing ad-hoc website 'Financial Crime Information Centre' (Europol 2011: 24). In 2012, it was invited to host the Permanent Secretariat for the newly created informal Anti-Money Laundering Operational Network (AMON), comprising experts and investigators from 25 EU Member States and several third countries (Europol 2012a).

Despite the growing relevance of financial and economic crime at the EU level and despite Europol's extensive practical, even part-formal involvement, integration in this issue area seemed far off at the time. Rules and procedures on financial and other information for the purposes of preventing, detecting or prosecuting criminal offences remained far from harmonised. Many longstanding problems in financial intelligence and police cooperation persisted, although the functional scope and demands constantly widened (Lannoo & Parlour 2021: 12). Aspects of finance increasingly mattered in more and more criminal issue areas and required the involvement of different practitioners' networks and authorities. Yet, law enforcement action remained ineffective, for example in the recovery of criminal assets, and joint efforts to manage institutional interdependencies and complexity were lagging behind (Europol 2016b: 4). Europol's role in relation to national FIUs was sidelined by the Commission's EU FIUs Platform, an expert group that had been launched in 2006 to facilitate FIU cooperation. In view of these persisting obstacles, Member States were undoubtedly interested in improving police cooperation. Especially subnational practitioners and police officers had an operational demand for central coordination and information exchange. This gave EU actors an opening to advocate EU police cooperation. They were able to effectuate some legislative changes, including the explicit mention of FIUs in the fourth AML Directive (Mouzakiti 2020: 355–356). Nonetheless, FIUs remained under the radar of national policymakers. Politically, money laundering and financial crime were not high-profile issue areas. The momentum that related forms of crime had gained among EU governments in the aftermath of 9/11 and the Madrid and London terrorist attacks had faded somewhat by 2010. European integration in this domain was neither a particular preference nor a priority among Member States.

The Jewish museum shooting in Brussels in May 2014 and the series of terrorist attacks across Île-de-France and Paris in January 2015 garnered a new momentum in the resolve of EU Member States to improve collective action in the fight against terrorism. By extension, this impacted state preference in favour of strengthening cooperation in relation to terrorist-financing and organised crime. Member States called upon the European Commission to include both as priority areas in the development of the renewed EU ISS and present it in spring 2015 (Council 2014e). For the years 2015–2020, "[...s]pecial attention should be given to any activity related to money laundering and reinvestments of related proceeds of crime, in particular aimed at infiltrating the legitimate economy" and in relation to terrorism financing (ibid.: 3–4).

In April 2015, the Commission presented the European Agenda on Security as a basis for EU cooperation and joint action on security (see Figure 5.11). The document renewed the ISS priorities and emphasised the fight against money laundering and terrorist financing as key objectives. The Agenda thus tightened the topical link between the areas of AML and CFT. It likewise brought existing operational demand and functional pressure to the forefront. Similar to cybercrime, financial and economic crime presented an increasingly cross-cutting phenomenon that sustained other crime areas and facilitated many criminal activities (Interviewees 33 & 38). Made visible by the terrorist attacks, this threat was officially acknowledged by EU policymakers in and throughout the 2015 Agenda. The document highlighted financial and economic crime as a priority issue area in combatting serious and organised cross-border crime as well as cybercrime in the EU (European Commission 2015b: 12). To equip police officials with "the capacity to turn the spotlight on the finance of organised crime" (ibid.: 17), the Agenda intended to strengthen information exchange and operational cooperation. To this end, it focused on Europol as key actor, single point of contact and "channel of first choice for law enforcement" cooperation (ibid.: 6).

The most significant provision of the European Agenda on Security for the field of financial crime derived from the decision to create the ECTC at Europol in 2016, which likewise foresaw the inclusion of AWF 'TFTP' and FIU.net within the new unit in Europol's operational department (ibid.: 13). Member States regarded "[...t]he forthcoming embedment of FIU.net with Europol[... as] enhance[...ing] capabilities in the fight against terrorist financing" (ibid.: 14). The Europol MB decision from May 2010 to incorporate FIUs at Europol was thus politically validated and elevated by the 2015 European Agenda, and against the backdrop of recent terrorist attacks. State preferences in favour of an integrated approach on counterterrorism likewise shaped integration preferences on the fight against financial and economic crime.

With a view to implementing the renewed ISS priorities – as set out by the European Agenda on Security – national policymakers advocated an integrated EU approach and improved law enforcement cooperation. In June 2015, the Council highlighted the importance of tackling money laundering and terrorist financing as well as strengthening financial investigations and information exchange (Council 2015e: 6–7). To this end, Member States instructed the different Council WGs with the preparation of measures. COSI was to "develop[...] a list of priority actions [...]by December 2015 at the latest" (ibid.: 10). A first implementation paper from July tasked COSI with monitoring the launch of the ECTC at Europol and the "link between organised crime and terrorism" (Luxembourg Presidency 2015: 6). The more operations-focused TWP was asked to address "cross-cutting issues" of counterterrorism such as data and financing (ibid.: 11). Finally, the Law Enforcement Working Party (LEWP) was to deal with the "financing of organised crime and the infiltration of the licit economy by organised crime" (ibid.: 16). Special emphasis was given to improving aspects of information- and knowledge-sharing. Although Europol was not explicitly mentioned in the Council conclusions, the European Agenda on Security had stressed the importance of enhancing its role and capabilities, and further action was now taken at working level to put this into practice.

The Paris attacks in November 2015 amplified EU action on financial crime and renewed political momentum to move along the FIU integration at Europol. EU actors and Member States alike called for the swift inclusion of FIU.net at the agency as a tool in the fight against terrorism (European Parliament 2015; Interviewees 27 & 31). In January 2016, FIU.net was officially embedded in Europol (Europol 2016a: 102). While this step further institutionalised EU cooperation, cross-border police cooperation on money laundering and terrorist financing remained far from perfect. This was likewise acknowledged by EU actors and deliberately leveraged to promote further integration among Member States. In its Action Plan for strengthening the fight against terrorist financing from February 2016, the European Commission announced a "mapping exercise[...] to identify practical obstacles to access to, exchange and use of information as well as operational cooperation" alongside a "supranational assessment of money laundering and terrorism financing risks" (European Commission 2016: 7). Based on this stocktaking, policy and legislative measures should be developed at the EU level. Additionally, action was to be taken on related issue areas like illegal cash movements, money laundering and criminal assets, and EU initiatives to be prepared jointly with Europol and others (ibid.: 10). These initiatives were presented as "building on existing EU rules" and continuing the priorities and measures stipulated by the European Agenda on Security (ibid.: 2). The European Commission thus combined arguments of functional pressure and institutional continuity to shape state preferences in favour of EU action. Emerging interdependencies in the areas of money laundering and terrorist financing as well as in cross-border cooperation structures had already in the past proven as effective means to sway Member States and advance the role of EU actors.

The Commission report on cooperation between EU FIUs from June 2017 – a staff working document prepared by national FIU officials – found a "significant number of obstacles" to operational and strategic cooperation (European Commission 2017a: 10). As key problems, the report identifies differences in the organisational structure and cultures of national FIUs, lack of access to relevant information and lack of a common understanding of the functions and types of analyses carried out by FIUs. To address these issues, the European Commission suggested strengthening its very own EU FIUs Platform and other tools within the EU AML regime but also FIU.net. The report explicitly recognised the value of the latter's embedment at Europol and welcomed its contribution to "the creation of synergies between FIU intelligence and law enforcement work" (ibid.: 3).

The ultimate impetus towards integrated EU solutions – including the creation of EFECC at Europol – came from domestic security and police officials (Interviewees 50 & 51). Functional spill-overs from economic and monetary integration in the EU gradually produced political spill-overs. The rise of financial and economic crime could not be satisfyingly dealt with by domestic actors or single Member States alone. Practitioners at the national level were increasingly attributing the persisting problems in the fight against money laundering, terrorist financing and related forms of crime to the discrepancy between rising structural interdependencies on the one hand and the institutional complexity and fragmentation of cooperation and policing efforts on the other. This first manifested itself within individual Member States. The impact of financial and economic crime cut across various policy domains and authorities. As illegal financial activities expanded in scale and scope, so did functional pressure on subnational practitioners to cooperate.

The UK acted as first mover in this issue area and as role model for action in other Member States and later at the EU level. This seems unsurprising in view of the UK's status as European and international financial hub with a large financial sector. In February 2015, it launched a Joint Money Laundering Intelligence Taskforce (JMLIT) "to enable financial sector institutions and law enforcement agencies to share and analyse information to prevent, detect and disrupt money laundering" (HO 2017: 4). JMLIT brings together officials from the private sector, the UK's tax, payments and customs authority, the National Crime Agency and the City of London Police (HO & HM Treasury 2017: 37). The unit had originally started as a pilot but was soon reinforced as operational cooperation platform and referenced in other policy instruments, such as the first National Risk Assessment (NRA) for Money Laundering and Terrorist Financing. The report followed a recommendation from the international Financial Action Task Force (FATF) and was presented in October 2015. It concluded that "the same factors which make the UK attractive for legitimate financial activity also make it attractive for criminals and terrorists" (ibid.: 4). To close intelligence and regulatory gaps, tackle legal and practical inconsistencies and improve the overall AML and CFT approach in the UK, the NRA identified three priorities: enhancing law enforcement responses, supervisory regimes and cross-border cooperation. Among its key objectives, the assessment underlined the importance of "transforming" information exchange between police agencies, supervisory authorities and the private sector (HO & HM Treasury 2015: 7). To this end, it recommended to "build[…] on the progress made through the JMLIT" as a priority in the national action plan that would follow in 2016 (ibid.).

The UK's holistic, risk-based approach and model of public-private partnership inspired other Member States. Similar central units and interdisciplinary platforms were established in Denmark, the Netherlands and Sweden (Lannoo & Parlour 2021: 19). This 'centre approach' and centralisation tendency among domestic authorities created an opening for EU actors to promote integration at supranational level. Member States could hardly argue against streamlined cooperation and integrative action at the EU level when they had already underlined the added value and importance of both at the national level. They had previously supported the establishment of focal points and operational centres at Europol (e.g. EC3 and ECTC) to address interdependencies in the fight against cybercrime and terrorism. This not only made opposing EU centralisation initiatives in the area of financial and economic crime politically difficult for government officials, but it also would have contradicted the functional and operational need voiced by domestic practitioners to improve collective action.

Accordingly, in 2017, Europol instigated the launch of a pilot platform modelled after the UK's JMLIT. In December 2017, it launched the Europol Financial Intelligence Public Private Partnership (EFIPPP). This would ultimately pave the way for the creation of EFECC. Similar to JIMLIT, the main objective of EFIPPP is to improve strategic and operational collaboration and facilitate information exchange among Europol, different competent authorities (also FIUs) and financial institutions (Maxwell 2020: 79). Hosted by Europol, the partnership may be regarded as an example of external differentiation. Its fifteen state members include not only EU Member States but also third countries (Australia, Switzerland, the UK and the US). Additionally, 25 banking institutions participate in EFIPPP. The network is governed by a Steering Group, comprising Europol and eight other members and supported by a permanent secretariat at Europol, composed of seconded staff members from Europol, law enforcement agencies, FIUs and financial institutions (ibid.: 80). EFIPPP meets quarterly and discusses priority topics defined by the Steering Group. Currently, three WGs exist to deal with (1) the analysis of threats and typologies, (2) mapping legal gateways for information exchange and (3) the impact of COVID-19 on financial crime (AMLC 2020). The partnership has been promoted internationally by Europol and others as trailblazer for integrated action in the fight against financial crime. In January 2018, Europol's Executive Director Rob Wainwright proudly called the partnership "the first transnational financial information sharing mechanism" (Europol 2018c).

By 2018, Europol had established itself as an actor in this issue area and related EU police cooperation and information exchange were thriving. Various measures and actions were taken at the EU level in the same year. They include a Commission proposal (COM(2018) 213 final) from April 2018 to facilitate "the use of financial and other information for the prevention, detection, investigation or prosecution of certain criminal offences." The proposed directive (which has meanwhile been adopted) stipulated indirect access for Europol (through ENUs) to national centralised bank account registries or data retrieval systems. This constituted a direct reaction to Europol integration entrepreneurship. In 2017, Europol had stressed a lack of access to financial and especially bank account information. This, the agency argued, hampered its analytical and support capacity and thereby hindered EU police cooperation (Europol 2017: 2). Member States seemed to respond to these functional arguments. In December 2018, they adopted a set of operational measures to strengthen law enforcement in the fight against migrant smuggling (Council doc. 15250/18). This included the improvement of financial intelligence cooperation within the EU. Concretely, the Council pledged to "[s]trengthen Europol's [...]capacity to support financial investigations and asset recovery[...,] in particular by facilitating access to information from[...] FIUs, [...]AROs and Customs agencies" (ibid.: 5 & 16).

Europol actively sought to cultivate this political momentum. The Europol Strategy 2020+ that was adopted in December 2018 highlights financial and economic crime as a priority area. To strengthen the delivery of "agile operational support" and tackle cross-border organised crime groups and networks, Europol announced to "put more focus on investigating high-value targets, financial investigations and asset recovery" (Europol 2018a: 4).

Two developments put a damper was on the integration momentum. First, the embedment of FIU.net at Europol "proved both legally and technically complicated," especially its integration with SIENA (Mouzakiti 2020: 371). A 2017 Europol Roadmap for the future development of FIU.net aimed at centralising the system as a possible remedy. However, this was met with reluctance by multiple FIUs. Domestic concerns about data protection and ownership clashed with Europol's integration attempts (EU FIU Platform 2018: 5–6). As a consequence, Europol reworked the Roadmap and guidance was requested from the EDPS and the Europol Cooperation Board, which comprises representatives from national supervisory authorities and the EDPS (Mouzakiti 2020: 372). In the meantime, the operational momentum of EU cooperation on financial intelligence issues was curbed if not put to a halt altogether. A Commission report from July 2019 noted that "recurrent technical difficulties in the functioning of the FIU.net" were still making it "cumbersome for FIUs to share information" and pressed for the swift resolution of "questions raised by the FIUs, relating in particular to data protection compliance issues" to enable Europol to continue updating the system (European Commission 2019: 14).

Second, parallel developments at the EU level had direct implications on the evolution of FIU.net as well as on EU police cooperation, data processing and the role of Europol. The year 2018 was "the year of data protection" in the EU (Mouzakiti 2020: 363). In May, the GDPR went into effect and the deadline for the incorporation into national law of the Police Data Protection Directive expired. Against this backdrop, the Europol Cooperation Board in September 2019 responded to Europol's request for advice on the embedment of FIU.net. It did not find existing arrangements or planned provisions "consistent with Europol's mandate" (Pellegrini 2019). In December, the EDPS confirmed this view. He declared the incorporation of FIU.net into SIENA as infringing data protection rules and legal limitations of the Europol Regulation (EDPS 2020a: 18). As a consequence, the EDPS imposed a ban on related data processing by Europol. FIU.net should be transferred to another entity. In view of the importance of related information exchange, a relatively generous deadline for this transfer was set with December 2020. While this development presented a blow to Europol's role and the (at least technical) integration of police cooperation, it highlighted the relevance of functional pressure to cooperate; domestic operational authorities had pushed for embedding FIU.net at Europol for years and effectuated its formal incorporation in 2016 – in the absence of a legal basis.

A (at least interim) solution came in May 2020. In the light of the rapidly unfolding COVID-19 crisis, the topic of financial and economic crime was moving up on the political and operational agendas of the Member States. The scale and scope of illegal activities in the EU in relation to the pandemic was increasing noticeably. A Europol report from March 2020 warned against the risk of criminal exploitation of the quickly emerging and highly profitable pandemic economy. It underlined the significant "potential for substantial financial damage" to Member States in relation to the expanding "market for product counterfeiters, fraudsters and profiteers" (Europol 2020b: 7–8).

This offered opportunities for EU actors to position themselves and promote their services. The COVID-19 crisis presented a favourable moment for supranational policy entrepreneurship: to advertise EU policy venues and police cooperation as solutions to transnational threats affecting the Member States. The need to manage uncertainty arising from the complex risks, consequences and interdependencies of the pandemic rendered national policymakers open to EU proposals for a way forward (Interviewees 47–53). In the middle of a growing societal polarisation, politicisation and climate of fear, decisive collective action at European level was able to gain traction. Actors like Europol and the European Commission successfully harnessed this political momentum. In May 2020, the European Commission presented an Action Plan to strengthen EU preventive measures against money laundering and terrorist financing. Citing Europol and the risen criminal threat due to COVID-19, the Commission stressed the urgent need to ensure effective cooperation on financial and economic crime (European Commission 2020b: 21). With a view to resolving the deadlock in the development of FIU.net, the European Commission would work towards an appropriate

"EU coordination and support mechanism for FIUs" and would temporarily host FIU.net in the meantime, starting at the end of 2020 (ibid.: 29). This option was embraced by the EDPS in July (EDPS 2020).

Next to FIU.net, the Commission's Action Plan dealt with various larger developments in relation to the EU AML/CFT framework. These included the establishment of an EU single rulebook, strengthening implementation and information exchange, and the creation of a central EU-level supervisory Authority for AML and CFT (AMLA). Concrete proposals were put forward as part of a comprehensive legislative package in July 2021. It foresees i.a. enhancing law enforcement access to financial information, further strengthening the powers of EU FIUs and setting up the AMLA as a "centrepiece of an integrated AML/CFT supervisory system" and specifically as a "support and coordination hub" for the cooperation and information exchange among FIUs (COM(2021) 421 final: 3–4). This would transfer the management of FIU.net to the soon-to-be-created AMLA (ibid.: 9). At the time of writing, the proposals are still under discussion.

Europol likewise leveraged the critical window provided by the COVID-19 crisis. In June 2020, it formally launched the EFECC. The European Commission, in its Action Plan from May, had already acknowledged Europol's plans for "concentrat[...ing] all financial intelligence and economic crime capabilities in a single entity" (European Commission 2020b: 30). The Action Plan noted "that the EFECC would be a natural counterpart to the EU support and coordination mechanism for FIUs and that the two entities might develop solutions to boost exchanges of information, particularly in cross-border cases" (ibid.).

The official establishment of the Centre at Europol one month later resulted from the explicit demand and preference of European Member States for more support from Europol on financial and economic crime (Europol 2021: 74). National law enforcement capabilities alone could not effectively tackle the growing scale and scope of this criminal issue area. At the same time, parallel developments in the institutional environment of the EU – such as the establishment of a European Public Prosecutor's Office (EPPO) tasked with investigating crimes affecting the financial interests of the EU – made economic crime a priority topic and heightened the need to improve integration and collective action, with spill-over effects for police cooperation (ibid.).

The pandemic provided a convenient window of opportunity for EU actors like Europol to play on this functional integration pressure and on state preferences, which were already increasingly in favour of improved EU cooperation. Politicisation in relation to high-profile criminal cases and the COVID-19 crisis turned the spotlight to persisting shortcomings of cooperation arrangements targeting financial and economic crime and of existing AML/CFT regimes. A strategic Europol report that accompanied the launch of the EFECC cited COVID-19 as a key development requiring the further development of police cooperation in this area (Europol 2020a). The existing threat landscape – exacerbated by the pandemic – made it the "right time" for the creation of such a centre at Europol (ibid.: 20). The interconnectedness of financial and economic crime with other issue areas – as "key enabler for all other types of serious and organised crime"- required a central cooperation platform, namely EFECC (ibid.: 19). Europol built on previous institutional developments within the agency and at the EU level to justify this move. Already in 2018, the Europol Strategy 2020+ had named financial and economic crime as a priority area and paved the way for further action at Europol.

The aim behind EFECC was to (1) provide operational, analytical and technical support, (2) facilitate information exchange and cooperation among competent authorities and (3) bring together relevant expertise and stakeholders from the private and the public sector (ibid.: 19–20). It would be a key partner of the newly created EPPO and its bridge to the law enforcement community in the EU. "Initially," the centre was to support Member States through eight different analysis projects on "fraud against public and private finances, money laundering, asset recovery, corruption, product and currency counterfeiting" (ibid.: 20). The term "initially" potentially indicates a wider ambition beyond these areas and activities. Not even two years into operations, the EFECC today also lists "tax crime, euro counterfeiting and intellectual property crime" among issue areas under its responsibility. The "only pre-requisites to be eligible for EFECC Operations support are that the case affects one or more Member States and involves a criminal offence in respect of which Europol is competent" (Europol 2022). This is arguably not only testimony to Europol's growing self-perception as actor in its own right within EU police cooperation, but it also demonstrates an expectation of future path-dependency, spillovers and unintended consequences that mirrors the experience from previous centres at Europol.

Despite the successful launch of EFECC and Europol's relatively ambitious aim for the centre's role in EU police cooperation, its practice leaves much to be desired. In 2021, Europol itself observed that the "demand for financial intelligence support to Member States' investigations remains higher than the centre's capacities and further efforts need to be made in expanding EFECC services towards all forms of corruption as a new area of work" (Europol 2021: 7). Additionally, well-known obstacles to EU cooperation on financial and economic crime persist. The success and effectiveness of AML/CFT regimes and policy measures still remain behind expectations (Lannoo & Parlour 2021: 19). Particularly FIU cooperation can and must be further improved. To this end, some argue in favour of turning FIU.net into a centralised platform (ibid.). These shortcomings possibly leave room for further integration in the future or at least for the institutional development of EU police cooperation. In its Programming Document for the years until 2023, Europol has already committed to consolidate the internal and external dimensions of cooperation at its EFECC (Europol 2021: 75–76). This includes objectives like the establishment of a Joint Financial Intelligence Group at Europol, the development of a customs cooperation function within the EFECC, cooperation with the EPPO, the monitoring of relevant pandemic-related trends and the preparation for "any potential new task arising from the Action Plan [...]published by the Commission on 7 May 2020" (ibid.: 76).

It remains to be seen how Europol and the Member States decide to build on existing institutional and cooperation arrangements and if they decide to integrate further or prefer to keep structures informal and decentralised. This will most likely also depend on the evolution of the COVID-19 crisis and will be affected by parallel EU developments such as the implementation of the Commission's AML/CFT package from July 2021. The (at the time of writing on-going) Russian invasion of Ukraine since 24 February 2022 and the adoption of international economic and financial sanctions drew further attention to the issue area and presented additional opportunity for EU action and policy entrepreneurship. To enforce sanctions and prevent listed individuals from evading restrictive measures, the European Commission in March established a 'Freeze and Seize' Task Force comprising officials from the Commission, Europol, Eurojust, other EU agencies and national contact points of the Member States. The Task Force will not only facilitate information exchange among its members but also strategic and operational coordination in the seizure and confiscation of respective assets (European Commission 2022b). Additionally, the EU – together with G7 countries and Australia – launched an international 'Russian Elites, Proxies, and Oligarchs (REPO)' Task Force. If these cooperation formats prove successful, the Russian-induced crisis could present yet another window for supranational integration initiatives in the area of AML and the fight against financial and economic crime.

The Europol Regulation

Next to the institutional development of Europol via operational centres and its subsequently strengthened role in these issue areas, Member States advanced formal integration through amending the agency's legal framework. The Europol Regulation effectively replaced the ECD on 1 May 2017, not even ten years after Member States had chosen to transfer Europol to the EU framework and making it the Union's official law enforcement agency. While the importance of the Regulation for the institutional development of the organisation and EU police cooperation should not be overstated, it "has continued the trend to extend the powers of the agency" (Santos Vara 2018: 447). Among other things, it gives Europol more say and leeway in the initiation of operational cooperation and joint analytical projects and strengthens the role of the EU *vis-à-vis* the Member States in the agency's governance. Especially the European Commission gained considerable influence through the new legal framework, including in the management of Europol's external affairs, institutional and budgetary oversight as well as strategic guidance and priority-setting (European Parliament 2019). However, Europol remains a decentralised EU agency to date whose main purpose is to "support and strengthen action by the competent authorities of the

Member States" as well as "cooperation among law enforcement authorities" in the EU (Art. 3(1) & 1(1), Regulation (EU) 2016/794).

Spill-Over Effects and Path-Dependency as Crucial Enablers

This chapter has illustrated that interdependence in and among different issue areas was permanently on the rise and continues to grow in recent years. Yet, state preferences on the Europol Regulation were first and foremost shaped by political spill-overs from earlier integration decisions, most notably, the 2007 Lisbon Treaty. The Regulation itself recalls: "Article 88 of the Treaty provides for Europol to be governed by a regulation to be adopted in accordance with the ordinary legislative procedure" (recital 2 in the preamble). By the time the ECD was adopted, it was arguably already overhauled (Interviewee 29). Or, as an EU official phrased it: "with the Regulation, Europol was 'lisbonised' from an institutional point of view" (Interviewee 34). Although the Treaty provided the EU with legal personality and explicitly stipulated the adoption of a regulation as Europol's legal framework, it took six years before the European Commission first presented a draft regulation to the Member States in early 2013 (European Commission 2013). Next to the political spill-overs – or perhaps unintended consequences – of the Lisbon Treaty, the proposal for the Europol Regulation came amidst a larger integration trend in JHA: from stand-alone intergovernmental solutions to integrated "one-stop shop" solutions at the EU level (Interviewees 28, 30, 31, 34 & 44).

Path-dependency and functional pressure from spill-overs played key roles in shaping state preferences towards further integration and in favour of the Regulation. Europol had been emerging as central hub of EU police cooperation for over a decade, and increasingly presented a reliable institutional platform and trust basis for law enforcement authorities to work together (Interviewees 13 & 22–24). Member States faced an increasing demand for the continuity of these channels and had themselves developed an interest in EU initiatives. Domestic political expectations alongside positive experiences with Europol's operational output and track record constituted the main driving forces in this regard (Interviewees 12, 14, 22 & 27). Most European governments preferred to continue EU police cooperation and extend the benefits generated in single issue areas to more domains of policing and internal security. Thus, Europol and EU police cooperation benefited directly from functional and political spill-over effects that ultimately shifted state preferences towards a new regulatory framework with more powers for the EU level.

Commission Entrepreneurship and Cultivated Spill-Overs

Over the last decade, cultivated spill-overs have increasingly influenced Member States. Especially the European Commission's power in the policy domain of JHA has grown consistently and considerably, partially because of the general development of the EU, and in part thanks to the Commission's proactive integration advocacy and promotion of supranational policy venues in the area of security (Interviewees 6, 15, 23 & 33). As this chapter has demonstrated, Commission representatives frequently pushed for more centralisation and a larger role for the Commission itself in the coordination of related policies and initiatives. Very often, as this book likewise shows, Commission entrepreneurs successfully justified this position through a supposed functional need to counter growing interdependencies and collective action problems. However, in line with the adage "who has the information has the power," institutional self-interest played an at least similar motivating factor (Interviewee 46). The Commission's uniformity initiative with regard to decentralised EU agencies presents one such example. Whereas the institution's influence in centralised EU agencies was already considerable, the adoption of a common approach on decentralised ones offered an opportunity to further extend its mandate and power *vis-à-vis* the Member States (Interviewees 15, 29 & 46). Centralising information exchange at Europol and police databases at the EU level entailed a gain in the powers of EU actors and especially the European Commission. The Europol Regulation presented an opportunity to this end.

Preceding the formal regulation proposal in early 2013, Commission officials had conducted scoping talks with Member State representatives and EU actors in 2010 and 2011 (European Commission 2013: 4). The first draft version embodies a significant number of changes at Europol and within EU police cooperation that bear testimony to the strong negotiating position, institutional self-interest and investment of Commission representatives. Some of these proposals were rejected by the Member States, while others succeeded in being integrated in the final legislative text, even against the will of European governments (Interviewees 27, 29, 34 & 35). Europol and its new legal framework presented an entry point for Commission entrepreneurship and an opportunity to expand the latter's role in EU JHA and its influence within the still strongly intergovernmental realm of police cooperation.

The first draft regulation would have strengthened the powers of EU actors and diminished the ones of the Member States in various regards. The European Commission originally suggested a much more significant degree of formalisation and centralisation of Europol (Interviewees 6, 27, 29 & 34). Although Member States acknowledged the Lisbon Treaty's requirement to replace the ECD, they did not see the need for additional formalisation less than a decade after the last legislative framework had entered into effect. They disagreed on the extent to which the Commission should be involved in the organisation's governance, and how far the uniformity initiative for EU agencies should apply to Europol (ibid.). The European Commission had lobbied for the merger of Europol and the European Police College (CEPOL) – a move that would have even further increased the Commission's influence, not just in one agency (Art. 1(2), European Commission 2013). However, Member States quickly rejected the Commission's primarily budgetary and efficiency arguments. The suggestion to consolidate both organisations was deleted at the beginning of 2014 (Council 2014a).

By contrast, another pro-integration proposal was included in the final regulation. The Lisbon Treaty had formally empowered the European Commission to conclude cooperation agreements with third parties/countries on behalf of the EU (European Commission 2013: 74). Preparations for the extension of Europol's external relations were already under way even before the regulation was adopted and Member States faced considerable pressure from the European Commission and the European External Action Service (EEAS) to provide the EU with more leeway in the new legal framework (Haber 2017: 8). A similar stipulation in the first draft regulation foresaw relative autonomy for Europol in setting operational priorities without having to rely on national decision-making or endorsement. It built on previous efforts of supranational policy entrepreneurs and acknowledged the "possibility to develop [EU] centres to fight specific forms of crime" (European Commission 2013: 7). This proposal was included in the final Regulation, effectively allowing the agency to establish "Union centres of specialised expertise" (Art. 4(1)(l)).

Notwithstanding the success of Commission advocacy in some respects, a few highly ambitious suggestions were vehemently opposed by the Member States. The Commission originally recommended to include the option of down-sizing decision-making within Europol's Management Board in urgent cases by establishing a "small-sized Executive Board" (European Commission 2013: 10). Comprising the Management Board's chairperson and three other members as well as one Commission representative, such an Executive Board might have significantly reduced the power of the Member States and relatively strengthened the Commission's position (Art. 22(4), ibid.). In the words of Germany's Management Board member: "This proposal failed due to opposition from a majority of the Member States, above all because such a committee would provide only selective representation" (Schlatmann 2016: 44f.). Concerning decision-making and relative power distribution within Europol's strategic oversight and guidance, the Commission was not able to assert itself and shift state preferences; supranational advocacy lost against governmental sovereignty concerns (Interviewees 6, 27, 31, 33 & 34).

Supranational Advocacy on the Rise: The Regulation as an Example of a Changing Trend?

Whereas the policy process of the Europol Regulation demonstrated strong supranational entrepreneurship, "the Member States won on crucial points" (Interviewees 29 & 35). Nevertheless, a number of concessions demonstrate the growing strength of supranational advocacy. These include the stronger involvement of EU actors in Europol's governance, particularly on data protection, parliamentary oversight, operational priority-setting, budgetary planning and external relations (Interviewees 15, 21, 27, 31 & 33). Next to functional spill-overs from the overall development of EU integration and path-dependency within police cooperation, the Commission benefited tremendously from an early mover advantage. As key initiator of the Regulation, it was in a favourable position to shape the interests and preferences of Member States on the institutional development of Europol.

Supranational entrepreneurship on the Europol Regulation leveraged functional and especially public pressure to influence state preferences positively towards deeper integration. The European Commission already framed its first proposal accordingly in 2013. Contextualising the draft version, it emphasised that "the EU has seen an increase in serious and organised crime as well as more diverse patterns in crime" and that Eurobarometer data consistently demonstrated crime to be "one of the five main concerns of EU citizens" (European Commission 2013: 2 & 3). This approach successfully impacted state preferences for two main reasons. First, the functional or common-sense argument to continue developing Europol arguably applied to more or less every Member State (Interviewees 14, 25, 26, 31, 34 & 35). From a practical and operational point of view, rising internal and external interdependencies required additional professionalisation or centralisation of EU police cooperation. Europol and other EU actors could offer unique cross-national products and services, including access to funding and pooled resources (Interviewees 27 & 35). In view of previous integration steps and investments in the agency, "it simply made sense in every way" to further strengthen collective action and activities at the EU level (Interviewee 34). The tools and services of Europol and the Commission had become key instruments of EU police cooperation.

Second, political expectations and politicisation made Member States highly susceptible, if not vulnerable, to these common-sense arguments and supranational policy entrepreneurship in favour of further formalising Europol. European governments themselves frequently "use[d] the EU to sell things to their constituencies which they would not otherwise have been able to sell" (Interviewee 40). This deliberate pro-EU politicisation of domestic security issues and the strategic employment of the EU level as multiplier of attention to threats challenging the Member States in turn created public-political pressure on national policymakers to continue this path (Interviewees 14, 15, 21, 27 & 43). Where governments had previously presented and discursively justified Europol and the EU as preferred policy venues for police cooperation, it was difficult to suddenly argue against further strengthening both. In the negotiations on the Europol Regulation, the European Commission harnessed this public perception to affect state preferences. Deliberate politicisation, the instrumentalisation of public opinion, had been emerging for some time as "tool of legitimisation for the EU in the area of JHA" (Interviewee 23). The Commission had increasingly positioned itself as protector of internal security and developed according to discursive strategies (Interviewees 25, 26, 34 & 35). Member States, against it, had to offer few or relatively weak 'counter narratives' to the strong pro-integration advocacy of supranational policy entrepreneurs.

Additionally, the lack of a homogeneous preference situation among Member States opened a window of opportunity for Commission entrepreneurship. Contrary to EU actors, European governments did not demonstrate a unified position on EU police cooperation (Interviewees 27, 29 & 33). Their preferences varied greatly in line with the extent to which individual countries felt affected by interdependencies. Asymmetries thus played a crucial role in diversifying states' positions on the degree of formalisation at Europol. Countries with the highest levels of interconnectedness preferred deeper integration, while those with comparatively less interconnectivity or sufficient national networks favoured a weak draft regulation or even differentiated models of integration (Interviewees 12, 14 & 22–24). The lack of a unified preference situation enabled Commission and EU officials to successfully push some of their proposals, even against the will of governments. This included the larger role for the European Parliament in relation to Europol (Díaz de Mera 2014). The proposal for the JPSG originated from the Parliament itself. It was jointly promoted with the Commission and ultimately included in the final regulation despite reluctance from some Member States (Interviewees 14 & 34).

Supranational policy entrepreneurship, leveraging functional and public pressure, can arguably explain how the Europol Regulation came about. Against the backdrop of spill-over effects and path-dependency, EU actors used political expectations to assert pro-integration positions in the draft and strengthen supranational venues within EU police cooperation. Post-crisis politicisation generated by the terrorist attacks in Paris added momentum and pressure in this respect. Compared to previous institutional developments and integration at Europol, state preferences did not significantly change in the policy process leading to the adoption of the Europol Regulation. However, the process illustrates the growing influence of supranational advocacy in EU police cooperation. Although the European Commission did not essentially shift state preferences towards deeper integration, it succeeded in determining the negotiations on a number of points through the deliberate instrumentalisation of political expectations and public pressure. While this strategy perhaps succeeded in moving the preferences of EU governments in some regards – including towards centralisation in information-exchange, more operational leeway for Europol and a larger role for the Commission – it more often functioned as "political blackmail" in the negotiations on the Regulation (Interviewee 27). In an age of EU agencies, European governments could politically hardly oppose supranational initiatives for collective action and the further development of common institutions. Although the importance of the Europol Regulation should not be overstated, it possibly brought Europol one step closer to being an increasingly important, autonomous platform connecting local, national and global levels. Or, in the words of one interviewee: "Operationally, Europol remains largely driven by the Member States and close to developments on the ground. Institutionally, it is developing more and more towards the EU and a certain autonomy" (Interviewee 31).

Brexit and Other Developments – Looking Back and Moving Forward?

While it might seem like the Europol Regulation was the successful culmination of a historic integration process – which it was at the time – the institutional evolution of EU police cooperation did not stop there. The new legal framework has not been Europol's "happily ever after." Much remained imperfect and much has happened since then. Shortly after the Europol Regulation was adopted on 11 May 2016, the UK voted to leave the EU, throwing not only their own country but also the EU as a whole into political turmoil. Although the UK has in the meantime officially withdrawn from the EU, the consequences of the British referendum continue to affect Europe and EU police cooperation. Additionally, Jihadist terrorism challenged the still fledgling Europol and its newly founded ECTC. In July and December 2016, two vehicle-ramming attacks in Nice and Berlin claimed the lives of almost 100 people and injured more than 300. They were only the first of many similar attacks over the following years, illustrating the proliferation of altered methods and new types of attack. Terrorist organisations were beginning to increasingly rely on the Internet to "remotely inspir[e...] and direct[...] attacks" and make "terrorism accessible to the masses" (Harrsion 2018). Low-tech attacks by terrorist groups and radicalised individuals continue to pose a serious threat to European governments and citizens. Practically anyone can use a knife or vehicle to attack large crowds and public spaces anywhere. Finally, the evolving transnational activities of organised crime groups required further strengthening Europol and EU police cooperation. In July 2020, it became known that organised criminal networks had been using EncroChat, an encrypted phone network, to coordinate and conduct their illegal operations around the globe. EncroChat was successfully dismantled by a JIT of officials from France, the Netherlands, Europol and Eurojust. The operation demonstrated "the global scope of serious and organised crime and the connectivity of criminal networks who use advanced technologies to cooperate on a national and international level" (Europol 2020c). It triggered an unprecedented number of criminal investigations all over the EU as well as responses at political and law enforcement level to better fight criminal structures and networks and their illicit exploitation of digital and communication technology. Both continue to challenge security authorities and policymakers today. The persistence of the COVID-19 pandemic after it first broke out in Europe in early 2020 and the subsequent surge in the use of the Internet, digital tools and electronic communication has likewise had an impact on the activities of criminals and terrorists. Additionally, all these developments have affected EU police cooperation and further strengthened the role and involvement of Europol and other EU actors.

EU Police Cooperation Post-Brexit

On 23 June 2016, British EU membership was put to a public vote. In a referendum, British nationals were asked to decide whether the UK should remain part of or leave the EU. A slight majority (52%) voted in favour of 'Brexit' and thus determined the fate of their country. However, the details remained unsettled for some time. A Withdrawal Agreement was only signed in January 2020. Although the UK formally left the EU on 31 January 2020 at midnight Brussels time, Brexit would only take full effect after a transition period until 31 December. During this time, the cornerstones of the future relationship between the EU and the UK were negotiated. It was concluded just in time before the end of the transition period: on 30 December 2020 the Brexit agreement (officially: Trade and Cooperation Agreement (TCA)) was signed. Its entry into force in 2021 not only ended an era of British membership, but it also brought a three-and-a-half-year long period of political uncertainty to a close. Despite the Brexit agreement, much remains to be settled, consequences and implications remain to be seen.

Although the UK has always held a special status within EU cooperation on JHA matters, it has frequently opted into measures in this area and shaped the political debate and action at European level. EU police cooperation has been driven and influenced substantially by British security culture, its policing models and methods, and has benefitted in no small part from the UK's intelligence leads, information-sharing and data input. This applies not only to Europol but also to most relevant European cooperation platforms and databases. The UK for instance issued "approximately 20% of the total number of national security alerts on the SIS II system" in 2017 (HM Government 2018a: 21).

The TCA contains, within Part Three, an agreement on law enforcement and judicial cooperation in criminal matters (see Table 5.1). It contains provisions for 13 issue areas "in relation to the prevention, investigation, detection and prosecution of criminal offences and the prevention of and fight against money laundering and financing of terrorism" (Art. 522). A particular emphasis lies on data exchange (automated transfers and established information systems) on the one hand and the participation in EU police cooperation and agencies (specifically Europol and Eurojust) on the other. This is unsurprising, since the UK

TABLE 5.1 Titles of the EU-UK Law Enforcement Agreement

Title I: General Provisions
Title II: Exchanges of DNA, Fingerprints, and Vehicle Registration Data (Prüm)
Title III: Transfer and Processing of Passenger Name Record Data (PNR)
Title IV: Cooperation on Operational Information
Title V: Cooperation with Europol
Title VI: Cooperation with Eurojust
Title VII: Surrender
Title VIII: Mutual Assistance
Title IX: Exchange of Criminal Record Information
Title X: Anti-money Laundering and Counter Terrorist Financing
Title XI: Freezing and Confiscation
Title XII: Other Provisions
Title XIII: Dispute Settlement

has presented one of the most significant "contributors of data, information and expertise" (Piquet 2020) and simultaneously "one of the main users" of Europol's services (Monroy 2021). At the same time, the UK has benefited tremendously from EU police cooperation. In 2014, it had rejoined 35 pre-Lisbon police and criminal justice measures, which Theresa May – then Home Secretary – described as "vital to stop foreign criminals from coming to Britain, deal with European fighters coming back from Syria, stop British criminals evading justice abroad, prevent foreign criminals evading justice by hiding here, and get foreign criminals out of our prisons" (EUC 2016: 9). For the UK, some of the most important EU instruments include the Prüm framework, SIS II, ECRIS, Passenger Name Records (PNR), the European Arrest Warrant (EAW) and cooperation via Europol (EUC 2016: 10). In 2018, in the middle of the Brexit negotiations, a British government paper observed:

> Without the UK's participation in, and contribution to, these data exchange tools, there would be a significant loss of capability which would reduce the UK's and the EU's ability to protect citizens across Europe. This would mean EU law enforcement agencies lose the ability to identify serious criminals and missing persons as they cross the UK border. It would also result in a reduction in the UK's and the EU's ability to identify and track terrorist networks across Europe.
>
> *(HM Government 2018b: 57)*

Under the TCA, the UK retains access to Prüm, ECRIS and PNR data, which comprise DNA profiles, fingerprints, vehicle registration data, information extracted from criminal records and PNR data for flights between the UK and the EU. Titles II, III and IX stipulate the conditions, including rules for data receipt and processing and other obligations and requirements placed on the UK. However, access to ECRIS, SIS II and the EAW "is not preserved in a formal sense" (King & Scarlett 2021). Rather, the TCA seeks to replicate existing arrangements or envisage alternative ones for these instruments. To maintain access to ECRIS, the UK is for example required to build its own technical infrastructure. Yet, the "development and operation of its own interconnection software" (Annex 44) can only approximate or mirror the previous state of affairs and could make information-exchange and investigations in the UK "slower under the new arrangements" (EUC 2021: 21). With regard to SIS II, Wilson (2021) observes "[s]ignificant discontinuity" from previous arrangements: a "loss of the fully automated and integrated flow of information from 29 countries into UK police and border control systems via SIS II." This concerns especially "real-time data on persons and objects of interest including wanted and missing persons" (EUC 2021: 22). The alternative (manual) route to obtain this or similar information via Interpol systems does not nearly suffice to offset the loss in capabilities after Brexit. This likewise applies to the EAW. The UK has had to leave the EU's common extradition system. Relying only on Interpol channels for the exchange of arrest warrants and extradition data is no feasible alternative for British authorities to guarantee the same standards, as possibilities through Interpol are much more limited in scope and depth (Monroy 2021). In place of the EAW, the TCA (Title VII) foresees a "mechanism of surrender" (Art. 596) intended to replicate the EU's extradition model for "acts punishable by a custodial sentence[...] of at least 12 months" (Art. 599). Although the surrender provisions could contribute to the continuity of cooperation in this area, it remains to be seen how they play out in practice. As always, the devil will be in the details.

A second critical issue area of the TCA concerns police cooperation and participation in Europol. Rather than maintaining the UK's membership and direct involvement in the agency, Title V foresees the establishment of "cooperative relations" between the UK and Europol (Art. 564). With the end of the transition period, the UK has lost its first-hand access to Europol's databases and analysis projects. It no longer formally participates in Europol and JITs, which presents a "[s]ignificant loss of continuity" for the UK (Wilson 2021). Under the TCA, both the EU and the UK commit themselves to "mutual cooperation in preventing and combating serious crime, terrorism and forms of crime which affect a common interest covered by a Union policy." The functional scope of cooperation remains the same as under the Europol Regulation. Although the UK is no longer part of Europol through the EU, it "shall designate a national contact point to act as the central point of contact" (Art. 568(1)), including for the exchange of information. To ensure consistent, fast and effective operational cooperation, the TCA foresees the reciprocal secondment of liaison officers to Europol and the UK. It also focuses on information-sharing and "ensuring that data exchanges [...]can take place as quickly as possible, and to consider the incorporation of any new processes and technical developments which might assist with that objective" (Art. 572). This highlights the importance of this topic as a key element of post-Brexit cooperation at Europol.

At the time of writing, it remains unclear what post-Brexit cooperation at Europol will look like in practice. The (currently still on-going) revision of Europol's mandate and the legislative proposal for a Police Cooperation Code might have additional implications for EU-UK police cooperation and British access to relevant data and capabilities. As the UK is no longer a member of the EU, it is not involved in related negotiation and decision-making processes. It has formally lost its role and influence in the institutional and operational development of Europol. Whether or to what extent the UK might still shape EU police cooperation at Europol as a non-Member State remains to be seen. The same applies to future cooperation arrangements with Europol. Operational details, working and administrative arrangements still have to be specified and need to prove themselves. Their negotiation will be an exclusive matter for Europol and the UK, with no role for EU Member States. It will determine the shape and extent of practical cooperation as well as British access and involvement regarding Europol's analytical or operational products and services. Monroy (2021) presumes that the TCA's reference to "crime prevention methods" (Art. 567(e)) might concern cooperation within Europol's ECTC – a centre in whose establishment the UK played an important role. Securing British participation in the ECTC is probably not only in the interest of the UK but also Europol and EU Member States with a view to guaranteeing effective European police cooperation on counterterrorism.

Of course, operational police cooperation is not limited to Europol. Title IV specifies arrangements and rules for future EU-UK cooperation on operational information. It seeks to enable police and customs authorities to exchange relevant data in relation to "(a) [...]criminal offences; (b) [...]criminal penalties; (c) [...]threats to public safety; and (d) [...]money laundering and the financing of terrorism" (Art. 563(1)). However, the UK's lack of access to SIS II and the EIS will likely adversely impact the quality and effectiveness of cooperation with competent authorities in the EU. This will in large part depend on the willingness of Member States to (also) use bilateral or Interpol channels for communication and data-sharing (Arnell et al. 2021: 271).

Next to provisions for the broader fields of information exchange and operational cooperation via Europol, the TCA stipulates rules and objectives for the specific issue area of AML/CFT (Title X). The following Title (XI) deals with the freezing and confiscation of property. Under the TCA, British and European competent authorities, including FIUs, should "cooperate in preventing the use of their financial systems to launder the proceeds of all criminal activity, including drug trafficking and corruption, and to combat terrorist financing" (Art. 653(1)). While the TCA's stipulations remain overall vague and focus on "support[ing] international efforts" rather than European or EU ones, the practical need for swift and reliable information exchange will presumably link working arrangements in this area to action and efforts at the EU level. Europol's ECTC and EFECC both present key platforms for EU police cooperation in the fight against money laundering and terrorist financing. Other on-going and future EU developments in these fields might likewise affect UK-EU cooperation. In July 2021, a comprehensive package of legislative proposals to strengthen the EU's rules on AML and CFT was adopted and remains to be implemented (AML/CFT 2021).

A mere legal analysis of the TCA and post-Brexit law enforcement arrangements does not necessarily "correspond to operational performance and professional influence" and may not reflect the reality of practical cooperation (Wilson 2021; Interviewees 47 & 51). The TCA only fully entered into force on 1 May 2021. It is therefore still too early at the time of writing to tell the exact implications for both UK-EU police cooperation and EU police cooperation as a whole. A Partnership Council – comprising both EU and UK representatives – oversees the implementation of the agreement and acts as institutional oversight mechanism (TCA Art. 7). It may amend parts of the TCA within its first years of application, where deemed necessary (Art. 7(4)). Additionally, the TCA foresees a regular "review [of] the implementation [...]five years after the entry into force" (Art. 776). Part Three on law enforcement and judicial cooperation in criminal matters complements this clause with further review provisions for specific cooperation arrangements (cf. EUC 2021: 14).

Until then, it remains difficult to predict the consequences of Brexit for EU police cooperation. It seems clear that the TCA will have implications in the areas of information exchange, operational cooperation and institutional development of Europol and European law enforcement cooperation. According to Arnell et al. (2021: 267) "[t]he danger in the area of police cooperation and information exchange is that changes in one area will negatively impact upon another. Sadly, this has to an extent happened" in the case of Brexit. At the same time, it is in the interest of all Parties to ensure that future EU-UK police cooperation is as close as possible to its previous state, or at least as fast and effective as possible under the new arrangements. While the UK is no longer an EU Member State and must be treated as a third country by the EU, it remains part of multilateral platforms and settings that likewise affect EU cooperation. Examples include the CTG or the Police Working Group on Terrorism (PWGT) (Monroy 2021). Both groups also comprise EU governments as members and cooperate with Europol, which even holds observer status in the PWGT and records related information in SIS II. Whether and to what extent the UK can use these settings to retain access to European information systems, to participate in operational cooperation or even shape EU police cooperation at the strategic and political level remains to be seen. "The effectiveness of [working…]arrangements will be tested by events in the period ahead. The consequences […]are not yet clear" (King & Scarlett 2021). Only time will tell how well the TCA is able to guarantee the continuity of EU(-UK) police cooperation post-Brexit.

Towards the Future of European Cross-Border Policing: The Europol Regulation 2.0 and EU Police Cooperation Code

This likewise applies to Europol, existing operational arrangements and the future of EU police cooperation. In January 2020, the European Commission announced a revision of Europol's mandate to "reinforce operational police cooperation" in its Work Programme for 2020 (European Commission 2020a: 7). This proposal was reiterated in July 2020, when the European Commission presented an ambitious new EU Security Union Strategy for the period until 2025. The Strategy included plans for an EU 'Police Cooperation Code' to improve operational effectiveness. In December 2020, a concrete legislative proposal to update the Europol Regulation was published. It foresaw some rather significant changes to the organisation's mandate that sparked controversy in the negotiations. At the time of writing, in early 2022, the legislative proposal has been amended several times. In February 2022, the Council and the European Parliament provisionally agreed on the text. When the revised Europol regulation is adopted – presumably this summer – it will yet again strengthen Europol's mandate. And it will have been – also yet again – the result of interdependencies as well as of policy entrepreneurship from subnational and EU officials.

The European Commission first announced to revise the agency's legal framework in 2019. The original Europol Regulation (Art. 68) stipulated the regular evaluation and review of Europol's "impact, effectiveness and efficiency" and tasked the Commission to conduct according assessment by "1 May 2022 and every five years thereafter." However, the ultimate choice to launch an inception impact assessment in 2020 was driven by discussions at operational level in the Member States about growing interdependencies (Interviewee 53). Police officers and practitioners were increasingly feeling and voicing the impact of digitalisation and emerging technologies on serious criminal offences that were perpetrated online or enabled by cyber and technological means. Additionally, transnational organised crime groups were infiltrating and undermining the legal economy of Member States, increasingly using licit structures for illicit activities (Interviewees 47–49). Especially the growing volume of electronic means of payment, online banking and digital financial channels offered considerable opportunities for criminal profits. Against it, European law enforcement authorities and Europol were limited in their capacity and capabilities to respond to these developments. While criminals were operating across physical and digital borders, exploited new technologies to conduct illegal business and build their criminal enterprises, police officers were lacking the technological means and legal competencies to crack down on these activities, tackle encrypted networks and collect or follow digital evidence. What is more, law enforcement authorities lacked the necessary information and data to launch investigations (ibid.). At the EU level, where cross-country links could be identified from existing data sets, legal limitations prevented Europol from receiving and processing personal data from the private sector. This inevitably produced functional pressure on law enforcement authorities to improve and further develop EU police cooperation.

These operational concerns and needs were first raised at the EU level by subnational experts and police officers in the Council's LEWP in 2019 (Council 2019b: 3). They highlighted the growing role of the private sector and big data in cross-border investigations and pressed for improving operational police cooperation accordingly. In December 2019, the input from the working level was turned into political action when European ministers adopted Council conclusions on Europol's cooperation with private parties. In view of "the need for European law enforcement to address ongoing technological developments" the Council stressed "the urgent operational need for Europol to request and receive data directly from private parties" and asked the Commission to take this into account in its review of Europol's legal framework (ibid.: 5).

In January 2020, the Commission published its Work Programme 2020 and announced that it would "strengthen the Europol mandate[...] to reinforce operational police cooperation" (European Commission 2020a: 7). A first inception impact assessment was presented in May 2020 amidst the quickly spreading COVID-19 pandemic in Europe. The European Commission intended to finalise its review of Europol's mandate by September and aimed at presenting a legislative proposal by the end of 2020 (ibid. 2020c). Although the original impetus to further boost the agency's role had come from subnational levels and was driven by functional pressure from interdependencies, the legislative process illustrates the logic of EU policy entrepreneurship and growing influence of the European Commission. While no concrete proposal was on the table yet in the spring of 2020, the Commission – as in previous cases – harnessed the power of functional and political pressure to establish the importance of the EU level, justify its own role and prepare the ground for future supranational integration initiatives. Building on the discussions in the Member States and at the Council, the Commission cited "emerging security threats," "limitations of Europol's current legal basis" and "calls from Member States for stronger EU support for the work of their law enforcement authorities" as the rationale behind its initiative to revise Europol's mandate (ibid.). It additionally harnessed pressure from the unfolding pandemic crisis by emphasising the "increase of tele and remote working across all sectors," which was expanding the (digital) attack surface and opportunities for criminal exploitation.

As regards the timing, the European Commission seems to have been motivated primarily by calls from the Member States and the opportunity for deeper integration. It acknowledged itself that very little time had passed since the entry into force of the Europol Regulation in May 2017. As a consequence, it was too soon for a comprehensive assessment of the functioning of its legal framework and any review would be "non-representative." Yet, the European Commission prepared an evaluation and presented an ambitious proposal for a revised Europol Regulation in December 2020. It was published alongside and linked to the new EU Counter-Terrorism Agenda as well as to a legislative proposal for improving the SIS.

Drawing on crisis momentum from COVID-19 and recent terror attacks, and citing the operational demand and growing use of Europol's services by the Member States, the Commission suggested to strengthen Europol's mandate in four key areas:

- **Cooperation with private parties**, especially in relation to the areas of cross-border communication, banking and transport services, **and with third parties;**
- **Response to emerging threats and new developments,** particularly in the areas of cybercrime, financial crime and terrorism, as well as regarding research and innovation;
- **Initiation of cross-border investigations**, equipping Europol with the right to "request[...] the competent authorities of a Member State to initiate, conduct or coordinate an investigation of a crime which affects a common interest covered by a Union policy, without the requirement of a cross-border dimension of the crime concerned" (European Commission 2020e: 3);
- **Big data challenge for law enforcement**, inter alia (1) enabling Europol to process and analyse large and complex datasets, and (2) updating Europol's data protection rules.

Additionally, the proposal foresaw the possibility for Europol to enter data into the SIS on the suspected involvement of a third country national in an offence falling within Europol's mandate. It also sought to continue and strengthen the 'centre approach.' The proposal highlighted the success of Europol's operational centres, especially the ECTC. At the initiative of the German Council Presidency, EU Interior Ministers had first underscored this in response to the terrorist attacks in Paris, Vienna, Dresden, Nice and other European cities (ibid.: 2). This illustrates yet again how politicising events foster political momentum and windows of opportunity in EU police cooperation. It likewise confirms the role of Germany as a motor of integration and potentially the importance of holding the Council Presidency as a positive influence on state integration preferences. In October 2020, reacting to the Commission's announcement of a legislative proposal by the end of 2020, Germany had already gathered EU home affairs ministers to discuss the future of Europol and provide input to the Commission. Due to the pandemic the meeting was only held virtually. Originally, the German Presidency had planned the event as a two-day high-level conference in Berlin to discuss the institutional development of Europol – which presented a key pillar of its presidency. German policymakers and practitioners were even revisiting Kohl's vision for a "European FBI" (Interviewees 48 & 50). The outcome document – a joint declaration titled 10-point plan on the future of Europol – favourably shaped the Commission's legislative proposal. It incorporated key points of the ministerial declaration: bolstering Europol's role in information-sharing and as analysis and coordination hub for EU police cooperation. Nevertheless, the declaration fell short of German expectations. Despite naming Europol as "important example" of "highly successful cooperation," ministers emphasised that policing presented a "core area of Member State sovereignty" (German Presidency 2020: 1). The document portrays a discrepancy between functionally-driven integration preferences to further institutionalise cooperation and political preferences to safeguard national competencies and power in this policy domain and vis-à-vis EU policy entrepreneurs.

Unsurprisingly, the Commission's proposal for a revised Europol mandate and particularly the parts that had come from or built on input from the Members States was overall well received. Adapting Europol to new and emerging threats, addressing operational or legal shortcomings and managing the institutional complexity of EU police cooperation were uncontentious issues. Especially domestic police officials and others working at the frontlines of police cooperation welcomed the proposal to strengthen Europol's mandate by boosting its ability to process large and complex datasets in support of criminal investigations, consolidating its role in fighting serious crime and developing new technologies in response to law enforcement needs (Interviewees 48 & 52–53). Improving information exchange and cooperation with third and private parties at the EU level were functionally-driven solutions to problems of internal and external interdependencies.

By contrast, some provisions included in the Commission's proposal caused considerable controversy, even resistance, at the political level. And the Commission was fully aware from the beginning that some of its suggested policy options might cause tension. When it published the original proposal, it explicitly noted how Member States – despite overall supporting a stronger mandate for Europol – were "conscious of the importance of their national sovereignty in the area of law enforcement from an operational and procedural perspective" (European Commission 2020e: 8). Yet, supranational policy entrepreneurship was sufficiently established for the Commission to take the chance and present a number of ambitious integration proposals. First, it suggested the possibility for Europol to request Member States to investigate a crime, even in cases without a cross-border dimension but which affects a common EU interest. Europol's current legal framework already enabled it to request the initiation of a criminal investigation although only in cases affecting two or more Member States. In practice, this possibility has never been used by Europol. Nevertheless, Member States vehemently opposed this new policy option.

Second, Member States were overall opposed to the Commission's proposal to enable Europol to enter data into the SIS on the suspected involvement of third country nationals in an offence falling within Europol's mandate. They strongly rejected the proposal to create a new alert category within the SIS to be used exclusively by Europol, under which it could directly insert alerts into the system (Interviewees 52–53). Seeking to maintain control, Member States watered down the legislative text by suggesting Europol could propose the entry of data or alerts "in the interest of the Union," yet domestic authorities would decide whether or not to act upon such a proposal and ultimately insert data or alerts into the SIS (Council 2021: 3). Member States thus retained the sole right to initiate action and control over data.

Third, the issue of data protection flared up anew in the negotiations on revising Europol's mandate. The Commission's original proposal emphasised the importance of further aligning data processing at Europol with EU data protection provisions and strengthening parliamentary scrutiny. It acknowledged concerns of the EDPS about personal data handling at Europol. Shortly before the Commission's presentation of a proposal for revising Europol's mandate, the EDPS had – in September 2020 – published a Decision on "Europol's big data challenge" and transmitted it directly to Europol and the Member States (EDPS 2020). In relation to the processing of personal data and large datasets, the EDPS had opened an investigation to analyse concerns about data protection and compliance, "in particular with the principles of purpose limitation, data minimisation, data accuracy, [and] storage limitation" (ibid.: 3). The analysis found that Member States were sending increasingly larger volumes of data to Europol and that the agency was using techniques of digital forensics and big data to be able to manage this challenge and "provide them back with intelligence products" (ibid.: 5). This, the EDPS found, did indeed not comply with Europol's legal framework. The Decision formally admonished Europol and requested it to devise a plan and concrete measures within six months.

The Commission considered this development in its proposal for strengthening Europol's mandate. Citing an even earlier EDPS Decision from December 2019, the Commission acknowledged the "inconsistency between the safeguards on categories on data subjects set out in [the 2016 Europol Regulation...], and situations where Europol acts as a service provider to Member States regarding their bilateral exchanges of data on crimes" (European Commission 2020d: 43). The Commission's proposal for a revised Europol Regulation included substantial changes in the agency's data protection framework, such as clarifying the role of the data protection officer at Europol and further specifying existing provisions along with introducing new ones, especially concerning compliance with fundamental rights and the processing of personal data. It also foresaw strengthening the supervisory roles of the EDPS and the JPSG.

The preferred policy options concerning data protection at Europol differed substantially between the Member States and EU actors. The deliberations in the Council and the European Parliament demonstrated the primarily political nature of this issue. From a functional or operational perspective, no immediate change was required. Neither was the topic high on the public radar nor had a crisis revealed deficits or a need to act. Consequently, Member States did not develop a preference to further integrate in the area of data protection. On the contrary, driven by sovereignty concerns, Member States overall rejected supranational integration initiatives in relation to Europol's data protection regime. However, politically, they could not assert this preference. First, political spillovers from the EU's regulatory framework in other areas (e.g. data protection, fundamental rights and agency governance) made it difficult to argue against this trend in the police domain and at Europol. Second, substantial policy entrepreneurship by the European Parliament pushed Member States to concede integration on some points and grant a stronger role to EU actors in data protection. Examples include the establishment of a fundamental rights officer at Europol and the possibility for the JPSG to participate in MB meetings for political, non-operational topics (Interviewee 52).

While the Council and European Parliament were still discussing how to ensure a balance between data protection and operational cooperation, various exchanges between Europol and the EDPS took place over the course of 2021. Unsatisfied with Europol's action plan and progress reports, the EDPS asked the agency to clarify data retention provisions and specify a maximum time limit for uncategorised data, for which he recommended six months, "after which such datasets should be permanently deleted" (ibid.: 4). This was too short in Europol's view and not foreseen in its current legal framework. In October 2021, it requested a deferral of an EDPS decision on the matter until the negotiations on the revised Europol Regulation were concluded. Nevertheless, the EDPS published a Decision on 10 January 2022 on the retention of datasets without Data Subject Categorisation at Europol (Cases 2019-0370 & 2021-0699). The Decision considered the processing of any uncategorised data unlawful and ordered Europol to "proceed to data subject categorisation[...] within six months" and otherwise delete the datasets (ibid.: 13).

At the time of writing, the revised Europol Regulation has still not been adopted. The EDPS Decision from January 2022 has sped up the work by the Council and the European Parliament on Europol's new legislative framework. Both reached a provisional political agreement on 1 February, which addresses the EDPS' concerns and further aligns Europol with the EU data protection regime (European Commission 2022a). The Council and the European Parliament ultimately agreed on and formally adopted the proposal in May 2022, allowing the regulation to enter into force on 28 June – just two days short of the EDPS' deadline. Without this much needed agreement and legal amendment by July 2022, Europol would have failed to meet the demands of the EDPS and would have been required to erase any uncategorised datasets. The amended regulation gives Europol a support role in the screening of foreign direct investments into the EU and in relation to the SIS. Europol will be able to propose to Member States to enter data on third-country nationals into the SIS and issue information alerts on foreign terrorist fighters. By contrast, it will not be able to request Member States to investigate a crime in cases without a cross-border dimension.

The revision of the Europol mandate illustrates the same challenges and driving factors that have shaped national integration preferences on police cooperation in the EU since the early 2000s and today. Most notably, functional pressure to integrate or at least institutionalise police cooperation continues to grow in line with internal and external interdependencies affecting the EU's security. The need to manage emerging transnational threats and growing complexity, for instance in relation to digital technologies or big data, strongly informs state preferences to jointly devise effective solutions at central level and cooperate via Europol and EU policy venues. By contrast, Member States tend to remain hesitant, even reluctant about integration on primarily political points with little functional pressure. Frequently, spill-over effects from other policy areas (like data protection) increase the practical need to integrate, while supranational policy entrepreneurs leverage this functional pressure and their growing political weight to lobby towards strengthening EU cooperation structures and the competencies of EU actors, and effectuate further integration. These same drivers and their impact on state preferences are also visible in other integration initiatives such as the Commission's ambitious proposal for an EU police cooperation code from December 2021, which includes proposals for a recommendation on operational police cooperation, a directive on information exchange and a regulation on automated data exchange (European Commission 2021). In many ways, this initiative could mark a peak of EU police cooperation to date and could advance integration, as it seeks to consolidate processes, structures and actors under one umbrella. Whether this will indeed be the case and to what extent the Commission's integration initiative can succeed remains to be seen.

Institutional Choice in a Nutshell: State Preferences on the Three Dimensions of Differentiated Integration

Although relatively little time has passed since the adoption of the ECD in April 2009, the process leading to its replacement with the Europol Regulation in 2016 and to the proposal for a revised Europol mandate in 2020 exhibit striking and on-going changes in the influence of driving factors on state preferences within EU police cooperation. Whereas supranational policy entrepreneurship already increased in its relevance in the early 2000s, the advocacy and power of EU actors in this area has arguably risen even further until today. Next to Europol, the European Commission succeeded in extending its role and establishing itself as an accepted, well-respected entity. Functional and political spill-over effects – most notably from the Lisbon Treaty – facilitated the maturation of supranational policy entrepreneurship. Politicisation formed a crucial part in enabling the growing influence of EU actors on state preferences. The deliberate and strategic leverage of public pressure often created the necessary political momentum to boost the stance of supranational integration advocates and their proposed initiatives.

The establishment of operational centres at Europol, the adoption of the Regulation and proposal for a revised mandate form the most recent events in a chain of developments towards deeper integration of EU police cooperation. While the legal and practical changes towards formalisation should not be overstated, they have clearly situated Europol amidst the European agencification trend and strengthened the role of supranational actors in JHA. The importance of increasingly centralising information flows and exchange at the EU level should not be underestimated. With the creation of a centre approach at Europol and the replacement of the ECD with a regulation, Europol and the European Commission have effectively broadened their influence in vertical decision-making. As in the previous case studies, internal and external interdependencies acted as important drivers of state preferences to this end. However, supranational policy entrepreneurship mattered even more. This chapter has shown how EU actors successfully harnessed functional pressure from high interdependence to produce cultivated spill-overs. Member States were accordingly influenced to favour additional centralisation and ultimately establish the EC3, ECTC, EMSC and EFECC – an observation that likewise partially holds with regard to the Europol Regulation.

At the same time, the institutional changes and developments at Europol between 2009 and 2022 demonstrate a simultaneous growth of differentiated integration within EU police cooperation. While the establishment of operational centres at Europol and the adoption of the Regulation have certainly contributed to the organisational consolidation and formalisation of processes at the agency, some issue areas, tools and functions remain below or outside the EU level. Technological, strategic and operational standards continue to differ, as does the political will of Member States and law enforcement authorities to cooperate via Europol. Informal networks and subgroups often parallel but also complement the work done at the EU level and in formal policy venues. Most interviewees stressed the importance of smart division of labour and the need for 'coalitions of the willing' to advance cooperation and integration in the long run. Asked about the drivers of state preferences in this respect, respondents agreed that two factors could primarily explain differentiated integration and primarily determined whether European governments were willing to join an avant-garde group or not. On the one hand, asymmetrical levels of interdependence and affectedness matter as shapers of Member States' political will to integrate further. The case studies in this book clearly confirm that high degrees of interdependence form a necessary condition for pro-integration preferences. In turn, strongly asymmetrical levels of interconnectivity might be able to account for diverging state preferences and the emergence of avant-garde groups in single issue areas and even within formal cooperation fora. Second, subnational policy entrepreneurship can explain the persistence of informal horizontal networks and modes of governance within EU police cooperation, including at Europol. Where formal channels cannot satisfy operational needs for speed and efficiency, or in areas where policymakers are unwilling to pursue centralisation, domestic security and police officials often emerge as trailblazers themselves and initiate the creation of informal subgroups at working level to manage common threats. In contrast to this positive instigation of differentiation, subnational entrepreneurs may also resort to informal networks and coalitions because of insufficient trust in formal channels and only slowly progressing 'socialisation' to EU police cooperation. Irrespective, subnational policy entrepreneurship often drives differentiation, be it as a means of flexible integration or bureaucratic resistance. As a mix of formal and informal modes of governance, EU police cooperation and Europol thus continue to present examples of differentiated integration to date.

This chapter has confirmed various hypotheses. First, high interdependencies were present as a necessary condition in every case. Even where they did not constitute the primary driver of state preferences, functional pressure to integrate mattered as motivating force at highest political levels. Second, supranational policy entrepreneurship emerged as one key driving factor of state preferences after the ECD. Benefitting from path-dependency and spill-over effects, the influence of EU actors was growing visibly. The Europol Regulation and its 2020 revision as well as all operational centres at Europol originated in one way or another from supranational proposals. In this context, differentiation – or rather flexible integration – has become a vital part of supranational policy entrepreneurship and the long-term strategies of EU actors. Finally, politicisation was frequently present as complementary driving force alongside interdependence and/or supranational policy entrepreneurship. The role of crises should be particularly stressed in this respect. Recent terror attacks and the 2014–2015 migrant and refugee crisis presented windows of opportunity for a shift in the preferences of Member States towards further integration at Europol. Regardless of particular integration preferences – whether governments had an actual interest in long-term integration of EU police cooperation or merely prioritised EU action as a form of venue-shopping to evade domestic pressure and contestation – supranational actors could build on post-crisis momentum to advance political and cultivated spill-overs. At the time of writing, the same dynamic can be observed with regard to the Russian-Ukrainian conflict, for example in relation to coordinating a joint EU response to the refugees from the region or with regard to fostering information exchange and preventing sanctioned individuals from circumventing restrictive measures in the EU.

Regardless of the strength of driving forces and political resolve in the Member States, integration at Europol still faces many obstacles to date. Although more and more domestic officials are familiar with the agency, and Europol has increasingly developed into a socialisation platform, lack of trust and persisting bureaucratic resistance remain key problems in practice. Whether Europol and EU police cooperation continue to struggle or strategically manoeuvre between differentiation and integration could ultimately hinge on supranational policy entrepreneurship and the extent to which EU actors manage to connect both. What is clear, irrespective of the concrete institutional development and future of Europol, is that EU police cooperation is here to stay. Although Europol is unlikely to evolve into Kohl's vision of a European FBI anytime soon, growing interdependencies and security crises will undoubtedly continue to motivate Member States to cooperate at European level and further develop police cooperation in the EU.

CONCLUSION AND DISCUSSION

EU police cooperation to date remains a long way from full integration. Intergovernmental settings and sovereignty concerns continue to collide with multi-level governance and the initiatives of EU actors. Nonetheless, over time, Member States have increasingly opted for moving this issue area into EU policy venues and have equipped supranational actors with more and more powers in the process. The evolution of European police cooperation and particularly the institutional development of Europol demonstrate progressive integration on all three dimensions of differentiated integration, a trend that is still on-going: a gradual 'deepening' and 'widening' of EU police cooperation and an extension of its functional scope (see Figure C.1).

On the basis of the empirical and theoretical literature, this book has sought to investigate how and to what extent interdependence, politicisation and policy entrepreneurship shape the integration preferences of Member States in EU police cooperation. It has traced the influence of these driving factors throughout the policy processes predating four consecutive milestones in the institutional development of the latter: (1) the 1976 Trevi Group; (2) the 1995 Europol Convention establishing Europol; (3) the 2009 Europol Council Decision naming Europol official EU agency and (4) the 2016 Europol Regulation, including the proposal for its revision in 2020. All these arguably constitute significant qualitative 'quantum leaps' in the integration of EU police cooperation (see Figure C.1). In sum, differentiation initiatives – rather than deriving from anti-integration sentiments – provided temporary strategies of Member States to cope with cooperation pressure in areas where full integration was not possible. More often than not, they presented means of advancing integration in the long run. The asymmetrical effects of driving factors thus explain why governments opt for venue-shopping and avant-garde approaches in single issue areas. In this light, it seems less puzzling that diverging modes of cooperation, governance

DOI: 10.4324/9781003262176-7

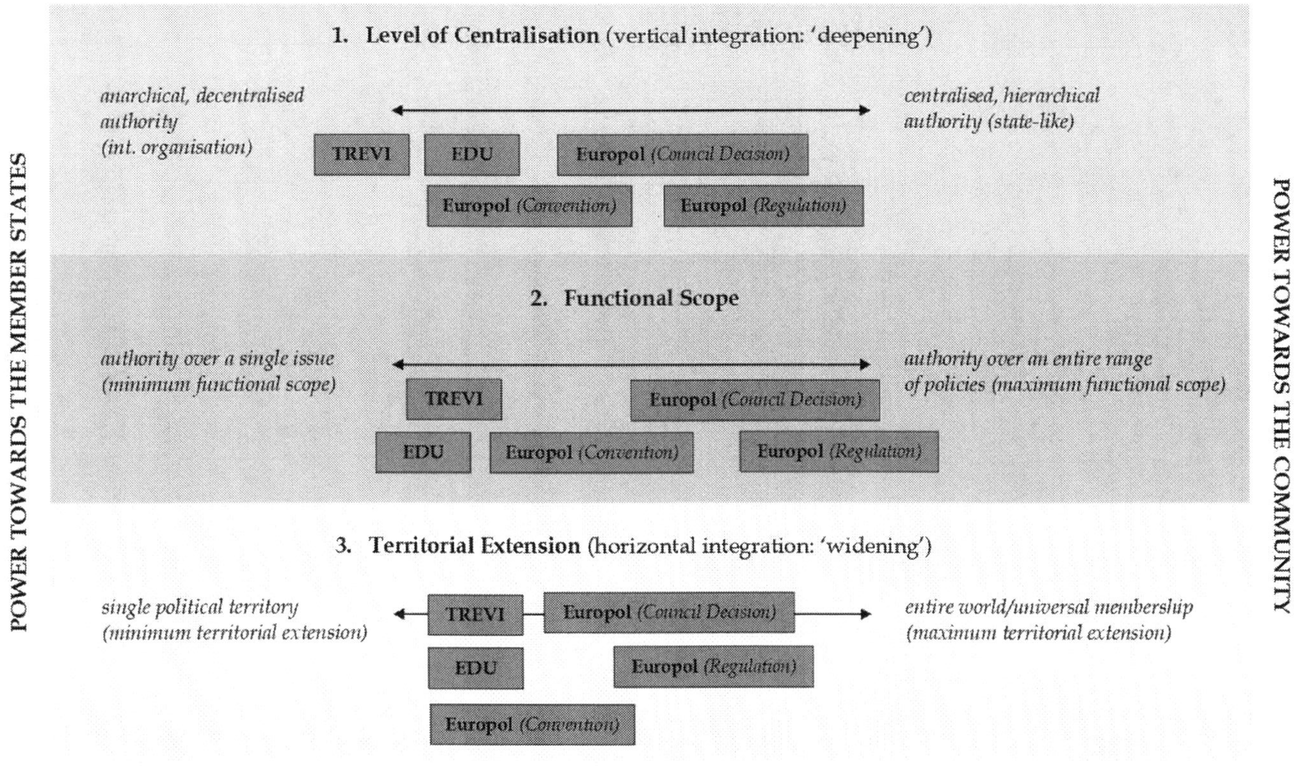

FIGURE C.1 EU Police Cooperation 1976–2022: Institutional Choice on the Three Dimensions of Differentiated Integration

Compiled by the author, based on Leuffen et al. (2013)

and integration continue to exist and evolve alongside one another in EU police cooperation. While the explanatory power of drivers varies across these case studies, that is, over time and issue areas, a number of common findings emerge.

Interdependence, Politicisation and Policy Entrepreneurship: Drivers of State Integration Preferences and Their Causal Mechanisms

First, high interdependence seems to always positively impact the integration preferences of Member States and seems to present a necessary condition for the latter; the causal mechanism at work here is functional pressure. The higher the interconnectedness in concrete issues, the less able single governments are to manage problems unilaterally and the more they experience a practical necessity to cooperate with other countries. This functional need often becomes manifest in the growing inability of domestic levels to cope with threats and safeguard internal security, or the increasing occurrence and frequency of coordination and collective action problems. The analysis thus confirms hypothesis H1. The higher the interdependence in security issues, the more likely Member States are to favour EU police cooperation and integration. It appears to matter less whether interdependencies arise from an external interconnectedness in common threats and challenges, or from internal institutional linkages. Both types produce functional pressure on Member States to cooperate if not integrate. Since the 1970s, internal interdependence has especially increased in line with the development of the EU and progressively reinforced, perhaps even overtaken external interdependence as pro-integration driver within EU police cooperation.

Second, politicisation appears to constitute a sufficient condition for pro-integration preferences only in conjunction with one of the other factors. This book has not found strong evidence for the independent impact of politicisation. Instead, its analysis demonstrates the complementary role of public pressure and salience as amplifiers of other causal mechanisms. Particularly crises and shocks present critical moments or 'windows of opportunity' to this end. When politicising events suddenly raise the visibility of particular issue areas, they often ignite a public-political debate on the appropriateness or consequences of policy choices. This in turn creates public pressure on policymakers to act in order to prevent societal contestation, and thereby generates political momentum. While politicisation may act as both enabler and impediment to EU police cooperation, the case studies more often exhibit a positive effect of high salience and public pressure on integration preferences. Especially the combination with high interdependence or supranational policy entrepreneurship caused Member States to favour EU police cooperation and integration. Where politicising events illustrate existing interdependencies, as in the case of terror attacks, they reinforce integration pressure by raising the public visibility of existing functional needs to cooperate. This makes it considerably more difficult for governments to argue against enhancing EU police cooperation – an effect that was often successfully harnessed by supranational actors to shift state preferences towards further integration. Consequently, this book concludes that high politicisation tends to act as amplifier of other pro-integration drivers in the area of internal security and policing. It may not produce an independent effect on state preferences, but the single or aggregate effects of politicising events generate public and political pressure to act that renders governments more vulnerable to the influence of interdependencies or policy entrepreneurship. On the contrary, this book's analysis has not found evidence that high politicisation makes it less likely that Member States favour EU police cooperation and integration or any cooperation at the EU level. Hypotheses H2.2 and H2.3 may thus be cautiously rejected.

Third, supra- and subnational policy entrepreneurship increasingly matter as shapers of pro-integration preferences on EU police cooperation. They both harness functional and public pressure in their advocacy of cooperation at the EU level. In the light of a quickly expanding interconnectedness in common threats and institutions, they frame integration and securitising measures at transnational level as a necessary – if not the only – response to growing problems of coordination and collective action. On the other hand, policy entrepreneurs deliberately leverage public pressure to shift state preferences towards 'more' rather than less EU; they invoke a public demand for European cooperation or integration and frame politicising events like terror attacks accordingly. Whereas subnational actors have arguably evolved from bureaucratic resistance to cautious integration enthusiasts since the 1970s, their role and influence is largely asymmetrical across Member States and hinges on the respective national system and security tradition. By contrast, supranational actors – especially the European Commission and Europol – present steadily growing drivers of pro-integration preferences on EU police cooperation. Benefitting from path-dependency and spill-over effects, their influence has expanded visibly, especially over the past decade. EU actors have increasingly leveraged politicisation to this end. The findings of this book therefore strongly confirm hypothesis H3, the positive relationship between high policy entrepreneurship and pro-integration preferences. Concerning the potential impact of subnational advocacy on differentiation preferences, the case studies provide no sufficient evidence to validate hypothesis H4: that high subnational policy entrepreneurship makes it less likely that Member States favour EU police cooperation and integration, and more likely that they prefer differentiation and decentralised, informal modes of cooperation.

Driving Factors across Issue Areas and Time

A number of issue- and time-specific conclusions may be drawn. The case studies illustrate that politicisation may have the largest effect on state preferences – even if indirectly as a window of opportunity – in high-profile issue areas of police cooperation. Amongst others, terrorism and illegal migration arguably generate relatively more public pressure and higher salience, and crises or shocks tend to be more visible in these fields. By comparison, low-profile or more technical areas like vehicle-related crime and cybercrime debatably spawn less politicisation. In these issue areas, the effects of politicisation on state preferences are thus rather limited, and integration is perhaps primarily pushed by functional pressure from interdependence. This diverging impact of driving factors across issue areas is likewise reflected in the discursive strategies of policy entrepreneurs. The discourse of the European Commission in high-profile policy domains for instance strongly harnesses public pressure and political momentum from politicising events. Against it, frames and narratives within more operational settings and issue areas rather focus on functional needs to advance EU police cooperation.

Two more observations can be made regarding the influence of driving factors over time. First, interdependence has steadily grown from the early days of European police cooperation in the 1970s until today and has consistently shaped government preferences in favour of integration. Particularly globalisation and digitisation have increased external interconnectedness of EU Member States, while their internal or institutional linkages have skyrocketed in line with the general development of the EU and have become progressively more relevant as driving factors. However, the impact of functional pressure on state preferences has arguably flattened somewhat recently. Although interdependencies remain a necessary causal condition of governmental pro-integration stances, they have been sidelined by other, increasingly more important influences on state preferences like supranational policy entrepreneurship.

Changes in the nature of policy entrepreneurship over time constitute the second observation. Whereas supranational policy entrepreneurship was barely or not at all present in earlier cooperation stages, it has emerged as key shaper of state preferences on EU police cooperation in recent years. Especially the European Commission and Europol have progressively assumed roles as strong pro-integration lobbyists, most notably since the Lisbon Treaty and the ECD. Growing path-dependency alongside functional and political spill-over effects increasingly enabled cultivated spill-overs and the success of integration initiatives, as illustrated by the Europol Regulation. This seems to confirm new intergovernmentalist tenets that preference formation and EU integration have become more and more interconnected since the 1990s. At the same time, supranational policy entrepreneurs have also become more flexible in their advocacy, again supporting a new intergovernmentalist hypothesis; EU actors indeed appear to act strategically in their integration initiatives, not per se promoting full-fledged integration but embracing opportunities for entrepreneurship as they arrive. The case studies demonstrate that supranational institutions may even support differentiation and avant-garde groups with a view to producing cultivated spill-overs in the long run.

The effect of subnational policy entrepreneurship on state preferences on EU police cooperation likewise changed between the 1970s and 2022. While domestic security and police officials initially supported cooperation but resisted integration, they have perhaps become cautious integration enthusiasts in some regards today. The early 2000s still demonstrate a strong advocacy in favour of differentiation and decentralisation, as can be seen in the launch of EUCARIS, Prüm and other initiatives. Nevertheless, path-dependency and the functional benefits of common institutions like Europol may now be increasingly transforming bureaucratic resistance into pro-integration advocacy at operational levels. Supranational policy entrepreneurship and a certain socialisation at European level have further boosted this development. At the same time, the role of subnational actors and their influence on state preferences in the integration of EU police cooperation is only changing gradually. More research is thus needed to confirm this observation.

Shaping Preferences across the Three Dimensions of Differentiated Integration

Next to this book's general findings and the issue- and time-specific effects of driving factors, the strength of their impact on state preferences appears to vary across the three dimensions of differentiated integration. While the case studies clearly demonstrate interdependence as necessary causal condition for pro-integration preferences on all dimensions, it possibly acts as strongest interest shaper on the functional scope of EU police cooperation, complemented by subnational policy entrepreneurship. By comparison, politicisation and supranational advocacy seem to primarily drive state preferences on vertical and horizontal integration. Asymmetrical effects of these factors across Member States and integration dimensions possibly explain instances of differentiated integration. When the causal mechanisms at work are significantly stronger in some countries than in others, the resulting functional or public pressure may push a subgroup of governments to favour and advance integration amongst themselves.

Concerning the effect of interdependencies on state preferences across the three dimensions of differentiated integration, the analysis of EU police cooperation between 1976 and 2022 exhibits a particularly strong influence with regard to the functional scope. High external, issue-specific interdependencies seem to primarily push governments towards expanding cooperation to more issue areas. At the same time, internal or institutional interdependencies complement this effect and additionally act as drivers of centralisation preferences. In this context, subnational policy and security officials arguably often play a key role. Although subnational policy entrepreneurship may not be a key explanatory factor of pro-integration preferences on the functional scope of EU police cooperation. However, the findings of this dissertation confirm the new intergovernmentalist hypothesis that "problems in domestic preference formation have become standalone inputs into the European integration process" (Bickerton et al. 2015b: 714). Where subnational actors are faced with national constraints to manage heightened security threats – often arising from growing interdependencies – they tend to promote venue-shopping at the EU level (cf. Guiraudon 2000, 2003). Particularly the early 2000s illustrate how subnational policy entrepreneurship frequently shapes state preferences in favour of police cooperation on more and more issue areas, and even centralisation. At the same time, strong asymmetries among European law enforcement authorities often result in the promotion of differentiated integration or even differentiation. Differences in the institutional interconnectivity, the degree of influence on the respective government, and the predominant threats at operational level may explain why some subnational policy entrepreneurs advocate integration and successfully contribute to an according preference of their national government, while others prefer differentiation or fail to impact higher political levels at home.

Against it, politicisation and supranational advocacy matter most as interest drivers on the dimensions of vertical and horizontal integration. Whereas interdependencies have to be present as well for Member States to prioritise the latter two, high salience and public pressure perhaps more importantly shape preferences towards formal, publicly visible cooperation formats. Highly politicised issue areas related to policing and internal security more often yield pro-integration attitudes among affected governments than not. Additionally, the analysis of the case studies finds that the office of the Council presidency potentially has a positive impact on integration preferences. Holding the Council presidency possibly particularly exposes governments to public and political expectations, and the influence of pro-EU pressure. Nevertheless, further research is needed to validate this conclusion and determine the significance of the Council presidency as actual interest shaper of Member States or mere 'enabling factor' for the impact of other drivers. Irrespective, this dissertation finds that politicisation alone does not suffice. Instead, it seems to act as window of opportunity for the impact of supranational policy entrepreneurship. EU actors seem to harness the momentum and public pressure arising from politicising events to shape state preferences in favour of vertical and horizontal integration. Especially since the early 2000s, this could be observed in the aftermath of multiple crises. The impact of supranational policy entrepreneurship on centralisation preferences has grown significantly until today; it has arguably begun to replace interdependence as primary driver in this respect. Although interdependencies continue to matter as necessary driver of state preferences towards integration, supranational policy entrepreneurship and crisis politicisation gained significant influence as shapers of the priorities of Member States concerning Europol and EU police cooperation since at least 2010. Europol's operational centres and its new legal framework, the Regulation as well as its revision, bear testimony to the increasing influence of EU actors.

At the same time as integration, differentiation – or rather flexible integration – has possibly become a vital part of EU police cooperation (see Figure C.1). Interestingly, the case studies seem to suggest that differentiation initiatives in this area tend to be moved into EU policy venues in the long run. Rather than impeding integration, it appears, approaches of differentiated integration are often adopted by Member States as deliberate integration strategies or to overcome political deadlock and institutional obstacles. Additionally, this dissertation finds that asymmetries in the impact of different driving factors can explain this phenomenon, as they yield diverging preferences across countries and on the three dimensions of differentiated integration. The analysis of EU police cooperation between 1976 and 2022 shows that the respective strength of single drivers ultimately determines not only preference formation on vertical and horizontal integration as well as the functional scope of European police cooperation but also the probability of preference di- or convergence among Member States.

The Road Ahead: Outlook into the Future

EU police cooperation has changed considerably since its inception as the Trevi Group in 1976. It has developed from a semi-formal intergovernmental platform outside any EC/EU structures to an official EU law enforcement agency and central hub for information exchange among Member States. Although police cooperation remains a core state powers and governments still dominate governance at Europol, they are possibly losing control over the process. The early 2000s illustrate this. While EU governments deliberately opted for enhancing Europol's role, they did not originally intend to integrate it into the supranational framework. Yet, the more issue areas Member States added to its responsibilities and the more powers they gave to the agency, the more path-dependency and spill-overs they created that increasingly justified Europol as an actor itself. Notwithstanding explicit integration preferences and initiatives of some Member States, unintended consequences of initial cooperation decisions have thus contributed significantly to shaping future integration.

At the same time, functional pressure to cooperate, if not integrate, continues to rise. Next to an interconnectedness in threats through digitisation and globalisation amongst others, intra-EU interdependencies continue generate a need to work together across borders. Particularly structures, systems and procedures developed in the area of internal security and policing now produce progressive internal linkages that challenge Member States with new coordination and collective action problems. In this context, EU actors matter more and more as central administrators, brokers and coordinators, as demonstrated by the ongoing efforts to improve the interoperability of EU information systems amongst others. This trend is likely to continue. Especially Europol and the European Commission have developed an expanding policy entrepreneurship in the past years and will certainly sustain their support of the Member States in the future as well as the proactive promotion of EU policy venues.

Regardless of the strength of driving forces and political resolve in the Member States, integration at Europol still faces many obstacles to date. Although more and more domestic officials are familiar with the agency, and Europol has increasingly developed into a socialisation platform, lack of trust and persisting bureaucratic resistance remain key problems in practice. Whether Europol and EU police cooperation continue to struggle or strategically manoeuvre between differentiation and integration could ultimately depend on supranational policy entrepreneurship and the extent to which EU actors manage to connect both.

This is perhaps even truer in the light of 'Brexit' and a growing Euroscepticism across European governments – a political climate that likewise poses challenges to the area of police cooperation. The tension between EU collective action, if not integration, in this field and national sovereignty concerns will undoubtedly continue to matter and shape its further institutional development.

Against this backdrop, differentiated integration is highly likely to form an integral part of EU police cooperation in the future. The role of avant-garde groups and flexible integration might become an even more important tool for Member States to cope with the domestic manifestations of cross-national interdependencies in areas where integration preferences fail to converge. Their role as trailblazers for long-run integration will likewise continue to matter and affect state preferences as well as the further development of Europol. Irrespective of the concrete shape this will take, it seems clear that EU police cooperation is here to stay. Although Europol is unlikely to evolve into Kohl's vision of a European FBI anytime soon, growing interdependencies and security crises will undoubtedly continue to motivate Member States to cooperate at European level and further develop police cooperation in the EU. Time will tell.

APPENDIX

Categories and Criteria of Qualitative Structured Content Analysis

Category	*Definition*	*Coding rules*
I1: high interdependence	High conviction or certainty of dependence on others in given issue area or activity (implicit or explicit), i.e. • conviction of general and/or specific need for collective action, and/or • recognition of excessive demands on single government efforts/ unilateral solutions, and/or • recognition of relevance of cooperation for obtaining a national goal and/or joint policy outcome	Significant or various mentions of high interdependence, no comment should doubt the high level of interdependence Otherwise code "medium/ neutral interdependence"
I2: medium/ neutral interdependence	Partial, incoherent conviction of dependence on others, or uncertainty about interdependence	No or only sporadic and isolated mentions of interdependence that do not qualify as either "high" or "low"

(Continued)

DOI: 10.4324/9781003262176-8

Category	*Definition*	*Coding rules*
I3: low interdependence	High conviction or certainty of independence from others (implicit or explicit), i.e. • conviction of no general or specific need for collective action, and/or • conviction of satisfying response from single governments and unilateral solutions, and/or • conviction of irrelevance or low importance of cooperation for obtaining a national goal and/or joint policy outcome	Significant or various mentions of low interdependence or high independence, no comment should doubt the low level of interdependence Otherwise code "medium/ neutral interdependence"
I4: level of interdependence not deducible	Mention of the defined aspects, but comments do not clarify nature of relationship between different actors	
P1: high politicisation	Strong conviction or certainty of high politicisation (implicit or explicit), i.e. • significant saliency through considerable media, public and political interest, or politicising events (e.g. terror attacks), and/or • significant direct or indirect public/political pressure on policymakers from home and abroad (e.g. (in-)directly arising from the saliency of an issue, public opinion polls, citizens' and interest groups' demands), and/or • deliberate politicisation by policymakers, e.g. securitising moves by government and opposition	Significant or various mentions of high politicisation, no comment should doubt the high level of politicisation Otherwise code "medium/ neutral politicisation"
P2: medium/ neutral politicisation	Partial, incoherent conviction of politicisation, or uncertainty about public pressure	No or only sporadic and isolated mentions of politicisation that do not qualify as either "high" or "low"
P3: low politicisation	Low conviction of public pressure, strong certainty of low or absent politicisation (implicit or explicit), i.e. • lack of media, public and political interest, or politicising events (e.g. terror attacks), and/or • lack of direct or indirect public/ political pressure on policymakers from home and abroad, and/or • deliberate depoliticisation by policymakers	Significant or various mentions of low or no politicisation, no comment should doubt the low level of politicisation Otherwise code "medium/ neutral politicisation"

(Continued)

Category	*Definition*	*Coding rules*
P4: level of politicisation not deducible	Mention of the defined aspects, but comments do not clarify nature of politicisation	
E1: high influence of policy entrepreneurship	Strong conviction or certainty of high influence of supra-/subnational policy entrepreneurs (implicit or explicit), i.e. • stronggeneralpresenceandinvolvement in the decision-making and policy process, and/or • significant passive engagement of through procedural, legal or institutional settings, and/or • significant (pro-)active engagement in the stages of preference formation, negotiation or institutional choice, and/or • significant consultation by governments, and/or • transnational networks and synergies between supra-/subnational actors: interest groups coalition-building	Significant or various mentions of high influence of supra-/subnational policy entrepreneurs, no comment should doubt the high level of influence Otherwise code "medium/neutral influence of supra-/subnational policy entrepreneurs"
E2: medium/neutral influence of policy entrepreneurship	Partial, incoherent conviction of influence of supra-/subnational policy entrepreneurs, or uncertainty about their role	No or only sporadic and isolated mentions of supra-/subnational policy entrepreneurs that do not qualify as either "high" or "low" influence
E3: low influence of policy entrepreneurship	Low conviction of the influence of supra-/subnational policy entrepreneurs, strong certainty of no or limited influence (implicit or explicit), i.e. • low or lack of general presence and involvement in the decision-making and policy process, and/or • insignificant or no passive engagement in procedural, legal or institutional settings, and/or • little or no (pro-)active engagement in the stages of preference formation, negotiation or institutional choice, and/or • little or no consultation by governments, and/or • lack of transnational networks and synergies between supra-/subnational actors: few or no interest groups coalition-building	Significant or various mentions of low or no influence of supra-/subnational policy entrepreneurs, no comment should doubt the low level of influence Otherwise code "medium/neutral influence of supra-/subnational policy entrepreneurs"

(Continued)

Category	*Definition*	*Coding rules*
E4: level of influence of policy entrepreneurship not deducible	Mention of the defined aspects, but comments do not clarify nature of influence of supra-/subnational policy entrepreneurs	

BIBLIOGRAPHY

2015 Charlie Hebdo Attacks Fast Facts. (2018, December 24). https://edition.cnn.com/2015/01/21/europe/2015-paris-terror-attacks-fast-facts/index.html

AA – German Federal Foreign Office.

(1973, May 10). *Note on 'Vorbereitung einer europäischen Konferenz über innere Sicherheit'*. Political Archive of the German Federal Foreign Office. (PA/AA, B 21, Bd. 108870)

(1974, March 1). *Draft internal working paper, attached to the letter from 19 March 1974, concerning 'Ausarbeitung des Berichts zur Europäischen Union'*. German Federal Archives. (BArch B 106/78851)

(1976, May 20). *'Express letter' (Schnellbrief) to the Federal Minister of the Interior, concerning "Konferenz der EG-Staaten über innere Sicherheit; hier: Vorbereitendes Treffen der hohen Beamten am 25. Mai in Luxemburg"*. German Federal Archives. (BArch B 106/78830)

Aden, H.

(1998). *Polizeipolitik in Europa. Eine interdisziplinäre Studie über die Polizeiarbeit in Europa am Beispiel Deutschlands, Frankreichs und der Niederlande*. Opladen/Wiesbaden: Westdeutscher Verlag.

(Ed.). (2015). *Police cooperation in the European Union before and after the Treaty of Lisbon: Opportunities and Limitations*. Baden-Baden: Nomos.

AFP. (2015, August 16). Merkel says migrants bigger challenge for EU than Greek debt crisis. http://news.yahoo.com/merkel-says-migrants-bigger-challenge-eu-greek-debt-181432878.html

Algeria hostage crisis: Country by country. (2013, January 25). *BBC News*. https://www.bbc.com/news/world-africa-21116623

Amicelle, A., & Chaudieu, K. (2018). In Search of Transnational Financial Intelligence: Questioning Cooperation between Financial Intelligence Units. In C. King, C. Walker, & J. Gurulé (Eds.), *The Palgrave Handbook of Criminal and Terrorism Financing Law* (649–676). Cham: Palgrave Macmillan.

AML/CFT – Anti-money laundering and countering the financing of terrorism legislative package. (2021, July 20). https://ec.europa.eu/info/publications/210720-anti-money-laundering-countering-financing-terrorism_en

Amr, H., & Ferris, E. (2009). Introduction. In H. Amr, E. Ferris, K. Koser, & S. Schmeidl (Eds.), *Displacement in the Muslim World: A Focus on Afghanistan and Iraq* (5–7). Washington D.C.: Human Development Task Force: 2009 U.S.-Islamic World Forum, The Saban Center for Middle East Policy at Brookings.

Anderson, M.

(1989). *Policing the World: Interpol and the Politics of Police Co-operation.* London: Clarendon Press.

(1993a). The British Perspective on Internationalization of Police Cooperation in Western Europe. In C. Fijnaut (Ed.), *The Internationalization of Police Cooperation in Western Europe* (19–40). Arnhem: Gouda Quint.

(1993b). The French Police and Cooperation in Western Europe. In C. Fijnaut (Ed.), *The Internationalization of Police Cooperation in Western Europe* (49–84). Arnhem: Gouda Quint.

Anderson, M., Den Boer, M., Cullen, P.J., Gilmore, W., Raab, C., & Walker, N. (1995). *Policing the European Union.* Oxford: Clarendon Press.

Andersen, S.S., & Eliassen, K.A. (Eds.). (1993). *Making Policy in Europe: The Europeification of National Policy-Making.* London: SAGE Publications Ltd.

Andreas, P., & Nadelmann, E. (2006). *Policing the Globe.* Oxford: Oxford University Press.

Angel. (1977, May 17). *Letter to T.J.B. George (EID, FCO), concerning "Co-operation between Ministries of the Interior: Abolition of Frontier Passport Controls".* The National Archives of the UK. (FCO 30/3420)

Anti Money Laundering Centre NL. (2020, October 26). AMLC in Europol Financial Intelligence Public Private Partnership Steering Group (EFIPPP). https://www.amlc.eu/amlc-in-europol-financial-intelligence-public-private-partnership-steering-group-efippp/

Arlacchi, P. (1986). *Mafia Business – The Mafia Ethic and the Spirit of Capitalism.* (M. Ryle, Trans.). London: Verso.

Armstrong. (1975, July 31). *Letter to M.D. Butler (FCO).* The National Archives of the UK. (FCO 30/2614)

Arnell, P., Bock, S., Davies, G., & Wörner, L. (2021). Police Cooperation and Exchange of Information under the EU–UK Trade and Cooperation Agreement. *New Journal of European Criminal Law, 12*(2), 265–276. https://doi.org/10.1177/2032284421995572

Avramopoulos, D. (2015, July 9). Parliamentary questions (reference: E-004621/2015) – Answer given by Mr Avramopoulos on behalf of the Commission. http://www.europarl.europa.eu/doceo/document/E-8-2015-004621-ASW_EN.html?redirect

Baker-Beall, C. (2016). *The European Union's Fight against Terrorism: Discourse, Policies, Identity.* Manchester: Manchester University Press.

Balzacq, T. (2008). The Policy Tools of Securitization: Information Exchange, EU Foreign and Interior Policies. *JCMS: Journal of Common Market Studies, 46*(1), 75–100.

Balzacq, T., Bigo, D., Carrera, S., & Guild, E. (2006). Security and the Two-Level Game: The Treaty of Prüm, the EU and the Management of Threats. *Centre for European Policy Studies (CEPS), 234.*

Balzacq, T., & Léonard, S. (2013). Information-Sharing and the EU Counter-Terrorism Policy: A 'Securitisation Tool' Approach. In C. Kaunert & S. Léonard (Eds.), *European Security, Terrorism and Intelligence: Tackling New Security Challenges in Europe* (127–142). Basingstoke: Palgrave Macmillan.

Barnett, M.N., & Sikkink, K. (2008). From International Relations to Global Society. In C. Reus-Smit & D. Snidal (Eds.), *The Oxford Handbook of International Relations* (62–83). Oxford: Oxford University Press.

Baun, A. (1987). An Interesting Development within Interpol: The Technical Committee on Cooperation in Europe. *International Criminal Police Review, 405*, 24–25.

BBC.

(1975, October 3). 1975: London's Spaghetti House siege ends. http://news.bbc.co.uk/onthisday/hi/dates/stories/october/3/newsid_4286000/4286414.stm

(2000, June 19). 58 dead in port lorry. http://news.bbc.co.uk/2/hi/uk_news/796791.stm

BDK – Bund Deutscher Kriminalbeamter. (2015). Europäische Gemeinschaft – auch für die Kriminalpolizei; 2. Fachtagung Kripo International des Bundes Deutscher Kriminalbeamter – 10. und 11. April 1974 in Wiesbaden. https://www.bdk.de/web/kripo-inter/archiv/1974/1974

Beach, D., & Pedersen, R. (2016). *Causal Case Study Methods: Foundations and Guidelines for Comparing, Matching, and Tracing*. Ann Arbor, MI: University of Michigan Press.

Bebe, O. (2015, June 10). *Securitising the Internet: The Making of an EU Internet Referral Unit at Europol (*Master thesis). Leiden University, Leiden.

Bell, J.B. (2013). *The IRA, 1968–2000: An Analysis of a Secret Army*. London: Frank Cass Publishers.

Bennett, A., & Checkel, J.T. (Eds.). (2015). *Process Tracing: From Metaphor to Analytic Tool*. Cambridge: Cambridge University Press.

Benyon, J., Turnbull, L., Willis, A., Woodward, R., & Beck, A. (1993). *Police Co-operation in Europe: An Investigation*. University of Leicester: Centre for the Study of Public Order.

Berry, M., Garcia-Blanco, I., & Moore, K. (2016). *Press Coverage of the Refugee and Migrant Crisis in the EU: A Content Analysis of Five European Countries – Report Prepared for the United Nations High Commission for Refugees (December 2015)*. http://www.unhcr.org/56bb369c9.html

BfV – German Federal Office for the Protection of the Constitution. (1984, April 11). *Telefax to the German Federal Ministry of the Interior (BMI) concerning "Zusammenarbeit in der Terrorismusbekämpfung mit Großbritannien"*. German Federal Archives. (BArch B 106/106870)

Bickerton, C.J., Hodson, D., & Puetter, U.

(Eds.). (2015a). *The New Intergovernmentalism: States and Supranational Actors in the Post-Maastricht Era*. Oxford: Oxford University Press.

(2015b). The New Intergovernmentalism: European Integration in the Post-Maastricht Era. *JCMS: Journal of Common Market Studies, 53*(4), 703–722.

Bigo, D.

(1996). *Polices en réseaux. L'expérience européenne*. Paris: Presses de Sciences Po.

(2002). Security and Immigration: Toward a Critique of the Governmentality of Unease. *Alternatives: Global, Local, Political, 27*(1), 63–92.

(2014). The (In)securitization Practices of the Three Universes of EU Border Control: Military/Navy – Border Guards/Police – Database Analysts. *Security Dialogue, 45*(3), 209–225.

Bigo, D., Carrera, S., Guild, E., Guittet, E.-P., Jeandesboz, J., Mitsilegas, V., … Scherrer, A. (2015). *The EU and its Counter-Terrorism Policies after the Paris Attacks* (CEPS Paper in Liberty and Security in Europe No. 84). Brussels: Centre for European Policy Studies.

Bischoff. (1984, April 19). *Memo on 'Zusammenarbeit mit Großbritannien; hier: Ministerbesuch in London'*. German Federal Archives. (BArch B 106/106870)

BKA – German Federal Criminal Police Office.

(1976a, January 21). *Report, attached to the memo by Horst Herold from 2 February 1976, concerning 'Schaffung einer Europäischen Paß-Union; hier: Abbau der Grenzkontrollen innerhalb der Europäischen Gemeinschaft (EG)'*. German Federal Archives. (BArch B 106/78853)

(1976b, September 7). *Letter addressed to the Federal Minister of the Interior, concerning 'Europäische Konferenz für Innere Sicherheit am 25. Juni 1976 in Luxemburg'*. German Federal Archives. (BArch B 106/78831)

Block, L. (2011). *From Politics to Policing: The Rationality Gap in EU Council Policy-Making*. The Hague: Eleven International.

BMI – German Federal Ministry of the Interior.

(1973a, February 2). *Resolution concerning 'Sitzung der Ständigen Konferenz der Innenminister der Länder am 2. Februar 1973 in Bonn; Punkt 14A: Verbesserung der internationalen Zusammenarbeit auf dem Gebiet der Verbrechensbekämpfung'*. German Federal Archives. (BArch B 106/39571)

(1973b, June 12). *Internal memo on 'Vorbereitung einer Europäischen Konferenz über Innere Sicherheit; Ergebnisvermerk über eine Besprechung am 16. Mai 1973 im BMI'*. German Federal Archives. (BArch B 106/39571)

(1974a, March 6). *Situation report, attached to the letter of the Federal Ministry of the Interior to the other Federal Ministries from 6 March 1974, concerning '[...] die Behandlung der Probleme im Zusammenhang mit der Aufhebung grenzpolizeilicher Kontrollen an den Grenzen zwischen den Mitgliedsstaaten der EG'*. German Federal Archives. (BArch B 106/78851)

(1974b, August 23). *Internal memo: 'Ergebnisvermerk über eine Besprechung mit Ressorts, BfV, BKA und Referaten im BMI am 15. August 1974'*. German Federal Archives. (BArch B 106/39571)

(1975a). *Draft memo for the German Chancellor, attached to a letter from the Federal Ministry of the Interior to the Federal Foreign Office dated 20 November 1975, concerning '[...]die Sitzung der Regierungschefs der EG-Staaten am 1./2. Dezember 1975 in Rom'*. German Federal Archives. (BArch B 106/78853)

(1975b). *Report on "Internationalisierung des anarchistischen Terrors; hier: Intensivierung der Zusammenarbeit bei der Bekämpfung des internationalen Terrorismus – Anlage 2 zu II.5"*. The National Archives of the UK (TNA). (FCO 30/2614)

(1975c, September 15). *Situation assessment on 'Internationale Verbindungen deutscher Terroristen – Anlage 1 zu II.5'*. The National Archives of the UK. (FCO 30/2614)

(1976a, February 9). *German translation of a note from the British Government: "Note der Britischen Regierung"*. German Federal Archives. (BArch B 106/78830)

(1976b, April 27). *Draft memorandum, attached to an internal memo from 27 April 1976, in preparation for the ministerial conference on internal security on 29 June 1976*. German Federal Archives. (BArch B 106/106774)

(1976c, September 6). *Internal memo: 'Ergebnisvermerk über die Besprechung am 2. September 1976 im BMI'*. German Federal Archives. (BArch B 106/78831)

(1978a). *Report on: "Zu TOP 4 – 'Ausarbeitung der Präsidentschaft zur Frage eines ständigen Sekretariats und zur Verlängerung des Vorsitzes in den Arbeitsgruppen'"*. German Federal Archives. (BArch B 106/78849)

(1978b, September 19). *'Gespräch des Generaldirektors der französischen Polizei, Herrn Solier, unter Hinzuziehung von Herrn Lacarriere und Herrn Abteilungsleiter IS in Begleitung von RR Dr. Schneider (IS 3) am 8. September 1978 in Paris,' enclosed to a note from RR Schneider concerning 'TREVI-Zusammenarbeit'*. German Federal Archives. (BArch B 106/106776)

(1978c, September 25). *Internal memo concerning "Sitzung der Arbeitsgruppe TREVI I, Bekämpfung des Terrorismus' am 20./21. September 1978 in Bonn"*. German Federal Archives. (BArch B 106/106777)

(1982, May 5). *Memo concerning "Erörterung der Problematik des organisierten Verbrechens durch TREVI"*. German Federal Archives. (BArch B 106/106869)

(1983a, November 10). *Memo concerning 'Auswertung einer in Großbritannien durchgeführten Untersuchung zur Terrorismusbekämpfung'*. German Federal Archives. (BArch B 106/106870)

(1983b, November 23). *Memo concerning 'Besuch PStS Spranger in London am 14./15.11.1983'*. German Federal Archives. (BArch B 106/106870)

(1985a). *Beilage; Erweiterung der TREVI-Zuständigkeit auf schwere Gewalttaten und das organisierte internationale Verbrechen sowie Informationsaustausch über Störungen der öffentlichen Ordnung*. German Federal Archives. (BArch B 106/106819)

(1985b). *Sitzung des TREVI-Ausschusses der Hohen Beamten in Rom am 31. Mai 1985; Vorbereitung des Ministertreffens – Ausweitung der TREVI-Zuständigkeit auf schwere Straftaten und das internationale organisierte Verbrechen*. German Federal Archives. (BArch B 106/106819)

(1985c). *Translation of Scalfaro paper, titled '"Sicherheit für Europa" – Projekt der europäischen Zusammenarbeit bei der Bekämpfung des Terrorismus, der Kriminalität und der Drogen'*. German Federal Archives. (BArch B 106/106819)

(1985d, April 19). *Internal memo: 'Vermerk über die Besprechung zwischen BM Dr. Zimmermann und dem italienischen Innenminister Scalfaro am 18. April 1985'*. German Federal Archives. (BArch B 106/106819)

(1985e, May 17). *Report on 'Gespräch AL P/PR BKA am 16. Mai 1985'*. German Federal Archives. (BArch B 106/106819)

(1985f, June 4). *Extract from the situation report of 4 June 1985: "TREVI-Treffen der Hohen Beamten in Rom am 30./31. Mai – Ministertreffen am 21. Juni"*. German Federal Archives. (BArch B 106/106819)

(1986, March 12). *Translated minutes: 'Bericht über die Sitzung der TREVI AG I in Den Haag am 28. Januar 1986'*. German Federal Archives. (BArch B 106/106846)

(1992, June). *Report of the German Federal Intelligence Service (BND) on 'Gefährdungspotential des internationalen Drogenhandels'*. German Federal Archives. (BArch B 106/137936)

Bochmann. (1974, July 4). *Communication from the German Minister of the Interior concerning 'Vorbereitung einer europäischen Konferenz über innere Sicherheit; hier: Beschlüsse der Ständigen Konferenz der Innenminister der Länder am 14. Juni 1974'*. German Federal Archives. (BArch B 106/39571)

Boeden. (1984, April 18). *Memo to the German Federal Ministry of the Interior (BMI) concerning "Polizeiliche Zusammenarbeit mit Großbritannien"*. German Federal Archives. (BArch B 106/106870)

Boge, H. (1985). Komplizierte Verfahrensvorschriften und schwerfällige Geschäftswege. Lage und Perspektiven der internationalen Verbrechensbekämpfung. *Kriminalistik*, *39*, 38–45.

Boge & Schneider. (1979, September). *Internal memo on "TREVI-Zusammenarbeit – Sitzung des Ausschusses Hoher Beamter am 25. September 1979 in Dublin"*. German Federal Archives. (B/106/106834)

Boin, A. (2005). Crisis Management as Political Communication. In *The Politics of Crisis Management: Public Leadership under Pressure* (69–90). Cambridge: Cambridge University Press.

Boin, A., & 't Hart, P. (2003). Public Leadership in Times of Crisis: Mission Impossible? *Public Administration Review*, *63*(5), 544–553.

Boin, A., 't Hart, P., Stern, E., & Sundelius, B. (2005). *The Politics of Crisis Management: Public Leadership under Pressure*. Cambridge: Cambridge University Press.

Borger, A.C.J., Tokyo, J.M. in, & Macalister, T. (2013, January 25). Timeline of the In Amenas siege. *The Guardian*. https://www.theguardian.com/world/2013/jan/25/in-amenas-timeline-siege-algeria

Börzel, T.A.
(1998). Organizing Babylon – On the Different Conceptions of Policy Networks. *Public Administration, 76*(2), 253–273.
(2002). *States and Regions in the European Union: Institutional Adaptation in Germany and Spain*. Cambridge: Cambridge University Press.

Börzel, T.A., & Risse, T. (2017). From the Euro to the Schengen Crises: European Integration Theories, Politicization, and Identity Politics. *Journal of European Public Policy, 25*(1), 83–108.

Boserup, R.A., & Martinez, L. (2018). *Europe and the Sahel-Maghreb Crisis (No. 3)*. Copenhagen: Danish Institute for International Studies (DIIS).

Bossong, R. (2013). *The Evolution of EU Counter-Terrorism: European Security Policy after 9/11*. New York, NY: Routledge.

Bossong, R., & Hegemann, H. (2018). The Governance of Internal Security: Beyond Functionalism and the Finality of Integration? In A. Ripoll Servent & F. Trauner (Eds.), *The Routledge Handbook of Justice and Home Affairs* (19–29). Abingdon: Routledge.

Bossong, R., & Lavenex, S. (2016). Governance and EU Internal Security. In R. Bossong & M. Rhinard (Eds.), *Theorizing Internal Security in the European Union* (86–108). Oxford: Oxford University Press.

Boswell, C., Geddes, A., & Scholten, P. (2011). The Role of Narratives in Migration Policy-Making: A Research Framework. *British Journal of Politics and International Relations, 13*(1), 1–11.

Bourbeau, P. (2013). *The Securitization of Migration*. London: Routledge.

Bourne, J. (2011). Spaghetti House Siege: Making the Rhetoric Real. *Race & Class, 53*(2), 1–13.

Bracht.
(1975a, August 27). *Internal memo to the Minister of the Interior, concerning 'Ihr Gespräch mit dem Innenminister der Französischen Republik am 22. August 1975; hier: Vorbereitung einer Konferenz der für die innere Sicherheit verantwortlichen Minister der Mitgliedsstaaten der Europäischen Gemeinschaften (EG)'*. German Federal Archives. (BArch B 106/78829)
(1975b, November 11). *Draft letter from the Federal Minister of the Interior, Werner Maihofer, to Roy Jenkins, British State Secretary for the Home Department*. German Federal Archives. (BArch B 106/78829)
(1975c, November 13). *Memo to the Federal Minister of the Interior: 'Informationsvermerk für das Gespräch des Herrn Ministers mit dem französischen Innenminister am 21. November 1975 in Paris'*. German Federal Archives. (BArch B 106/78829)
(1976a, June 11). *Memo at the request of the Federal Minister of the Interior from 9 June 1976, concerning 'Vorbereitung einer Europäischen Konferenz für Innere Sicherheit; hier: Ergänzung der auf Beamtenebene erarbeiteten Papiere durch eine politische Willenserklärung der Minister'*. German Federal Archives. (BArch B 106/78831)
(1976b, July 2). *Internal memo concerning 'Europäische Konferenz für innere Sicherheit am 29. Juni 1976 in Luxemburg; hier: Ergebnisse'*. German Federal Archives. (BArch B 106/78831)
(1976c, October 5). *Internal memo concerning 'Europäische Zusammenarbeit "Innere Sicherheit"; hier: Umsetzung der Ministerbeschlüsse von Luxemburg durch die am 24. September 1976 in Den Haag beschlossenen Arbeitsgruppen'*. German Federal Archives. (BArch B 106/106774)

Brady, H.E., & Collier, D. (Eds.). (2004). *Rethinking Social Inquiry: Diverse Tools, Shared Standards*. Lanham, MD: Rowman & Littlefield.

Brandt, W. (1969, October 28). Government Declaration by Willy Brandt, delivered to the Bundestag. Bonn.

Brimelow. (1975, October 13). *Letter to Arthur Peterson (HO)*. The National Archives of the UK. (FCO 30/2614)

Brisard, J.-C. (2015). The Paris Attacks and the Evolving Islamic State Threat to France. *CTC Sentinel*, *8*(11), 5–8.

Bruggeman, W. (2016). ...on Europol's past and future. In Europol, *1998-2016 – Looking Back, Moving Forward: One Hundred Meetings of the Europol Management Board* (26–30). Luxembourg: Publications Office of the European Union.

Brussels Jewish museum shooter 'an angry French teen' who was radicalised in jail. (2019, March 8). *France 24*. https://www.france24.com/en/20190308-brussels-jewish-museum-attack-mehdi-nemmouche-french-teen-radicalised-jail

Bullard. (1975, September 2). *Telegram No 696 concerning "Visit of the Minister of State, Home Office"*. The National Archives of the UK. (FCO 30/2614)

Bundesrat. (1994, October 5). Printed Matter [Drucksache] 909/94 of the German Bundesrat, titled 'Entwurf für einen Rechtsakt des Rates über die Ausarbeitung des Übereinkommens über die Errichtung eines Europäischen Polizeiamts (Europol)'.

Bundestag (Deutscher).

5. Wahlperiode.

(1968a). *Drucksache V/2525*.

(1968b). *Drucksache V/2855*.

(1968c). *Plenarprotokoll 05/206*.

6. Wahlperiode.

(1970). *Drucksache VI/703*.

(1972). *Drucksache VI/3186*.

7. Wahlperiode.

(1975a). *Drucksache 7/3303*.

(1975b). *Plenarprotokoll 07/155 – Deutscher Bundestag. Stenographischer Bericht. 155. Sitzung. Bonn, Donnerstag, den 13. März 1975* (10731(B) ff.).

17. Wahlperiode.

(2012). *Printed Paper 18/41 – 'Restructured Analysis Work Files (AWFs) at EU police agency Europol'*.

18. Wahlperiode.

(2015a). *Druckssache 18/4413*.

(2015b). *Printed Paper 18/4413 – 'Development of the German Federal Criminal Police Office "Check the Web" project, which was originally launched to monitor the Internet, into a referral unit for unpleasant content.'*

Bunyan, T.

(1993). Trevi, Europol and the New European State. In T. Bunyan (Ed.), *Statewatching the New Europe. A Handbook on the European State* (15–36). London: Statewatch.

(Ed.). (1997). *From Trevi to Maastricht – Key Texts on Justice and Home Affairs in the European Union: 1976-1993* (Vol. 1). London: Statewatch.

(2006a). The EU's Police Chief Task Force (PCTF) and Police Chiefs Committee. *Statewatch Analysis*.

(2006b). The "Principle of Availability". *Statewatch Analysis*.

Bures, O.

(2012). Informal Counterterrorism Arrangements in Europe: Beauty by Variety or Duplicity by Abundance? *Cooperation and Conflict*, *47*(4), 495–518.

(2018). EU Counter-Terrorism: Glass Half-Full or Half-Empty? In A. Ripoll Servent & F. Trauner (Eds.), *The Routledge Handbook of Justice and Home Affairs* (157–168). Abingdon: Routledge.

Busch, H.

(1995). *Grenzenlose Polizei? Neue Grenzen und polizeiliche Zusammenarbeit in Europa.* Münster: Westfälisches Dampfboot.

(1996). EUROPOL – Eigenständiger Organismus mit Zukunft. *Bürgerrechte & Polizei (CILIP), 53*, 21–29.

(1999). *Polizeiliche Drogenbekämpfung – eine internationale Verstrickung.* Münster: Westfälisches Dampfboot.

Busch, H., & Monroy, M. (2017). *Who Drives EU Counter-Terrorism? On the Legislation of the European Union* (V. Langer, Trans.). Statewatch.

Busch, H., Funk, A., Kauß, U., Narr, W.D., & Werkentin, F. (1985). *Die Polizei in der Bundesrepublik.* Frankfurt; New York, NY: Campus.

Busuioc, M., Curtin, D., & Groenleer, M. (2011). Agency Growth between Autonomy and Accountability: The European Police Office as a 'Living Institution'. *Journal of European Public Policy, 18*(6), 848–867.

Callaghan.

(1975a, August 22). *Telegram No 424 concerning "Visit of Lord Harris".* The National Archives of the UK. (FCO 30/2614)

(1975b, October 17). *Telegram No 330 concerning "MIPT: Meeting of Community Ministers of the Interior".* The National Archives of the UK. (PREM 16/390)

Camera dei Deputati. (1979). *Disegno di legge: Ratifica ed esecuzione della Convenzione europea per la repression del terrorismo, aperta alla firma a Strasburgo il 27 gennaio 1977, presentato il 22 novembre 1979.*

Caporaso, J.A. (2009). Is There a Quantitative-Qualitative Divide in Comparative Politics? The Case of Process Tracing. In T. Landman & N. Robinson (Eds.), *Sage Handbook of Comparative Politics* (67–83). Thousand Oaks, CA: Sage Publications.

Carpenter, D.P., & Krause, G.A.

(2012). Reputation and Public Administration. *Public Administration Review, 72*(1), 26–32.

(2014). Transactional Authority and Bureaucratic Politics. *Journal of Public Administration Research and Theory, 25*(1), 5–25.

Carr. (1973, March 19). *Minute from Robert Carr to the Prime Minister concerning "Terrorism: The IRA", n.d., enclosed to a letter to L.P. Wright (Home Office), concerning "Security of Explosives".* The National Archives of the UK. (HO 371/43)

Carrapiço, H., & Farrand, B. (2018). Cyber Crime as a Fragmented Policy Field in the Context of the Area of Freedom, Security and Justice. In A. Ripoll Servent & F. Trauner (Eds.), *The Routledge Handbook of Justice and Home Affairs* (146–156). Abingdon: Routledge.

Carrapiço, H., & Trauner, F. (2013). Europol and Its Influence on EU Policy-Making on Organized Crime: Analyzing Governance Dynamics and Opportunities. *Perspectives on European Politics and Society, 14*(3), 357–371.

CEP – Counter Extremism Project.

(2017a, January 4). Amedy Coulibaly. https://www.counterextremism.com/extremists/amedy-coulibaly

(2017b, April 19). Mehdi Nemmouche. https://www.counterextremism.com/extremists/mehdi-nemmouche

Chalk, P. (1996). *West European Terrorism and Counter-Terrorism: The Evolving Dynamic.* London: Macmillan Press LTD.

Charlie Hebdo attack: Three days of terror. (2015, January 14). *BBC News.* https://www.bbc.com/news/world-europe-30708237

Chrisafis, A. (2015, January 12). Charlie Hebdo attackers: Born, raised and radicalised in Paris. *The Guardian*. https://www.theguardian.com/world/2015/jan/12/-sp-charlie-hebdo-attackers-kids-france-radicalised-paris

Christou, G., Croft, S., Ceccorulli, M., & Lucarelli, S. (2010). European Union Security Governance: Putting the 'Security' Back in. *European Security*, *19*(3), 341–359.

Clarke, C. (2005, July 15). Letter from the Home Secretary to Rt Hon David Davis MP and Mr Mark Oaten MP. https://publications.parliament.uk/pa/cm200506/cmselect/cmhaff/462/462we03.htm

Clemente, D. (2013). *Cyber Security and Global Interdependence: What Is Critical?* London: Chatham House.

Cobain, I. (2010, July 7). London bombings: The day the anti-terrorism rules changed. *The Guardian*. https://www.theguardian.com/uk/2010/jul/07/london-bombings-anti-terrorism

Collier, D. (2011). Understanding Process Tracing. *PS: Political Science & Politics*, *44*(4), 823–830.

Corbin, K. (2009, March 12). Lessons from the Russia-Georgia Cyberwar. *InternetNews*. http://www.internetnews.com/government/article.php/3810011/Lessons+From+the+RussiaGeorgia+Cyberwar.htm

Council (of the European Union).

(1994). Note from Chair of Working Party on Europol to Steering Group II; Subject: Revised version of the Convention on the establishment of Europol (10324/94).

(2005a, November 24). The European Union Strategy for Combating Radicalisation and Recruitment to Terrorism (14781/1/05).

(2005b, November 30). The European Union Counter-Terrorism Strategy (14469/4/05).

(2005c, December 1). Press Release: 'The European Union Strategy for Combating Radicalisation and Recruitment to Terrorism' (14390/05).

(2007a, February 15). Press Release 5922/07 – 2781st Council meeting – Justice and Home Affairs.

(2007b, May 29). Council meeting of 22-23 May: Council Conclusions (8457/3/07) on cooperation to combat terrorist use of the Internet ('Check the Web').

(2008). Council Conclusions on a Concerted Work Strategy and Practical Measures against Cybercrime, 2987th Justice and Home Affairs Council meeting, 27-28 November.

(2010a, February). Internal Security Strategy for the European Union: Towards a European Security Model (5842/2/2010).

(2010b, April 26). Council Conclusions Concerning an Action Plan to Implement the Concerted Strategy to Combat Cybercrime, 3010th General Affairs Council meeting, Luxembourg.

(2013, December 3). Background – Justice and Home Affairs Council – Thursday 5 and Friday 6 December in Brussels.

(2014a, February 19). Proposal for a Regulation[...]on the European Union Agency for Law Enforcement Cooperation and Training (Europol) and repealing Decisions 2009/371/JHA and 2005/681/JHA – Discussion paper (6476/14).

(2014b, October 8). Background – Justice and Home Affairs Council – Thursday 9 and Friday 10 October in Luxembourg.

(2014c, October 13). Foreign Fighters: Follow-up on the Conclusions of the European Council of 30 August 2014 (14160/14).

(2014d, December 2). Background – Justice and Home Affairs Council – Thursday 4 and Friday 5 December in Brussels.

(2014e, December 4). Council Conclusions on the Development of a Renewed European Union Internal Security Strategy.

(2015a). *Conclusions of the Council of the EU and of the Member States meeting within the Council on Counter-Terrorism* (Press Release No. 848/15). http://www.consilium.europa.eu/en/press/press-releases/2015/11/20-jha-conclusions-counter-terrorism/

(2015b). Outcome of the Council Meeting – 3422nd Council Meeting Justice and Home Affairs – 9 November (13870/15).

(2015c, January 16). Outline of the Counter-Terrorism Strategy for Syria and Iraq, with Particular Focus on Foreign Fighters (5369/15).

(2015d, March 2). 'Fight against Terrorism: Follow-up to the Statement of 12 February by the Members of the European Council and to the Riga Joint Statement of 29 January by the Ministers of Justice and Home Affairs of the EU – Implementation of Measures' (6606/15).

(2015e, June 16). Council Conclusions on the Renewed European Union Internal Security Strategy 2015–2020 (doc. 9798/15).

(2018, September 13). Working Party on Terrorism (TWP). https://www.consilium.europa.eu/en/council-eu/preparatory-bodies/working-party-terrorism/

(2019a, March 4). Infographic – Irregular Arrivals to the EU, 2008–2019. https://www.consilium.europa.eu/en/infographics/irregular-arrivals-since-2008/

(2019b, December 2). Council Conclusions on Europol's Cooperation with Private Parties (14745/19).

(2021, October 13). Proposal for a Regulation[...]amending Regulation (EU) 2018/1862 on the establishment, operation and use of the Schengen Information System (SIS) in the field of police cooperation and judicial cooperation in criminal matters as regards the entry of alerts by Europol – Mandate for Negotiations with the European Parliament (12800/21).

Council of Europe. (1977, January 27). *European Convention on the Suppression of Terrorism.*

Council on Foreign Relations. (n.d.). A Timeline of the U.S. War in Afghanistan. https://www.cfr.org/timeline/us-war-afghanistan

Cowhey, P., & Mueller, M. (2009). Delegation, Networks, and Internet Governance. In M. Kahler (Ed.), *Networked Politics: Agency, Power, and Governance* (173–193). Ithaca, NY: Cornell University Press.

Crelinsten, R.D., & Schmid, A.P. (Eds.). (1993). *Western Responses to Terrorism.* New York, NY: Frank Cass Publishers.

Cross, M.

(2007). An EU Homeland Security? Sovereignty vs. Supranational Order. *European Security, 16*(1), 79–97.

(2011). *Security Integration in Europe: How Knowledge-based Networks Are Transforming the European Union.* Ann Arbor, MI: University of Michigan Press.

(2014, January 9). European Integration and Security Epistemic Communities. http://www.e-ir.info/2014/01/09/european-integration-and-security-epistemic-communities/

Crozier, M. (1964). *The Bureaucratic Phenomenon.* Chicago, IL: University of Chicago Press.

CTC – EU Counter-Terrorism Coordinator.

(2014, November 24). Report on the implementation of the EU Counter-Terrorism Strategy (Council doc. 15799/14).

(2015, January 17). EU CTC input for the preparation of the informal meeting of Justice and Home Affairs Ministers in Riga on 29 January 2015 (Council doc. DS 1035/15).

Cusack, J.T. (1974). Response of the Government of France to the International Heroin Problem. In L.R.S. Simmons & A.A. Said (Eds.), *Drugs, Politics and Diplomacy: The International Connection* (229–256). London: Sage.

d'A Collings. (1976, August 2). *Internal memo from the European Integration Department to A. Campbell (Private Secretary of Anthony Crosland, Secretary of State, FCO), concerning "Terrorism: European Council Declaration"*. The National Archives of the UK. (FCO 98/211)

Dahlke, M.

(2006). *Der Anschlag auf Olympia '72; Die politischen Reaktionen auf den internationalen Terrorismus in Deutschland*. München: Peter Lang GmbH, Internationaler Verlag der Wissenschaften.

(2011a). Bundesrepublik Deutschland. Innenpolitisches Primat der Antiterrorismuspolitik. In *Demokratischer Staat und transnationaler Terrorismus; Drei Wege zur Unnachgiebigkeit in Westeuropa 1972–1975* (Vol. 90, 41–164). München: Oldenbourg Verlag.

(2011b). *Demokratischer Staat und transnationaler Terrorismus; Drei Wege zur Unnachgiebigkeit in Westeuropa 1972–1975*. München: Oldenbourg Verlag.

Dalferth, S. (2008). *How EU Policy in the Fight against Serious Crime Affects National Regulatory Structures in Germany and England*. Jacobs University Bremen.

Darley, M. (2010). Cooperation in Policing Schengen Area Borders: The Czech Republic/Austrian Example. *Penal Issues*, 1–4.

de Graaf, B.

(2010a). Counter-Narratives and the Unintentional Messages Counterterrorism Policies Unwittingly Produce: The Case of West-Germany. In National Coordinator for Counterterrorism (Ed.), *Countering Violent Extremist Narratives* (12–19). The Hague.

(2010b). *Theater van de angst. De strijd tegen terrorisme in Nederland, Duitsland, Italië en Amerika*. Amsterdam: Boom.

(2015). Terrorismus als performativer Akt. Die Bundesrepublik, Italien und die Niederlande im Vergleich. In J. Hürter (Ed.), *Terrorismusbekämpfung in Westeuropa: Demokratie und Sicherheit in den 1970er und 1980er Jahren* (93–116). Berlin: De Gruyter Oldenbourg.

de Wilde, P., Leupold, A., & Schmidtke, H. (Eds.). (2018). *The Differentiated Politicisation of European Governance*. Routledge.

de Witte, L. (1993). The Belgian Perspective on the Internationalization of Police Cooperation in Western Europe. In C. Fijnaut (Ed.), *The Internationalization of Police Cooperation in Western Europe* (85–100). Arnhem: Gouda Quint.

Deflem, M. (2002). *Policing World Society: Historical Foundations of International Police Cooperation*. Oxford: Oxford University Press.

Den Boer, M.

(2010). Towards a Governance Model of Police Cooperation in Europe: The Twist between Networks and Bureaucracies. In F. Lemieux (Ed.), *International Police Cooperation: Emerging Issues, Theory and Practice* (42–61). London: Willan Publishing.

(2014). Police, Policy and Politics in Brussels: Scenarios for the Shift from Sovereignty to Solidarity. *Cambridge Review of International Affairs*, *27*(1), 48–65.

Den Boer, M., Hillebrand, C., & Nölke, A. (2008). Legitimacy under Pressure: The European Web of Counter-Terrorism Networks. *Journal of Common Market Studies*, *46*(1), 101–124.

Den Boer, M., & Wiegand, I. (2015). From Convergence to Deep Integration: Evaluating the Impact of EU Counter-Terrorism Strategies on Domestic Arenas. *Intelligence and National Security*, *30*(2–3), 377–401.

Devichand, M. (2016, January 3). How the world was changed by the slogan 'Je Suis Charlie'. *BBC News*. https://www.bbc.com/news/blogs-trending-35108339

Devuyst, Y. (1998). Treaty Reform in the European Union: The Amsterdam Process. *Journal of European Public Policy, 5*(4), 615–631.

Díaz de Mera García Consuegra, A. (2014). *Report on the proposal for a regulation[...]on the European Union Agency for Law Enforcement Cooperation and Training (Europol) and repealing Decisions 2009/371/JHA and 2005/681/JHA*. Brussels: European Parliament.

Diez Medrano, J. (2003). *Framing Europe: Attitudes to European Integration in Germany, Spain, and the United Kingdom*. Princeton, NJ: Princeton University Press.

Dingelstad-Frankova, I. (2013). Europol Involvement in the EU THB Combat. *Pan European University in Bratislava*.

Dokumentation 11/72 – 'Gefahr für unsere Demokratie'. Schlußkundgebung anlässlich der 17. Bundestagung des Evangelischen Arbeitskreises der CDU/CSU am 12. März 1972. (1972). Pforzheim.

Drabek, T. (1994). Disaster in Aisle 13 Revisited. In K. J. Tierney & R. R. Dynes (Eds.), *Disasters, Collective Behavior, and Social Organization* (26–44). Newark, NJ: University of Delaware Press.

Dupont, B. (2004). Security in the Age of Networks. *Policing and Society, 14*(1), 76–91.

Dyson, K., & Sepos, A. (2010). Differentiated Integration as Design Principle and as a Tool in the Political Management of European Integration. In K. Dyson & A. Sepos (Eds.), *Which Europe? The Politics of Differentiated Integration* (3–23). New York, NY: Palgrave Macmillan.

EDPS.

(2020a). European Data Protection Supervisor Opinion (5/2020) on the European Commission's action plan for a comprehensive Union policy on preventing money laundering and terrorism financing.

(2020b). EDPS Decision of 17 September 2020 relating to EDPS own inquiry on Europol's big data challenge.

Ehrhart, H.-G., Hegemann, H., & Kahl, M. (2014). Towards Security Governance as a Critical Tool: A Conceptual Outline. *European Security, 23*(2), 145–162.

Eilstrup-Sangiovanni, M. (2009). Varieties of Cooperation. Government Networks in International Security. In M. Kahler (Ed.), *Networked Politics, Agency, Power, and Governance* (194–227). Ithaca, NY: Cornell University Press.

EReg – Association of European Vehicle and Driver Registration Authorities.

(2017a). EUCARIS General Assembly. https://www.ereg-association.eu/news-items/eucaris-general-assembly/

(2017b). Signing of the EUCARIS Protocol. https://www.ereg-association.eu/news-items/signing-of-the-eucaris-protocol/

ESC – European Scrutiny Committee.

(2006). *Select Committee on European Scrutiny – Twenty-Eighth Report: Document 7 'Co-operation between Asset Recovery Offices of the Member States'* (Session 2005-06). UK House of Commons.

EU FIU Platform. (2018, March 6). Minutes of the 35th Meeting of the EU FIU Platform.

EUC – European Union Committee.

(2008). *Europol: Coordinating the Fight against Serious and Organised Crime* (29 Report of Session 2007–08, HL Paper 183). London: House of Lords.

(2010). *Protecting Europe against Large-Scale Cyber Attacks* (5th Report of Session 2009-10, report with evidence, HL Paper 68). London: House of Lords.

(2015). *Home Affairs Sub-Committee: EU Action Plan against Migrant Smuggling – Evidence Volume*. London: House of Lords.

(2016). *Brexit: Future UK–EU Security and Police Cooperation* (7th Report of Session 2016-17 – HL Paper 77). London: House of Lords.
(2021). *Beyond Brexit: Policing, Law Enforcement and Security* (25th Report of Session 2019–21 – HL Paper 250). London: House of Lords.
EUCARIS – European Car and Driving Licence Information System.
(2017a). Legal basis. https://www.eucaris.net/general-information/legal-basis/
(2017b). Origin. https://www.eucaris.net/general-information/origin/
European Commission.
(1993). *Bulletin of the European Communities, No. 10, 1993.*
(1995, July 5). Press release – 'Third Pillar To Be Restructured'.
(2002). Proposal for a Comprehensive Plan to Combat Illegal Immigration and Trafficking of Human Beings in the European Union (2002/C142/02).
(2004, October 20). Communication[...]on Prevention, preparedness and response to terrorist attacks (COM/2004/698 final).
(2005, September 21). Terrorist recruitment: A Commission's Communication addressing the factors contributing to violent radicalisation (MEMO/05/329).
(2006a). Proposal for a Council Decision establishing the European Police Office (EUROPOL), and Explanatory Memorandum (COM/2006/817 final).
(2006b). Proposal for a Council Framework Decision on the exchange of information under the principle of availability (COM/2005/490 final).
(2006c, July 10). Communication[...]on Policy priorities in the fight against illegal immigration of third-country nationals (COM/2006/0402 final).
(2007). Communication[...]: Towards a general policy on the fight against cyber crime (COM/2007/267).
(2009a, March 9). Commission Staff Working Document: Third annual report on the development of a common policy on illegal immigration, smuggling and trafficking of human beings, external borders, and the return of illegal residents (SEC/2009/320 final).
(2009b, March 30). Communication[...]on Critical Information Infrastructure Protection – 'Protecting Europe from large scale cyber-attacks and disruptions: Enhancing preparedness, security and resilience' (COM/2009/149 final).
(2010a). The EU Internal Security Strategy in Action: Five steps towards a more secure Europe (MEMO/10/598).
(2010b, July 19). Communication[...]: Overview of information management in the area of freedom, security and justice (COM/2010/385).
(2010c, August 26). Communication[...]: A Digital Agenda for Europe (COM/2010/245 final/2).
(2010d, November 22). Communication[...]: The EU Internal Security Strategy in Action: Five Steps towards a more secure Europe (COM/2010/673 final).
(2012a). *Cyber Security* (Special Eurobarometer No. 390).
(2012b, January 12). Frequently asked questions: The European Cybercrime Center EC^3 (MEMO/13/6). http://europa.eu/rapid/press-release_MEMO-13-6_en.htm
(2012c, March 28). Communication[...]: Tackling Crime in our Digital Age: Establishing a European Cybercrime Centre (COM/2012/140 final).
(2012d, April 4). Commission Staff Working Document (SWD/2012/0081 final) – Impact Assessment – [...]Proposal for a Regulation of the European Parliament and of the Council on simplifying the transfer of motor vehicles registered in another Member State within the Single Market.
(2013, March 27). Proposal for a Regulation[...]on the European Union Agency for Law Enforcement Cooperation and Training (Europol) and repealing Decisions 2009/371/JHA and 2005/681/JHA (COM/2013/173 final).

(2015a). *Europeans' attitudes towards security* (Special Eurobarometer No. 432).
(2015b, April 28). Communication[...]: The European Agenda on Security (COM/2015/185 final).
(2015c, May 13). Communication[...]: A European Agenda on Migration (COM/2015/240 final).
(2015d, May 27). Communication[...]: EU Action Plan against migrant smuggling (2015–2020) (COM/2015/285 final).
(2015e, October 14). Communication[...]: Managing the refugee crisis: State of Play of the Implementation of the Priority Actions under the European Agenda on Migration (COM/2015/510 final).
(2016, February 2). Communication[...]on an Action Plan for strengthening the fight against terrorist financing (COM/2016/50 final).
(2017a, June 26). Commission Staff Working Document on improving cooperation between EU Financial Intelligence Units (SWD/2017/275 final).
(2017b, November 20). European e-Justice Portal – Criminal records. https://e-justice.europa.eu/content_criminal_records-95-en.do?init=true
(2017c, March 14). Prüm Decisions. https://ec.europa.eu/home-affairs/content/pr%C3%BCm-decisions_en
(2019). Report from the Commission to the European Parliament and the Council assessing the framework for cooperation between Financial Intelligence Units (COM/2019/371 final).
(2020a, January 29). Commission Work Programme 2020 (COM/2020/37 final).
(2020b, May 13). Communication[...]on an Action Plan for a comprehensive Union policy on preventing money laundering and terrorist financing (2020/C 164/06).
(2020c, May 14). Inception Impact Assessment (Ares/2020/2555219).
(2020d, December 9). Commission Staff Working Document – Impact Assessment Report (SWD/2020/543 final).
(2020e, December 9). Proposal for a Regulation[...]amending Regulation (EU) 2016/794, as regards Europol's cooperation with private parties, the processing of personal data by Europol in support of criminal investigations, and Europol's role on research and innovation (COM/2020/796 final).
(2021, December 8). Police Cooperation Code: Boosting police cooperation. https://ec.europa.eu/commission/presscorner/detail/en/ip_21_6645
(2022a, February 1). Political agreement on stronger mandate for Europol. https://ec.europa.eu/commission/presscorner/detail/en/IP_22_673
(2022b, March 17). Enforcing sanctions against listed Russian and Belarussian oligarchs: Commission's "Freeze and Seize" Task Force steps up work with internationalpartners.https://ec.europa.eu/neighbourhood-enlargement/news/enforcing-sanctions-against-listed-russian-and-belarussian-oligarchs-commissions-freeze-and-seize-2022-03-17_de
(n.d.). The history of the Euro. https://ec.europa.eu/info/about-european-commission/euro/history-euro/history-euro_en

European Council.
(1986). *European Council on 26 and 27 June 1986; Presidency Conclusions (SN 2178/3/86).* The Hague.
[1989]. (1997). 'The Palma Document' Free Movement of Persons. A Report to the European Council by the Coordinators' Group (Madrid, June 1989). In Bunyan (Ed.), *From Trevi to Maastricht – Key Texts on Justice and Home Affairs in the European Union: 1976–1993* (Vol. 1, 12–16). London: Statewatch.

(1991a). *European Council on 28 and 29 June 1991; Presidency Conclusions (SN 151/3/91).* Luxembourg.
(1991b). *European Council on 9 and 10 December 1991; Presidency Conclusions (SN 271/1/91).* Maastricht.
(1997). Amsterdam European Council 16 and 17 June 1997 – Presidency Conclusions [Press release]. http://www.europarl.europa.eu/summits/ams1_en.htm
(1999). *Conclusions of the Presidency of the European Council, 15–16 October 1999.* Tampere. http://www.europarl.europa.eu/summits/tam_en.htm
(2004, March 25). Declaration on Combatting Terrorism (doc. 7906/04), Brussels.
(2015a). Informal meeting of the Heads of State or Government Brussels, 12 February 2015 – Statement by the members of the European Council. https://www.consilium.europa.eu/en/press/press-releases/2015/02/12/european-council-statement-fight-against-terrorism/
(2015b). *Special meeting of the European Council, 23 April 2015 – statement.* https://www.consilium.europa.eu/en/press/press-releases/2015/04/23/special-euco-statement/

European Council, & Council of the European Union. (2018, October 25). Timeline: Foreign terrorist fighters and recent terrorist attacks in Europe. https://www.consilium.europa.eu/en/policies/fight-against-terrorism/foreign-fighters/history-foreign-fighters/

European Parliament.
(2015, December 2). Question for written answer E-01530415. https://www.europarl.europa.eu/doceo/document/E-8-2015-015304_EN.html
(2018, October 20). Legislative Train Schedule – 'Single Market: Simplifying the Transfer of Motor Vehicles Registered in Another Member State'. http://www.europarl.europa.eu/legislative-train
(2019, March). Legislative Train Schedule: Area of Justice and Fundamental Rights – Europol Regulation. http://www.europarl.europa.eu/legislative-train

Europol – European Police Office.
(2000). *Europol Annual Report 1999.*
(2001). *Europol Annual Report 2001.*
(2003). *Europol Annual Report 2002.*
(2004). *Europol Annual Report 2004.*
(2008, March 19). *Europol Work Programme 2009.*
(2009, September 15). Frequently Asked Questions (FAQ) on the association of Third Parties to Europol's AWFs (File no. 3300-381).
(2011). Europol Review: General Report on Europol Activities.
(2012a, January 30). International Anti-Money Laundering Operational Network (AMON) launched. https://www.europol.europa.eu/media-press/newsroom/news/international-anti-money-laundering-operational-network-amon-launched
(2012b, May 31). EUROPOL: New AWF Concept Guide for MS and Third Parties.
(2012c, July 10). Trafficking in Human Beings in Europe: The Perspective of Europol – Document prepared by Europol for the Special Committee on Organised Crime, Money Laundering and Corruption.
(2012d). *Check the Web.* Counter Terrorism Unit. https://www.asktheeu.org/en/request/1822/response/7002/attach/html/8/Partial%20Access%20CtW%20Presentation%202012.pdf.html
(2013). *Serious and Organised Crime Threat Assessment (SOCTA) 2013.* https://www.europol.europa.eu/activities-services/main-reports/serious-and-organised-crime-threat-assessment

(2014a). *European Union Terrorism Situation and Trend Report (TE-SAT) 2014.*
(2014b). *First Year Report – European Cybercrime Centre (EC3).*
(2015a). *'EU Internet Referral Unit at Europol – Concept note' (7266/15).*
(2015b). *Europol Review 2014: General Report on Europol Activities.*
(2015c, November 23). Enhancing counter terrorism capabilities at EU level: European Counter Terrorism Centre (ECTC) at Europol and counter terrorism related information sharing (Council doc. 14244/15).
(2016a). *1998–2016 – Looking Back, Moving Forward: One Hundred Meetings of the Europol Management Board.* Luxembourg: Publications Office of the European Union.
(2016b). *Does crime still pay? Criminal Asset Recovery in the EU.* https://www.europol.europa.eu/media-press/newsroom/news/does-crime-still-pay
(2016c). *European Union Terrorism Situation and Trend Report (TE-SAT) 2016.*
(2016d). *Migrant smuggling in the EU.*
(2016e). *The Internet Organised Crime Threat Assessment (IOCTA) 2016.*
(2016f, February 22). Europol launches the European Migrant Smuggling Centre. https://www.europol.europa.eu/newsroom/news/europol-launches-european-migrant-smuggling-centre
(2017). *From suspicion to action – Converting financial intelligence into greater operational impact.* Luxembourg: Publications Office of the European Union.
(2018a). *Europol Strategy 2020+.*
(2018b, January). European Counter Terrorism Centre – ECTC. https://www.europol.europa.eu/about-europol/european-counter-terrorism-centre-ectc
(2018c, February 1). Europol, Thomson Reuters and the World Economic Forum launch coalition to fight financial crime and modern slavery. https://www.europol.europa.eu/media-press/newsroom/news/europol-thomson-reuters-and-world-economic-forum-launch-coalition-to-fight-financial-crime-and-modern-slavery
(2020a, June 5). *Enterprising criminals – Europe's fight against the global networks of financial and economic crime.* https://www.europol.europa.eu/publications-events/publications/enterprising-criminals-%E2%80%93-europe%E2%80%99s-fight-against-global-networks-of-financial-and-economic-crime
(2020b, March 27). *Pandemic profiteering: How criminals exploit the COVID-19 crisis.* https://www.europol.europa.eu/publications-events/publications/pandemic-profiteering-how-criminals-exploit-covid-19-crisis
(2020c, July 2). Dismantling of an encrypted network sends shockwaves through organised crime groups across Europe. https://www.europol.europa.eu/media-press/newsroom/news/dismantling-of-encrypted-network-sends-shockwaves-through-organised-crime-groups-across-europe
(2021, January 29). Europol Programming Document 2021–2023.
(2022, February 23). European Financial and Economic Crime Centre – EFECC. https://www.europol.europa.eu/about-europol/european-financial-and-economic-crime-centre-efecc
(n.d.-a). European Migrant Smuggling Centre – EMSC. https://www.europol.europa.eu/about-europol/european-migrant-smuggling-centre-emsc
(n.d.-b). Europol Analysis Projects. https://www.europol.europa.eu/crime-areas-trends/europol-analysis-projects
(n.d.-c). Our Thinking. https://www.europol.europa.eu/about-europol/our-thinking
Eurostat. (n.d.). *Eurostat Asylum statistics.* https://ec.europa.eu/eurostat/statistics-explained/index.php/Asylum_statistics

Ewart-Biggs.

(1974a, August 28). *Telegram No 916 concerning "M Giscard D'Estaing on the construction of Europe"*. The National Archives of the UK. (PREM 16/78)

(1974b, August 28). *Telegram No 918 concerning "My Telegram No 916: Giscard's European Policy"*. The National Archives of the UK. (PREM 16/78)

Fabbrini, S. (2013). Intergovernmentalism and Its Limits: Assessing the European Union's Answer to the Euro Crisis. *Comparative Political Studies, 46*(9), 1003–1029.

Fägersten, B.

(2010). Bureaucratic Resistance to International Intelligence Cooperation – the Case of Europol. *Intelligence and National Security, 25*(4), 500–520.

(2016). For EU Eyes Only? Intelligence and European Security (Vol. Brief No. 8). European Union Institute for Security Studies.

Farnung, H. (2018). *Speaking at panel 1C on 'European Data Exchange,' 21. European Police Congress, 6–7 February*. Berlin.

FCO – British Foreign and Commonwealth Office.

(1974). *European drug co-operation*. The National Archives of the UK. (FCO 33/2297)

(1975a). *"Draft passage for record of Anglo-German Information Talks 25–26 September 1975; Item II.5: Co-operation in the campaign against international terrorism and in internal security questions", n.d., enclosed to a letter dated 29 September 1975 from A.M. Warburton to M.C. Wood concerning "International Terrorism"*. The National Archives of the UK. (FCO 30/2614)

(1975b). *'Proposed meeting of EEC Ministers of Interior, 1975': Collection of letters, notes and draft papers*. The National Archives of the UK. (FCO 30/2614)

(1975c). *Record of an Informal Discussion between the Foreign Ministers of the European Community at the Villa Reale di Marlia, Lucca on 18 and 19 October, 1975*. The National Archives of the UK. (FCO 30/2614)

(1975d, October 28). *Letter from German Federal Minister of the Interior Maihofer to British Secretary of State for the Home Office Lord Harris*. The National Archives of the UK. (FCO 30/2614)

(1975e, November 27). *"Capital Punishment for Terrorism – Mr Jenkins", Verbatim Service 226/75*. The National Archives of the UK. (FCO 30/2615)

(1976a). *Brief for the Secretary of State (Home Office) concerning "Professor Maihofer's Visit"; enclosed to a letter from A.S. Baker (Police Dept, HO) to Mr Philipps, concerning "Professor Maihofer's Visit", from 16 January 1976*. The National Archives of the UK. (FCO 30/3161)

(1976b). *Internal document concerning "Proposed German Draft UN General Assembly Resolution on the Taking of Hostages", n.d., received in registry on 3 September 1976*. The National Archives of the UK. (FCO 98/211)

(1976c, February 13). *Note by the United Nations Department (FCO), concerning "European Political Cooperation: Ministerial Meeting, Luxembourg, 23/24 February; Item No 4 International Aspects of Terrorist Problem"*. The National Archives of the UK. (FCO 98/211)

(1976d, July 15). *Letter from I.M. Sinclair, concerning "Terrorism"*. The National Archives of the UK. (FCO 98/211)

(1976e, July 28). *Letter concerning "Initiative at the United Nations on Terrorism", from "Presidency The Hague COREU to all Coreu Priority"*. The National Archives of the UK. (FCO 98/211)

(1976f, July 28). *Letter from P.M. Foster to A.D.S. Goodall (Western Europe Department), concerning "Terrorism"*. The National Archives of the UK. (FCO 98/211)

(1977, May 5). *Letter from J.H. Mallett (Migration and Visa Dept) to Mr Lance (EID, FCO), concerning "Meeting of EEC Ministers of the Interior"*. The National Archives of the UK. (FCO 30/3420)

Ferris, E. (2009). Iraqi Displacement: The Need for Solutions. In H. Amr, E. Ferris, K. Koser, & S. Schmeidl, *Displacement in the Muslim World: A Focus on Afghanistan and Iraq* (22–33). Washington D.C.: Human Development Task Force: 2009 U.S.-Islamic World Forum, The Saban Center for Middle East Policy at Brookings.

Fifoot. (1976, July 23). *Letter from Paul Fifoot to P.M. Maxey, concerning "Terrorism"*. The National Archives of the UK. (FCO 98/211)

Fijnaut, C.

(1992a). Naar een Gemeenschappelijke regeling van de politiële samenwerking en de justitiële rechtshulp. In C. Fijnaut, J. Stuyck, & P. Wytinck (Eds.), *Schengen: Proeftuin voor de Europese gemeenschap?* (89–117). Antwerp: Gouda Quint.

(1992b). Policing Western Europe: Interpol, TREVI and Europol. *Police Studies*, *15*(3), 101–106.

(Ed.). (1993). *The Internationalization of Police Cooperation in Western Europe*. Arnhem: Gouda Quint.

(2016). *The Containment of Organised Crime and Terrorism: Thirty-Five Years of Research on Police, Judicial and Administrative Cooperation*. Leiden: Brill/Nijhoff.

Fijnaut, C., & Hermans, R.H. (Eds.). (1987). *Police Cooperation in Europe*. Lochem: Van den Brink.

FMI – Ministère de l'Intérieur France.

(1978, September 26). *Note from Treyssac to the Directeur Général de la Police Nationale*. French Archives Nationales. (AN 19960183/30)

(1986, 1989). *Press articles and notes concerning 'Attentats de Paris/attentats terrorisme 1986-1989'*. French Archives Nationales. (AN 19920345/11)

Franko, K., & Gundhus, H.O.I. (2015). A Divided Fraternity: Transnational Police Cultures, Proximity, and Loyalty. *European Journal of Policing Studies*, *3*(3–4).

French Presidency. (2000, October 12). Proposal for the extension of Europol's mandate to the fight against cybercrime (Council doc. 12224/00).

French terror attacks: Victim obituaries. (2015, January 13). *BBC News*. https://www.bbc.com/news/world-europe-30724678

Fretwell. (1975, October 10). *Note to Mr Kerr, concerning "Meeting of the Community Ministers of the Interior"*. The National Archives of the UK. (FCO 30/2614)

Frevel, B., & Rogers, C. (2016). Community Partnerships (UK) vs Crime Prevention Councils (GER): Differences and Similarities. *The Police Journal*, *89*(2), 133–150.

Friedrichs, J. (2008). *Fighting Terrorism and Drugs: Europe and International Police Cooperation*. New York, NY: Routledge.

Friesendorf, C. (2007). *US Foreign Policy and the War on Drugs: Displacing the Cocaine and Heroine Industry*. New York, NY [etc.]: Routledge.

Gardner, N.R. (1979). Drug Abuse: The Italian Response. *Drug Enforcement*, *6*(1), 13–15.

Genschel, P., & Jachtenfuchs, M.

(Eds.). (2014). *Beyond the Regulatory Polity? The European Integration of Core State Powers*. Oxford: Oxford University Press.

(2017). *From market integration to core state powers : The Eurozone crisis, the refugee crisis and integration theory* (RSCAS Working Paper No. 2017/26). Florence: European University Institute, Robert Schuman Centre for Advanced Studies.

George, A.L., & Bennett, A. (2004). *Case Studies and Theory Development in the Social Sciences*. Cambridge, MA: MIT Press.

German Presidency, A. (2020, October 21). Declaration of the Home Affairs Ministers of the European Union – Ten points on the future of Europol. https://www.eu2020.de/eu2020-en/news/pressemitteilungen/10-point-plan-on-the-future-of-europol-agreed/2408888

Gévaudan, H. (1985). *La bataille de la 'French Connection': Récit*. Paris: Lattès.
Giddens, A. (1986). *The Constitution of Society: Outline of the Theory of Structuration*. Berkeley, CA: University of California Press.
Giering, C. (1997). *Europa zwischen Zweckverband und Superstaat : Die Entwicklung der politikwissenschaftlichen Integrationstheorie im Prozeß der europäischen Integration*. Bonn: Europa-Union-Verlag.
Gläser, J., & Laudel, G. (2010). *Experteninterviews und qualitative Inhaltsanalyse als Instrumente rekonstruierender Untersuchungen* (4th ed.). Wiesbaden: VS Verlag.
Græger, N., & Lindgren, W.Y. (2018). The Duty of Care for Citizens Abroad: Security and Responsibility in the In Amenas and Fukushima Crises. *The Hague Journal of Diplomacy*, *13*(2), 188–210.
Grande, E., & Kriesi, H. (2016). Conclusion: The Postfunctionalists Were (Almost) Right. In S. Hutter, E. Grande, & H. Kriesi (Eds.), *Politicising Europe: Integration and Mass Politics* (279–300). Cambridge: Cambridge University Press.
Grant, R.W., & Keohane, R.O. (2005). Accountability and Abuses of Power in World Politics. *American Political Science Review*, *99*(1), 29–43.
Gregory, F.E.C. (1991). Police Cooperation and Integration in the European Community: Proposals, Problems, and Prospects. *Terrorism*, *14*(3), 145–155.
Groenleer, M. (2009). *The Autonomy of European Union Agencies: A Comparative Study of Institutional Development*. Delft: Eburon Uitgeverij B.V.
Guiraudon, V. (2000). European Integration and Migration Policy: Vertical Policy-Making as Venue Shopping. *JCMS: Journal of Common Market Studies*, *38*(2), 251–271.
(2003). The Constitution of a European Immigration Policy Domain: A Political Sociology Approach. *Journal of European Public Policy*, *10*(2), 263–282.
Haas, E.B. (1958). *The Uniting of Europe: Political, Social, and Economic Forces, 1950–1957*. Notre Dame, IN: University of Notre Dame Press.
Haas, P.M. (1992). Introduction: Epistemic Communities and International Policy Coordination. *International Organization*, *46*(1), 1–35.
Haber, E.
(2015). *Druckssache 18/3910 – Kleine Anfrage des Abgeordneten Andrej Hunko u.a. und der Fraktion DIE LINKE: Maßnahmen der EU-Polizeiagentur Europol hinsichtlich ausländischer Kämpfer*. German Federal Ministry of the Interior.
(2017). *Druckssache 18/13105 – Kleine Anfrage des Abgeordneten Andrej Hunko und der Fraktion DIE LINKE: Bekämpfung des sogenannten E-Smuggling durch die Polizeiagentur Europol*. German Federal Ministry of the Interior.
Hafner-Burton, E.M., & Montgomery, A.H. (2009). Globalization and the Social Power Politics of International Economic Networks. In M. Kahler (Ed.), *Networked Politics: Agency, Power, and Governance* (23–42). Ithaca, NY: Cornell University Press.
Hall, P.A., & Taylor, R.C.R. (1996). Political Science and the Three New Institutionalisms. *Political Studies*, *44*(5), 936–957.
Harrington. (1985, September 9). *Translated letter: 'Schreiben des Home Office vom 9. Sept. 1985 an das Justizministerium in Luxemburg'*. German Federal Archives. (BArch B 106/106846)
Harrsion, S. (2018). Evolving Tech, Evolving Terror. *New Perspectives in Foreign Policy*, (15). https://www.csis.org/npfp/evolving-tech-evolving-terror
Hart, K. (2008, August 14). Longtime Battle Lines Are Recast in Russia and Georgia's Cyberwar. *The Washington Post*, D01.
Hay, C.
(2007). *Why We Hate Politics*. Cambridge: Polity Press.

(2008). Constructivist Institutionalism. In S.A. Binder, R.A.W. Rhodes, & B.A. Rockman (Eds.), *The Oxford Handbook of Political Institutions* (56–74). Oxford: Oxford University Press.

Hegemann, H., & Kahl, M.

(2016). (Re-)Politisierung der Sicherheit? Legitimation und Kontestation geheimdienstlicher Überwachung nach Snowden. *Zeitschrift Für Internationale Beziehungen, 23*(2), 8–42.

(2018). Security Governance and the Limits of Depoliticisation: EU Policies to Protect Critical Infrastructures and Prevent Radicalisation. *Journal of International Relations and Development, 21*(3), 552–579.

Henderson.

(1975a, April 25). *Telegram No 347 from British Embassy Bonn, concerning "Terrorist Attack on the Federal German Embassy at Stockholm"*. The National Archives of the UK. (FCO 33/2795)

(1975b, April 25). *Telegram No 349 from British Embassy Bonn, concerning "My Tel No 347: Terrorist Attack on West German Embassy in Stockholm"*. The National Archives of the UK. (FCO 33/2795)

Henzler, P. (2018). *Speaking at the panel discussion 'GTAZ & Co.: Strengthening of operational cooperation,' 21. European Police Congress, 6–7 February*. Berlin.

Heritier, A., & Knill, C. (2000). *Differential Responses to European Policies: A Comparison* (Max-Planck Project Group Reprint No. 2000/7). Social Science Research Network.

Héritier, A., Kerwer, D., & Knill, C. (2001). *Differential Europe: The European Union Impact on National Policymaking*. Lanham, MD: Rowman & Littlefield.

Herold, H. (1974). Zielvorstellungen für die Verbrechensbekämpfung in der EG. In Bund Deutscher Kriminalbeamter (Ed.), *Materialien für die Neuordnung der Verbrechensaufklärung und Verbrechensverhütung in Europa*. Berlin.

(1975a, July 21). *Letter to the Federal Ministry of the Interior, concerning 'Grobkonzept für die polizeiliche Zusammenarbeit mit Frankreich'*. German Federal Archives. (BArch B106/106861)

(1975b, August 25). *Situation assessment at the request of Werner Maihofer, Minister of the Interior, concerning 'Vorbereitung einer europäischen Innenministerkonferenz; hier: Sollvorstellungen für die polizeiliche Zusammenarbeit'*. German Federal Archives. (BArch B 106/78829)

(1976a, February 2). *Letter addressed to the state criminal police offices, the state Interior Ministers and the Federal Ministry of the Interior, concerning "Europäische Paß-Union; hier: Abbau der Grenzkontrollen innerhalb der EG"*. German Federal Archives. (BArch B 106/78853)

(1976b, September 7). *Letter to the Federal Minister of the Interior concerning "Europäische Konferenz für Innere Sicherheit am 25. Juni 1976 in Luxemburg"*. German Federal Archives. (BArch B 106/78831)

Herschinger, E., & Jachtenfuchs, M. (2012). Informell oder institutionalisiert? Die Internationalisierung der inneren Sicherheit. *Politische Vierteljahresschrift, 53*(3), 493–514.

Herschinger, E., Jachtenfuchs, M., & Kraft-Kasack, C.

(2011). Scratching the Heart of the Artichoke? How International Institutions and the European Union Constrain the State Monopoly of Force. *European Political Science Review, 3*(03), 445–468.

(2013). Transgouvernementalisierung und die ausbleibende gesellschaftliche Politisierung der inneren Sicherheit/Transgovermentalization and the lack of social politicization of domestic security. In M. Zürn & M. Ecker-Ehrhardt (Eds.), *Politisierung der Weltpolitik* (190–212). Berlin: Suhrkamp.

Herzog, S. (2011). Revisiting the Estonian Cyber Attacks: Digital Threats and Multinational Responses. *Journal of Strategic Security*, *4*(2), 49–60.

HM Government.

(2018a, May). *Framework for the UK-EU Security Partnership*. https://assets.publishing.service.gov.uk/government/uploads/system/uploads/attachment_data/file/705687/2018-05-0_security_partnership_slides__SI__FINAL.pdf

(2018b, July). The future relationship between the United Kingdom and the European Union – Cm 9593.

HO – British Home Office.

(1969, December 11). *Draft paper on "Law and Order", enclosed to a letter from E.M. to the Minister of State (Home Secretary), concerning "Government Achievements"*. The National Archives of the UK. (HO 287/2223)

(1974a). *Collection of media articles following the London Tower bomb blasts of 17 July 1974*. The National Archives of the UK. (HO 306/129)

(1974b, July 23). *Note from S.G. Norris (Private Secretary) to A.S. Baker, Brennan, FitzGerald et al., concerning "Supply Debate on Public Safety and Decline in Respect for the Law"*. The National Archives of the UK. (HO 306/129)

(1975a). *Draft Letter from the Home Secretary to Monsieur Poniatowski, Ministre de l'Interior, Paris*. The National Archives of the UK (TNA). (FCO 30/2614)

(1975b). *Home Secretary's engagement diaries, 1975*. The National Archives of the UK. (HO 317/26)

(1975c, May 20). *Brief concerning "Meeting of European Ministers of Justice, 22 May 1975, International Terrorism", enclosed to a letter from C.H. Prior on behalf of Mr Brennan to Vincent Evans*. The National Archives of the UK. (HO 306/129)

(1977a). *Draft Brief, Visit of Herr Genscher: 24 January – Terrorism (Defensive)*. The National Archives of the UK. (HO 306/137)

(1977b). *Draft paper on "Conference of Ministers of the Interior (Meeting on 31 May, 1977, London) Abolition of Frontier Passport Controls within the European Community", n.d.; enclosed to letter from N.A. Nagler (HO) to Mr P.L. Taylor, concerning "EEC Ministers of the Interior", dated 2 May 1977*. The National Archives of the UK. (FCO 30/3420)

(2006). *Report of the Official Account of the Bombings in London on 7th July 2005 (HC 1087)*. London.

(2017). *Impact Assessment (HO0289): Criminal Finances Act – Information Sharing*.

HO (Home Office) & HM Treasury.

(2015). *National risk assessment of money laundering and terrorist financing 2015*.

(2017). *National risk assessment of money laundering and terrorist financing 2017*.

Hof, T.

(2011). *Staat und Terrorismus in Italien 1969–1982*. Munich: Oldenbourg Verlag.

(2015). Anti-Terrorismus-Gesetze und Sicherheitskräfte in der Bundesrepublik Deutschland, Großbritannien und Italien in den 1970er und 1980er Jahren. In J. Hürter (Ed.), *Terrorismusbekämpfung in Westeuropa: Demokratie und Sicherheit in den 1970er und 1980er Jahren* (7–34). Berlin: De Gruyter Oldenbourg.

Hollande, F. (2015). Discours du président de la République devant le Parlement réuni en Congrès. Versailles. http://www.elysee.fr/declarations/article/discours-du-president-de-la-republique-devant-le-parlement-reuni-en-congres-3/

Holzinger, K., & Schimmelfennig, F. (2012). Differentiated Integration in the European Union: Many Concepts, Sparse Theory, Few Data. *Journal of European Public Policy*, *19*(2), 292–305.

Hooghe, L., & Marks, G.

(2001). *Multi-level governance and European integration*. Lanham, MD: Rowman & Littlefield.

(2009). A Postfunctionalist Theory of European Integration: From Permissive Consensus to Constraining Dissensus. *British Journal of Political Science*, *39*(1), 1–23.

Hutter, Swen, Grande, E., & Kriesi, H. (Eds.). (2016). *Politicising Europe: Integration and Mass Politics*. Cambridge: Cambridge University Press.

Huysmans, J. (2006). *The Politics of Insecurity: Fear, Migration and Asylum in the EU*. London: Routledge.

Ikenberry, G.J. (2001). An Institutional Theory of Order Formation. In G.J. Ikenberry (Ed.), *After Victory: Institutions, Strategic Restraint, and the Rebuilding of Order after Major Wars*. (50–79). Princeton, NJ: Princeton University Press.

Imbert, P. (1989). Do We Need a British FBI? *Police Review*, *5020*, 1416–1417.

IMK – German Standing Conference of State Interior Ministers.

(1973a, February 2). *Sitzung am 2. Februar 1973 in Bonn (Protokollauszüge und Schriftwechsel)*. German Federal Archives. (BArch B 106/39854)

(1973b, November 30). *Sitzung am 30. November 1973 in Bonn (Beschlußprotokoll und Schriftwechsel)*. German Federal Archives. (BArch B 106/39856)

(1995, March 20). *Report to the German Standing Conference of State Interior Ministers, concerning 'Vorschläge für Eckpunkte zur Umsetzung der Europol-Konvention in nationales Recht. Bericht der ad-hoc-Arbeitsgruppe Europol des AK II'*.

(2017). Ständige Konferenz der Innenminister und -senatoren der Länder – Aufgaben und Arbeitsweise. http://www.innenministerkonferenz.de/IMK/DE/aufgaben/aufgaben-node.html;jsessionid=DEEED310E66854C8EB192A605306D44E.1_cid365

Irrera, D. (2018). Organized Crime: Balancing National Sensitivities with Global Necessities. In A. Ripoll Servent & F. Trauner (Eds.), *The Routledge Handbook of Justice and Home Affairs* (136–145). Abingdon: Routledge.

Jachtenfuchs, M., Friedrichs, J., Herschinger, E., & Kraft-Kasack, C. (2008). *Policing among nations : Internationalizing the monopoly of force* (Working paper No. 28). Berlin: Hertie School of Governance.

Jeffreys-Jones, R. (2007). The Idea of a European FBI. In L.K. Johnson (Ed.), *Strategic Intelligence: Counterintelligence and Counterterrorism: Defending the Nation against Hostile Forces* (Vol. 4, 73–96). New York, NY: Praeger.

Jenkins. (1975, October 14). *Minute from the Home Secretary to Prime Minister Harold Wilson*. The National Archives of the UK. (PREM 16/390)

Johnston, L., & Shearing, C. (2003). *Governing Security: Explorations in Policing and Justice*. London: Routledge.

Jones, C. (2015). *Briefing – Counter-terrorism: What the EU is discussing after the Paris attacks*. Statewatch.

Jones, T., & van Steden, R. (2013). Democratic police governance in comparative perspective: Reflections from England & Wales and the Netherlands. *Policing: An International Journal of Police Strategies & Management*, *36*(3), 561–576.

Jupille, J., & Caporaso, J.A. (1999). Institutionalism and the European Union: Beyond International Relations and Comparative Politics. *Annual Review of Political Science*, *2*(1), 429–444.

Kahler, M. (2009). *Networked Politics: Agency, Power, and Governance*. Ithaca, NY: Cornell University Press.

Karamanou, A. (2000). *Report (A5-0312/2000), of 27 October 2000*. Brussels: European Parliament.

Kassim, H., & Le Galès, P. (2010). Exploring Governance in a Multi-Level Polity: A Policy Instruments Approach. *West European Politics*, *33*(1), 1–21.

Kaunert, C.

(2007). "Without the Power of Purse or Sword": The European Arrest Warrant and the Role of the Commission. *Journal of European Integration, 29*(4), 387–404.

(2010a). The Area of Freedom, Security and Justice in the Lisbon Treaty: Commission Policy Entrepreneurship? *European Security, 19*(2), 169–189.

(2010b). Towards Supranational Governance in EU Counter-Terrorism? – The Role of the Commission and the Council Secretariat. *Central European Journal of International & Security Studies, 4*(1), 8–31.

(2011). *European Internal Security – Towards Supranational Governance in the Area of Freedom, Security and Justice?* Manchester: Manchester University Press.

Kaunert, C., & Léonard, S. (2012). The Development of the EU Asylum Policy: Venue-Shopping in Perspective. *Journal of European Public Policy, 19*(9), 1396–1413.

Kaunert, C., Leonard, S., & Occhipinti, J.

(2013). Agency Governance in the European Union's Area of Freedom, Security and Justice. *Perspectives on European Politics & Society, 14*(3), 273–284.

(Eds.). (2015). *Justice and Home Affairs Agencies in the European Union*. London: Routledge.

Kaunert, C., Léonard, S., & Pawlak, P. (Eds.). (2012). *European Homeland Security: A European Strategy in the Making?* London: Routledge.

Keck, M.E., & Sikkink, K. (1998). *Activists beyond Borders: Advocacy Networks in International Politics*. Ithaca, NY: Cornell University Press.

Kickert, W.J.M., & Meer, F.-B. van der. (2011). Small, Slow, and Gradual Reform: What can Historical Institutionalism Teach Us? *International Journal of Public Administration, 34*(8), 475–485.

King, J., & Scarlett, J. (2021, January 18). The Future of UK–EU Security Cooperation. https://rusi.org/explore-our-research/publications/commentary/future-uk-eu-security-cooperation

Kingdon, J.W. (2003). *Agendas, Alternatives and Public Policies* (2nd ed.). New York, NY: Longman (1st ed. 1984).

Kirchner, E.J., & Sperling, J. (2007). *EU Security Governance*. Manchester: Manchester University Press.

Kleine, M., & Pollack, M. (2018). Liberal Intergovernmentalism and Its Critics. *JCMS: Journal of Common Market Studies, 56*(7), 1493–1509.

Knelangen, W.

(2001). *Das Politikfeld innere Sicherheit im Integrationsprozess : Die Entstehung einer europäischen Politik der inneren Sicherheit*. Opladen: Leske + Budrich.

(2006). Die innen- und justizpolitische Zusammenarbeit der EU und die Bekämpfung des Terrorismus. In E. Müller & P. Schneider (Eds.), *Die Europäische Union im Kampf gegen den Terrorismus : Sicherheit vs. Freiheit?* (140–162). Baden-Baden: Nomos-Verlag.

Koenig, N. (2015). *A Differentiated View of Differentiated Integration* (Policy Paper No. 140). Berlin: Jacques Delors Institut.

Koenig-Archibugi, M. (2004). Explaining Government Preferences for Institutional Change in EU Foreign and Security Policy. *International Organization, 58*(1), 137–174.

Kohler-Koch, B., & Rittberger, B. (2006). The 'Governance Turn' in EU Studies. *JCMS: Journal of Common Market Studies, 44*(1), 27–49.

Kölner Stadt-Anzeiger. (1974, June 15). *Innenminister für EG-Konferenz über Sicherheit*. German Federal Archives. (BArch B 106/39571)

König, F. (2015). *The Art of Collective Response in Global Health Governance: Competing Frames, the Public Sphere and Pandemic Crises* (QEH Working Paper Series, No. 206). Oxford: University of Oxford.

Koremenos, B., Lipson, C., & Snidal, D. (2001). The Rational Design of International Institutions. *International Organization, 55*(4), 761–799.

Korns, S.W., & Kastenberg, J.E. (2009). Georgia's Cyber Left Hook. *Parameters, 38*(4), 60–76.

Koser, K., & Schmeidl, S. (2009). Displacement, Human Development, and Security in Afghanistan. In H. Amr, E. Ferris, K. Koser, & S. Schmeidl (Eds.), *Displacement in the Muslim World: A Focus on Afghanistan and Iraq* (8–21). Washington D.C.: Brookings Institution.

Kratochwil, F.V. (1991). *Rules, Norms, and Decisions: On the Conditions of Practical and Legal Reasoning in International Relations and Domestic Affairs.* Cambridge: Cambridge University Press.

Kriesi, H. (2016). The Politicization of European Integration. *JCMS: Journal of Common Market Studies, 54*(S1), 32–47.

Krings, G. (2018). *Opening speech at the 21. European Police Congress, 6-7 February.* Berlin.

Krzyżanowski, M., & Ledin, P. (2017). Uncivility on the Web: Populism in/and the Borderline Discourses of Exclusion. *Journal of Language and Politics, 16*(4), 566–581.

Krzyżanowski, M., Triandafyllidou, A., & Wodak, R. (2018). The Mediatization and the Politicization of the "Refugee Crisis" in Europe. *Journal of Immigrant & Refugee Studies, 16*(1–2), 1–14.

Labour Party (UK). (1974, February). *Labour Party General Election Manifesto: 'Let us work together – Labour's way out of the crisis'.*

Lammert, M.

(2015). Ein neues Analysemodell für die historische Terrorismusforschung? Securitization-Prozesse in Frankreich und Deutschland in den 1970er und 1980er Jahren. In J. Hürter (Ed.), *Terrorismusbekämpfung in Westeuropa: Demokratie und Sicherheit in den 1970er und 1980er Jahren* (200–215). Berlin: De Gruyter Oldenbourg.

(2017). *Der neue Terrorismus: Terrorismusbekämpfung in Frankreich in den 1980er Jahren.* Berlin; Boston, MA: De Gruyter Oldenbourg.

Lance. (1976, February 18). *Letter to Maxey (UN Department), concerning "European Political Co-Operation: Ministerial Meeting Luxembourg 23/24 February".* The National Archives of the UK. (FCO 98/211)

Landtag Rheinland-Pfalz. (1974). *Drucksache 7/2788 – Kleine Anfrage des Abgeordneten Haberer (CDU): Errichtung einer Europäischen zentralen Polizeibehörde "Europol".* German Federal Archives. (BArch B 106/39571)

Lange, H.-J. (1999). *Innere Sicherheit im Politischen System der Bundesrepublik Deutschland.* Opladen: Leske + Budrich.

Lannoo, K., & Parlour, R. (2021). *Anti-Money Laundering in the EU – Time to Get Serious.* Brussels: Centre for European Policy Studies.

Laursen, F., & Vanhoonacker, S. (Eds.). (1992). *The Intergovernmental Conference on Political Union. Institutional Reforms, New Policies and International Identity of the European Community.* Dordrecht: Brill/Nijhoff.

Lavenex, S. (2010). Justice and Home Affairs. Communitarization with Hesitation. In H. Wallace, M. Pollack, & A. R. Young (Eds.), *Policy-Making in the European Union* (457–477). Oxford: Oxford University Press.

Lavenex, S., & Wagner, W. (2007). Which European Public Order? Sources of Imbalance in the European Area of Freedom, Security and Justice. *European Security, 16*(3–4), 225–243.

Léonard, S. (2007). *The European Union and the 'Securitization' of Asylum and Migration: Beyond the Copenhagen School's Framework* (PhD thesis). University of Wales, Aberystwyth.

Léonard, S., & Kaunert, C. (2011). Reconceptualizing the Audience in Securitization Theory. In T. Balzacq (Ed.), *Securitization Theory: How Security Problems Emerge and Dissolve* (57–76). Abingdon: Routledge.

Leruth, B. (2014). *Differentiated Integration in the European Union: A Comparative Study of Party and Government Preferences in Finland, Sweden and Norway* (PhD in Politics). University of Edinburgh, Edinburgh.

Leuffen, D., Rittberger, B., & Schimmelfennig, F.

(2013). *Differentiated Integration: Explaining Variation in the European Union.* London: Palgrave Macmillan.

(2015). The European Union as a System of Differentiated Integration: Interdependence, Politicization and Differentiation. *Journal of European Public Policy, 22*(6), 764–782.

Leupold, A. (2015). A Structural Approach to Politicisation in the Euro Crisis. *West European Politics, 39*(1), 84–103.

Lewis, J.A. (2002). *Assessing the Risks of Cyber Terrorism, Cyber War and Other Cyber Threats.* Washington, D.C.: Center for Strategic and International Studies.

Lindberg, L.N., & Scheingold, S.A. (Eds.). (1970). *Regional Integration: Theory and Research.* Cambridge, MA: Harvard University Press.

Loader, I. (2002). Policing, Securitization and Democratization in Europe. *Criminal Justice, 2*(2), 125–153.

Luiijf, E., Besseling, K., & de Graaf, P. (2013). Ten National Cyber Security Strategies: A Comparison: Critical Information Infrastructure Security. Presented at the 8th International Workshop on Critical Information Infrastructures Security, Amsterdam.

Luxembourg Presidency. (2015, July 14). Renewed European Union Internal Security Strategy Implementation Paper (Council doc. 10854/15).

Maaßen, H.-G. (2018). *Keynote address titled 'Networked security in times of networked risks – Risk control in the 21st century,' delivered at the 21. European Police Congress, 6-7 February.* Berlin.

MacGregor, S. (1998). Pragmatism or Principle? Continuity and Change in the British Approach to Treatment and Control. In R. Coomber (Ed.), *The Control of Drugs and Drug Users: Reason or Reaction?* (131–154). Amsterdam: Harwood.

Mahoney, J. (1976). 22b Balcombe Street London. The Television Siege. *European Broadcasting Review, 27,* 16–18.

Maihofer, W. (1975, September 18). *Letter from the German Minister of the Interior, Werner Maihofer, to the French Minister of the Interior, Michel Poniatowski.* German Federal Archives. (BArch B 106/78829)

Malmström, C. (2011, April). *It's Time to Take Cyber Criminals Offline.* SPEECH/11/260, Brussels.

March, J.G., & Olsen, J.P.

(1989). *Rediscovering Institutions: The Organizational Basis of Politics.* New York, NY: The Free Press.

(1995). *Democratic Governance.* New York, NY: Free Press.

(2006). Elaborating the 'New Institutionalism'. In R.A.W. Rhodes, S.A. Binder, & B.A. Rockman (Eds.), *The Oxford Handbook of Political Institutions.* Oxford: Oxford University Press.

Maricut, A. (2016). *The Institutional Development of the EU's Area of Freedom, Security and Justice: Roles, Behaviors, and the Logic of Justification.* Central European University, Budapest.

Markoff, J. (2008, August 12). Before the Gunfire, Cyberattacks. *The New York Times.* https://www.nytimes.com/2008/08/13/technology/13cyber.html

Marx, D. (2018). *Speaking at the panel discussion 'GTAZ & Co.: Strengthening of operational cooperation,' 21. European Police Congress, 6–7 February.* Berlin.

Mastenbroek, E., & Kaeding, M. (2006). Europeanization beyond the Goodness of Fit: Domestic Politics in the Forefront. *Comparative European Politics*, *4*, 331–354.

Maxwell, N. (2020). *Five years of growth in public–private financial information-sharing partnerships to tackle crime* (Future of Financial Intelligence Sharing research programme). Royal United Services Institute.

Mayring, P. (2010). *Qualitative Inhaltsanalyse: Grundlagen und Techniken* (11th ed.). Weinheim: Beltz.

Meade, R.C. (1990). *Red Brigades: The Story of Italian Terrorism*. New York, NY: Palgrave Macmillan.

Meichtry, S., Bisserbe, N., & Faucon, B. (2015, January 14). Paris Attacker Amedy Coulibaly's Path to Terror. *Wall Street Journal*. https://www.wsj.com/articles/paris-attackers-path-to-terror-1421204761

Merk.

(1973a, April 25). *Draft invitation letter to BfV and BKA for a meeting on 'Vorbereitung einer Europäischen Konferenz über innere Sicherheit'*. German Federal Archives. (BArch B 106/39571)

(1973b, April 25). *Internal memo concerning 'Vorbereitung einer Europäischen Konferenz über innere Sicherheit'*. German Federal Archives. (BArch B106/106879)

(1974a, February 7). *Internal memo: 'Ergebnisvermerk über eine Besprechung im französischen Innenministerium am 5. Februar 1974 zur Vorbereitung einer Europäischen Konferenz über innere Sicherheit'*. German Federal Archives. (BArch B 106/39571)

(1974b, February 7). *Internal memo on 'Vorbereitung einer Europäischen Konferenz über innere Sicherheit; hier: Abstimmung mit der französischen Regierung'*. German Federal Archives. (BArch B 106/39571)

(1974c, August 2). *Internal memo on 'Europäische Konferenz über innere Sicherheit; hier: Bildung einer deutsch-französischen Arbeitsgruppe für allgemeine Fragen der inneren Sicherheit'*. German Federal Archives. (BArch B 106/39571)

(1976a, May 26). *Internal memo for the Federal Minister of the Interior, concerning 'Europäische Konferenz für Innere Sicherheit; hier: Vorbereitende Sitzung der zuständigen hohen Beamten (Abteilungsleiter bzw. Generaldirektoren) am 25. Mai 1976'*. German Federal Archives. (BArch B 106/106774)

(1976b, September 6). *Speaking points for the Federal Minister of the Interior in advance of the meeting of the IMK, concerning 'Innenministerkonferenz am 16./17. September 1976 in Hamburg; hier: Unterrichtung über Europäische Konferenz für Innere Sicherheit am 29 Juni 1976 in Luxemburg'*. German Federal Archives. (BArch B 106/78831)

Merk & Bahners. (1973, June 12). *Memo concerning 'Vorbereitung einer Europäischen Konferenz über Innere Sicherheit; Ergebnisvermerk über eine Besprechung am 16. Mai 1973 im BMI'*. German Federal Archives. (BArch B 106/39571)

Merk & Bracht.

(1976a, June 15). *Internal memo to the Minister of the Interior concerning 'Vorbereitung einer Europäischen Konferenz für Innere Sicherheit; hier: Ergänzung der auf Beamtenebene erarbeiteten Papiere durch eine politische Willenserklärung der Minister'*. German Federal Archives. (BArch B 106/78831)

(1976b, October 16). *Internal memo concerning 'Europäische Zusammenarbeit "Innere Sicherheit"; hier: Erfahrungen in der ersten Sitzungsrunde der fünf Arbeitsgruppen – Überlegungen für weiteres Vorgehen'*. German Federal Archives. (BArch B 106/106774)

Meyer-Sahling, J.-H., & Yesilkagit, K. (2011). Differential Legacy Effects: Three Propositions on the Impact of Administrative Traditions on Public Administration Reform in Europe East and West. *Journal of European Public Policy*, *18*(2), 311–322.

Migration to Europe in charts. (2018, September 11). *BBC News*. https://www.bbc.com/news/world-europe-44660699

Milward, A.S. (1992). *The European Rescue of the Nation State*. London; New York, NY: Routledge.

Mitsilegas, V., Monar, J., & Rees, W. (2003). *The European Union and Internal Security: Guardian of the People?* London: Palgrave Macmillan UK.

Monar, J.

(2001). The Dynamics of Justice and Home Affairs: Laboratories, Driving Factors and Costs. *JCMS: Journal of Common Market Studies, 39*(4), 747–764.

(2003). Justice and Home Affairs: Europeanization as a Government-Controlled Process. In K. Dyson & K. Goetz (Eds.), *Germany, Europe, and the Politics of Constraint* (309–324). Oxford: Oxford University Press.

(2007). Common Threat and Common Response? The European Union's Counter-Terrorism Strategy and its Problems. *Government and Opposition, 42*(3), 292–313.

(2011). The Role of the European Union in Transnational Violence Risk Management. In M. Kahl (Ed.), *The Transnationalisation of Risks of Violence* (120–138). Baden-Baden: Nomos.

Monar, J., & Morgan, R. (Eds.). (1994). *The Third Pillar of the European Union: Cooperation in the Fields of Justice and Home Affairs*. Brussels: European Interuniversity Press.

Monroy, M. (2021, January 2). Brexit agreement: Close EU police cooperation with the UK continues. https://digit.site36.net/2021/01/02/brexit-agreement-close-eu-police-cooperation-with-the-uk-continues/

Moravcsik, A.

(1993). Preferences and Power in the European Community: A Liberal Intergovernmentalist Approach. *JCMS: Journal of Common Market Studies, 31*(4), 473–524.

(1998). *The Choice for Europe: Social Purpose and State Power from Messina to Maastricht*. Ithaca, NY: Cornell University Press.

Moravcsik, A., & Nicolaïdis, K. (1999). Explaining the Treaty of Amsterdam: Interests, Influence, Institutions. *JCMS: Journal of Common Market Studies, 37*(1), 59–85.

Moravcsik, A., & Schimmelfennig, F. (2009). Liberal Intergovernmentalism. In A. Wiener & T. Diez (Eds.), *European Integration Theory* (67–88). Oxford: Oxford University Press.

Morehouse, C., & Blomfield, M. (2011). *Irregular Migration in Europe*. Washington D.C.: Transatlantic Council on Migration, Migration Policy Institute.

Moreno-Lax, V. (2018). The EU Humanitarian Border and the Securitization of Human Rights: The 'Rescue-Through-Interdiction/Rescue-Without-Protection' Paradigm. *Journal of Common Market Studies, 56*(1), 119–140.

Morgan, N. (2014). *The heroin epidemic of the 1980s and 1990s and its effect on crime trends – then and now* (Research Report No. 79). London: Home Office.

Mouzakiti, F. (2020). Cooperation between Financial Intelligence Units in the European Union: Stuck in the middle between the General Data Protection Regulation and the Police Data Protection Directive. *New Journal of European Criminal Law, 11*(3), 351–374. https://doi.org/10.1177/2032284420943303

Moysey, S.P. (2008). *The Road to Balcombe Street: The IRA Reign of Terror in London*. London: Routledge.

Mühl, B. (2011, August). *EU Asset Recovery Offices and the CARIN Network*. Vienna.

Muller, A. (2018, November 15). Fourniret, itinéraire d'un prédateur. *Le Figaro*. http://www.lefigaro.fr/actualite-france/2018/02/16/01016-20180216ARTFIG00357-fourniret-itineraire-d-un-predateur.php

Müller, T. (2015). Europäisierung der inneren Sicherheit. In B. Frevel (Ed.), *Polizei in Staat und Gesellschaft, Politikwissenschaftliche und soziologische Grundzüge* (73–89). Hilden: Verlag Deutsche Polizeiliteratur.

Münch, H. (2018). *Keynote address titled 'Challenges and possible solutions for the federal security architecture,' delivered at the 21. European Police Congress, 6–7 February*. Berlin.

Nadelmann, E. (1993). *The Internationalization of Police Cooperation in Western Europe*. Pennsylvania, PA: Pennsylvania University Press.

Nail, T. (2016). A Tale of Two Crises: Migration and Terrorism after the Paris Attacks. *Studies in Ethnicity and Nationalism*, *16*(1), 158–167.

Nairne. (1974, September 11). *Steering brief addressed to Lord Bridges: "Preparation for Summit Dinner on 14 September"*. The National Archives of the UK. (PREM 16/78)

National Council. (2006, April 21). 1155 der Beilagen zu den Stenographischen Protokollen des Nationalrates XXII. GP – Staatsvertrag – Materialien. https://www.parlament.gv.at/PAKT/VHG/XXII/I/I_01155/fnameorig_050447.html

Nazario, J. (2009, June). *Politically Motivated Denial of Service Attacks*. Presented at the Conference on Cyberwarfare, Cooperative Cyber Defence Centre of Excellence, Tallinn, Estonia.

Neumann, G.L. (2012). The Brakes that Failed: Constitutional Restriction of International Agreements in France. *Cornell International Law Journal*, *45*(2), 257–365.

Niemann, A. (2006). *Explaining Decisions in the European Union*. Cambridge: Cambridge University Press.

Niemann, A., & Schmitter, P. (2009). Neofunctionalism. In A. Wiener & T. Diez (Eds.), *European Integration Theory* (2nd ed., 45–66). Oxford: Oxford University Press.

Niemeier, M. (2007). Die Zukunft von Europol. *Integration*, *30*(3), 292–301.

Niemeier, M., & Zerbst, P. (2007). Der Vertrag von Prüm – vertiefte grenzüberschreitende Zusammenarbeit zur Kriminalitätsbekämpfung in der EU; Die Überführung des Vertrages von Prüm in den Rechtsrahmen der EU. *ERA Forum*, *8*(4), 535–547.

Noelle, E., & Neumann, E.P. (Eds.). (1974). *Jahrbuch der öffentlichen Meinung. 1968–1973*. Allensbach: Verlag für Demoskopie.

North, D.C. (1990). *Institutions, Institutional Change and Economic Performance*. New York, NY: Cambridge University Press.

Oberloskamp, E.

(2012). Das Olympia-Attentat 1972. Politische Lernprozesse im Umgang mit dem transnationalen Terrorismus. *Vierteljahrshefte Für Zeitgeschichte*, *60*(3), 321–352.

(2015). Die Europäisierung der Terrorismusbekämpfung in den 1970er Jahren: Bundesdeutsche Akteure und Positionen. In J. Hürter (Ed.), *Terrorismusbekämpfung in Westeuropa: Demokratie und Sicherheit in den 1970er und 1980er Jahren* (219–238). Berlin: De Gruyter Oldenbourg.

(2017). *Codename TREVI: Terrorismusbekämpfung und die Anfänge einer europäischen Innenpolitik in den 1970er Jahren*. Boston/Berlin: De Gruyter Oldenbourg.

Occhipinti, J.D.

(2003). *The Politics of EU Police Cooperation: Toward a European FBI?* London: Lynne Rienner Publishers.

(2015). Still Moving Toward a European FBI? Re-Examining the Politics of EU Police Cooperation. *Intelligence and National Security*, *30*(2–3), 234–258.

Olsen, J.P.

(1996). Europeanization and Nation-State Dynamics. In S. Gustavsson & L. Lewin (Eds.), *The Future of the Nation State: Essays on Cultural Pluralism and Political Integration*. London: Routledge.

(1997). European Challenges to the Nation State. In B. Steunenberg & F. v. Vught (Eds.), *Political Institutions and Public Policy* (157–188). The Hague: Kluver Academic Publishers.

Ottis, R. (2008). Analysis of the 2007 Cyber Attacks against Estonia from the Information Warfare Perspective. In D. Remenyi (Ed.), *Proceedings of the 7th European Conference on Information Warfare and Security (30 June – 1 July 2008, University of Plymouth)* (163–168). Reading: Academia Publishing Limited.

Paoli, L. (2014). How to Tackle (Organized) Crime in Europe? The EU Policy Cycle on Serious and Organized Crime and the New Emphasis on Harm. *European Journal of Crime, Criminal Law and Criminal Justice, 22*(1), 1–12.

Paravicini, G., & Cerulus, L. (2016, April 28). Belgian police knew since 2014 that Abdeslam brothers planned 'irreversible act'. *POLITICO*. http://www.politico.eu/article/belgian-police-knew-since-2014-that-abdeslam-brothers-planned-irreversible-act/

Park, J. (2015). Europe's Migration Crisis. *Council of Foreign Relations*, 311–325.

Parusel, B., & Schneider, J. (2011). *Annual Report on Migration and International Protection Statistics 2009*. Nuremberg: Federal Office for Migration and Refugees.

Peek, J. (1994). International Police Cooperation within Justified Political and Juridical Frameworks: Five Theses on TREVI. In J. Monar & R. Morgan (Eds.), *The Third Pillar of the European Union: Cooperation in the Fields of Justice and Home Affairs* (201–208). Brussels: European Interuniversity Press.

Peek, J., & Hoefman, M. (1993). The Dutch Perspective on Internationalization of Police Cooperation in Western Europe. In C. Fijnaut (Ed.), *The Internationalization of Police Cooperation in Western Europe* (101–112). Arnhem: Gouda Quint.

Pellegrini, F. (2019). *Report of the chair of the Europol Cooperation Board to the Joint Parliamentary Scrutiny Group*. Brussels. https://www.europarl.europa.eu/cmsdata/188163/23_17h30_18h30_PROF%20PELLEGRINI_ecb_speech_jpsg_20190922-original.pdf

Peterson. (1975, September 30). *Note from the Permanent Under-Secretary of State (HO) to Thomas Brimelow*. The National Archives of the UK. (FCO 30/2614)

Pfahl-Traughber, A., & Berndt, U. (1999). Extremismus und Innere Sicherheit. In W. Weidenfeld & K.-R. Korte (Eds.), *Handbuch zur deutschen Einheit, 1949–1989–1999* (353–367). Frankfurt am Main: Campus Verlag.

Pierson, P. (1996). The Path to European Integration: A Historical Institutionalist Analysis. *Comparative Political Studies, 29*(2), 123–163.

Piquet, A. (2020, December 11). The post-Brexit police cooperation: An act of tightrope walk [Queen Mary University of London]. https://www.qmul.ac.uk/nexteuk/publications/blog/items/the-post-brexit-police-cooperation-an-act-of-tightrope-walk-.html

Pollack, M.

(1994). Creeping Competence: The Expanding Agenda of the European Community. *Journal of Public Policy, 14*(2), 95–145.

(2019). Institutionalism and European Integration. In A. Wiener, T. A. Börzel, & T. Risse (Eds.), *European Integration Theory* (3rd ed.). Oxford: Oxford University Press.

Powell. (1974, November 29). *Minute from C.D. Powell (British Embassy Bonn) to J.A. Shepherd (WED, FCO), concerning "Security Measures in the Aftermath of the Von Drenkmann Murder"*. The National Archives of the UK. (FCO 30/2690)

Presidency & CTC (Counter-Terrorism Coordinator). (2015, November 16). Follow-up to the recent terrorist attacks in Paris (Council doc. 14122/15).

Prime Minister's Office (UK).

(1974, November 22). *Extract from the Prime Minister's Speech at Newham*. The National Archives of the UK. (PREM 16/2085)

(1976, June 14). *Letter from Oliver Wright (British Embassy, Bonn) to Anthony Crosland MP (HM Principal Secretary of State for Foreign and Commonwealth Affairs), concerning "German Federalism"*. The National Archives of the UK. (PREM 16/894)

(1979). *Home Office Statistical Bulletin, "Statistics on the Prevention of Terrorism (Temporary Provisions) Act 1974 and 1976 – First Quarter 1979*. The National Archives of the UK. (PREM 16/2085)

Princen, S., & Rhinard, M. (2006). Crashing and Creeping: Agenda-Setting Dynamics in the European Union. *Journal of European Public Policy, 13*(7), 1119–1132.

Prior. (1975, November 14). *Letter to the Foreign and Commonwealth Office, the Law Officers' Department et al., concerning "Terrorism – Proposed Council of Europe Convention"*. The National Archives of the UK. (HO 291/1853)

Proyecto de Ley Orgánica por la que se modifica la Ley Orgánica 10/1995, de 23 de noviembre, del Código Penal, en materia de delitos de riesgo provocados por explosivos. (Aprobada por el Consejo de Ministros en su reunión de 11 de marzo de 2005.)

Puetter, U. (2012). Europe's Deliberative Intergovernmentalism: The Role of the Council and European Council in EU Economic Governance. *Journal of European Public Policy, 19*(2), 161–178.

Pütter, N. (1991). EKA, EDIU und EUROPOL. *Bürgerrechte & Polizei (CILIP), 40.*

Quillé, M. (2009). *Key note address: Current threats and future challenges posed by cybercrime.* Presented at the Octopus Interface Conference on Cooperation against Cybercrime (10 March), Council of Europe, Strasbourg.

Ragin, C.C. (1987). *The Comparative Method: Moving beyond Qualitative and Quantitative Strategies*. Berkeley, CA: University of California Press.

Rapoport, D.C. (2013). The Four Waves of Modern Terror. International Dimensions and Consequences. In J. M. Hanhimäki & B. Blumenau (Eds.), *An International History of Terrorism: Western and Non-Western Experiences* (282–310). London; New York, NY: Routledge.

Rauh, C., & Zürn, M. (2014). Zur Politisierung der EU in der Krise. In M. Heidenreich (Ed.), *Krise der europäischen Vergesellschaftung? Soziologische Perspektiven* (121–145). Wiesbaden: VS Verlag für Sozialwissenschaften.

Rauschgift: Wie Dr. No; Südamerikas und Asiens Drogenbosse streben auch im Westen nach der Macht – dieses Ziel unterstellen ihnen Geheimdienstler. (1992, January 6). *Der Spiegel, 2*, 125–126.

Rekawek, K., Matějka, S., Szucs, V., Beňuška, T., Kajzarová, K., & Rafay, J. (2018). *Who Are the European Jihadis? Project Midterm Report*. GLOBSEC. https://www.globsec.org/publications/who-are-european-jihadis-from-criminals-to-terrorists-and-back/

Requate, J., & Zessin, P. (2007). Comment sortir du 'terrorisme'? La violence politique et les conditions de sa disparition en France et en République Fédérale d'Allemagne en comparaison 1970-années 1990. *European Review of History, 14*(3), 423–445.

Rhinard, M. (2018). Public Policy Approaches and the Study of European Union Justice and Home Affairs. In A. Ripoll Servent & F. Trauner (Eds.), *The Routledge Handbook of Justice and Home Affairs* (41–55). Abingdon: Routledge.

Rhodes, R.A.W.

(1996). The New Governance. Governing without Government. *Political Studies, 44*(4), 652–667.

(2008). Policy Network Analysis. In R.E. Goodin, M. Moran, & M. Rein (Eds.), *The Oxford Handbook of Public Policy* (425–443). Oxford: Oxford University Press.

Richardson, J.J. (1996). *European Union: Power and Policy-Making.* London: Routledge.

Risse, T., Cowles, M.G., & Caporaso, J.A. (2001). Europeanization and Domestic Change: Introduction. In M.G. Cowles, J.A. Caporaso, & T. Risse (Eds.),

Transforming Europe: Europeanization and Domestic Change (1–20). Ithaca, NY: Cornell University Press.

Rittberger, B., & Wonka, A. (Eds.). (2012). *Agency Governance in the EU.* Abingdon: Routledge.

Rittberger, B., Biermann, F., Guérin, N., Jagdhuber, S., & Weiss, M. (2017). *'Explaining Uneven EU Integration Trajectories: A Comparison of the Euro Crisis and the Refugee Crisis' – paper prepared for the European Union Studies Association (EUSA) Conference.* Miami.

Rittberger, B., Leuffen, D., & Schimmelfennig, F. (2014). Differentiated Integration of Core State Powers. In P. Genschel & M. Jachtenfuchs (Eds.), *Beyond the Regulatory Polity? The European Integration of Core State Powers* (189–210). Oxford: Oxford University Press.

Robinson, N., Disley, E., Potoglou, D., Reding, A., Culley, D., Penny, M., ... Millard, J. (2012). *Feasibility study for a European Cybercrime Centre – Prepared for the European Commission – Final Report TR-1218-EC.* RAND Europe.

Rüger, C. (2012). *Europäische Außen- und Sicherheitspolitik. (K)ein Thema für die Öffentlichkeit. Die außen- und sicherheitspolitische Rolle der EU im Blickwinkel von öffentlicher Meinung und Medien.* Baden-Baden: Nomos.

Rupprecht, R.

(1991). Brauchen wir Europol? – Zukunftsgedanken an der Schwelle zum neuen Jahr. *Die Polizei, 82*, 293–299.

(1993). Internationalization of Police Cooperation in Western Europe: The German Perspective. In C. Fijnaut (Ed.), *The Internationalization of Police Cooperation in Western Europe* (41–48). Arnhem: Gouda Quint.

Rupprecht, R., & Hellenthal, M.D. (1994). Internal Security and the Single Market. In R. Rupprecht, M.D. Hellenthal, & W. Weidenfeld (Eds.), *Internal Security and the Single Market* (17–53). Gütersloh: Bertelsmann Foundation Publishers.

Sabbati, G., & Poptcheva, E.-M. (2015). *Irregular Immigration in the EU: Facts and Figures.* European Parliamentary Research Service. https://epthinktank.eu/2015/04/27/irregular-immigration-in-the-eu-facts-and-figures/

Salt, J., & Almeida, J. C. (2006). International Migration in Europe. Patterns and Trends since the mid-1990s. *Revue Européenne Des Migrations Internationales, 22*(2), 155–175.

Sandholtz, W., & Stone Sweet, A. (Eds.). (1998). *European Integration and Supranational Governance.* Oxford: Oxford University Press.

Santos Vara, J. (2018). The EU's Agencies: Ever More Important for the Governance of the Area of Freedom, Security and Justice. In A. Ripoll Servent & F. Trauner (Eds.), *The Routledge Handbook of Justice and Home Affairs* (445–457). Abingdon: Routledge.

Saupe, A. (2010). Von "Ruhe und Ordnung" zur "inneren Sicherheit" – Eine Historisierung gesellschaftlicher Dispositive. *Zeithistorische Forschungen/Studies in Contemporary History, 7*, 170–187.

Scharpf, F. (1985). Plädoyer für einen aufgeklärten Institutionalismus. In H.-H. Hartwich (Ed.), *Policy-Forschung in der Bundesrepublik Deutschland. Ihr Selbstverständnis und ihr Verhältnis zu den Grundfragen der Politikwissenschaft* (164–170). Opladen: Westdeutscher Verlag.

Schäuble, W. (1990). Europa ohne Grenzen – eine sichere Gemeinschaft. *Europa-Archiv, 6*, 203–212.

Schimmelfennig, F.

(2015). Efficient Process Tracing: Analyzing the Causal Mechanisms of European Integration. In A. Bennett & J.T. Checkel (Eds.), *Process Tracing: From Metaphor to Analytic Tool* (98–125). Cambridge: Cambridge University Press.

(2017). European Integration (Theory) in Times of Crisis. A Comparison of the Euro and Schengen Crises. *Journal of European Public Policy, 25*(7), 969–989.

Schjolberg, S. (2014). *The History of Cybercrime: 1976–2014*. Norderstedt: Books on Demand.

Schlatmann, A. (2016). …on the MB's competences de jure and in practice under the Europol Regulation. In *Europol, 1998-2016 – Looking Back, Moving Forward: One Hundred Meetings of the Europol Management Board* (44–46). Luxembourg: Publications Office of the European Union.

Schmidt, V.A. (2018). Rethinking EU Governance: From 'Old' to 'New' Approaches to Who Steers Integration. *JCMS: Journal of Common Market Studies, 56*(7), 1544–1561.

Schmitter, P.

(1969). Three Neo-Functional Hypotheses about International Integration. *International Organization, 23*(1), 161–166.

(2005). Ernst B. Haas and the Legacy of Neofunctionalism. *Journal of European Public Policy, 12*(2), 255–272.

Schneider. (1979, April 27). *Note on 'TREVI-Zusammenarbeit; hier: Sitzung der Arbeitsgruppe I am 11./12. April 1979 in Paris'*. German Federal Archives. (BArch B 106/78834)

Schober, K. (2017). *Europäische Polizeizusammenarbeit zwischen TREVI und Prüm. Mehr Sicherheit auf Kosten von Freiheit und Recht?* Heidelberg: C.F. Müller.

Schout, A., & Wolff, S. (2016). The 'Paradox of Lisbon': Supranationalism-Intergovernmentalism as an Administrative Concept. In F. Laursen (Ed.), *The EU's Lisbon Treaty: Institutional Choices and Implementation* (21–40). London: Routledge.

Schreiber. (1985, June 3). *Letter to MR Siegele, titled 'Für Ministerialrat Dr. Siegele'*. German Federal Archives. (BArch B 106/106819)

Schröder, O. (2015). *Antwort vom 14. April auf die Kleine Anfrage des Abgeordneten Andrej Hunko u. a. und der Fraktion DIE LINKE: 'Maßnahmen der EU-Polizeiagentur Europol gegen sogenannte "Illegale Immigration"'(BT-Drucksache 18/4522)*. Berlin: German Federal Ministry of the Interior.

Schroeder, U.C. (2011). *The Organization of European Security Governance : Internal and External Security in Transition*. Hoboken: Routledge.

Schütze, R. (2015). *European Union Law*. Cambridge: Cambridge University Press.

Schwarz, H.

(1973a, January 4). *Interview (ZDF Heute, 21:15) with Heinz Schwarz, Minister of the Interior of Rhineland-Palatinate and Chairman of the Standing Conference of State Interior Ministers (IMK): 'zu Fragen von INTERPOL und EUROPOL'*. German Federal Archives. (BArch B 106/39571)

(1973b, December 27). *Interview (ZDF Heute, 19:00) with Heinz Schwarz, Minister of the Interior of Rhineland-Palatinate and Chairman of the Standing Conference of State Interior Ministers (IMK): 'zu den Plänen einer europäischen Innenministerkonferenz'*. German Federal Archives. (BArch B 106/39571)

Scipioni, M. (2018). Failing Forward in EU Migration Policy? EU Integration after the 2015 Asylum and Migration Crisis. *Journal of European Public Policy, 25*(9), 1357–1375.

Seawright, J., & Gerring, J. (2008). Case Selection Techniques in Case Study Research: A Menu of Qualitative and Quantitative Options. *Political Research Quarterly, 61*(2), 294–308.

Selchow, S. (2016). The Construction of "European Security" in the European Union in a Changing Global Environment: A Systematic Analysis. *European Security, 25*(3), 281–303.

Senato (della Repubblica). (1976). *Tipografia del Senato: 'Repressione e prevenzione dell'abuso di stupefacenti e sostanze psicotrope: Indagine conoscitiva'*. Rome.

Shakarian, P., Shakarian, J., & Ruef, A. (2013). How Cyber Attacks Augmented Russian Military Operations. In *Introduction to Cyber-Warfare; A Multidisciplinary Approach* (23–32). Waltham, MA: Elsevier Inc.

Sheptycki, J.W.E.

(2000). The 'drug war' learning from the paradigm example of transnational policing. In J.W.E. Sheptycki (Ed.), *Issues in Transnational Policing* (201–228). London, New York: Routledge.

(2002). *In Search of Transnational Policing: Towards a Sociology of Global Policing*. Aldershot: Ashgate.

Siegele, G. (1992). Von TREVI bis Europol – Die Entwicklung der zwischenstaatlichen Kooperation im Bereich der öffentlichen Sicherheit. In R. Morié, M. Murck, & R. Schulte (Eds.), *Auf dem Weg zu einer europäischen Polizei. Rahmenbedingungen, Aufgaben und berufliches Selbstverständnis* (132–147). Berlin: Richard Boorberg Verlag.

Siegele & Lümmen. (1985, March 11). *Internal memo concerning "Sitzung des Arbeitskreises II der Arbeitsgemeinschaft der Innenministerien der Bundesländer am 14./15. März 1985".* German Federal Archives. (B/106/106819)

SMJ – Spanish Ministry of Justice. (2006). *Sumario No 20/2004 – El auto de procesamiento por el 11-M.* Madrid: Administración de Justicia.

Solier. (1978, August 26). *Telefax from the Directeur Général de la Police Nationale to Loewenich (BMI).* French Archives Nationales. (AN 19960183/28)

South, N. (1998). Tackling Drug Control in Britain: From Sir Malcolm Delevigne to the New Drugs Strategy. In R. Coomber (Ed.), *The Control of Drugs and Drug Users: Reason or Reaction?* (87–106). Amsterdam: Harwood.

Sperling, J., & Webber, M. (2014). Security Governance in Europe: A Return to System. *European Security, 23*(2), 126–144.

Storbeck, J.

(2001, December 3). 'Wir sind in Grenzbereichen'/Interviewer: S. Schreiber [Transcript]. *DER SPIEGEL, 49.* http://www.spiegel.de/spiegel/print/d-20899551.html

(2016). ...on Europol's first years. In Europol, *1998-2016 – Looking Back, Moving Forward: One Hundred Meetings of the Europol Management Board* (21–24). Luxembourg: Publications Office of the European Union.

Streicher.

(1975, October 13). *Internal memo, referring to the letter of the British Embassy from 15 September 1975, concerning 'Europäische Konferenz für innere Sicherheit; hier: Einladung des Herrn Ministers zu einem Besuch in London'.* German Federal Archives. (BArch B 106/78829)

(1976, February 17). *Memo for the Federal Minister of the Interior, concerning 'Vorbereitung der Europäischen Konferenz für Innere Sicherheit; hier: Vorbereitende Gespräche mit der dänischen und luxemburgischen Seite'.* German Federal Archives. (BArch B 106/78829)

Streicher & Bracht.

(1975a, November 4). *Internal Memo concerning 'Europäische Konferenz für Innere Sicherheit; hier: Britische Initiative im Rahmen der Europäischen Politischen Zusammenarbeit'.* German Federal Archives. (BArch B 106/78829)

(1975b, December 9). *Memo for the Federal Minister of the Interior, concerning 'Umsetzung der Beschlüsse des Europäischen Rates vom 1./2. Dezember 1975; hier: Vorbereitung einer Europäischen Konferenz für innere Sicherheit'.* German Federal Archives. (BArch B 106/78829)

(1976, January 30). *Memo for the Federal Minister of the Interior, concerning 'Vorbereitung einer Europäischen Konferenz für Innere Sicherheit; hier: "Pakt gegen den Terrorismus"'.* German Federal Archives. (BArch B 106/78829)

Stubb, A. C.-G. (1996). A Categorization of Differentiated Integration. *JCMS: Journal of Common Market Studies, 34*(2), 283–295.

Tallberg, J. (2003). The Agenda-Shaping Powers of the EU Council Presidency. *Journal of European Public Policy, 10*(1), 1–19.

Tekin, F. (2015). Differentiated Integration: Ever More Relevant for Police Cooperation after the Treaty of Lisbon? In H. Aden (Ed.), *Police Cooperation in the European Union under the Treaty of Lisbon* (81–98). Baden-Baden: Nomos.

Thomson, I. (2008, August 12). Georgia gets allies in Russian cyberwar: Estonia and Poland offer assistance. *V3*. https://www.v3.co.uk/v3-uk/news/1997915/georgia-allies-russian-cyberwar

Thomson, R. (2008). The Council Presidency in the European Union: Responsibility with Power. *JCMS: Journal of Common Market Studies, 46*(3), 593–617.

Tomkins.

(1975a, September 24). *Telegram No 925 concerning "Armstrong's visit to the Ministry of the Interior"*. The National Archives of the UK. (FCO 30/2614)

(1975b, November 27). *Telegram No 1170 concerning "My Telegram No 1087: European Council: French Attitudes"*. The National Archives of the UK. (PREM 16/398)

UK Presidency. (2005, October 3). *Council conclusions on intelligence-led policing and the development of the Organised Crime Threat Assessment (OCTA) (Doc. 10180/4/05)*. Brussels.

UNHCR – Refugee population statistics database. (n.d.). "Refugee Data Finder." United Nations High Commissioner for Refugees. https://www.unhcr.org/refugee-statistics/download/?url=3HMho5

UNODC – United Nations Office on Drugs and Crime. (2003). *Global Illicit Drug Trends 2003*. New York, NY: United Nations Publications.

Van Asselt, M.B.A., & Renn, O. (2011). Risk Governance. *Journal of Risk Research, 14*(4), 431–449.

Van Berkel, M. (2017, September). *Europol Criminal Assets Bureau; Ensuring crime does not pay*. Presented at the Annual Police Experts Meeting: 'Crime Should Not Pay: Illicit Financial Flows and Confiscation of Criminal Assets. Countering Financial Proceeds of Criminal Networks', Vienna.

Van Buuren, J. (2012). Runaway Bureaucracy? The European Police Chiefs Task Force. *Policing, 6*(3), 281–290.

van der Meulen, N., Jo, E.A., & Soesanto, S. (2015). *Cybersecurity in the European Union and Beyond: Exploring the Threats and Policy Responses* (Study for the LIBE Committee). Brussels: European Parliament.

Virta, S. (2013). Governing Urban Security in Finland: Towards the 'European Model'. *European Journal of Criminology, 10*(3), 341–353.

von Boetticher, C.U. (2003). *Report (A5-0106/2003), of 27 March 2003*. Brussels: European Parliament.

von der Gablentz. (1975, October 24). *Memo from the Federal Foreign Office to the Federal Minister of the Interior, Werner Maihofer, concerning 'Europäischer Rat am 1./2. Dezember in Rom; hier: Britischer Vorschlag für eine Konferenz der neun Innenminister der EG-Staaten im ersten Halbjahr 1976'*. German Federal Archives. (BArch B 106/78829)

Von Hippel, K. (Ed.). (2005). *Europe Confronts Terrorism*. New York, NY: Palgrave Macmillan UK.

von Rottenburg.

(1973, January 30). *Internal memo 'gemäß Besprechung mit Herrn ORR Dr. Nicksch in Ergänzung zu der Vorlage vom 22. Januar 1973 vorgelegt'*. German Federal Archives. (BArch B 106/39571)

(1974, March 6). *Communication from the German Minister of the Interior concerning 'Probleme im Hinblick auf den Abbau grenzpolizeilicher Kontrollen an den innergemeinschaftlichen Grenzen zwischen den Mitgliedsstaaten der EG; hier: Sachstandsbericht'*. German Federal Archives. (BArch B 106/78851)

Waeraas, A., & Maor, M. (2015). *Organizational Reputation in the Public Sector*. New York, NY: Routledge.

Walden. (1975, September 19). *Note from G.G.H. Walden (UK Embassy, Paris) to D.J. Wright (FCO), concerning "Poniatowski"*. The National Archives of the UK. (FCO 30/2614)

Wall, S. (2013). *The Official History of Britain and the European Community, Vol. II: From Rejection to Referendum, 1963-1975*. New York, NY: Routledge.

Wallace, W. (1983). Less Than a Federation, More Than a Regime: The Community as a Political System. In H. Wallace, W. Wallace, & C. Webb (Eds.), *Policy-Making in the European Community* (403–436). New York, NY: Chichester.

Warntjen, A. (2007). Steering the Union. The Impact of the EU Presidency on Legislative Activity in the Council. *JCMS: Journal of Common Market Studies, 45*(5), 1135–1157.

Weinhauer, K. (2006). Zwischen 'Partisanenkampf' und 'Kommissar Computer': Polizei und Linksterrorismus in der Bundesrepublik bis Anfang der 1980er Jahre. In K. Weinhauer, J. Requate, & H.-G. Haupt (Eds.), *Terrorismus in der Bundesrepublik. Medien, Staat und Subkulturen in den 1970er Jahren* (Vol. 42, 244–270). Frankfurt am Main; New York, NY: Campus Verlag.

Welt am Sonntag. (1974, March 31). *Newspaper article: 'Europol und Eurocourt: Kripo-Jagd ohne Grenzen'*. German Federal Archives. (BArch B 106/39571)

White, S.P. (2018). *Understanding Cyberwarfare: Lessons from the Russia-Georgia War*. Modern War Institute at West Point.

White Paper on National Defence and Security *[Livre Blanc sur la Défense et la Sécurité Nationale]*. (2008). Paris: Odile Jacob/La Documentation Française.

Wilson, T.J. (2021). EU-UK criminal justice and security cooperation after Brexit: A perspective. *Forensic Science International: Synergy, 3*, 100144. https://doi.org/10.1016/j.fsisyn.2021.100144

Windhoff-Héritier, A. (1983). "Policy" und "Politics"–Wege und Irrwege einer politikwissenschaftlichen Policy-Theorie. *Politische Vierteljahresschrift, 24*(4), 347–360.

Wintour, P. (2005, August 6). Blair vows to root out extremism. *The Guardian*. https://www.theguardian.com/politics/2005/aug/06/terrorism.july7

Wittschen. (1975, July 21). *Internal memo concerning 'Polizeiliche Zusammenarbeit mit Frankreich zur Bekämpfung des Terrorismus; hier: Kurzanalyse zu dem vom Präsidenten des BKA am 21. Juli 1975 übermittelten Grobkonzept'*. German Federal Archives. (BArch B106/106861)

Wolff, S.

(2008). Border Management in the Mediterranean: Internal, External and Ethical Challenges. *Cambridge Review of International Affairs, 21*(2), 253–271.

(2015). Integrating in Justice and Home Affairs: A Case of New Intergovernmentalism Par Excellence? In C.J. Bickerton, D. Hodson, & U. Puetter (Eds.), *The New Intergovernmentalism: States and Supranational Actors in the Post-Maastricht Era* (129–145). Oxford: Oxford University Press.

Wolff, S., & Mounier, G. (2012). A Kaleidoscopic View on the External Dimension of Justice and Home Affairs. *European Foreign Affairs Review, 17*(2), 143–162.

Wolff, S., & Schout, A. (2013). Frontex as Agency: More of the Same? *Perspectives on European Politics and Society, 14*(3), 305–324.

Wonka, A. (2015). The party politics of the Euro Crisis in the German Bundestag: Frames, Positions and Salience. *West European Politics*, *39*(1), 125–144.

Wood. (1975, September 4). *Note to Sir Vincent Evans, concerning "International Terrorism"*. The National Archives of the UK. (FCO 30/2614)

Wright. (1976, July 1). *"Note of a Conversation between the Prime Minister and the Federal German Chancellor after Lunch in the Chancellery in Bonn on Wednesday 30 June 1976"*. The National Archives of the UK. (PREM 16/894)

Wright, V. (1994). Reshaping the State: The Implications for Public Administration. In W.C. Müller & V. Wright (Eds.), *The State in Western Europe: Retreat Or Redefinition?* (102–137). London: Frank Cass Publishers.

Zachert. (1985, May 20). *Memo for the Minister of the Interior, concerning 'Zusammenarbeit der EG-Staaten im Bereich der Inneren Sicherheit; hier: Italienische Initiative zur Verbesserung der Zusammenarbeit'*. German Federal Archives. (BArch B 106/106819)

Zachert, H.-L. (1992). Europol – Mehr Schlagkraft gegen das Verbrechen in Europa. In *BKA-Vortragsreihe* (Vol. 37, 9–19). Wiesbaden: German Federal Criminal Police Office.

Zahariadis, N. (2013). Building Better Theoretical Frameworks of the European Union's Policy Process. *Journal of European Public Policy*, *20*(6), 807–816.

Zaun, N. (2018). The European Commission in Justice and Home Affairs: Pushing Hard to Be a Motor of Integration. In A. Ripoll Servent & F. Trauner (Eds.), *The Routledge Handbook of Justice and Home Affairs* (409–420). Abingdon: Routledge.

Ziercke, J. (2018). *Speaking at panel 1C on 'European Data Exchange,' 21. European Police Congress, 6-7 February*. Berlin.

Zürn, M. (2013). Politisierung als Konzept der internationalen Beziehungen. In M. Zürn & M. Ecker-Ehrhardt (Eds.), *Die Politisierung der Weltpolitik. Umkämpfte internationale Institutionen* (7–35). Berlin: Suhrkamp.

Zürn, M., & Ecker-Ehrhardt, M. (Eds.). (2013). *Die Politisierung der Weltpolitik: Umkämpfte internationale Organisationen*. Berlin: Suhrkamp.

INDEX

Note: Page references in *italics* denote figures, in **bold** tables and with "n" endnotes.

Made in the USA
Las Vegas, NV
28 October 2024

8201743d-7657-4e1a-88cf-fdc3041e6337R01